UGLY STORIES

*of the Peruvian
Agrarian Reform*

A book in the series

LATIN AMERICA OTHERWISE:
LANGUAGES, EMPIRES, NATIONS

A series edited by
Walter D. Mignolo, Duke University
Irene Silverblatt, Duke University
Sonia Saldívar-Hull, University of Texas, San Antonio

UGLY STORIES *of the Peruvian Agrarian Reform*

ENRIQUE MAYER

Duke University Press   Durham and London   2009

Printed in the United States of
America on acid-free paper ∞

Designed by Heather Hensley

Typeset in Minion Pro by Tseng
Information Systems, Inc.

Library of Congress Cataloging-
in-Publication Data appear on the
last printed page of this book.

This book was published with
the assistance of The Frederick W.
Hilles Publication Fund of
Yale University.

To the memory of
Héctor Martínez Arellano

CONTENTS

Latin America Otherwise: Languages, Empires, Nations is a critical series. It aims to explore the emergence and consequences of concepts used to define "Latin America" while at the same time exploring the broad interplay of political, economic, and cultural practices that have shaped Latin American worlds. Latin America, at the crossroads of competing imperial designs and local responses, has been construed as a geocultural and geopolitical entity since the nineteenth century. This series provides a starting point to redefine Latin America as a configuration of political, linguistic, cultural, and economic intersections that demands a continuous reappraisal of the role of the Americas in history, and of the ongoing process of globalization and the relocation of people and cultures that have characterized Latin America's experience. *Latin America Otherwise: Languages, Empires, Nations* is a forum that confronts established geocultural constructions, rethinks area studies and disciplinary boundaries, assesses convictions of the academy and of public policy, and correspondingly demands that the practices through which we produce knowledge and understanding about and from Latin America be subject to rigorous and critical scrutiny.

In 1969, Peru, under the rule of a military dictatorship, initiated one of the most extensive projects of agrarian reform witnessed in Latin America. Revolutionary in its goals, Peru's land reform eliminated colonial legacy relations of personal servitude and coerced labor; it also initiated a process of land distribution aimed at reversing centuries-old patterns of concentrated land ownership. This project was so far-reaching that its impact is comparable to the abolition of slavery in North America. Yet, over the following three decades, much of this program, including the creation of agrarian cooperatives and cultural initiatives promoting native tradition, was all but abandoned. Moreover, during these decades, Peru imploded, trapped in the throes of a civil war spawned by Shining Path and enflamed by a government with an entrenched hatred of the highlands and a disregard for human rights and reshaped by a neoliberal economic logic that excoriated government intervention in production and consumption in favor of a market system that reinstalled Peru's enormous social inequalities.

Surprisingly, Peru's agrarian reform and its consequences have been little studied. Even more surprisingly, the understandings and perceptions of those who were party to this venture have been virtually ignored—that is, until now. Enrique Mayer has put together a stunning, innovative volume of memory-stories of peasants, politicians, teachers, merchants, government officials, landowners, day laborers, shopkeepers, and anthropologists (including himself) whose intertwined lives and remembrances construct this tableau of Andean political upheaval. Through an orchestration of voices, Mayer not only brings us close to lived experiences, he makes us take part in these sometimes shared, sometimes conflicting, and always complex perceptions. Mayer, the narrator-anthropologist-analyst-commentator, juxtaposes memories in dramatic readings of events and passions, sensibilities and apprehensions. The reader joins the stories, entering into dialogue with Mayer and his interlocutors. This is Latin America and Latin Americans in a momentous period of history—seen, envisioned, explained, and presented, Otherwise.

In July 1969, at the age of twenty-five, I was aboard a Chilean cargo ship returning to Peru after a decade of study at both the University of London and Cornell. The ship stopped in the northern port of Talara. I went ashore, took a local bus to the end of its run on a beach, and there observed some fishermen land their catch in the heavy surf of the Pacific Ocean. I bought some and a woman offered to cook it for me. Watching marine birds circle in the sky and eating the most delicious fried fish of my life, I was told that a few weeks previously the army had expropriated the privately held sugar estates, the richest and most productive agricultural enterprises in the country. Thirty-two years later, in 2001, I was walking with my wife, Lidia Santos, on another beach. This time I was in East Haven, Connecticut. I told her that I wanted to write a book about the momentous agrarian reform, which I had lived through from the moment that I landed in Peru and which I had followed throughout my professional life, in such a way that Peruvian readers would recognize themselves or others through the stories that I would tell. Surprised, Lidia turned to me, saying, "Then why are you writing this book in English?"

I persevered because I told myself an English text would acquire a more universal tone dealing with important human predicaments such as ideological disputes about private property, the rights and wrongs of expropriation, and the merits and difficulties of collective production and of revolutionary reforms gone astray. These are part of the history of the twentieth century throughout the world. Such a book in English could portray for a new international generation what it was like to live through a revolution. Here I want to deeply acknowledge the writerly talent and loving companionship of Lidia Santos.

I started this project in 1988 during a fellowship at the Woodrow Wilson International Center for Scholars in Washington, D.C., where I wrote four chapters that I eventually discarded as my focus shifted away from a policy-oriented case study full of statistics and diagrams to a more people-oriented kind of oral history. At the Wilson Center, I benefited from advice by Professors William P. Glade and Richard M. Morse, co-directors of the Latin American Program at that time. In retrospect, I came to realize that 1988 was too early to write about the unraveling of the agrarian reform in Peru because it was still an ongoing process. I waited until the 1990s to rethink the project. Two small grants from the Arnold Beckman Award of the Research Board of the University of Illinois at Urbana-Champaign in 1992 and 1993 allowed me to travel to Peru to begin again.

Very special thanks go to Anne Marie Hocquenghem, who took me to Piura and introduced me to several expropriated landlords and to *ingeniero* Mario Ginocchio. The interviews in Piura in 1994 were a viability test of people's willingness to talk openly about their memories of the agrarian reform. With funding from the John Simon Guggenheim Foundation in 1996, a Yale sabbatical, and a small grant from the Social Science Research Council, I began the new project with the help of many colleagues in Peru. At the Centro Peruano de Estudios Sociales (CEPES), I gratefully acknowledge Fernando Eguren, Juan Rheinek, Mariano Valderrama, Jaime Urrutia, Bertha Consiglieri, Carlos Monge, Flavio Figallo, José Luis Rénique, Custodio Arias, the secretaries who did the rapid transcription (Beatriz Huaytán, Teresa Prado, and Lourdes Cánepa), and especially Danny Pinedo, who diligently worked with me during that whole year. The CEPES and its staff provided an institutional base, infrastructure, contacts, knowledge, companionship, and the opportunity to enjoy their gourmet rooftop lunches. At the Instituto de Estudios Peruanos (IEP), I thank Julio Cotler for giving me permission to write a postmodern book, Carlos Iván Degregori for intellectual stimulation, Cecilia Blondet, Efraín Gonzales de Olarte, Carolina Trivelli, and Víctor Caballero Martín for friendship and encouragement. I am especially grateful to onetime associates of the IEP, Hortensia Muñóz and Marisol de la Cadena, who steadfastly encouraged me to keep writing.

Throughout 1996, when not traveling around the country for interviews, I sat in an apartment in San Isidro going over transcriptions of my recordings and chuckling to myself at the humorous stories I was privileged to have been told by so many people throughout the country. I thank them with all my heart. Many people helped me in the field, in Huancayo (Nivardo and Victor Santillán), Ayacucho (Jefrey Gamarra and Enrique

González Carré), Cusco (Jorge Villafuerte and Genaro Paniagua), Puno (Ricardo Vega and Raúl Rodríguez), Trujillo (Elías Minaya), and Lima (María Benavides, Ricardo Letts, Alejandro Camino, Luis Soberón, José Portugal at the Office of Comunidades Campesinas, and many more people at other institutions). I thank my family, too: my mother, Elizabeth de Mayer; my sisters, Maria Scurrah and Renate Millones; my nephew, Mateo Millones; and my brothers-in-law, Martin Scurrah and Luis Millones. At CEPES, the IEP, the Centro de Estudios Rurales Bartolomé de las Casas in Cusco, and all of the libraries of the provincial universities where we researched, I thank the librarians at their respective documentation centers. Two memorable seminars, one at the CEPES and the other at the IEP where I read aloud some of the stories I had collected, were occasions where I absorbed the positive reactions of the audience whom I had asked for help in how one could structure a book with this material.

Summers at my home on the beach at East Haven were dedicated to converting the interview material into chapters at an excruciatingly slow pace of more or less one chapter per summer. The scholarship of the anthropologist Rodrigo Montoya, the economist José María Caballero, and the sociologist Fernando Eguren is crucial for an understanding of the reform, and my readings of their works and conversations with them over the years are reflected in the tenor of this book. At Yale, I give special thanks to Richard Burger, Jim Scott, Kay Mansfield, and the colleagues at Agrarian Studies. Natalia Sobrevilla and Vladimir Gil listened patiently and gave me encouragement. Benjamin Orlove read an early version of the manuscript and gave me a thumbs up message. César Rodriguez, the curator of the Latin American Collection, was also especially helpful. Paul Gootenberg at SUNY Stonybrook invited me to give a lecture for its Center for Latin American Studies in 1997, and it was there that I tried out the first chapter of my draft on an academic audience. I thank him and other audiences that responded to presentations of further chapters at Hampshire College, Colby College, Fairfield University, Connecticut College, the Seminario Permanente de Investigacion Agraria (SEPIA) in Trujillo, the Yale Agrarian Studies program, the Center for Latin American Studies at Pittsburgh, and the Yale Department of Anthropology. Elisabeth Enenbach diligently worked with me in editing the manuscript, and I thank her for her thoroughness and for paying attention to who said what when, and to whom.

I did not want to use a camera during my field trips because photography is a crutch to remembering given that it fixes events in space and time through the viewfinder of the photographer holding the camera. Instead I decided to hunt for images produced by others during the times of the agrarian reform. This turned out to be quite an exciting chase. I am grateful to the filmmaker Federico García Hurtado, the photojournalist Carlos ("El Chino") Domínguez, the artist Jesús Ruiz Durand, and Máximo Gamarra, Hugo Neira, and Teo Chambi. Also, I am grateful to the staff of TAFOS (Talleres de Fotografía Social), a project in the 1980s and 1990s that provided young people in diverse communities with cameras to photograph what they thought important; the photos are now stored at the Pontificia Universidad Católica del Perú. Thanks go to Brigitte Maass and Briklin Dwyer for the pictures taken at my behest. At Yale, Karina Yager and Mark Saba produced the maps; William K. Sacco, Joseph Szaszfai, and Jude Breidenbach at Yale Media Services generated the digital images for this book. Special thanks are also due to Valerie Millholland and the staff for production help at Duke University Press.

Memory

This book deals with memories as its principal source. During my field-work in 1995–96, I traveled all over Peru with Danny Pinedo and a small battery-powered tape recorder to interview people who had lived through the agrarian reform (1969–99). The idea came to me a couple of years be-forehand, when I was asked by a friend in Lima about my next research project, and I said that it would be the agrarian reform. The disgusted look on his face made me change my stance, and I corrected myself: "Not the reform, but the history of the reform."

He brightened up, saying that that was an interesting topic, and im-mediately launched into a long and detailed narration of how the agrarian reform had affected him personally. It was fascinating. I then knew that the idea of collecting oral histories or testimonies (I prefer to call them stories) had great potential. In contrast with the dry accounts full of statistics and class analysis that characterize the literature on the Peruvian agrarian re-form, the stories I collected were so vivid that I resolved to base the whole project around the memories people have of the reform.

Armed with a Guggenheim Fellowship and a sabbatical, I conducted the bulk of the interviews that year. Danny was, at that time, a student who had completed his course work in the Anthropology Department at the Uni-versity of San Marcos in Lima, and he agreed to participate in this project. I was affiliated with the Centro Peruano de Estudios Sociales (CEPES), the members of which knew the past and present rural conditions of Peru very well. I had maintained my interest in the agrarian reform for many years and my colleagues at CEPES helped me to roughly sketch out what issues I wanted to interview people about and where. I selected places that I remembered due to their notoriety or because they were emblematic to

Map 1 Peru with main locations mentioned in the text. Drawn by K. Yager.

the reform process, or because I was familiar with the area from previous fieldwork. In each place, Danny and I reviewed the local history of the area and completed a bibliographic search in local university libraries. Then we identified potential people to interview and, after tracking them down and getting them to agree to tell us their stories, we interviewed them. We ended with about eighty interviews, each about ninety minutes, revolving around one particular estate, region, or process. We tried to gather material with as many versions from as many perspectives as possible. Separately we interviewed the exlandlords, the expropriators, the government officials, the local politicians, the peasant leaders, the activists, the officials of the cooperatives, and the farming families in each region. Once each interview was transcribed, we sent a copy of each transcription to the person we had interviewed and asked if he or she had any comments, corrections, or deletions. We incorporated these into the final transcripts.[1] We also mentioned that we would use their names unless they preferred to remain anonymous (only two persons chose that option). Danny was a good travel companion, a great intellectual partner, and a committed anthropologist.

Memory

What is a memory? In some respects it is a way to relive the past. It is always associated with an emotional state. When, during my interviews, after people began to feel comfortable with the recorder and with me, I could really tell that they were remembering. They began to be oblivious of their surroundings, their gazes turned inward, and their eyes shone. And they intensely came to experience some very crucial moments of their past. Most of these were very painful. Charged with emotion and awash in sentiments, they relived these moments as they told me their stories and enlisted my full empathy. They sweated, cried, raised their voices, and even laughed embarrassedly. These moments were dreamlike, and they could be recaptured afterward by some telltale signs in their narration. I began to notice that this particular moment of remembering had come when the person started adding contextual detail to corroborate time and place. There was a clear positioning of the storyteller vis-à-vis another person. The storytellers remembered or (more likely) reconstructed exact quotable dialogue. There was always a moral or ethical issue at stake, with the narrator taking the "ethical" stance and the quoted interlocutor the unethical one. The point of each story was the narrator's intent of safeguarding his or her own personal dignity. The narrator asked the anthropologist to share in his or her moral outrage in the face of an unjust accusation, an unfair treatment, a suffered indignity, or a flagrant injustice. This point was often signaled by a bitter laugh.

My recordings were not open ended or free flowing. I sometimes questioned hard and used a loose structure of the principal events of the agrarian reform to get the narrator to move on to other topics. None of the stories I gathered were neutral about the agrarian reform. I found no one, not one person who wanted to tell me that he or she was happy with the way the agrarian reform worked itself out. Although most agreed that the country did need an agrarian reform at that time, they disagreed about the way it was brought about. I note that most of the time my interviewees were materially, socially, and economically much better off than before the reform. This is true for the peasants. It holds too for many, though not all, of the expropriated landlords who went into business and moved to the city, or the activists, many of whom are now employed by NGOs working on sustainable development. The employees of the government, now retired, remember the failures that came after adjudication of land into cooperatives, or how from their positions of power they saw how so much went wrong despite their reportedly good intentions and honest efforts.

It would be naïve to believe that the people told me the dry and factual truth, and even more simple minded to have personal experiences stand for larger social processes unleashed by the massive process of expropriation and redistribution of land begun by the revolutionary military government of Juan Velasco Alvarado in 1969, a process that took thirty years to work itself out. I realized this when I began to hear certain stories that were told to me as if they were firsthand experiences being repeated by others as if these stories had also happened to them. Here is an example:

Rafael Seminario, a landowner harried by lawsuits revolving around the expropriation of his hacienda, crossed the main plaza in Piura and was accosted by a shoeshine boy.

"Señor, shoeshine?"
"No!"
"Shall I just remove the soil? (¿Le quito la tierrita?)"
"Ah! You too want to take my land?"

This joke is much more effective if it is told as if one had personally experienced it. The people I interviewed mixed personal memories, shared experiences, popular opinions produced at that time or collectively elaborated afterward, apt examples kept in mind as cautionary tales, unconfirmed gossip, and political opinions. All of these were shaken together into a cocktail of meanings that poured into the tape recorder. Finding it impossible and unnecessary to sort them out, or to separate truth from exaggeration, I paid more attention to the narrative quality and what it sought to illustrate.

I was interested in eliciting how people's lives had changed because of the reform, and how they personally experienced important events. When they look back, what do Peruvians remember of the reform, and how do they evaluate it? The erratic changes in government policy and acts of resistance defined contexts and circumstances for action. I was interested in documenting the *tumbos de la vida* of different kinds of people over the thirty-year span of the reform, and how individuals navigated those troubled times. *Tumbos de la vida* cannot really be translated as "career patterns," but rather as how to survive when one is buffeted around on very rough roller-coaster rides.

We all know that memory is selective and changes according to context, and this is not quite the point in this book. Just as the many radio interviews that Studs Terkel collected in books such as *Hard Times* (1971) about the Great Depression in the United States provided atmosphere, color, and human content to large-scale events, my intention was to stitch the memories together into a larger narrative. Yet, when I tried to emulate Terkel's style, I realized that his books are effective only if the reader has a certain background or contextual knowledge of the events about which the individuals are reminiscing—in other words, if there is a collective memory that bounces with, reflects, and refracts the individual's own. In the case of the Peruvian agrarian reform, there is no "official story," let alone a "history" of the reform or of Velasco's military leftist government that might lay out some guidelines along which people can order their own remembrances.

On the contrary, the current neoliberal atmosphere has satanized the Velasco government for every evil that befell Peru and which needs to be repaired. "*Guayabera* socialists" (from the Cuban button-down silk shirt that became the symbolic dress for leftists in Peru) were made fun of in editorials, and Velasco's angry face was frequently reproduced to remind people of his errors. The mood was dark during the middle of the Fujimori regime, when I was conducting the interviews for this book, as the society slowly became aware of the devastating destruction and death toll caused in Peru by the uprising of the Maoist Sendero Luminoso, or Shining Path. There were opinion makers who circulated the accusation that Velasco's left-wing regime had spawned the terrible Shining Path uprising. My research ended before the Peruvian Truth and Reconciliation Commission was established in December 2000 to conduct nationwide hearings, some of which were televised. Only then did the real horror of what had happened come to the fore. By that time, giving testimony and telling the truth became part of a national process of understanding and reflection. The stories of little people began to matter importantly.

During the time that I was interviewing, however, the situation was different. There was a very strong push to keep silent and to forget about the civil war. It had to do with the very recent collapse of Shining Path and the manner in which it occurred. People were just emerging from a war, and events were far too close to be comfortably remembered without pain, terror, and fear of consequences if one talked. This had to do with the way Shining Path collapsed, with desertions, informants, arbitrary prison sentences for the guilty and not-guilty alike, and the lack of a clear "accounting," which only began once the Truth and Reconciliation Commission commenced its work. This somber mood may have colored the people's recollections about the agrarian reform that preceded the period of political violence.

Memory research comes to the rescue of forgetting and deliberate erasure, and this book intends to do this by remembering the good, the bad, and the ugly through the tales of people who lived in those times. I hope that every reader, no matter what his or her current political position or received wisdom about the agrarian reform, can empathize with one or several of the personal stories I have selected to be part of this book. My regrets about those I had to leave out because they would have made the book impossibly long have made the writing process even more difficult than I envisioned. This book is not a history of the agrarian reform, but an invitation to readers to remember and reflect, to tell each other more stories about those times, to reminisce, and to ponder what was important to them and to the nation as events unfolded forty years ago. Many readers will have been born after Velasco's times and wonder what they were like. Grandparents, parents, and children will be stimulated to reminisce with this book.

Agrarian issues have made good stories, but they are hard to write. I looked for literary models to guide me. I take great comfort that Nikolai Gogol's *Dead Souls* (1996 [1842]) was so difficult for him to write that he never finished it (the book ends in mid-sentence and he destroyed the second part of his trilogy). Mixing satire, the absurd, and hilarious farce, Gogol tells how Chichikov, the corrupt main character, visits decaying rural estates in order to buy the dead souls of serfs—and, in the process, portrays the rural Russia of his times in unforgettable ways. George Orwell in *Animal Farm* (1945) uses allegory to point to betrayals and difficulties that arise under the collectivization of farms, but the book was hijacked for anti-Communist propaganda purposes. In contrast, *Fanshen: A Documentary of Revolution in a Chinese Village* (1966), by William Hinton, is a participant observer's extraordinary account of the Chinese agrarian reform in the village of Long Bow after the triumph of Mao's revolution of 1947. It was compelling reading for me as an anthropologist as I was living through another agrarian reform in Peru in the 1970s. Microcosmic accounts were also models for the Peruvian novelist Ciro Alegría. Writing in the *indigenista* and realist mode, he produced a village epic of heroic community resistance against nasty landlord intentions in which good and evil are clearly delineated in *El mundo es ancho y ajeno* (1941). José María Arguedas's *Yawar fiesta* (1941), which contains more complex characters, used the local context of Puquio in Ayacucho to unfold a more nuanced and profoundly moving psychological portrayal of *hacendados*, peasants, and townspeople locked in conflict and hate.

I was helped in how to structure my tale of stories for a whole nation by reading V. S. Naipaul's *India: A Million Mutinies Now* (1990). It provided me with another model. Naipaul lets his interviewees speak, but he orders the tale, he chooses the context in which to let them speak, and he decides the sequence of events in order to tell his story about the rise of political religious fundamentalism. Naipaul did not like the India that he saw in 1990, and he distilled his unease, his dislike, and his European conservative viewpoint through the tales and observations of those people's narrations. I love my country, I was enthused by the prospect of an agrarian reform really changing my country for the better, and I was upset that it did not work out—and horrified with the violence and killing that came afterward. However, unlike Naipaul, I attempt with the memories that people shared with me to paint a more positive view of the agrarian reform than the one that currently is in fashion.

Each chapter is a story in a very literal way. It has a narrative structure, characters, descriptions, dialogues, and a beginning, a middle, and an end. I constructed the stories from the interviews, memories, and reports from my fieldwork and from scholarly works into larger wholes. In each story I roughly follow the chronological sequence of the reform process, intertwining various points of view from my interviewees and my own scholarly comments. I am the narrator. I fashioned these stories out of the material of the interviews and I include my own memories as well. However, I tried to keep myself as much in the background as possible and let the people do the telling. When necessary, I connected them to keep the story going. I also make comments in notes to contextualize and amplify what was impossible to include in the main text, and in them I provide a bibliographic guide with commentary about the issues brought out in the main text. Furthermore, in the notes I chronicle the treatment of the agrarian reform in literature, film, and testimony to explore the degree to which the reform has become part of the cultural milieu of the past or the present.

Although *testimonio* literature also made its mark in Peru, only three publications deal with the specifics of Velasco's reform: Lino Quintanilla (1981), a member of Vanguardia Revolucionaria (VR; the Revolutionary Vanguard party) who was sick and disappointed at subsequent failures, told the anthropologist Rodrigo Montoya how he abandoned his lower-middle-class family and job and married a peasant woman to help peasants organize invasions of landed estates in Andahuaylas in the highlands of southern Peru in 1974. Another testimonial was published by Charlotte Burenius (2001), wherein Zózimo Torres gives an account of the rise and fall of a cooperative named Huando; she is the granddaughter of the owners, he the union leader of the workers on the same estate. The anthropologists Ricardo Valderrama and Carmen Escalante (1986) published the bitter memories of a serf (*pongo*), who remembered the cruelty of a nearly demented and sick woman owner of an hacienda shortly before the agrarian reform expropiated her in the department of Huancavelica. My book hopes to encourage other personal accounts to enrich our understanding of Peru's tumultuous twentieth century.

The first chapter provides the context of the Velasco regime and gives an overview of the agrarian reform, its antecedents, execution, and the difficulties that followed. It ends with a very positive retrospective opinion of the reform by a member of Velasco's government, Francisco Guerra, a specialist in political science whom I interviewed in 1996. The structure of the story of the agrarian reform is rather simple and can easily be told. The hacienda system that had developed out of Peru's colonial society was extremely unjust and oppressive. Peasants and workers had struggled against it for centuries, and intellectuals had denounced it for a long, long time.

Land was extremely concentrated in large estates. While the first agrarian reform in Latin America came with the Mexican Revolution of 1910, the age of agrarian reforms reached the rest of the continent after the Second World War. In Peru, massive peasant movements in the 1950s and 1960s finally pushed the first government of Fernando Belaúnde Terry to pass an agrarian reform law in 1964. But the implementation of that reform was slow and ineffective. In 1968, Belaúnde was overthrown by a leftist military government led by Juan Velasco Alvarado, who then implemented a drastic and thorough program of expropriations beginning in 1969. Expropriated land was then collectively adjudicated in the form of cooperatives. Shying away from the more drastic forms of collectivization implemented by Communists in the Soviet Union and the Eastern European countries that fell under the sway of the Soviet bloc, cooperatives were a milder, yet imposed model for social change that left-leaning intellectuals favored in Latin America in the postwar era. However, the Peruvian cooperative models for agriculture did not prosper, and they began to falter. When the country returned to civilian rule in the 1980s, members of the cooperatives organized to dismantle them and to distribute the land among themselves. This book highlights the struggles that were involved in dismantling the collective enterprises that technocratic elements of the military regime had invented, in all good faith, to project a new kind of society out of the reform process.

Each chapter therefore tells of expropriation, the experiences under collective models of social experimentation, the people's subsequent disillusion when the experiments failed, and the ensuing efforts made by collectives' members to capture the land away from government control. Thus expropriation, adjudication, and decollectivization are three phases of the process. The particular details of how this worked itself out in each place, however, make up the stuff of the captivating stories that I managed to collect.

one

AGRARIAN REFORMS

Relevant Presidential Regimes and Hopefuls in Chronological Order

MANUEL PRADO UGARTECHE (1939–45), a conservative president who was aligned with oligarchy.

VÍCTOR RAÚL HAYA DE LA TORRE (1895–1979), the founder of the APRA (Alianza Popular Revolucionaria Americana, or American Popular Revolutionary Alliance). This persecuted, amnestied, and perennial presidential hopeful espoused a program that included calls for radical agrarian reforms.

MANUEL ODRÍA AMORETTI (1948–56), a conservative military general who was opposed to agrarian reform.

MANUEL PRADO UGARTECHE (1956–62), a president who, in his reelected period, faced massive peasant uprisings in the Cusco region.

GENERAL RICARDO PÉREZ GODOY (1962–63), head of a military junta. To oversee a failed election, he declared a limited agrarian reform in the Cusco region to curb the peasant uprising.

FERNANDO BELAÚNDE TERRY (1963–68), an elected president of Peru, implemented the first agrarian reform.

JUAN VELASCO ALVARADO (1968–75), an army general who led the Revolutionary Government of the Armed Forces.

FRANCISCO MORALES BERMÚDEZ CERRUTI (1975–80), an army general who overthrew Velasco and initiated the "second phase" of the military's revolutionary regime.

FERNANDO BELAÚNDE TERRY (1980–85), a reelected president who allowed the dissolution of agrarian cooperatives and oversaw the retreat of the government's reform policies. The Shining Path began an armed uprising in Ayacucho during his regime.

ALAN GARCÍA PÉREZ (1985–90), the first member of APRA to be elected president. García tried to validate the speedy collapse of agrarian reform cooperatives in the highlands and supported political and economic measures to consolidate some of the agrarian institutions created by the Velasco regime. As president, he faced the brunt of the Shining Path insurgency; he was reelected in 2006.

ALBERTO FUJIMORI (1990–2000), an elected president who implemented neoliberal policies and reversed the remaining statutes of the agrarian reform, allowing unlimited private property and the sale of land. Fujimori privatized collapsing sugar cooperatives; arrested the leader of Shining Path in Lima in 1992; killed hostage-takers of guests in the Japanese embassy, ending armed uprisings in 1997; and resigned in 2000 under a cloud of corruption.

Velasco's Revolution

Juan Velasco Alvarado's government (1968–75) was revolutionary for its time. It was the first moment in which Peru confronted foreign corporations with entrenched privileges. Its nationalism was different because it incorporated indigenous, popular, and Andean people and their cultural themes, widening the imagined community of the nation. It undertook a serious attempt at income redistribution, and it organized a range of programs for the poor in the city and in the countryside. The growth and impact of state enterprises and industrial import substitution programs were being touted as successes elsewhere in Latin America, and Peru's attempt seemed appropriate for those years. Going against Iron Curtain and Cold War policies to open relations with Mao's China, the Soviet Union, and the Eastern Bloc countries, as well as maintaining friendly relationships with Cuba (coupled with nonalignment), was very progressive. Above all, the regime is remembered for executing Latin America's most radical agrarian reform, the subject of this book. This was carried out without bloodshed.

The revolution from above began at dawn on October 3, 1968, when tanks from the armored division of the army rumbled from across the Rimac River in Lima toward the presidential palace with an elite corps of *rangers*. They entered the presidential palace, arresting a startled President Fernando Belaúnde and shipping him off to Buenos Aires. General Velasco (the chief of the armed forces) and his small group of co-conspirators were joined by top-ranking officers of the air force and navy to form the Revolutionary Government of the Armed Forces (Gobierno Revolucionario de las Fuerzas Armadas), which was to stay in power for twelve years.

Its legacy is still controversial, but there is no doubt that the military's initial left-wing shift and sweeping reforms of practically every aspect of social, economic, and political life were an important watershed for the country. In five years of Velasco's presidency, the military rigorously implemented in top-down, corporatist, and undemocratic ways a slew of profoundly radical reform measures. Coming fast and without warning, one after another, these changes left citizens dizzy and reeling. Dirk Kruijt (1989; 1994), a Dutch sociologist, aptly called it a "revolution by decree."

It was the second time within five years that a military junta had stepped in to break an impasse that civilian regimes could not resolve. The Belaúnde government was blocked by a coalition in Parliament that perversely impeded the implementation of the reforms that he had promised in his election campaigns. Velasco's government surpassed these promises and carried forward many of the dreams for change that progressives had desired for decades. He also introduced innovations such as worker participation in industry—even though they fizzled—that were interesting attempts to reduce the great income inequalities and distances between social classes that were part of Peru's legacy from its colonial, aristocratic, and oligarchic republican past.

Despite its obsession to control them, the junta vastly expanded the political participation of previously un- or underrepresented sectors of society. The popular classes in towns, villages, indigenous communities, and shantytowns were involved in projects and programs that ultimately advanced their incorporation as citizens. The government treated them with greater respect than ever before, discouraging forms of social injustice and everyday humiliation. At the same time, the Velasco style clipped the wings of the elites, breaking up their self-assurance and the privileges they had taken for granted, partly by ridicule and partly by imposing new, more popular horizontal forms of treatment for everyone (those not in uniform, that is). It was the first government ever to execute significant income redistribution in a society of great inequalities. It completed the abolition of all forms of servitude in rural estates, a momentous shift in the history of the Andes, akin to the abolition of slavery in the Americas. It glossed over the racial/ethnic issues that divide Peruvian society by using the neutral class-derived word *campesino* (peasant), banishing the word *indio*.

However, this was done in ways that produced unease and negative reactions. New organizations were created with difficult alphabet-soup acronyms, each controlled by a colonel sitting in the commanding seat as overseer, intervener, or director. Yet within local institutions, a kind of supervised democracy was to function with the less powerful placed on top (if they exceeded the government's limitations, these institutions were subject to "intervention"). Government bureaucracy and state enterprises expanded enormously and invaded new spheres of life; every low-level functionary assumed the air of a barrack sergeant. A tiresome nationalist propaganda machine, which coupled heavily socialized rhetoric with an increasingly muzzled and expropriated press, dominated the scene. Opposing ideas or persons were labeled counterrevolutionary or denounced as dangerous. A paranoid atmosphere generated by ubiquitous spying secret service organizations soured political culture. Public discussion, though not forbidden, was restricted. Private debate, in contrast, was intense. Stealth and intrigue in the timing and imposition of new revolutionary measures meant to keep opposition forces off balance was frustrating and immobilizing to civilians in all walks of life, even to those who supported—often critically—the imposed measures.

Above all, it was a period in which government activity was imbued with a complex technocratic discourse. Reform measures were implemented through the imposition of "models" derived from beliefs that a scientifically correct formula could be designed and enforced to change human character and behavior, thus bringing about a reduction of class conflict and inequality, and the achievement of social cohesion. Velasco's revolutionaries wished to utilize social engineering to create a new, proud, and nationalist Peruvian who was fully participant in a humanitarian society and economy that was neither capitalist nor communist, but fiercely national and patriotic.

My professional debut as a young anthropologist coincided with my only encounter with Velasco. He inaugurated the Congress of Americanists in 1971, where I presented my first paper. A couple hundred foreign and local scholars were seated in a school patio; in front of us on a raised platform under a tent, the general in a green uniform was surrounded by other uniformed dignitaries. Sitting with him were José Matos Mar, an anthropologist and the convener of the congress, and a selection of eminent scholars. After the national anthem and other formalities, Velasco began a short

Figure 1 General Juan Velasco Alvarado heading a political rally in Lima on June 7, 1975. Archive of the photographer Carlos Domínguez. © Carlos Domínguez.

speech with a smoker's raspy voice, but he was interrupted by a protest led by Jacqueline de la Puente, the French widow of the guerrilla leader Luis de la Puente Uceda. Security personnel in civilian clothing who were mixed in with the audience immediately rose and began to move forward. Matos had foreknowledge of this and asked the general if a spokesperson of the group could say a few words. The general accepted. The linguist Alfredo Torero (who was not given a microphone and therefore was inaudible to the audience) asked Velasco, since he was a revolutionary, to give amnesty to the jailed guerrillas of 1965 who had fought for the same ideals as he. Velasco responded in a friendly way, saying that those in prison had been tried in courts and therefore had to complete their sentences. He also said that he would think about it. The ceremony continued. However, as soon as the president left, those whom the secret service had seen murmuring and accompanying Jacqueline were arrested. Matos Mar had to intercede for their release the next day. A couple of months later, amnesty for the guerrillas was granted.

Velasco's popularity as El Chino (a nickname that quickly stuck because of his slanted eyes) among lower classes, workers, and peasants grew slowly as he implemented the reforms that benefited them (fig. 1).[1] Half the middle classes abhorred him (although they gained from expanding employment opportunities), and landowners had reason enough to fear him because he attacked them frontally. Industrialists were split: most were against, those that collaborated became rich. Foreign-owned companies dedicated to export production were expropriated, but those industrial enterprises and financial institutions that adjusted to the conditions of a rapid and badly designed import substitution industrialization program had a place in the new economy. Political parties were left in limbo and Parliament was closed. Civilian opposition was not treated kindly. Organized unions affiliated with left-wing parties were divided by the creation of parallel pro-Velasco organizations, demobilizing them with rough tactics. The threat of the military boot was always palpable. The regime deported individuals or removed them from office, closed down institutions that were troublesome, or created rival parallel ones as measures of political control. Yet while his regime was opressive, it did not jail many people, nor kill anyone. Peruvian friends of mine used a funny expression: they said Velasco's was a *dictablanda* instead of a *dictadura*, a soft instead of a hard dictatorship, and I agreed.

Cultural life was nationalized, favoring performances by Peruvian folk artists. Handicraft clay pots became fashionable over imported china at dinner parties, and *velasquista* youth put on ponchos and played the panpipes in Miraflores, a middle-class suburb of Lima. Government institutions freely appropriated Incan and indigenous cultural elements in images, names, and symbols. *Fútbol* was also absorbed into the revolution when the national team played in the World Cup competition in Mexico in 1970 (¡viva el Perú, carajo!). Santa Claus was banned as a symbol of American consumerism and replaced by *el niño Manué* to celebrate a more authentic Peruvian Christmas. The military also flaunted its own privileges, and black Dodge Coronet sedans (assembled in Peru) became a common military status symbol. The period also saw an incredible expansion of intellectual debate, with an emphasis on the social sciences, spilling into public and private spheres . . . and I was a privileged member of this group. I could explain to others what an "irreversible change in the structure of society" was supposed to mean and why the military said it would stay in power until then. It suited me fine!

I was born to middle-class European parents and grew up in Huancayo, a city in the central highlands of Peru. My parents often visited *hacendados* on their estates, and their and my disgust with the way the indigenous people were pushed around stayed with me, so much so that as a teenager I wanted to be a journalist to denounce injustices. I became an anthropologist instead, graduating from Cornell University. At that time, Cornell had strong intellectual connections to Peru in economics, political science, sociology, and anthropology. I was attracted to this university because Professor Alan Holmberg and his Peruvian collaborator Mario Vásquez had started an experiment on a highland hacienda wherein the serfs were liberated, and which was purported to demonstrate that it had provided a model of how to implement a successful agrarian reform (Mayer 2006).

Following progressive thought in Latin American studies of the 1960s in graduate school, I ended every term paper I wrote on Peru by demanding an authentic agrarian reform as a necessary precondition for development and social integration. I sported a beard and long, curly hair. I landed back in Peru in 1969, doing ethnographic fieldwork for a year in a bilingual Quechua- and Spanish-speaking indigenous peasant community in the central Andes. I then affiliated myself with the Instituto de Estudios Peruanos (IEP) and the Pontificia Universidad Católica del Perú (PUCP), both places where the debate for, against, and about the reforms of the military government was intense. I shared an apartment in Miraflores with my married sister and many a foreign graduate student researching aspects of the Velasco revolution. Our place was an intense debating forum. In principle, I agreed with the government's reform aims, yet was critical toward the way it went about them. I did not actively join the regime or any opposition leftist political party, but it was exciting to live in a revolution.

In February 1973, Velasco suffered a sudden serious illness. An aneurism required heavy blood transfusions and the amputation of his leg. Although he recovered, his leadership in the period after his resumption of office was weakened. He was left isolated and became so mistrustful that his prestige and power eroded. The inner core of revolutionary generals was outmaneuvered by air force and navy officers with less revolutionary fervor. In 1976, while the military was secretly looking for ways to replace him, he was ousted in an internal coup by General Francisco Morales Bermúdez. The latter's regime, from 1975 to 1980, announced the continuation of the original revolution—it was called the "second phase"—but actually reversed it. Morales Bermúdez's government was beset with economic troubles (forced to cut back on expenditures and devalue currency); surrounded by hostile dictatorships in Brazil; Chile, Argentina, and Ecuador;

uneasy in its relationships with the United States and international lenders; and facing widespread internal unrest and opposition. The regime became much more repressive than that of Velasco, who, isolated and sick, died on December 24, 1977. Unexpectedly, seventy thousand people showed up at his funeral.

Human rights statistics for the Morales Bermúdez period were not made public, but union smashing, persecution, and arbitrary arrests were common. Constitutional guarantees were suspended and Lima was under strict curfew for months. In spite of this repressive atmosphere, protests against government measures grew, culminating in two impressive general strikes on July 19, 1977, and February 27–28, 1978. Ten days after the first one, Morales Bermúdez announced that the military intended to return to its barracks. In 1978 he convened a constituent assembly (presided over by an aging Haya de la Torre), which was ratified in 1979. General elections were held in May 1980, and the very same deposed Fernando Belaúnde assumed a new civilian government on July 28, 1980.

In 1978, in the darkest days of the second phase, I was offered a job in Mexico. At the airport, where much paperwork was required to show compliance with currency restrictions, taxes, legal deposits, and so on, the emigration officer folded the documents into my passport. He then handed them back, saying, "Congratulations, Mr. Mayer; you are leaving the country. I wish I could join you." That day the government employees had held a huge demonstration to protest the dismissal of 30 percent of the employees.

Sixteen years later, in 1994, I was in Piura, the birthplace of Velasco. I wanted to see the house where he had lived in his youth in the poorer neighborhood of Castilla, the "wrong" side of the town. Asking for directions, I was turned away. "It is a dangerous area and not safe for people like you," said a man. "Besides, there is nothing to see." It was true, in all Piura there was not one single monument to Velasco; no street, plaza, or bridge was named for him. There were many statues of Miguel Grau (a naval hero from the times of the Chilean War), but El Chino was remembered secretly in the *barrios* and the rural areas. The subsequent regimes of Belaúnde, García, and Fujimori, with their officially promoted public culture, have done their best to undo his policies and to erase his memory.

The Agrarian Reform

The 1940s and early 1950s were a time when intellectuals in Latin America, Europe, and the United States focused on the study and the denunciation of the dominance of the large-estate *latifundium* regime and began to debate how it could be changed. In the Andean region, where most of the serf and rural populations were also Indian, the abuse with which they were treated was seen as particularly egregious. Given the racist connotations of that time, landowners argued that dividing the lands among ignorant and primitive Indians on a hacienda was not appropriate without educating them first, otherwise such division would lead to a fragmentation of property and low productivity. José Carlos Mariátegui (the founder of Peru's socialist party) already had argued the reverse as early as 1928. He said that the "Indian problem" (what to do about integrating the indigenous rural population) was a land problem, not only an educational or cultural one. He and other early socialist thinkers such as Hildebrando Castro Pozo also reasoned that the Andean tradition of collectivism could be adapted to modern *latifundios* to be transformed into community-based cooperatives, and to very small holdings (*minifundios*), which likewise could be aggregated.[2]

For scholars, politicians, and technocrats, the most notorious need for reform was in the so-called traditional or feudal hacienda system entrenched in the highland sierra regions of the country. The almost mythical prototype of a highland hacienda was owned by an absentee landlord, administered by a local employee, and had a resident indigenous serf population (called *colonos* or *yanaconas)* that was permitted to grow crops and pasture animals on the owner's land in exchange for work on the hacienda's own (demesne) lands. Because the owners derived rent from their property and the serfs were not free to move elsewhere, the words feudal or semi-feudal were used to describe the despotic and exploitative conditions under which these haciendas operated, regardless of the symbolic pay in money or in coca leaves that the hacienda called "wages."[3] A reform that would abolish serfdom and see to the disappearance of the traditional hacienda could therefore remove a source of shame with which Peruvian society was burdened among Latin American nations.

In contradistinction, indigenous communities (*comunidades de indíge-*

nas) of free peasants (that is, those not tied to hacienda peonage), with an institutional past rooted in the colonial system of tributary populations, gained a measure of state protection in the 1920s. At that time, the government began to issue certificates of official recognition to collectively owned territories of colonial origin (petitioning Indians had to demonstrate that they had occupied their lands "since time immemorial"), in which members cultivated land individually and herded their animals in the community's natural pastures. Land was held as common property, but each family had access to very little of it, and endemic poverty was characteristic of indigenous communities. Indigenous communities had been subject to dispossession from expansionist landlords and had litigated and resisted heroically. When talk about reform began, these communities were considered, alongside the serfs of the haciendas, as legitimate and justified beneficiaries of land restitution.

There were other land-related issues that intellectuals described as being in need of reform. On the irrigated desert coastal plains, a capitalist plantation economy had developed with the rise of world markets for primary products such as sugar and cotton (the sugar plantations were often foreign owned). Smallholders bitterly resented the plantations' territorial expansion at their expense, in addition to the exploitative labor practices into which they were forced as proletarization took hold. The landowning classes ruled with an iron fist and dominated regional politics. Plantations were assailed by left-leaning intellectuals as clear examples of the distorting effects of capitalism and imperialism, resulting in a strangulating dependency dictated by the developed countries' need for cheap raw materials. Right-wing intellectuals, in contrast, saw these estates in a positive light as technological progress, Peru's incorporation into modernity, and a source of foreign exchange—and, therefore, not in need of reform. Calls for agrarian reform in Peru thus had different reasons in different regions. In the highlands, the progressive argument had it that feudalism needed to be abolished in order to bring about capitalist development. On the coast, the socialist argument insisted that the owners of plantations had to be expropriated because they were too capitalist.

How these ideas translated to laws, programs, and policies will briefly be reviewed below. In keeping with the popular tradition of remembering time periods by presidential regimes, I will highlight the main aspects of the agrarian reform in chronological order, using the headings of the governments that presided over them. We begin in the late 1950s and early 1960s.

Manuel Prado, 1939–45; Manuel Odría, 1948–56; Manuel Prado, 1956–62

While conservative anti-reform elements maintained power from 1939 to 1962, serious challenges to the status quo were accumulating. As the historian Peter Klaren (1973) has shown, the expansion of sugar estates in the northern coast area had provided the opportunity for the birth in 1924 of the radical party Alianza Popular Revolucionaria Americana (APRA), whose founder, Víctor Raúl Haya de la Torre, included calls for agrarian reforms in his platform. Proscribed by the military dictator Manuel Odría in 1948, the party went underground, while a succession of civilian and military dictatorships bolstered by an alliance of the coastal plantation oligarchy and regional highland landowning classes ruled the country for twenty-three years. Clamping down on rural and urban unrest, and persecuting union leaders, they postponed any kind of reform. Under an agreement to support Manuel Prado's election for a second term, the APRA was allowed to return to legality in 1956, and much chastised and hungry for power, it began to compromise on its initial principles and reformist flavor. However, during those years, the APRA and the pre-Castro Communist party did quietly support peasant struggles against landowners in the countryside and promoted the unionization of workers on the coastal plantations.

Socialists of those times argued that one could not change an agrarian regime without a preceding revolution such as those shown by the Mexican, Russian, or Chinese cases. Moreover, Marxists believed that they could bring about this revolution through the exacerbation of agrarian conflicts. The time was ripe. There was a violent agrarian reform in Bolivia's MNR (Movimiento Nacionalista Revolucionario, or Bolivian Nationalist Revolutionary Movement) revolution of 1952–56, with massive invasions of haciendas. Fidel Castro expropriated the Cuban sugar estates in 1959 after his triumph, and Peru was surely going to be next. But agrarian reforms also had a conservative bent. The Allies had won the Second World War, but it brought about the Cold War. In Japan and South Korea, the United States applied agrarian reforms to remove the power of aristocratic landowning classes, hoping to create a progressive-conservative, smallholding, family-based farmer class in its own ideological democratic image of its historical development in the North, Midwest, and Great Plains regions (the slave plantations in the South had been broken up after the U.S. Civil War). During the same period after the Second World War, on the other side of the Iron Curtain, in Russia and China, land reform meant collectivization and state intervention in Eastern European countries that fell under Soviet influence.

In the competition for spheres of influence in Latin America at the height of the Cold War, the United States developed alternatives to Communist agitation, and its push for an administratively managed redistribution of land was a priority enshrined in John F. Kennedy's Alliance for Progress program. This was subscribed to by Latin American governments, as a measure to prevent the spread of Communism, at Punta del Este, Uruguay in 1961; this was the same conference that expelled Cuba from the Organization of American States. The Organization of American States then set up an intergovernmental organism called the Interamerican Committee for Agricultural Development, and in Spanish Comité Interamericano de Desarrollo Agrícola (CIDA), based in Chile and directed by Solon Barraclough.[4] Peru was certainly considered by CIDA to be overripe for an agrarian reform. It published an exhaustive 500-page study called *Tenencia de la tierra y desarrollo socio-económico del sector agrícola — Perú* (1966) that became the basic document that everyone consulted and cited. (The document is referenced under Inter-American Committee on Agricultural Development [1966] to facilitate electronic searches.) The study took a whole year to complete and involved a series of international and Peruvian experts. As the report makes clear, Peru's diverse climate and history had produced one of the most complex and unequal land tenure systems on the continent. Based on the analysis of the agricultural census of 1961, which counted each agricultural unit, CIDA divided these into four types, based mainly on the size of the unit. These ranged from the large *latifundium* and the private- or corporate-owned estate, down to the single-family peasant farm, and ending with units whose lands were so small as to render them unviable as farms. It also found it useful to distinguish between the conditions on the industrialized coastal region and in the more traditional and backward highlands.

As can be seen in table 1 regarding the fertile irrigated coast, CIDA calculated that for 1961, fewer than one thousand large estates (CIDA called them large multifamily units) had 80 percent of the surface area. The medium-

TABLE 1 Coast

Peru: Estimated Values by Number and Surface of Agricultural Units by Economic Category for the Coast, 1961.

Agricultural Units

TENURE SYSTEM	NUMBER OF UNITS		SURFACE		
	Total Units	Percentage	Total in 1,000 Ha	Percentage	Average Ha Per Type of Unit
Large Multifamily (> 500 Ha)	920	1.7	1,036.0	80	1,126.1
Medium Multifamily (10 to 50 Ha)	2,000	3.7	78.0	6	39.0
Family Units (3–10 Ha)	6,200	11.4	52.0	4	8.4
Subfamily or Nearly Landless (< 3 Ha)	45,200	83.2	129.0	10	2.9
Totals	54,320	100	1,295.0	100	23.8

Note: Ha = hectare of irrigated land
Source: Prepared by the Interamerican Committee for Agricultural Development based on data of the First National Agricultural Census and documents of CRAV, CIDA, and CIDA/IRAC case studies and some regional reports. *Tenencia de la tierra y desarrollo socio-económico del sector agrícola — Perú*, p. 56. My translation.

sized technically operated farms, considered by all as socially desirable, were only 3.7 percent of the total units, with only 6 percent of the land. Single-family small units, from three to ten hectares, were 11.4 percent of the units, with only 4 percent of the land. The nearly landless category (called subfamily units by the CIDA), with land under three hectares, was numerically the largest with 83.2 percent of the total, but with only 10 percent of the land. The process of land concentration had been driven by a national and foreign industrial bourgeoisie, a powerful capitalist class with strong institutional presence in government affairs.

The CIDA calculated that the highlands of Perú, as shown in table 2, had

TABLE 2 Highlands

Peru: Estimated Values by Number and Surface of Agricultural Units by Economic Category for the Highlands, 1961.

Agricultural Units

TENURE SYSTEM	NUMBER OF UNITS		SURFACE		
	Total Units	Percentage	Total in 1,000 Ha	Percentage	Average Ha Per Type of Unit
Large Multifamily	8,912	1.3	11,450	75.0	1,284.8
Medium Multifamily	19,100	2.7	760	5.0	39.8
Family Units	88,500	12.5	724	4.8	8.2
Subfamily or nearly landless	590,730	83.4	722	4.7	1.2
Communities	808	0.1	1,604	10.5	1985.1
Totals	708,050	100	15,260	100	21.6

Definitions

	Irrigated (Ha)	Rain-fed Land (Ha)	Pasturage (Ha)
Large Multifamily	> 100	> 100	> 2,500
Medium Multifamily	10–100	50–100	500–2,500
Family	3–10	10–50	100–500
Subfamily	< 3	< 10	< 100

Note: Ha = hectare
Source: Prepared by the Inter-American Committee for Agricultural Development based on data of the First National Agricultural Census and documents of CRAV, CIDA, and CIDA/IRAC case studies and some regional reports. *Tenencia de la tierra y desarrollo socio-económico del sector agrícola—Perú*, p. 107. My translation.

thirteen times the number of agricultural units in the coastal region, but fifteen times more land. However, the maldistribution was just as evident as it was on the coast. Large multifamily haciendas represented only 1 percent of the nearly three-quarter million units but controlled 75 percent of the land. At the other end of the spectrum, 590,000 nearly landless families had 4.7 percent of the land. The desired single-family farm represented only 12.5 percent of all units, encompassing less than 5 percent of the land with a mean of 8.2 hectares per family. Officially recognized indigenous communities in 1966 were 0.1 percent of the legal units and had 10.5 percent of the land, but if the number of community members were to be counted in each, then the number in substandard family holdings would have increased (communities invariably included a large number of the poor family units). According to the CIDA, very few highland haciendas were modernizing by themselves through increasing productivity, paying proper wages to workers, or providing the government-mandated educational and integration programs for Indian serfs.

A restudy of land tenure conditions based on the agricultural census of 1972 found that the CIDA study, so universally accepted, was nonetheless in error for the highlands. José María Caballero, an economist who became the leading expert on agrarian reform in Peru and one of its most respected critics, pointed out that large estates were by no means the dominant form of landholding in the highlands, and that false impressions had led to misconstrued policy options. Hacienda domination was a myth, and Caballero hinted at the political motivations and statistical errors that produced it: "The progressive sectors each from their point of view considered—more than rightly—that highland *hacendados* were a dead weight and impediment to development, and as they took up the fight for an agrarian reform, they were inclined to promote an exaggerated image of how much land they concentrated, in the same way that landlords themselves were interested in presenting an embellished picture of themselves" (Caballero 1981a, 93–94, my translation). Caballero questioned the simplistic meaning of one hectare that the CIDA economists had used. Given the complex ecology of the highlands, one hectare of irrigated land in favorable climatic conditions below 3,000 meters above sea level is equivalent to 51.6 hectares of *puna* grasslands above 4,000 meters. Using these equivalencies to correct land tenure data in terms of standardized hectares, Caballero (1981a, 96–103) found that the predominant units (98 percent) were small units (unequally distributed between a large number of *minifundio* subfamily and family units and a smaller group of family farms from 2 to 50 hectares), with about 80 percent of the land. Thus there were far fewer large hacienda-like units (even in standardized hectares) than CIDA's numbers, and these tended to occupy the highland *puna* grasslands dedicated to sheep ranching. Although a landowner could socially strut around as an *hacendado*, the actual amount of land he controlled was far less than his legal title would suggest. The highlands faced an absolute shortage of land. The redistribution of land would therefore not solve many problems, since there was not that much of it to expropriate, and by the late 1960s the hacienda as an economic system was in severe decline. Nonetheless, since Caballero's study of 1981 came ten years after expropriation, the prevailing myth of hacienda domination in the highlands was to be the guiding idea justifying agrarian reform.

The implementation of a rapid modernization on these haciendas, once expropriated, was an explicit objective of any reform, somewhat in contradiction with the restitutive ideals of giving the land back to the indigenous population. Optimistically, the models that reformists worked with sought to achieve both. As we shall see later in this book, modernization of highland *puna* pasture management was already underway before the agrarian reform in the form of enclosure movements. These affected the communities and the resident peasant population, causing reform agents headaches about how to proceed as they were torn between restitution and the expansion of modernization.

By the late 1950s, population growth against a limited land base in the rural areas was producing a politically explosive situation in the highlands. Increasing rates of litigation, land occupations, conflicts between communities and haciendas, and shrill reports of *hacendado* abuses were amply discussed in the media and in intellectual circles. When large numbers of landless indigenous people started migrating to the cities and aggressively settling in slums surrounding the capital city of Lima, the ruling elites began to fear them, hoping that through agrarian reform they could stem the massive migratory trend.

The earliest commission to study a possible agrarian reform was set up in 1959, during Manuel Prado's second administration. It was lead by Pedro Beltrán, who was Prado's conservative premier, a prominent cotton hacienda owner in the Cañete Valley, and the owner of a newspaper. Predictably, that commission and Beltrán's newspaper, *La Prensa*, reported that instead of distributing land, the country should focus on opening new lands for colonization in the empty jungle portions of the country, as well as bringing about state-sponsored irrigation on the coast and green-revolution technology to improve productivity in the highlands. The coast with its capitalist plantations was deemed to be untouchable since it was generating foreign exchange.

The Rise of Fernando Belaúnde and a Brief Military Intervention, 1962–63

Beginning in 1956, a young progressive architect from Arequipa, Fernando Belaúnde Terry, challenged the oligarchy and competed with the APRA through a new political party called Acción Popular or Popular Action (AP). Belaúnde spent a whole year as a candidate visiting every village, town, and place in Peru, promising agrarian and other reforms. The bitterly fought election in 1962 between Odría, Haya de la Torre, and Belaúnde turned out to be inconclusive. A military junta staged a coup to break the impasse and called for renewed elections within one year. By that time, peasant unrest had become massive in the highland department of Cusco, and a small guerrilla camp was established by Luis de la Puente Uceda in a remote area of that department. To quell it, the military junta entered the region with a repressive campaign to contain the movement. This junta also implemented an agrarian reform limited to one province in the Cusco area (Convención y Lares). Thus, the first experience of a top-down reform by a military regime provided a precedent for the subsequent reform by Velasco.

Fernando Belaúnde, 1963–68

Belaúnde redoubled his electoral campaign, reaffirmed his promise to implement an agrarian reform, and won the elections in 1963. In anticipation, peasants in the highlands had occupied thousands upon thousands of hectares in staged "invasions" of hacienda lands that Belaúnde the candidate had condoned, but Belaúnde the president had to confront due to their illegality and the protests of landowners. The political scientist Howard Handelman in *Struggle in the Andes* stated, "The peasant mobilization of the early 1960s was unquestionably one of the largest peasant movements in Latin American history" (1975, 121). And the authors of the CIDA report (1966) saw the mobilization of what they estimated as three hundred thousand peasants in most of highland Peru at that time as a warning: the movements were intensifying, escalating, and radicalizing, requiring a solution in the most urgent terms.

The losing APRA joined the conservative Odría opposition in Parliament, abandoning its reformist principles yet once more. Belaúnde did not have a majority in Congress, and his regime's reform measures were constantly stymied in this fractious Parliament. Also, in 1965, during Belaúnde's first regime, two separate small guerrilla movements inspired by Ché Guevara established a tenuous foothold in the highland and jungle areas far away from Lima. They were quickly routed by the military. All the same, even the military became acutely aware that time was running out.

Belaúnde did keep his promise. He presented his agrarian reform laws to be debated in Parliament a month after his inauguration in August 1963. The other parties brought their own proposals soon after. The diverse interests and intense debate produced a compromised law that was promulgated on May 24, 1964. Among its strong points that immediately went into effect were the prohibition of personal services of any kind and the right of peasants to full ownership of their usufruct parcels, abolishing the status of serfdom (*yanaconaje* and *colonato*, the system by which a family was granted the use of a small plot of land in exchange for obligatory work for the owner). Peasants in indigenous communities were also guaranteed their communal possessions, and the law gave them high priority in the adjudication of expropriated lands based on demonstrated need and historically proven prior dispossession.

However, it was a weak law and difficult to implement. Conservative opposition groups had introduced a number of exceptions and loopholes that allowed landowners to minimize the impact of the law. Coastal plantations producing agro-export crops were exempt; so too were "efficiently" run haciendas anywhere in the country. How to characterize an efficient hacienda was slippery, and thus this categorization was an inducement to contest expropriation. Landowners were also given fairly generous land extensions that they could keep. In addition, they were encouraged to parcel up their haciendas under private initiative in the spirit of the reform by making portions of the hacienda available to landless families. The law provided very generous measures to compensate expropriated land and capital stocks, making each expropriation an expensive proposition. The law's procedural aspects required a series of complex steps safeguarding the rights of the landowner and permitting appeals to contest the reform agency's decisions. It gave the landowning class, backed by its well-paid lawyers, ample opportunities to protect its interests and to delay final decisions. Each expropriation required a presidential decree. As Susana Lastarria-Cornhiel (1989) shows, the pace of expropriation and adjudication under the first Belaúnde regime was exceedingly slow, and its impact minimal.[5]

The Belaúnde land reform law had envisioned promoting small- and medium-sized family farms, each endowed with full private property. Co-operativization of farms, the Belaúnde law stipulated, was to be encouraged on a voluntary basis. But, as the CIDA report (1966) pointed out, there was not enough land available to achieve these lofty aims. The CIDA had calculated available land base, or the number of hectares from haciendas that could be expropriated, and compared it against the number of land-less people deserving allocations and the minimum size of a viable farm to be given to each. They did not match up. Economists for the CIDA pre-dicted that on the coast, only 13 percent of the land need could be satisfied from the land base that could potentially be expropriated. In the high-lands, where the problem was more acute, their calculations indicated that only 4 percent of needed land would be become available. While 150,000 families could potentially benefit, that left 700,000 families out of con-sideration. Caballero's (1981a) assessment was even more dire as to what could be expropriated and redistributed or the effect that a potential reform could have had. However, he wrote the book with the benefit of hindsight. Velasco's experts were aware of these limitations and therefore sought to expropriate as much land as they could.

Juan Velasco Alvarado, 1968–75; Francisco Morales Bermúdez, 1975–80

By 1968 the Belaúnde regime was in severe trouble. Fractious disputes in Parliament, an indecisive weak president, a slew of scandals, and the mis-handling of a dispute with a petroleum concession owned by the United States, the International Petroleum Company, led to his ouster. Two days after the coup on October 9, 1968, Velasco's troops occupied the contested installations of the International Petroleum Company at Talara, signaling that this military regime would be very different.

Within one year came the second surprise, a secretly prepared and more radical agrarian reform law.[6] Compared to that of Belaúnde, this law did not allow exemptions and included punitive expropriation if social con-ditions on haciendas were not in compliance with existing rules. Agro-factories such as rice mills or sugar refineries were considered part of the property that could be expropriated.

The preferred form of adjudication was to be in the form of worker-managed cooperatives. Supercooperatives, as I have nicknamed variants specifically designed for the adjudication of highland sheep and cattle haciendas to indigenous communities, were named Sociedades Agrararias de Interés Social (SAIS), or Agrarian Societies of Social Interest (the operation of the SAIS system is discussed in chapter 6). Land was also to be adjudicated to individual peasant communities with the strong injunction not to divide up the land, but to develop a collective area with improved technology and a market orientation. If a group of peasants did not belong to a community, the agrarian reform labeled them *grupos campesinos* (peasant groups) in the hopes that they might in the future organize themselves into a cooperative or become a newly recognized peasant community. The law also stipulated that individuals could become recipients of adjudicated land. A special land court was to be installed to deal with litigation arising from a streamlined and better-financed national agrarian reform bureaucracy. In that court, landlords were treated with little sympathy. Compensation for expropriations was reduced and to be paid mostly in bonds, which could be redeemed for investments in industry. Adjudicated land was to be paid back to the government in the form of an agrarian debt over twenty years.

June 24, the summer solstice, had become enshrined as the revived Incan ceremony Inti Raymi in Cusco and El Día del Indio in Lima. Velasco chose that day in 1969 to announce the new laws in Lima. In his speech, he addressed all agricultural workers regardless of ethnic status as *campesinos* and said to them, "*Campesinos, el patrón ya no comerá de tu pobreza*" (the landlord is no longer going to eat from your poverty). The army took over the sugar estates on the northern coast two days later, indicating to the landlords that this time the agrarian reform was to be for real. Ten years later, the government had expropriated 15,826 properties and 9 million hectares. In the previous period from 1962 to 1968, in comparison, Belaúnde had expropriated 1 million hectares from 546 haciendas (Matos Mar and Mejía 1980, 171).

But Velasco's reform concentrated and collectivized land. Through cooperativization, the 15,000 expropriated units were consolidated into 1,708

Figure 2 General Enrique Gallegos Venero, the minister of agriculture, embraces a folklorically dressed-up member at the inauguration of a cooperative in Nazca on June 24, 1975. Archive of the photographer Carlos Domínguez. © Carlos Domínguez.

collective adjudications (reducing the number to one-ninth of the preexisting haciendas). Three hundred thousand families (twice the number that the CIDA had calculated) were named beneficiaries by including them as members of cooperatives. Far from distributing land, agrarian reform therefore consolidated land holdings, most often into unwieldy, large, territorially disperse units that incorporated a diverse mixture of forms of land tenure and production systems within their boundaries. The setting up of these new cooperatives was, of course, accompanied by much rhetoric. They were named after Incas, indigenous resistance heroes, or revolutionary thinkers. Generals attended adjudication ceremonies and in their speeches claimed that agrarian reform had expelled the owners, that it had returned the land to those who truly made it productive, and that it had given autonomy to the peasants (fig. 2). They emphasized that the cooperative was theirs to make it prosper, and the new *socios* (members) cheered wildly.

In setting up this system, the government pursued some very clear objectives, which can be briefly summarized as the intentions behind the reform. First, technological regression was to be avoided. Since in theory each hacienda consisted of a centralized area, which operated with greater technical efficiency and profitability than the other area where the peasants had their subsistence plots, the central productive system was to be maintained, improved, and enlarged.

Second, no internal land distribution was to take place, since any growth of land in the hands of inefficient peasants would imply a loss of technical efficiency.

Third, the benefits of agrarian reform would accrue to owner/workers through wages, social services, profit distribution, or development assistance to member communities, but not through increased access to land.

Fourth, the modern technology that supposedly operated in the centralized area was to be transferred to the member's individual lands and to the constituent communities, so that gradually the collective efficient area would grow and the peasant subsistence plots would diminish as the two areas were progressively integrated. The dynamism of the central part of the enterprise was to spread to the small peasant holdings contained within it. Thus, if all went well, the peasants would give up their subsistence plots over time and become full-time wage-earners/owners of their increasingly more efficient cooperatives.

Fifth, the enterprise was to capitalize on the profits to be made from the collective lands, so as to provide for investment funds to less-developed sectors of the unit.

Sixth, after a grace period of five years, the unit would be able to begin paying installments of the agrarian debt it owed the government (as the recipient of adjudicated land) out of the profits made from the lands that were worked collectively. This debt was to be repaid over a twenty-year period.

Seventh, until the agrarian debt was paid, the full titles of adjudication would not be turned over to the new units and, until then, the government reserved the right to oversee and intervene if the cooperative failed to move toward the objectives of agrarian reform.

Eighth, more beneficiaries of agrarian reform could be incorporated into each adjudication, with no need to worry about people/land ratios or the viable size of the smallest farms. Thus, political pressures caused by the demands of deserving people but insufficient land to allocate could be avoided. By making many people members of a cooperative and telling them that they were the owners, but not giving any of them any land, the ninth objective was achieved.

TABLE 3 Land Adjudicated and Beneficiary Families by Type of Unit (1969–78)

TYPE OF UNIT	NUMBER	EXTENSION IN HA	% LAND	# FAMILIES	% FAMILIES
SAIS	60	2,773,435	37	60,990	18
Cooperatives	502	2,127,166	29	103,699	31
Peasant Groups	743	1,586,396	21	43,922	13
Communities	403	726,227	10	109,709	33
Individuals	—	190,317	3	15,878	5
Totals	1,708	7,405,508	100	334,108	100

Note: Total extensions and number of families do not add up properly in original.
Source: Martínez Arellano 1980, 107.

Ninth, the peasants were politically demobilized since—in theory—they had been given land. It also made the statistics look good and thereby earned the reform applause from world experts, who praised how radical the Peruvian agrarian reform had been to give land to so many families. One such statistical table, derived from official sources, is shown in table 3.

The problems of land pressure were thus transferred, unsolved, from the old unjust system onto the newly adjudicated units. But unlike communist countries, the Peruvian reform did not really enforce collectivization with repression or brute force. During the ten years of military rule, there were many problems and conflicts within the cooperatives, troubles between the cooperatives and their land-hungry neighbors, and between communities and cooperatives. The government responded with top-down adjustments, lecturing and reorganizing the cooperatives and redesigning the enterprises.

By and large, very few cooperatives prospered. Though it is easy to document how the wages and benefits of the members increased for some years, the enterprises themselves began to decline and falter after a few years, and when it was hard to pay those costly wages members had so enthusiastically approved in previous general meetings, difficulties set in. Here I will not deal with the causes of this decline because the details are in chapter 5. Suffice it to say that Peru lost its lucrative cotton and sugar export sectors, and that it drastically increased its food imports over twenty years instead of stimulating a healthy agricultural sector. There is hardly a single positive statistic one can show until the mid-1980s, other than that about one-third of Peru's land got expropriated and cooperativized.

Several bureaucratic state service institutions were created to train cooperative workers to operate marketing boards, sugar cooperative supervisory boards, state fertilizer distribution companies, and other such bodies. Some of them, especially the agrarian bank, became obstacles to cooperative development instead of fostering its growth. Their effectiveness also decreased as money ran out during the successive economic crises. Already under the Morales Bermúdez regime of 1975–79, enthusiasm for the agrarian reform was waning and the government pulled much of the support it used to give to cooperatives in the form of credit, guaranteed markets and prices, technical aid, and political backing.

The beneficiaries of the agrarian reform, mainly the serfs on highland haciendas and the workers on the coastal plantations, were initially enthusiastic about the reform but soon began to chafe under the strictures of their cooperatives. Political participation in the government-imposed *campesino* federation, the Confederación Nacional Agraria (CNA, or National Agrarian Confederation) was at best lukewarm, although its inauguration with peasant delegates sitting in the hallowed seats of the parliament building did have a momentary political impact (fig. 3). Nor did land invasions cease despite the accelerated pace of expropriation. Land occupations initially were to speed up the expulsion of their owners, often with the connivance of government agencies. Other occupations were preemptive, to keep out competitors, and yet other conflicts arose when peasants refused to conform to their designated assignations in collective units. Karl Yambert (1989) describes how as early as 1973, in Piura, the members of the community of Catacaos invaded their own cooperative. Elmer Arze Espinoza's (1983) careful recounting of Piura peasant movements tells how discontented landless peasants and other excluded rural people used this age-old tactic to jockey for land that they would not otherwise have been awarded. Protests against adjudications perceived as unfair and mildly repressive government countermoves clouded the politics of agrarian reform throughout. In 1974 in the department of Andahuaylas, a wave of land occupations took the Velasco government by surprise—in that remote area, the reform agency, probably influenced by landlord connections, was exceedingly slow serving them with notifications of expropriation.

Figure 3 The inauguration of the Confederación Nacional Agraria (CNA). Delegates of beneficiaries of the agrarian reform use the Houses of Parliament, September 28, 1974. Archive of the photographer Carlos Domínguez. © Carlos Domínguez.

A second kind of land occupation occurred when discontented members of cooperatives pushed into the lands of the centralized areas that were supposed to be "off limits" to them, much of this stealthily and with the collusion of their administrators; in other cases, as described in chapter 5, these seizures of land took place as spectacular acts of disobedience and defiance. The tactics peasant movements had learned in the 1960s were successfully revived. Repossession of land that had nominally been adjudicated to them began tentatively during the military regime, accelerated in pace, and became bold throughout the second Belaúnde and García regimes, because the peasants realized that by that time governments were no longer interested in defending the cooperatives and the SAISes.

Intellectual reactions to Velasco's agrarian reform were also mixed. Initially, it was praised by progressives. While right-wing opposition was effectively silenced in the public sphere, criticisms and objections to the way the reform was being carried out came from the Left. Further left than the Velasco government, some of the objections were extremely radical.[7] An early analysis was so critical that the author chose a pseudonym in publishing it; Ramón Saldívar (in real life the economist César Benavides) characterized the Velasco reform as "bourgeois." Based primarily on an analysis of the new laws in relation to the CIDA report and focusing on financial aspects, he argued that because the reform compensated the bourgeois owners in money and forced the peasants to pay for the land as agrarian debt, the agrarian reform was thus reconstituting the old social classes in thin disguises and continuing the process of the accumulation of capital in the hands of the bourgeoisie (Saldívar 1974). As the agrarian reform officers began to take more and stricter control of the cooperatives, critics from the Left said that reformed agrarian cooperatives were examples of nationalist state capitalism, that power had been transferred from the landowning classes to the state but the modus operandi was still capitalist. For example, another anonymous writer, Pedro Atusparia (1977), in real life Rodrigo Montoya (1989, chapter 6), disentangled the complexities of the agrarian reform process to argue that when all ideology is unmasked, state capitalism was the real intent and design of the reform. Worker or peasant ownership of the reformed enterprises, these critics said, was a sham and a smokescreen.

A more devastating critique of agrarian reform was that by the economist José María Caballero (1980, 1981b). Although he found the description of the reform as a model of state capitalism an accurate one, he nonetheless called it a resounding failure because the objectives it set for itself were fairly conservative rather than revolutionary, and more importantly, because it failed to achieve its own limited objectives. Despite name changes, there was in fact a lot of continuity in the way the agrarian sector operated before and after the reform. The cooperatives did not function well and did not perform their important functions of growth and expansion; rather, they vegetated or declined. The complex mechanisms designed to compensate nonbeneficiaries through the distribution of profits for development hardly ever became operative and instead became a source of conflict. Peasants and workers did not like the cooperatives they were forced into, and the state was repeatedly forced to intervene, which made it unpopular. In terms of production, see Caballero's judgment: "Output performance during the reform years was poor but without any noticeable setbacks for which the agrarian reform may be held particularly responsible" (1981b, 35). On income distribution, Caballero cites expert studies that point out that it was relatively small, "of the order of 1% to 1.5% of National Income; and that the redistribution is biased, most of [it] going to the richest sectors of agrarian labor" (1981b, 35).

Taking advantage of the reshuffling of power and economic opportunity, new opportunists emerged as a new group of middle-class Peruvians. In a text originally written in 1974, Ricardo Letts, the son of middle-sized landholders, an agronomist, an enthusiast of agrarian reform, a leftist critic, a militant in the political party Vanguardia Revolucionaria (Revolutionary Vanguard), and a gadfly politician, used a lot of hyphenated words in his description of this new class fraction that benefited from the military's reformist model: "State-capitalism gives birth to a new class sector of the bourgeois class,[8] made up of high-ranking officers in alliance with administrators, managers, directors, high-level bureaucrats, all of whom become the beneficiaries of state capitalism, which arises from the control over the means of production and of the surplus value extracted from the workers in the enterprises: The capitalist-State-cooperative, the communal-social property-State enterprise, the social interest-State-enterprises and, of course, the State-bourgeois-capitalist-State enterprise itself" (Letts 1981, 170; my translation).

Almost twenty small, semi-clandestine, Marxist, left-wing political parties emerged during those years, and some of them began to support and organize peasant federations to oppose the government. Among them was a group with expertise in rural conditions, Vanguardia Revolucionaria (VR), which oversaw the growth of a peasant federation called the Confederación Campesina Peruana (CCP). The CCP grew steadily throughout the Velasco and Morales Bermúdez years and became an effective challenge to the government's own Confederación Nacional Agraria (CNA). Vanguardia Revolucionaria was behind the land occupations in Andahuaylas and Piura, and as disaffection with the way the cooperatives were functioning increased, it promoted further land occupations that are discussed in chapter 5.

Opposition to Velasco and Morales Bermúdez from the Left stimulated the growth of left-wing sentiment throughout the country, partly because Velasco's revolution had turned away from its initial radicalism as internal dissention among the armed forces veered the process to the right. The proliferation and growth of many factions of left-wing oppositional politics took three forms: 1) the support of unions and peasant movements that challenged the military's own worker and peasant federations, in the city and countryside, often in semi-clandestine form; 2) electoral participation toward the end of the military's regime in the Constitutional Assembly (where the Left garnered one-third of the total vote) and then the general elections, in which the Left failed to unite and lost; and 3) the growth of fractions of extreme Maoists who talked about armed struggle, among them a very tiny fraction of Maoists who had been expelled from other student organizations at the University of Huamanga and took the name Partido Comunista del Perú: Sendero Luminoso (Shining Path). This group began to infiltrate the countryside in the department of Ayacucho. Its first public act was to burn the ballot boxes in the village of Chuschi in the general election that brought Fernando Belaúnde back to the presidency in 1980.

Fernando Belaúnde Terry, 1980–85

Though Belaúnde in his first reign had favored an agrarian reform, he very diplomatically did his best to derail the Velasco reform in his second term in office. Though it was impossible to undo it à la Chile, where the landowners actually got their properties returned by Pinochet, Belaúnde passed a law that simply stated that since cooperatives were autonomous enterprises and not under state control, those cooperatives that wished to change their legal structure were free to do so. This set off an avalanche of cooperative dissolutions. Most cooperatives were terribly in debt, could not get credit, and lacked any entrepreneurial vision on how to save themselves. This process took place mostly on the coast where land was valuable and cash cropping viable, and where the members had enough experience in agriculture to make a go of it as independent smallholders. The failure of these cooperatives is likened by some observers to the collapse of collective agriculture in the Soviet Union, Eastern Europe, and the remarkable changes that took place in China with the increase in private entrepreneurship in the rural communes.

In the highlands, the landowning class was totally eliminated from the countryside. Even before Velasco's drastic measures, many owners had divided up their lands among heirs and their *colonos* to move to urban occupations. The total expropriation of those who had remained had left a power vacuum in rural areas. Most traditional feudal haciendas dissolved fairly rapidly into de facto and sometimes officially recognized indigenous communities (*comunidades campesinas*) without much fanfare or official notice. Sometimes the peasants on haciendas steadfastly refused to become cooperatives. A few expropriations went through a nominal phase of a co-operative or pre-cooperative structure, but they did not last long. The fact that communities won the most land in the highlands is an unintended consequence of the reform. It should be emphasized that the original Velasco reform had neither the patience nor the desire to create new communities or give them land because it considered them archaic and an impediment to agricultural change. They were supposed to be obedient participants in the modernizing efforts of the reform's intent—even as it meant that the reform was to contribute to their demise—but not be merely awarded land to continue to be underdeveloped peasant *comuneros*. Velasco's officials had repeatedly stated that their objective was to create wealth and distribute it, but not to spread poverty by breaking up economies of scale.

In fieldwork that César Fonseca and I did in 1984 in the Paucartambo Valley of Cusco, we found the following post-agrarian reform situation: In 1961 there were 169 haciendas in Paucartambo and 24 communities. In 1985 there were 4 agrarian cooperatives, 46 recognized *comunidades*, and not one hacienda. The agrarian cooperatives were in total economic collapse. They had sold their cattle and tractors, had no capital to start production again, and the members were in serious conflicts with each other. Soon after we concluded our fieldwork, they were dismantled by the government and the land was divided among the *socios*. The officially recognized communities, in contrast, were a more stable form of organization and grew from 16 in 1961 to 47 in 1986. Sixteen of them had received new land, and 18 newly constituted communities grew out of ex-hacienda lands. There were also 31 new *grupos campesinos* created by the government out of ex-haciendas, which functioned as *comunidades* but lacked the official recognition papers at the time. In due course, the government did provide them. Thus in total, 78 communities occupied the space of 161 ex-haciendas. Nationally, the number of recognized communities doubled from 2,228 when Velasco took over to 4,792, occupying more than one-third of the land in the sierra (Trivelli 1992) by the end of García's presidency.

Thus "from hacienda to community" is the story of agrarian reform for most of the highlands. In some cases there was a contentious detour of the setting up of cooperatives that quickly disintegrated. Belaúnde's second regime did nothing for the newly emerged ex-hacienda communities. He and his government began to fully embrace the neoliberal reforms that became dominant in the hemisphere under what was labeled the Washington Consensus. The support system for agrarian reform, already dwindling from the Morales Bermúdez regime, continued to shrink.

Also, importantly, the beginnings of radical insurgency by the Maoist leftist guerrillas of Shining Path began in the region of Ayacucho. This coincided with the Belaúnde regime, pushing the military into brutal counterinsurgency wars. Friendly generals who only a few years before had inaugurated cooperatives or paternalistically had presided over peasant organizations now commanded overwhelmingly powerful murderous army units that pursued entire villages in their hunt for subversives in the Ayacucho region.

Alan García Perez, 1985–90

Running for election against a growing but fractious newly emerged Left, Alan García, the leader of APRA, won the elections of 1985. Fiery and populist in his speeches, but severely hampered by a deepening economic crisis and the expansion of the Shining Path insurgency, García turned his efforts toward economic policies of the agrarian sector in terms of price supports, subsidies, and credit. He devised a populist rapprochement with the peasant communities. The statute governing internal relations within communities (promulgated by Velasco but neglected by Belaúnde) became a law approved by Parliament. He participated in face-to-face meetings with community leaders (*rimanakuy*) in each department and implemented micro-level development projects. Falling production (despite easier credit) amid runaway inflation was made up for by increasing food imports. Under García's government, the agrarian reform SAISes on sheep and cattle ranches in the department of Junín and Puno collapsed.

Over time the supercooperatives that had been set up under Velasco's reform had become larger versions of hacienda-like institutions through the infiltration of a managerial class of veterinarians and professionals who focused on improved production, on hardening their positions against encroachments by landless peasants in communities, and on developing political alliances with conservative elements in towns and regional governments. The managers had become an elite technocracy that generated little benefit to surrounding communities. A detailed case on how the SAIS Cahuide disintegrated in the department of Junín in 1987 is in chapter 6. At that same time, a wave of organized invasions in the department of Puno liquidated the forty-four agrarian reform cooperative institutions and divided them out mostly to communities. With those invasions, all land expropriated by Velasco finally was reappropriated by the peasants. The insurgency of Shining Path and the MRTA (Movimiento Revolucionario Túpac Amaru, or Túpac Amaru Revolutionary Movement) spread to other parts of the country and increased in Lima during García's regime.

Alberto Fujimori, 1990–2000

For the highlands, the takeover, dissolution, and distribution of cooperatives and SAISes in Puno marked the end of agrarian reform. Alan García's government ended in disgrace. He was booed as he handed over the presidential sash to Alberto Fujimori amid accusations of corruption and ineptitude, and for causing hyperinflation. He faced opprobrium by the business class for attempting to nationalize the banks, and hate by the Left for bombing prisons during a prison revolt led by Shining Path. He fled to exile in Colombia and evaded judicial proceedings against him. Mario Vargas Llosa, the writer, had become the candidate for the conservatives, arguing the neoliberal need for structural readjustment. He was opposed by the obscure but rapidly rising popular Japanese-Peruvian candidate who rode a tractor and trailer because he had been a rector of the Agrarian University. Alberto Fujimori, whose campaign promise was not to implement the bitter medicine of structural readjustment prescribed by Vargas Llosa's economists, won the election. Fujimori then implemented the bitter medicine anyway; it was called the *fujishock*. At enormous cost to the citizens, he stabilized the economy. He was also lucky in that the secret police had tracked down Abimael Guzmán, the leader of Shining Path, to his middle-class hideout in Lima and arrested him in 1992, resulting in the fizzling of the insurrection. In 1996 he demolished what was left of the other insurgent group, the MRTA, which had taken over the Japanese embassy and kept hostages.[9]

In agrarian policy, Fujimori completed the neoliberal agenda that was driven by free markets, cleaning up—so to speak—what Velasco had created. His minister of agriculture, Absalón Vásquez, the son of a worker from the Casa Grande sugar cooperative, oversaw the privatization and expropriation of the last remaining bastions of Velasco's sugar cooperatives on the northern coast. By then they were in the most miserable state, like Romanian agrarian collective factories with antiquated machinery and a huge labor force (the owners) that could not be fired (and those over sixty were demanding their pensions). Most of the sugar cooperatives had neglected production and had run up enormous debts to banks. Internal corruption was rife, supported by shady political deals in the region. The members of the sugar cooperatives did not think that parceling land was an option because they were tied to the refinery. The Fujimori government coercively offered to forgive the cooperatives' tax and social security debts if the members agreed to convert their collective ownership in the cooperatives into individualized and divisible shares. If they did not agree, bankruptcy procedures were to be implemented. The government then offered to help to sell off the ex-cooperatives to private investors. The members' shares were then bought cheaply by shady investors, gaining majority holdings for the board of directors. The new companies fired excess workers. Despite bitter opposition, the workers sought out joint ventures with capitalists instead but lost out. Since then the residences of the workers have become independent towns. Provision of water and electricity, education, and other benefits previously sustained by the cooperative were privatized; ex-owners/ex-workers now have to pay for these services.

If the dissolution of the SAISes in the highlands was messy, the breakup of the sugar cooperatives was far worse. Because the process had not yet concluded by the time I did my fieldwork, and although I did collect some very bitter recollections and very ugly stories from people in the sugar cooperatives, I have omitted them from this book.[10]

In agrarian policy, Fujimori's neoliberal restructuring and reduction of the state entailed the closing of the agrarian bank, the cancellation of all forms of subsidies and special credit to farmers, the shutting down of the agrarian reform office and the bureau responsible for peasant communities, and the dismantling of the state apparatus that had dealt with agrarian reform and rural development. He even sought to dissolve the communities by adopting the precedent of the Mexican constitution of 1991 that allows members to dissolve their community if a majority vote decides to do so in an assembly. Only a few *comunidades* close to urban areas were tempted to subdivide land to sell it as urban land. Fujimori's agricultural legislation removed the last vestiges of protectionist agrarian laws. Land was to be freely bought and sold without any top limits. In order to assist the creation of a land market with financial aid from the Inter-American Development Bank, a new land-titling program has begun to clean up the mess in titles caused by the diverse expropriations, restructuring, and redistributions, and to properly register private and communal property (Lastarria-Cornhiel and Barnes 1999). In military terms, his administration recognized and officialized peasant defense organizations (*rondas campesinas*) that collaborated with the army in routing out Shining Path from the rural areas in the central highlands.

Initially Fujimori was a popular president, but then he organized a coup against himself, rewriting the Constitution so he could create a rubber-stamp parliament. He insured support from the rural communities for his referendums, the approval of his new constitution, and reelection campaigns through personal helicopter landings on the plaza of every remote village. There, he would don a peasant poncho, wear the appropriate *campesino* headgear, and distribute presents—often computers that could not be used because there was no electricity. He gave money for small construction projects and he did put up a lot of school buildings, all painted bright orange to be easily recognizable as his personal gift. Then Fujimori would dance with the peasants and fly back to Lima. This was greatly appreciated.

So ended the era of agrarian reform with an excursion into chimerical cooperatives, which Velasco's social engineers had dreamed could solve everything. In the end, three hundred thousand families got some small plots of land, which they had to take forcibly from the cooperatives into which they were pushed. In the highlands, communities had to struggle to retrieve the actual land that had been expropriated in their name but which they had not been allowed to use. They did this by using the proverbial weapons of the peasants: they infiltrated the cooperative's lands, they increased the number of their cattle on the pastures, they inflated the number of members in the cooperatives. On the legal front, they agitated to deactivate the cooperatives, they staged land invasions, and they sought official recognition as communities. It is also true that what Western eyes recognize as capital infrastructure and agricultural technology was destroyed during the reform process. Small-scale, household-based rural peasant economies have become the predominant units of production in the countryside.

The whole process took seventy years. It fundamentally changed rural relationships and the country itself. The Peru of today is a very different place because of Velasco's revolution and its agrarian reform. Looking back today, the old questions that used to be asked about it—was it a success or a failure?—have become irrelevant. A good response is that the agrarian reform happened and it had many consequences, many of them still not completely understood. However, as you will read in the chapters that follow, the people who lived through it have all sorts of stories to tell about it. They tell these stories in the absence of an official history of the agrarian reform against which they can measure their own experiences. I start with the memories of a spirited supporter of the Velasco revolution. I interviewed Francisco Guerra García, a political scientist, in March 1996.

Pancho Guerra about SINAMOS

Francisco (Pancho) Guerra García was my colleague at the Catholic University in the late 1960s. A political scientist, he joined the Velasco regime with enthusiasm and continued defending it even after it became unpopular. In March 1996, I looked him up at the Centro de Estudios para el Desarrollo y la Participación (CEDEP, or Center for the Study of Development and Participation), an NGO made up of intellectuals dedicated to continuing the ideas and practices that had once fueled the Velasco revolution.[11] I asked for an interview with Pancho because he had been associated with SINAMOS (the Sistema Nacional de Movilización Social, or National System for Social Mobilization), the Velasco regime's most controversial institution.

It was set up in 1971 to support the political work of the revolution without becoming a political party itself; it was a bureaucracy instead. Many of my interviewees remembered SINAMOS as the scourge that caused everyone trouble. Administrators of cooperatives perceived SINAMOS's local promoters as gadflies whose preaching of revolutionary principles of a society of democratic participation and the inclusion of the excluded made their work difficult. They commonly accused the institution of being infiltrated by leftists bent on undermining the productivist aims of the new agrarian reform enterprises. At the same time, organizers of left-wing opposition found in the work of SINAMOS's agents their most effective obstacle, and, from their point of view, a demobilizing force in the countryside. The offices of SINAMOS were burned in Cusco in 1973 and in Lima on February 5, 1975 (during two days of rioting). In the end, everyone hated SINAMOS and it was closed down by Morales Bermúdez in 1976.

Yet it was one of the bolder institutions characteristic of the era in which the government tried to incorporate the masses while controlling them at same time. The intellectual civilian behind the idea was Carlos Delgado (also Velasco's speech writer), an anthropologist trained at Cornell University. It included former radicals and amnestied guerrillas, the so-called pragmatic leftists. David Scott Palmer, in his doctoral dissertation for Cornell, summarized SINAMOS's mission to "stimulate participation under the ultimate control of the military as the best way to insure that participation does not get out of hand" (1973, 132).

Pancho described the atmosphere in 1969:

> I was still a professor at the Catholic University when a friend called me on the phone to tell me that the agrarian reform would be radicalized and that it would start with the expropriation of the sugar estates. I reacted with complete doubt and disbelief that a military government would do such a thing. A radical agrarian reform had been what a whole generation of politicized leftists like me had long been dreaming about. I remember vividly the images on television of the armed forces rolling with tanks into the sugar refineries. That action persuaded me to join the regime.
>
> When SINAMOS was created, I was invited to take part, and I was really attracted to that kind of work. Initially it was a small group made up of people who came from different political camps. Some of us did not know the others. In several months of intense work we discussed the design of what would become the institution, how the organization could function. There was a great *espirit de corps* and we worked intensely.

With offices in every significant region of the country, SINAMOS was put together from seven preexisting bureaucracies already active in the countryside. Among these were the rural development office, the office of cooperatives, the bureau in charge of registering and recognizing indigenous peasant communities, organizations in the shantytowns, and a finance corporation. A mobilized citizen, according to Palmer, was to get involved with SINAMOS's activities only at the local "social interest" unit of participation: "Participation represents an opportunity for the citizen to bring about limited changes in the way a decision is implemented, but not the opportunity to intervene in the decision making process itself" (1973, 97), be it in his recently inaugurated cooperative or as a dweller in a newly established shantytown organization in a city. Palmer goes on to quote General Leonidas Figueroa, the head of the organization, in a speech: "'The government provides the structure of participation; the citizens may participate only to the degree that they accept the structure as given'" (1973, 97).

The headquarters of SINAMOS in Lima were located in an ugly concrete building (an example of the military's "brutalist" monumental architectural style) called the Centro Cívico in downtown Lima. But it also had a kind of think tank charged to devise long-term and large-scale political efforts (the Centro de Estudios de la Participación or the Center for the Study of Popular Participation). A group of elite intellectuals congregated in a beautiful villa in the middle of a park near the residence of the American ambassador, across the Avenida Arequipa. Nearby were the offices of the Ford Foundation in a modern skyscraper with Henry's Café on the ground floor. There one could drink espresso with the members of this select group and feel really close to individuals who were designing momentous changes on paper.

Coincidental with the Velasco years, the Brazilian military dictatorship had exiled many critics, among them the famous Brazilian anthropologist Darcy Ribeiro, who was welcomed to work in that think tank. I remember visiting him and I was introduced to another Brazilian exile, a friendly mathematician, whose job, I was told, was to construct a mathematical model of the Peruvian revolution. In those days there was much talk about the Peruvian model of the revolution and it has, of course, been widely discussed in the social science literature as corporatist.

So in 1996, I wanted to discuss models with Pancho Guerra, but he thought I was being ridiculous. I needled him.

ENRIQUE: Do you think about the great distance that there was between the models [of social participation in giant cooperatives] and the realities on the ground?

PANCHO [*after a long pause*]: I personally do not remember that in political discussions of those times models or their beauty were determining factors. . . .

ENRIQUE [*insisting*]: What was it in those times that built up great hopes that one could change people's mentalities by placing them in the correct box in an organizational chart?

PANCHO [*a somewhat irate response this time*]: I am talking from a purely political point of view. The agrarian reform set into motion strong political processes that in one way or another carried out the aims of radical change that had been demanded for a long time. The idea of implementing cooperatives was current here and elsewhere in Latin America and there were arguments dating from the 1930s by *apristas* and socialists like Hildebrando Castro Pozo that an Andean tradition of collective organizations would meld well with cooperatives. There were no other new ideas around.

The reform did produce a consensus because the people saw that what they had been struggling for so long began to be carried out. Other than landlords and conservative opposition, there were no new proposals that would have caused people to oppose it. More, I would say, people did find that what was being done did respond to all their illusions and their hopes. It was a legitimated process. Velasco's regime was very popular. In my case this was a decisive and strong factor. And if you ask me if it was worth it, I would say "yes" for the agrarian reform and "yes" for many other things that were done then. [*With emphasis*] The agrarian reform related to the people! Proof: no conflicts, no tensions, no prisoners, no bloodshed.

But more than that, I remember seeing the plazas so full of demonstrators as I never saw before. And above all with cheering peasants in places like Trujillo, Cusco, Arequipa. Extraordinary support! [fig. 4]

Pancho, like everyone else in those times, ruled out the direct distribution of land to individuals or communities.

PANCHO: What was not possible was to give land to all; in other words, to distribute in individual plots would have brought enormous difficulties in the process of distribution and greater problems especially in the big agro-industrial complexes to insure that their economic response would be better than what it had been before. That is was what was behind the notion of cooperatives. But once they had decided on the kind of model—mind you it was not made by SINAMOS, we came later—we had to support it.

ENRIQUE: So, what went wrong? In my interviews with local people they do talk badly about the cooperatives.

PANCHO: I do not think it is possible to generalize like that. It would be interesting to compare the conditions of these people before and after

Figure 4 Massive pro-Velasco demonstration in Chiclayo in 1975. Archive of the photographer Carlos Domínguez. © Carlos Domínguez.

the reform. My feeling is that they improved rather than the opposite, and I am not only talking economics but also in terms of social and political aspects. I think people have forgotten all the social welfare measures that were implemented while the cooperatives were operating.

One also needs to remember that once the second term of the Belaúnde regime was in place, it did its very best to take apart everything that had been built up previously. They [the Belaúnde regime] denied anything that could have been positive. And within the state apparatus the support institutions, technical assistance, and so on disappeared. This was done deliberately and if they did not disassemble more of it, it was because to do so would have been complicated and very difficult. Businesses suffered during those years too, so it should not surprise me that cooperatives were in trouble in the recession.

That the cooperatives parceled out the land among themselves was an endogenous process in the 1980s. We had a hard time accepting this. Had we done this in our NGO, we could have helped them to do a better job if we had anticipated it three or four years before it took place. We did not do it because we were psychologically and ideologically blocked. Since the model came from Velasco it was a difficult thing to accept and for us to change sides on this issue.

ENRIQUE: Why?

PANCHO: Because one gets stuck with what one was doing.

ENRIQUE: Because the model was beautiful?

PANCHO: Look here, Enrique! I am a practical person. You will not hear me talk about models. We did it because we thought it was good.

We thought it was good even though cooperatives have not functioned in any other part of the world!

ENRIQUE: What legacy did the agrarian reform leave?

PANCHO: [*Pauses and sighs.*] Every agrarian reform process is disorderly. It did not usher in a new order of economic and social relations. And also, it was left unfinished due to Velasco's illness.

ENRIQUE: What has to be done to clean it up?

PANCHO: Everything.

ENRIQUE: Is there a relationship between the effects of the agrarian reform and the political violence that followed?

PANCHO: I think that it was very little. I think that Abimael Guzmán (the leader of Shining Path) did not realize what profound effects the agrarian reform had in the highlands. And because the Velasco government had good relationships with the peasants, after the military changed its tactics, the peasants quickly supported the government's side with their own organizations, the *rondas campesinas*. The peasants' confrontation with Shining Path would not have been possible if before that there had not been an agrarian reform.

I remember a seminar here at a local university in which I participated.

After a while one of the participants threw the agrarian reform in my face.

"You are a *velasquista*."

I answered with two points: "Yes it is true. I am a *velasquista*. I am proud of being a *velasquista*. I want it to be clear that I am not an independent. As I understand it today, an independent is an improviser and opportunist. I am a man with a distinct political past and I have made mistakes. People who do things make mistakes." That was the first thing I said. The second was, "About the agrarian reform, permit me to say that I am convinced that if there had not been an agrarian reform, Shining Path would now be circling in the outskirts of Lima. Have you forgotten the enormous social distances, the poverty and misery, etc.? Now that you feel that the Shining Path insurgency is being controlled, are you going to forget those problems?"

To me he reiterated his thought. "I do think that the Shining Path would be circling Lima."

And I said, "Yes it is true that the peasant groups defeated the Shining Path in the countryside."

I am not quite sure whether Pancho said *gobernando* (governing) or *rondando* (circling), although I remember the stronger "governing." This issue is raised by both sides of the political spectrum. The Right has blamed the pseudo-communist *velasquistas* and *izquierdistas* for laying the groundwork that enabled the Maoist Shining Path to gain a foothold; at the same time, the Left argues, as Pancho did, that the Velasco reforms strengthened the peasantry and enabled it to defeat the insurgency. Nonetheless, the irony of implementing agrarian reforms to prevent revolutionary uprisings as was preached by the Alliance for Progress is complicated for the Peruvian case, because the decade of 1980–90 was one of terrible political violence that followed right on the heels of the agrarian reform. Chapter 6 describes the appalling consequences of the intervention of Shining Path in dismantling the SAIS Cahuide supercooperative in the department of Junín.

In the next chapter, I focus more directly on memory making during those early years of the regime. The chapter describes the making of a film about the agrarian reform in the late 1970s, which tells the story of the expulsion of the landlord from his hacienda in Cusco. That film fixes the memory making to the middle of the process of the reform, and allows me, the metanarrator, to go back to pre-reform days and then to move forward in time after the film was made to give an opportunity to those who remember the reform and the making of the film to reevaluate what they thought then with what they thought afterward. It shows how remarkably fluid the process of memory making really is.

two

HEROES AND ANTIHEROES

(With Danny Pinedo)

Cast of Characters in Order of Appearance

FEDERICO GARCÍA HURTADO, a filmmaker interviewed in Lima, July 2002.

OSCAR FERNÁNDEZ, the landlord of the hacienda Huarán. (He was not interviewed, but he played a leading role in the events narrated in this chapter.)

MARTA FERNÁNDEZ, the landlord's daughter. (She was not interviewed.)

MARIANO QUISPE, a legendary peasant leader from Huarán. (He was not interviewed.)

SATURNINO HUILCA, a famous peasant leader in the Cusco region. (He was not interviewed.)

HUGO NEIRA SAMANÉZ, a journalist interviewed in Lima, December 2006.

HUGO BLANCO GALDÓS, a leader of a massive anti-hacienda rebellion interviewed in Cusco, February 2001.

JOSÉ ZÚÑIGA LETONA, a peasant leader in Huarán. (He was not interviewed, but he played a leading role in the events narrated in this chapter.)

IGNACIO CCORIMANYA, a smallholder in Huarán interviewed by Danny Pinedo in Huarán, July 1996.

MARIO HERRERA HIDALGO, a leader in Huarán's cooperative, the actor who played Zúñiga in the film *Kuntur Wachana*, and an anthropologist. He was interviewed by Danny Pinedo in Cusco, July 1996.

CIRILO COBADES, a smallholder in Huarán interviewed by Danny Pinedo in Huarán, July 1996.

PAULINO SAIRITUPAC, a smallholder in Huarán interviewed by Danny Pinedo in Huarán, July 1996.

HILARIO QUISPE, a smallholder in Huarán interviewed by Danny Pinedo in Huarán, July 1996.

CARMEN CALDERÓN, a farmer and the daughter of a landowner in Cusco. She was interviewed in Lima, February 1996.

Filming the Reform

My first consulting job in Peru came with a small crisis in the Velasco neither-communist-nor-capitalist revolution. In 1975, the government instituted an education reform that involved a revision of the official nationwide primary school curriculum. A conservative journalist accused the ministry of introducing totally unacceptable Marxist topics that would undermine the stability of the country's children. While the education minister went on television to deny this, a group of scholars, myself included, was hired on the quiet to "de-Marxify" the curriculum as fast as possible. We spent days and nights removing the most doctrinaire and inane Marxist content while trying to keep the spirit of the educational reform. One of the points of the new curriculum was to dissuade the use of the old-fashioned national heroes (mostly military) and encourage teachers instead to deal with local history and, therefore, find unsung heroes for schoolchildren to emulate.

My task was to provide guidelines for local schoolteachers on how to elevate simple local folk to heroic status, and my examples tended to focus on peasants who dared to defy their landlords, communities that recuperated hacienda lands, and lawyers who defended Indians in courts against unjust accusations. I remember specifying that a hero must be dead, lest his or her heroic actions be contradicted by later unheroic behavior. Forty years later, I find myself in a similar situation, reviewing behaviors of actors in the agrarian reform process to consider how the social construction of local heroes and antiheroes at that time has weathered the aging process and how they fare in people's memories today. Here I deal with the more controversial figures, namely, leftist activists.

Figure 5 The logo of the agrarian reform produced by the Office of Promotion of the Agrarian Reform used a stylized image of Túpac Amaru. Designed by the artist Jesús Ruiz Durand. © Jesús Ruiz Durand.

Thus, this chapter is about how heroes are created and what happens to them with the passage of time. The Velasco government chose a very generic hero as a symbol of its revolution. It was the legendary eighteenth-century cacique Túpac Amaru, who had led an indigenous uprising in southern Peru but was defeated, captured, tried, and cruelly executed by the Spaniards in the plaza of Cusco in 1781. Everything revolutionary and nationalistic during the Velasco regime had the name Túpac Amaru. New statues, plazas, and streets were dedicated to him in every city. The Ministry of Agriculture and its agrarian reform posters had Túpac Amaru on them. Expropriated haciendas with aristocratic Spanish names were renamed after him, and even the state-run food distribution system had a stylized stencil symbol of Túpac Amaru with a black-brimmed, tall top hat and a stern face (Cleaves and Scurrah 1980, 208) (fig. 5). Images of Túpac Amaru gave a distinct visual aura to the Velasco times, much as Ché's emblem did for Fidel Castro's Cuba and Sandino's did for Nicaragua.

Heroic figures, however, live in narratives, deliberately manipulated by propaganda machines in the heat of conflict, and when the passionate issues lose their validity the narrative itself may be in need of severe editing. The suffering of indigenous peasants has had, in *indigenista* literature, a respectable pedestal in Latin America and its own heroic mode of telling the tale. In it, virtuous peasants vainly resisted but lost against the class of *gamonales* whose haciendas were impregnable kingdoms supported by the venality of the local power holders, the priests, and a corrupt justice system that sent brave resisters to infamous jails. *Indigenista* literature had a strong influence in creating pro-agrarian reform sentiment, and the good-guys-against-bad storyline, typical of the genre, was retold many times.[1] With the successes of revolutionary activists in the 1950s, the narrative turned the tables because peasants started to win.

Federico García Hurtado (born in Cusco in 1937) was a filmmaker employed by the Sistema Nacional de Movilización Social (SINAMOS), a political organ of Velasco's government, to develop pro-agrarian reform propaganda. As part of this work he converted one of the real cases of an expropriation into a feature film in which the peasants successfully struggled hard to free themselves from the *hacendado*. The film *Kuntur Wachana*, a Quechua name meaning "where the condors are born," opened in Lima in 1977 when the initial impetus of the Velasco reforms had already been dampened. It won two prizes in Moscow film festivals, and another prize in a festival in Benalmádena, Spain.[2] I remember seeing it when it first came out in the downtown, elegant Lima Cine Metro, which ordinarily showed Hollywood extravaganzas. My students urged me to go, saying that it was "very anthropological" because it told of real events in which the peasants themselves played their parts and told their own story. In fact, much of the dialogue was in Quechua with Spanish subtitles.

Kuntur Wachana combined the *indigenista* genre with Soviet realism to produce a solemn collective epic. Sergei Eisenstein's influence is visible in the use of spectacular landscapes in which snaking columns of peasants march to take over the lands that are rightfully theirs, while brooding, westernized Andean choral music composed by the Peruvian Celso Garrido Lecca plays in the background.[3] The characters of the intransigent landlord, Oscar Fernández, and his nasty daughter Marta are all the more effective in the film because the peasants described their behaviors to the film's directors. To make the contrast even clearer, Oscar Fernández and Marta Fernández usually appear in dark, interior settings in the hacienda house, whereas the heroic peasants were filmed in beautiful nature out in the open. The unscrupulous lawyers and the shifty police officers and priests are frightening on screen because they were played by local *cus-*

queños familiar with their roles, and the camera filmed them from angles that emphasized their ugliness. In contrast, the folk-heroic peasant leaders, if still alive, and their supportive urban union organizers from the city of Cusco played themselves in the film. Their zeal is palpable in stirring swearing-in ceremonies that induct peasants into the union. The peasants' Revolutionary Agrarian Federation Túpac Amaru of Cusco or Federación Agraria Revolucionaria Túpac Amaru Cusco (FARTAC), together with the Agrarian Cooperative No. 001 "José Zúñiga Letona" of the ex-hacienda Huarán (located near the provincial city of Calca in the Sacred Valley of the Incas in the department of Cusco), sponsored the film. It was an inspiring tale about the virtues of crossing social boundaries between Indians, urban proletarians, and leftist students as it recalled good heroic days.

The film is in two parts. Part 1 opens in 1958 and tells the story of Mariano Quispe, an Indian shepherd bonded to the hacienda Huarán to herd the *hacendado*'s sheep in the high *puna* lands of the hacienda. Because Mariano gave shelter to Saturnino Huilca, a legendary peasant union organizer, he is harassed by the *hacendado* and thrown into jail so that the latter can rid himself of agitators among his hacienda workers. After a long time, the lawyers of the workers' federation in the city of Cusco obtain his release, but when Mariano tries to return home he notices that the police are looking to rearrest him. Realizing that he is now a hunted man and seeking protection, he hikes over the mountains to Cusco to become a clandestine organizer. He is shown walking through freezing mountain passes, evading his pursuers, and then through open fields to other haciendas, meeting up with workers, doggedly organizing. In the film, Saturnino Huilca plays himself as Quispe's spiritual guide.

Not shown in the film is the background on Saturnino Huilca, the son of bonded peasants in the hacienda Chhuru in Paucartambo province (fig. 6). Huilca never went to school and remained a Quechua monolingual all his life. Around 1948, already an adult, he heard that a law had been passed that forbade unpaid labor on haciendas. He walked to Cusco to see if this were true and established contact with the labor union. The union supported his efforts to organize the peasants on his hacienda to demand the end of free labor.[4] This aroused the ire of landlords who harassed the indomitable Huilca, expelling him from their haciendas. Branded as an instigator, he took refuge in the mountains. Huilca was a tireless organizer and, in 1964

Figure 6 Saturnino Huilca, a peasant leader in Cusco. The caption reads, "The peasant enters the Peruvian political scene" (Neira 1964, 105). Courtesy of Hugo Neira.

and 1965, when the great waves of land invasions took place, Huilca rode their crests in triumph. In the 1970s when the Velasco agrarian reform was in full swing, Huilca, already an old man, had become a useful hero, and the government used him for propaganda. The journalist Hugo Neira published Huilca's oral testimony in 1974. Huilca was a good speechmaker, and the heavily edited Spanish version of his testimony vibrated with justified anger:

> I am a peasant from Cusco and I know perfectly well that in the provinces they hear my voice; they listen to what I have to say. They organize to create unions. And their leaders, with my words, achieved what they had set out to do. I told them that the struggle has to be well guided; it has to have good direction to achieve liberty. And they said to me, "This is the way we battle; our struggles give good results. The *hacendado*

has sent us to jail, but there we meet and form federations." As if they were brothers, they take care of each other. The peasants and the urban workers, they support each other. (Neira 1974, 52, my translation)

Huilca's testimony is full of anguished personal memories of unjustified imprisonment and of the miserable conditions of Cusco's jails. He gives lengthy details of his many legal battles and expresses his anger at being mistreated and insulted as an Indian and a communist to boot. Having Huilca in the film had an impact for those who knew who he was, although García, the director, spoiled it by portraying him as an indigenous Andean, poncho-clad prophet instead of the practical organizer that he really was.[5] Backed by stirring music, Huilca and Mariano Quispe sit on top of Huarán's sacred mountain (where the condors nest), and Huilca admonishes the weary Mariano Quispe to keep on fighting because "when they humiliate you and—forgetting your human condition—you react by remaining silent, then you already are a cadaver that stinks" (my translation). Fulfilling Huilca's exhortation to struggle for liberation around the countryside, Mariano Quispe in due time meets a traitor in the pay of the landlords. His new acquaintance offers him a cup of poisoned *chicha*, and Mariano dies a martyr. And this, the peasants of Huarán say even today, is the truth.

As part 2 of the film moves to 1969, the film's voice-over narrator explains that the Belaúnde government (1964–68) had severely repressed the unions and defeated the guerrillas of 1965 in southern Peru. This narration compresses a history known to viewers at that time, but its silences also make oblique statements about some popular figures deemed heroic but inconvenient to the Velasco regime. The reference was to Hugo Blanco, who is never mentioned by name in the film. Blanco was the leader of a massive anti-hacienda rebellion in 1963 and 1964, a few hundred kilometers downriver from Huarán in the tropical and mountainous Convención Valley. This area had a half century of profitable coffee and tea expansion. Huge tracts of land were appropriated into haciendas. The owners worked only a small section of them, but to attract labor they assigned uncultivated land to settlers in exchange for a number of working days without pay on the owner's land. The settlers in turn recruited subsettlers and assigned them further plots within their own in exchange for labor, which could be used either to substitute for the original settler's labor obligations to the *hacendado* or to develop the settler's own coffee or coca plantation.

Although described as feudal,[6] the expansion was market driven, and the organization of rural labor unions timidly took root as early as the 1940s, demanding cash payments for work, eight-hour work days, and freedom for settlers to sell their own coffee crop in the market instead of being forced to hand it over to the landlord at arbitrary low prices. In addition, they agitated for just compensation for the improvements that they had made on virgin territory in establishing flourishing coffee plantations when they had been expelled from their land by the landowner. This was a frequent occurrence, because this was how the haciendas expanded the areas they brought under cultivation.

The mobilized peasants were supported by the workers' union from the city of Cusco, which itself was controlled by the traditional communist party, which followed Moscow's orders not to "rock the boat" in Latin America too much. By the late 1950s, encouraged by the success of the Cuban Revolution, radical leftist groups that were defying the traditional communists began to emerge, and Hugo Blanco became a leading "heroic" but controversial figure in this movement. The grandson of landlords, Blanco came from Huanuquite in Paruro province in Cusco (Seligmann 1995, 120–23). His father, a lawyer who had defended Indians in their endless legal suits, gave Hugo a progressive upbringing. He studied agronomy in Buenos Aires but soon joined the Trotskyites, who tutored him in clandestine political work and taught him how to radicalize unions in Buenos Aires and later in Lima. In 1958, he organized a large demonstration against Vice President Richard Nixon's goodwill visit to Lima. To avoid his arrest, the small Trotskyite party sent him back to Cusco. There he began to organize revolutionary unions in the Convención Valley by becoming a subsettler (*allegado*) of a comrade settler (*arrendire*) on the hacienda Chaupimayo, which was owned by Alfredo Romainville, the renowned, most "evil" landlord of all time.[7]

From 1958 to 1963, Blanco's political work led to a huge and well-organized peasant movement that spread all over the Convención Valley and to the rest of the department. Blanco's brother-in-law, Vladimiro Valer, who was based with the workers' federation in Cusco, chartered a radicalizing program for the newly organized unions.

The Trotskyite Blanco had a clear confrontational strategy that escalated with each success. First, he pushed the peasants to strike on individual haciendas; then, as conflict developed, he encouraged road blockades to enforce combined strikes on several neighboring properties. Later, demonstrations in the region's towns preceded general regionwide strikes. The final stages involved outright occupation of the settlers' and subsettlers' plots within the hacienda. At the height of the movement, the peasants sought to expel their landlords and provoke a takeover of the whole hacienda. By that time, Blanco was famous throughout Peru. The sociologist Eduardo Fioravanti described his fame this way:

> Hugo Blanco became the undisputed leader of the peasant movement; his name traveled from mouth to mouth in the highlands and the country [and he became] a legendary and mythical figure. . . . Peasants from the Convención Valley were so devoted to him that his rivals could not criticize him in public lest they earn their violent opprobrium from the peasants who admired the man who alone had given them their land. His slogan "Land or Death" reverberated all over the country. (1974, 194, my translation)

Blanco himself, in his prison memoirs, retains some flavor of this success. In the paragraph below, he remembers the psychological impact of peasant protest meetings he organized in the city of Cusco:

> In Cusco, for centuries, the Indian had slouched along the streets with his *poncho* and his whispered Quechua; he had never dared, even when drunk, to mount the sidewalk or speak his Quechua out loud with his head held high. He was fearful of the *misti* (the non-Indian), who was the master of the city. He fled from the authorities or from whomever could force him to do a job for a pittance—or for nothing—; or who could force him to sell his few products brought from the countryside at any price offered him. The city of Cusco meant all that to the Indian, who was degraded and humiliated on the streets, the plazas, in stores, and public transportation. The city meant more, too: courts of law, the offices of lawyers and notaries public, the provincial jail, the landlord's residence, where frequently a peasant, his wife, or his children had to do unpaid domestic work.
>
> The mass meeting put the Indian on top of the monster. A concentration of *ponchos* in the main plaza, the heart of the city. On the rostrum erected on the Cathedral portico which dominates the plaza. The odor of coca and Quechua permeating the air. Quechua out loud from

the throat; Quechua shouted, threatening, tearing away centuries of oppression. An organized march down the main streets, before and after the meeting. Windows and doors of the powerful fearfully slammed shut at the advance of the multitudes, aggressive, insulting, threatening, shouting in Quechua truths silenced by centuries of Castilian Spanish. The Indian, the master of the entire street and the sidewalk. That's what the peasant meetings meant. (Blanco 1972a, 46–47)

Blanco must have felt very good, standing on that rostrum with the Indians. The film *Kuntur Wachana* ends with an epilogue showing one such demonstration taken from documentary footage: artificially bathed in red, it focuses on the crowds, and then zooms in on Saturnino Huilca giving a speech to a sea of poncho-clad cheering crowds.

Alarmed by the growing unrest in the Convención Valley as well as the confirmation of rumors that Cuban-style guerrilla bases had been established in remote sections of the valley, the military caretaker junta intervened in the Convención Valley in 1962. To take the initiative away from Blanco's followers, a limited agrarian reform law specific to the region was enacted. But police and army units trained in counterinsurgency also entered the valley to dismantle the movement. A year later, the military handed over the government to Belaúnde, whose electoral promises of pro-agrarian reform had unleashed further waves of land occupations across the nation.[8]

As Belaúnde's government moved into the Convención Valley in 1963 and 1964 with its own "demobilizing" land reform and counterinsurgency measures, Blanco's movement began to be persecuted. The pro-Soviet branch of the communist party pushed Blanco's group to the margins of the peasant federation. He responded by organizing a very small self-defense militia. Isolated from his union base and eluding capture, he was forced to attack a police post. He killed one policeman and wounded another, to whom he gave medicine from his own supply and made sure was adequately treated. In May 1963, Blanco was arrested and accused of being a guerrilla. He was held incommunicado for three years before he was tried by a military tribunal and sentenced to twenty-five years in prison.

When the Velasco coup took place in 1968, there were widespread clamors to give him and other guerrillas, as well as rural union organizers, amnesty. Upon their release, many joined the Velasco government. But Blanco was the last one to be set free because he declined to collaborate with the government, continuing instead to criticize it harshly. He was deported to Mexico in 1971. His memoirs, written in prison, *Tierra o muerte: Las luchas campesinas en Perú* (1972b), were translated into many languages and widely studied. Written in a polemic but also didactic tone, the memoir described in simple but vivid language Blanco's role in the movement, and argued that his way of organizing peasants would have led to massive support for revolutionary change. He disputed other leftist positions, distancing himself from the tepid pro-Soviet parties on the one hand and arguing against *foco guerrillero* positions a la Guevara and Debray on the other. Exiled by Velasco, he was a popular lecturer on U.S. and European campuses during the late 1970s. All of this background was purposefully compressed in the film into a brief, two-sentence narration.

Part 2 of the film *Kuntur Wachana* begins by showing two former guerrillas, José Zúñiga Letona and Efraín Solís, in 1969 as they are sitting in a train traveling back to Huarán, where Solís had his home. Solís and Zúñiga had been in the struggle in the Convención Valley and became friends in prison. Zúñiga married Solís's sister and took up the fight against the landlord in Huarán. The film shows how the peasants hemmed in the landlord under Zúñiga's leadership. The police politely decline to offer the landlord their usual protection, saying, "There are new winds blowing." The priests excuse themselves, and the lawyers' efforts become ineffective as the landlord unsuccessfully attempts to divide the peasants. In clandestine meetings between the organizers and union leaders from Cusco, Vladimir Valer, the peripatetic organizer, recommends patience with the bureaucratic processes because he trusts that the official Velasco reform will soon give them the land.

In the film, Marta Fernández, the daughter of the landlord, in desperation, commissions one of her faithful followers to arrange for the killing of Zúñiga. The opportunity presents itself at a soccer match between the hacienda team and its neighboring villagers. During the game, Zúñiga is viciously kicked by a player on the hacienda's team and dies of internal injuries two days later. And this murder, the peasants of Huarán say even today, is the truth, and thus Zúñiga also died a martyr.[9]

The resolve of peasants to avenge Zúñiga's assassination is shown in scenes of his tumultuous funeral. Toward the end, in the claustrophobic atmosphere inside the hacienda house, Marta Fernández despondently reads to the assembled landlord family. Seated around the dinner table, they listen to the contents of the second notification of the total expropriation of their lands as ordered by the government. The first one they had ignored.[10] And then, disturbed by noises coming from outside, Oscar Fernández opens a window and is faced with a collective mass of peasants staring him down. A close-up shot of his ashen face says it all.

Ignacio Ccorimanya, a peasant from Huarán, told Danny Pinedo in 1996 how he remembered the invasion. "Once they decided to invade," he said,

> We sent small groups to reconnoiter, to learn the habits of the *hacendado*, to find out when he got up, how he treated visitors, and so on. So we knew his weaknesses. He used to come down from his second-floor rooms to the patio to deal with peasants. So three people were to go at seven in the morning to request an audience with him. One of them said to Fernández that he wanted to see him because he wanted to arrange with him how to access pasture lands and that he would pay the rights. He responded, "All right, wait, I will come down."
>
> So Señor Oscar and his daughter came down to the patio and the other two peasants, who had taken wire with them, secured the small door so he could not get back upstairs (we were afraid that he might have arms or tear gas bombs hidden upstairs). Another person blew a whistle as a signal, and then all the people who had secretly crept into the area pushed into the patio. The *señorita* Marta wanted to escape, but gently they held her back. With a yellow face, Fernández screamed: "What do you want? Speak up!"
>
> "That the agrarian reform should come now!"
>
> "We want justice!"
>
> "There will be blood," we screamed back.
>
> And then the police came and they made sure that respect was shown, that nothing happened to us or to the hacienda lady.
>
> The *hacendado* was held until he signed a document that he had been detained unharmed by the peasants who had taken over the hacienda. He and his daughter then left for Cusco in their small car. Then we notified the government, the radio, and police forces. We left everything intact but stayed for three days until we were told that the expropriation process would be sped up. Then government agents came to measure

everything, to count the *hacendado*'s things. He was notified to leave the hacienda and to take his personal belongings. After that he never came back.[11]

The film director Federico García Hurtado specialized in a genre called *cine campesino*, itself a product of leftist artistic currents of the times and the Velasco revolution.[12] Under his direction SINAMOS, which was associated with the radical branch of the regime, produced propaganda documentaries that promoted the government's reforms. But he soon ran into trouble because the guidelines issued by the presidential office of communications demanded that films should not show negative images but be decidedly pro-government, positive, and optimistic. One case concerned the short SINAMOS documentary *Runan Caycu*, by Nora de Izcue (1973), who had filmed Saturnino Huilca's testimony about successive confrontations with *hacendados* and included mention of past violent encounters with the armed forces. Although the film was sponsored by one branch of government, it was unauthorized by another. Because of this censorship it was modified before it could be shown (Bedoya 1992, 202). García's own early SINAMOS documentaries *Tierra sin patrones* (1971) and *Huando* (1972), about conflicts within the implementation of the agrarian reform, were censored for the same reasons and later burned when SINAMOS was closed by the successor government of Morales Bermúdez.

Thus, when García had a second chance to express his ideas in filming *Kuntur Wachana*, he knew he had to tone down his militant views, and that is why Hugo Blanco's movement got such an oblique treatment in *Kuntur Wachana*. However, he did use segments of the Huilca footage from *Runan Caycu* to close his film.[13] He also knew that financial support from SINAMOS was drying up, and, by 1975, when Velasco was overthrown and the agency was disbanded, he had to seek other sources to fund this film. These are the reasons why the cooperative of Huarán not only participated in the making of the film but also in funding it.

In an interview in July 2002, Federico García reminisced with me about the difficulties he had had in making the film. It started with the ideological problems. Part of the difficulty was that he had been a revolutionary activist in his student days when the Hugo Blanco movement was in full swing. This occasionally placed him at odds with more conservative colleagues in the industry. Having grown up in the area, he knew the peasant leaders. When he began working for SINAMOS, he heard all these stories and realized that there was good material to make a larger artistic statement in a feature film. His proposal was accepted by the cooperative with great enthusiasm. The people were going to participate in the film; the crew was to be fed and housed without charge during this time. A subsidiary of the cooperative, called Producciones Huarán, was to own the film rights. A bureaucratic mechanism had to be found, so a proposal to create a social communications project that was compatible with SINAMOS's activities was proposed, and a budget of one million *soles* was approved. The project included radio broadcasting, a local press, theater, film, and puppet shows. All of these activities were carried out, and the filming began under cover of this project. The atmosphere was positive and enthusiastic throughout the filming phase, which ended just as the government of Velasco fell.

Then García's problems started. There was no more money, and the unprocessed film was deteriorating in its canisters. The cooperative managed to raise a bank loan to develop the film in a laboratory, but the laboratory was not equipped to process color film, so about 20 percent of the footage was lost. García made a first cut and completed a preliminary editing in Lima, but then he reached a technical dead end. During the period when his documentaries for SINAMOS were being burned, Federico García felt that elements within the military also sought to block his efforts at finishing this film. He and several colleagues were arrested and put into jail until a large protest staged by newspapers, film critics, and peasant federations managed to obtain his release.

The film could not be further processed in Peru. More money was found through the cooperative of Huarán and delivered to Federico García in La Paz, Bolivia. García traveled on to Buenos Aires and arrived during the era of the Videla military government. In the laboratory that was editing and processing the film, a jealous assistant editor denounced García as a communist. In that country and at that time, that was a very serious accusation. Federico García had to hide. With no money, he and his companions went camping until the film was ready. Feeling persecuted, García made arrangements to have the negatives sent to the Cuban Film Institute in Havana for safekeeping, and then he returned overland through Bolivia with Videla's and Hugo Banzer's police on the lookout for him at many a roadblock. The film was well hidden in the cooperative's pickup truck. When they arrived in Cusco, *Kuntur Wachana* was given its premiere in the presence of the leaders of the cooperative and to thunderous applause.

Film reviewers, however, concurred in pointing out some of the difficulties of the film. Ricardo Bedoya, a critic and film historian, gave a thoughtful retrospective evocation of the enterprise, which pointed out that it could have been attractive:

> The initial proposal was to engage in collective work in the creation of a drama designed from the point of view of its principal protagonists. However, the cinematic treatment of this proposal soon got lost because the filmmaker relied excessively on older, more traditional, ways of representation, leaving very little room to spontaneity, to the fusion of its parts, and to show the uncertainties and hesitations of a human group being filmed while they were remembering events that were from the past, but still fresh in their lives or of their parents. (1992, 210, my translation)

Bedoya went on to critique García's lyric escapades, the intrusion of heavy-handed Andean symbolism (the condors, the blowing of an ancient conch shell to signal the invasion), and the ostensive use of landscapes to make the film "an illustration of an exemplary tale that showed in all too obvious ways the many ideological intentions and dramatic devices that presided over its making" (Bedoya 1992, 211). He also felt that the stark duality between good *campesinos* and bad *hacendados* had been overdrawn.

García Hurtado's films, however, do stand out for their high technical quality and their focus on issues of social conflict in the Andes. His attempts to portray Andean peasant villagers played by themselves on screen was a daring innovation but unfortunately not as persuasive as hoped. *Kuntur Wachana* is the only full-length treatment of the agrarian reform in film.[14] Seen from the vantage point of today, it has the distinct flavor of the ponderous leftist polemic and didactic art that was part of the Velasco revolution and to which Federico García contributed a great deal.

However, in 1996 when Danny Pinedo, my assistant, interviewed people in Huarán, memories of *Kuntur Wachana* revealed that it ended as a bitter experience. Mario Herrera, a leader in the invasion and a member of the cooperative who was interviewed by Danny Pinedo in 1996 and who is also the author of a dissertation on Huarán (1994), recalls that back in 1975 everything was initially rosy. Federico García was enthusiastic about making the film. He talked a lot about how the cooperative was contributing to a totally new concept of producing revolutionary Third-World films. Solís also was eager, seduced by the idea that they all would become famous with their stirring story. Everyone had great fun making a participatory film. Paulino Sairitupac, a member of the cooperative, remembered how he was filmed, although the segment did not make it into the final version: "The film showed the kind of life we had during the hacienda. How they mistreated us, how the *hacendado* behaved, how he broke our *chicha* jars when we took too long a break. All of that we have reproduced in the film, just as it was, how he kicked the jars, how we were slapped, all that. We did it again exactly as it was for the film."

Rubén Ascue, a comrade of Solís and Zúñiga, got credited as a co-producer in his role as coordinator and *campesino* script writer. He later became a professional actor in García's other films. The cooperative claims to have used loans earmarked for agricultural production for the film, and to have borrowed cash from fellow cooperatives. According to people in Huarán, for six months the workers sacrificed their own wages to finance the laboratory work to process the film in Argentina. Everyone was full of illusions about how much money they were going to make from their film venture. According to Mario Herrera, García counted it out with his fingers for them: "*¡Compañeros!* At 60,000 dollars each copy!"

When the film was released, the holding company Producciones Huarán made hardly any income. Cirilo Cobades, another peasant from Huarán, said in his interview in 1996 that they had given money for the film because they thought it would be mutually beneficial.

We thought that all that money was necessary to finish the film, and when it was done, then there would be so much money for us. When the film was finished, it was shown in Lima and in two other haciendas here in the region. We had some income from that. So what did these people do? Without authorization they had bought another camera, a useless broken-down one, with a pretext that they wanted to continue to make educational films. García also demanded money he said he was owed, so that is how they spent it. Just then we owed the agrarian bank one million. When we demanded the balance from García, all he brought back was 412 *soles*. That is all! That number is engraved in my head because it was read out in an assembly.

Mario Herrera was commissioned by the cooperative to investigate and retrieve the funds from Federico García. According to García, Herrera was a *provocateur* who, manipulated by obscure forces, destroyed an ambitious project to create a center for social communication in Huarán based on their previous work and the success with the film. Herrera, in contrast, claimed that García had gotten himself rich with the film and had not returned what he owed to the cooperative. For years, García said, Herrera and the cooperative made his life impossible. A lengthy lawsuit embroiled both sides. With the participation of some intellectuals, relentless calumny was spread that García, the rich intellectual, had swindled poor innocent peasants. García was booed in Huarán several times. In Lima, it became a sport to publish slanderous articles in the press against García. In retaliation, García accused Herrera of forging a plot to undermine the revolution and denounced him as a CIA agent in nasty comments that appeared in the arts and culture sections of Lima's progressive magazines and in graffiti painted on Huarán's walls. The sport lasted for years, and García and Herrera are bitter enemies to this day. Forgotten were those agreeable days when García had recruited Herrera to play the role of Zúñiga Letona. Having failed to properly cast Zúñiga's role with professional actors from Lima, García told me he had found in Herrera the ideal actor. Brazen, small-bodied, dark, and curly haired, he could really play the role of a Cusco *cholo* that Zúñiga was.

Today the film has sunk into oblivion. When Danny asked whether the cooperative still showed it, Cirilo Cobades told him, "We used to have a copy of the film, but now I do not know where it is. It is deteriorated." In researching and writing this chapter, I have often asked my Peruvian colleagues if they remember the film *Kuntur Wachana*. Most do not.

Mario Herrera, Zúñiga's Double

It was difficult for me to understand José Zúñiga Letona as a person, apart from the conflation associated with soccer heroism and revolutionary martyrdom that is in the film. Danny's interviews in Huarán in the 1990s yielded a few points. Ignacio Ccorimanya remembers that he was of medium height, with dark skin and wavy hair (fig. 7). That he was an

Figure 7 Hugo Blanco, center, and companions on the penal island of El Frontón. To his immediate right is the real José Zúñiga Letona (from Blanco 1972a, 97). © Pathfinder Press.

outsider was important, born somewhere in the Convención Valley, said to be an illegitimate son of a peasant woman and a landowner, a stranger who came with his companions to organize the local people. To them his revolutionary credentials were impressive because Zúñiga told them, as remembered by Ccorimanya: "My parents were *hacendados*, and I made the poor people invade the property of my father."

His legitimacy in the area was enhanced by his marriage to Solís's sister from Arín. Cirilo Cobades listed the posts he had in regional organizations. "He had been in the Federation of Lares down in the Convención Valley,[15] here he was also secretary of the Provincial Federation of Peasants in Calca, later he was a leader in the community of Arín, so he was always moving around."

Mario Herrera was his friend, and Danny tracked him down in Cusco. Lying in bed with a high fever, he nonetheless consented to a four-hour interview. Mario Herrera is not a native of Huarán; he was born in Cusco in 1944, the son of unionized workers and himself a militant. During the 1960s, he led rallies, threw stones, endured tear gas, and organized unions in the countryside. He participated in many a heated dispute among the various factions of the extreme left, arguing endlessly about how to convert the peasant movement into the real revolution. He militated in support of groups for MIR (Movimiento de Izquierda Revolucionaria) guerrillas, and he was caught, arrested, and spent three years in jail. José Zúñiga, Herrera told us, was special because in his militant days he had been very close to Hugo Blanco. Zúñiga had participated in the assault on the police post, and when Blanco was arrested he eluded his captors and then joined the De la Puente guerrillas until they too were caught. Herrera met Zúñiga in jail and, upon his release, Zúñiga, who was physically sick and psychologically weakened, initially sought refuge in Herrera's house. According to Herrera,

> He had anemia, the beginnings of tuberculosis, and my mother gave him shelter. She accepted him as a son because he was an excellent *compañero*, very good and decent. He stayed for a year and could not work; he would get agitated and had problems. When he became uncomfortable he said to my mother, "Look, I know a *compañero* in Arín. I am going to visit him, because he has always invited me."
>
> And he came back after a week like Santa Claus, bringing fresh maize, cherries, cabbage, and whatnot. And so he started coming and going and once he stayed there for eight months, and I became alarmed. And when I saw him again, I said to him, "Hey! What is up with you?"
>
> "There is a landowner there who is a son of a bitch!"
>
> Still a bit burned I said to him, "Look *compadre*, be careful! We will be screwed if what happened to us before happens again."
>
> But he seriously wanted my support and I agreed. They used my house as a place to sleep when they needed to come to the city. The construction union I was leading provided funds for the struggle.

Thus a friendship between the younger militants Mario Herrera, Efraín Solís, Rubén Ascue (Solís's cousin), and José Zúñiga developed. The case of Huarán was important in Cusco because Oscar Fernández, the owner, had become the embodiment of the cause célèbre in resisting unionization, dividing the peasant movement, and subverting the government's intentions to expropriate him. In short, he was the exemplary "bad" landowner who had to be broken. Herrera's connections to the city, SINAMOS, the university, and the unions were important in organizing the wider support that led to Fernández's ouster.

Ignacio Huamán, whom Danny interviewed in 1996, has this version of Zúñiga's death:

He was a person who organized people. We were already with him for three years. Then in Arín there was this soccer match, and hacienda employees used to come, and there they injured José Zúñiga. He was kicked and fell to the ground with a crack in his head. It was an assassination faked like a play. The person who did this is called Maldonado, but who knows where he was from. And then out of *capricho* (anger) we invaded Huarán.

Mario Herrera told Danny the following:

I turned Zúñiga's death into a political assassination. Our newspapers wrote in our favor. We managed to arouse the people of the provincial city of Calca, and they responded. Zúñiga's funeral became an anti-landlord political rally. At that time, Fernández (backed by his family connections) had support from the Ministry of Agriculture, which was delaying the expropriation, whereas we were supported by SINAMOS, which encouraged us to invade. Even Velasco himself had to intervene. So we planned the invasion. I was always behind the scenes. The takeover was calculated with mathematical precision, planned with care at night. I assigned tasks and organized the logistics. I hid in a taxi in Arín, waiting for a signal so that I could then go and notify the newspapers and the radio. Because I was well known in Cusco, it was important that I remain invisible. It had to look like a spontaneous peasant invasion.

Then came the happiest day, in January 1973, the day that the generals came to give us the land. It was General Luis Uzátegui Arce who came, and he actually knew me from my organizing work in Cusco with the construction workers. All of a sudden he recognized me, as I was standing with a megaphone in my hand welcoming him and his retinue to Huarán. So he said to me, "Hey, Mario, I thought you were in civil construction, what are you doing here?"

And I responded, "General, I am in the struggle wherever it may be."

Soon afterward the tables were turned. Due to political infighting, Mario Herrera was pushed to the sidelines in his union in the city of Cusco. His buddy, Efraín Solís, in contrast, now the swanky president of the José Zúñiga Letona cooperative, with a pickup truck and all, found Herrera hard up in Cusco. So he said to him, "Brother, what are you doing here?

You are too valuable to waste your time here. Come to Huarán!" They gave Herrera a plot of land and assigned him administrative tasks.

Throughout the 1980s and 1990s, Huarán's case continued to interest me. During the 1970s, the anthropologist Juan Victor Núñez del Prado did fieldwork under my direction and explored the more complex political difficulties after it became an agrarian cooperative. After placing the hacienda under a special intervention committee run by a military officer, the experts decided that because of Huarán's high levels of productivity and the capacity shown by its leaders, it was to become a production cooperative. In those early years it was the government's favorite, supplied with much aid, advice, revolutionary experimentation, and sympathy. In 1996, twenty-five years later, Danny Pinedo spent four days there to find out what impact the film had had on the locality. The place looked derelict: the entrance was littered with broken-down rusty farm machinery, the orchards were neglected, and the signs and posters of the cooperative days were faded and covered with graffiti. The cooperative had almost completely dissolved. Nearly all of the land had been distributed to its individual members, its leadership was weak or nonexistent, animosity and resentment among its members were rife, and socialism was a bad word. The Left had splintered into many factions and fizzled, the peasant movements had disappeared, their unions and their federations disbanded.

Mario Herrera changed political parties five times before becoming disenchanted. He started as an APRA *rebelde* who had broken from the party to promote a failed guerrilla uprising that cost him time in jail, where he also met his lifelong buddies Efraín Solís and José Zúñiga. When he led the union of construction workers in Cusco, he was affiliated with the Soviet-sponsored Communist Partido Comunista Peruano (PCP). Lured by the reforms, he then became a follower of Velasco, but maintained, like most of the *velasquistas*, his primary loyalties to a vaguely defined critical left-wing position. In his debates with other leftists during various crises, the crucial considerations were not really about issues of principle or policy, but which faction of which group had which amount of blocking or facilitating capacity in the local Cusco power structure. He and everyone else accommodated accordingly. His own accommodation was "tactical," while that of the others he labeled "treasonous." He was PCP because his construction union was PCP; he supported the CNA (Confederación Nacional Agraria), a peasant organization organized by Velasco, and thus had to oppose the intellectuals who supported the CCP (Confederación Campesina Peruana), an opposition peasant confederation. The CNA stood for collectivism and endorsed cooperatives, whereas the rival CCP called them manifestations of state capitalism and encouraged peasants to disband them. When Velasco fell, Mario had many choices about which left-wing party to affiliate with and chose the one that advocated a continuation with the Velasco line, the PSR (Partido Socialista Revolucionario), because his income depended on the continued subsidy and support of the cooperative. When it was about to crumble, he urged that agricultural units be run with business criteria of efficiency and profitability in line with the clamorings of politicians who saw economic efficiency as the way to develop the country. When the cooperative turned itself into individual smallholders, he talked of the virtues of the peasant (*campesino*) way. One can read this as opportunism, as shifting with the major political winds that were blowing in the continent, or even as slow enlightenment as recognition of one's errors set in. There is also Federico García Hurtado's accusation that "wherever Mario Herrera goes, he provokes divisionism" to consider.

As with most of us, the disappearance of a left-wing option on a worldwide, Latin American, and Peruvian scene left Herrera perplexed. When leaders of peasant movements and urban unions turned into parliamentary candidates seeking votes, he was disgusted at how quickly they changed their thinking and their clothes, unaware of how he was shifting, too. With all of these changes, where did he define the principles that guided his actions? Herrera's interview of 1996 was filled with vicious epithets against his rivals, whom he easily labeled as opportunistic and shifty, but there was also a self-reflexive irony. At one moment in the interview he interrupted his diatribe to say, "And now I sound like a right-winger!" At other moments he was more precise. Accommodation was necessary because, he said, "I had to earn my beans." He claims that he did not abandon his principles, but that he became disillusioned with political activism. With a sneer he recalled all that left-wing enthusiasm about implementing collectivism. And with an equal grimace he disparaged the next factional dispute a few years later that sought to destroy that very same collectivism so eagerly trumpeted before. What really hurt him was the treacherous behavior among comrades who betrayed the solidarity among companions. He had contempt for those who shifted allegiances and disdain for the many who sold out for personal advantage. But he did the same. He made many enemies during his life, and he remembers them as "rats."

Behind the Scenes

The hacienda Huarán had produced maize on the floodplain, it had a large dairy operation, many hectares of planted eucalyptus trees, and extensive underutilized *puna* highlands. The extent of the property was about six thousand hectares, following two small river courses that descended from the snowy peaks. Much land was unsuitable for agriculture, but the hacienda had monopolized the best in the process of its consolidation. It did so at the expense of two ancient indigenous communities, Arín and Sillacancha, which, in 1971, had little and poor marginal lands in the valley area.

Reading Mario Herrera's thesis (1994), one can understand the rivalries between the two communities. The two villages had competed with each other to capture the hacienda. Arín, the poorer one, took a hostile attitude toward the landlord. The villagers often poached resources from it and were regarded by the owner as thieves. People from Arín tended to avoid entering into agreements with the landlord, whereas those from Sillacancha did provide free labor in exchange for access to grazing lands. Sillacancha's members survived with subsistence production and some marketable maize from their plots in their community lands and the raising of animals on Huarán's pastures. Arín's villagers, instead, had to migrate, many of them to the Convención Valley (there they learned union organizing). Sillacancha people, for that reason, had maintained a more cordial relationship with the owner in the classical patron-client relationship that characterized hacienda systems before the reform. Agitation to expropriate the landlord came from Arín, and it was sometimes opposed by Sillacancha. In the film, José Zúñiga skillfully averted an open confrontation between the people of Arín and Sillacancha that the landlord had in fact promoted. However, because Arín's migrants had more experience in organizing, as well as links beyond the hacienda, they led the push for expropriation. Riding on their success, they tended to manipulate decision making and monopolized the executive positions and their associated privileges in the cooperative afterward.

The reform process had privileged the combative Arín people by giving them a majority, among the 125 families that were approved by the government to become members of the cooperative. Only half the people from Arín and Sillacancha benefited in this way, whereas the other half ended up with no access to the cooperative's benefits. The latter therefore had no stake in making the cooperative succeed. Instead they provided a fertile forum from which it could be criticized, attacked, and undermined. They kept exerting pressure to find ways to access the cooperative's resources, either by poaching them or pressuring the leadership to extend membership benefits to them. In at least one instance, they tried to invade the cooperative at a moment when its internal weaknesses made this move tactically feasible. Under these pressures, the cooperative rallied to defend its territorial integrity, but it only just managed to do so.

According to Herrera's dissertation, the leaders in Arín's group became an entrenched elite in the cooperative, frequently enacting measures that favored themselves and their families to greater degrees than other members. Sillacancha's members eyed the Arín leadership with suspicion and formed an opposition group. However, it was a minority that could be outvoted or manipulated, but not without considerable internal conflict and petty political chicanery. Politics interfered with the cooperative, Mario Herrera told Danny. Their influence was heinous: "We had resources, and those starved politicos with no other occupation attempted to meddle and bewitch the leaders only to have a place and to feed from the trough. For example, I was on the electoral committee for six, seven years, and I saw how everything was rigged. And the peasants, just as you see them, so stupid, they were a useful instrument."

The cooperative had started off on and remained on a good economic footing for a few years, and, thanks to technical support from the agricultural agencies, it is said that it soon doubled production compared to the period under the former landlord. The cooperative benefited from a small economic boom that exported special Cusco maize to Japan. But the leadership made several unwise investments. The cooperative was given a large tract of land far away in the eastern jungle of Madre de Dios to develop into a cattle operation to absorb the excess population that the cooperative could not sustain. This venture turned into a financial trap as well as a personal disaster with the accidental death of several members who drowned in the Madre de Dios River while trying to cross it. The leaders of the cooperative bought another farm nearby but had to sell it at a loss a couple of years later. They also claim to have invested heavily in the film venture and to have never received any revenue for it. Taking advantage of easy reform-oriented credit from the Agrarian Bank, they later had great difficulty paying back their loans.

Labor discipline was also a contentious issue. In their own assessment, Sillacancha members saw themselves as workers with greater discipline who took greater care in preserving the cooperative's assets than Arín's careless members, yet all were paid the same salary and received the same benefits. Because many members also had access to subsistence plots, greater care and efforts were invested on these than on collective production. However, Arín's members depended more on wages for daily income than Sillacancha's, so it was the more "careless" work force that tended to predominate: those whose income came mainly from their plots showed up for work duties only to avoid falling below the required minimum so as not to lose their other privileges, such as below-cost purchases from their store, health benefits, or even the opportunity to take out loans from the cooperative, which few repaid.

Work was undisciplined. Ignacio Ccorimanya, a critic of the cooperative, remembered better times when he had worked for the hacienda in milk production. He said then he was paid punctually every two weeks in proportion to the milk he handed in.

> Six days you worked, and, at six o'clock, they paid. The packets were ready. But with the cooperative it was like a lawsuit to get paid. When I went to pick up my salary, they said, "There is no money." There was more discipline in the hacienda. They hurried them up; they only gave a half hour lunch break. With the cooperative, work is slow. They may arrive on time, but they hang around, chatting, laughing. That is not the way to work.

Stealing or taking advantage of cooperative property was rampant no matter how collective the ideology was. As with other cooperatives in Peru, the free-rider problem was difficult to handle, in part because the drastic inhumane punishments that had been the norm in the hacienda were no longer allowable. Memories of theft and other forms of malfeasance have their own dynamic. Everyone can tell stories about how they saw other people steal, but they, themselves, remained scrupulously honest. Of course!

Below is Mario Herrera's analysis, followed by some further interesting comments made by people whom Danny queried separately on this issue:

MARIO HERRERA: Thefts proliferated; if you did not pay attention they would steal your underpants. But then, how to deal with it? For example, a fellow had stolen a few thousand from the cooperative and was about to be "hanged." So what did the fellow do? He enrolled in this or that political group. And the politicians of that group would fight for him in the federations and so on. The leaders knew that so-and-so had stolen, but in order to keep the peace, they kept quiet, because if one accused the thief of being a thief, he would be your sworn enemy for the rest of your life. Yes, that is the way it was. It was terrible!

PAULINO SAIRITUPAC: Each leader who was voted into office always hid something from the cooperative, and it would later show up in their homes, and they even had their houses in the city.

DANNY PINEDO: Why do people steal?

CIRILO COBADES: There was no theft, only bad management, and that led people to think that there was theft. They did not organize the work well, they did not know how to administer.

DANNY PINEDO: If the cooperative was yours, why did you steal from yourselves?

CIRILO COBADES: No, we did not steal. That is what they say about us.

DANNY PINEDO: But why is there bad administration in the cooperative?

CIRILO COBADES: Because we have not been trained to higher levels.

MARIO HERRERA: Not everyone stole, for sure. There were some honest people, like Cirilo Cobades. He is very honest.

The pressure to distribute land generated constant problems in the cooperative. In the beginning, every member was given a subsistence plot, but as the next generation of the cooperative members started to form their own families they too began to demand additional allotments. They pointed out that the cooperative was not giving them employment. So allotments began to be made, including nicer pieces of land that were also given to some leaders and their well-connected relatives. Those who ended up with less than they thought they deserved began to protest, even those members who had land in either Sillacancha or Arín. The only way to resolve that conflict was to decide to have another land distribution to correct the errors of the first one. Once these initial distributions had been made, the pressure toward distributions down the line would not be contained.

In the late 1970s, the cooperative was in severe financial trouble. A proposal surfaced to reform the cooperative based on a strict business criterion and to do away with petty politics. The proposal implied the reorganization of the whole place, the correction of all the anomalies that had brought the cooperative to near bankruptcy. Among the mandates were the elimination of all established privileges, and the closing down of unproductive departments and all social services. The proposal called for tighter fiscal control and greater supervision of tools and materials, and worse, the dismissal of excess members. It was rejected by those in power, for it meant the loss of their own privileges.

So the pressure began for the outright dissolution of the cooperative and the division of its lands and assets among its members, led mostly by people from Sillacancha. When the second Belaúnde government issued the law in 1980 that allowed cooperatives to dissolve, the *sillacanchinos* had their opportunity. They succeeded, but not without a bitter struggle in which the leadership was accused in legal courts of mishandling assets, and they tried to organize an invasion of the land.

Those from Sillacancha, now mouthing socialist principles, were for equal proportions of land for each member (regardless of how much each one had in his own community), whereas the once collectivist cadres from Arín argued that land should be distributed according to the amount of work done for the cooperative. In the end, the latter faction won. Thus the originally landless, hostile, less disciplined, politicized Arín members who had dominated the cooperative since its inception ended up with larger shares of land than the others.

The herders in the *puna* highlands took the vast expanses of grassland with them and unaffiliated themselves from the cooperative. They had been largely marginalized from benefits or participation in the cooperative's affairs from the very beginning. But then, they had not been interested in them, either.

Only a shell of a service cooperative remained when Danny Pinedo and

I visited the place in 1996. Only twenty hectares of badly worked land still produced some maize for export. There were a few neglected cows in the stables. The eucalyptus plantations were being cut for sale, and the income was used to pay low salaries for the cooperative officers and nonmember day laborers. Yet, to us they spoke of grandiose plans to convert the hacienda house into a tourist hotel or develop water resources for fish farms. There was even a dream to build greenhouses to export flowers if only a foreign nongovernment organization (NGO) would come with the plans and the money. Huarán, however, had a bad reputation. According to Herrera, not one NGO would touch it with a ten-foot pole.

When, Herrera asked himself, did the solidary nucleus of Huarán break down? He answered with an Orwellian vision close to that found in *Animal Farm* (1945):

> When resources began to be available, when there was money!!! That is when the schemes and deviations started. And concretely, what never worked well was the productive side of the cooperative. The agronomists who were supposed to help run the place, and I say this with contempt, they were incompetent. People did not work, and the salaries were higher than the revenues. Their management of the resources was naïve, and no one ever knew how much maize had been harvested or sold.

But ultimately, he went on, the agrarian reform was a bag of contradictions. At issue was the state's push for collectivism against the people's innate individualism. "Don't forget that," he said to Danny. "All those leftists, the various shades of red and pink were more collectivist then, me too."[16] He went on to argue, "And we did not understand that all the peasant really wanted was his land and nothing else." Cooperation with and resisting all those (government and antigovernment) leftist agents was the peasants' strategy. Efraín Solís had told Herrera that participating in the government's programs was just a strategy to get hold of the land, "because afterwards, we will divide it up." Herrera admonished Danny: "So if you study the events carefully, you will arrive at the conclusion that they did this simply to please the government. And when the government went *pfft*, the land got divided up."

Asked to sum up the positive side of the reform, Herrera concluded the following:

So now, each one has his piece of land and is not interested in what happens to his neighbors or the institution. I see the positive side of the reform that lots of people have acquired their piece of land. There are many *compañeros* who never would have had their children in the university, each one with a computer. That makes me glad. I too am like that. I started off with nothing, and they gave me a piece of land, and it has helped me survive the crisis of the second Belaúnde regime and that of Alan García and today's Fujimori too.

Regarding to what end this experience served, Herrera stated:

It has served to think hard and deep. As I stitch all this history together, it was all about land. But then I sometimes ask myself, what have we done with the productive system? And this really invites me to live with a guilt complex. But I am no longer interested; I am not going to look to run things or to become president of anything. If you get involved and try to push what is not for the peasants, then they will just shrug you off, and the only thing that that produces is frustration.

I am a stranger in Huarán, more than I ever have been.

Where Are They Now?

Ignacio Ccorimanya wants the titles to his individual plots of land regularized and handed over to him. But the cooperative leaders have decided not to give them out, lest the peasants begin to sell their plots to outsiders. Cirilo Cobades has six children, two of them already in the university, one of them in the school of mining. "Without the reform, I would not have been able to educate them," he said to Danny. Hilario Quispe was vice president of the cooperative when Danny interviewed him and continued to defend it, seeing hope in its future projects. Paulino Sairitupac is content with what he has. The best times, he said, "[were] when we had our own cooperative, because with that we could sustain ourselves and live well." As he recalls, "It was not like the hacienda when we were always under the control of some supervisor. We could take *chicha* breaks and eat the lunch that our wives brought to us. Now we are peaceful, because the bad hacienda times are over."

Mario Herrera finished an anthropology degree at the University of Cusco. At the time of the interview, he was working on an irrigation project funded by the German government. When Danny and I went to look for him in Huarán, we saw his plot of land, fenced in with large stone walls. Inside a respectable house, his father responded to our call. He said that Mario was in Cusco and gave us the address. The father had moved in to take care of the farm because Mario was always busy with his job.

Oscar Fernández and his daughter are not always remembered as the "bad guys" they are portrayed as in the film.[17] A different picture emerged when Danny and I collated opinions our interviewees had in 1996. Carmen Calderón, the daughter of a neighboring landlord and herself a commercial farmer, had a vivid image of them:

> I knew something about them because my parents were friends with him and his daughter Marta. What the people said about him was not really true. But his hacienda was one of the most conflict-ridden ones in the region. And, it is true that the miss had a character. She was somewhat manly and was very demanding with her people. That is true. But to go from there to say that she had had people murdered or other things, that is absurd. Oscar Fernández was sort of stingy; he did not like to spend money. But to say that he did not give to his people is something else. On his property he lived well, with servants, with resources. He had everything. He treated himself well and ate good food.
>
> Oscar Fernández ended up an embittered man. He hated the government. He used to insult Velasco and wish him the worst kind of death. After the expropriation, he first went to Cusco, where he had a house to live in with his daughters and grandchildren. Afterward they moved to Lima. They sold the house in Cusco very cheaply. And in Lima he began to realize that he was running out of money. Marta had no job because she had no profession. The other daughter was a secretary in a bank, and her salary kept shrinking even as she had four children plus her father to maintain. Later she divorced. When she remarried, she moved elsewhere, abandoning Marta and her father. The two ended up living very poorly, surviving with help that friends would give them. Oscar died almost abandoned in a hospital and was buried in a poor man's grave. His grandchildren moved to the United States. One of them was my schoolmate, and he sometimes sends me a card and asks me if I still have my hacienda. I say "yes," and he responds, "Lucky you."
>
> The film? What an outrage!

Ignacio Ccorimanya:

Oscar Fernández was good. Everyone said that he was bad, but he wasn't. He could lose his temper, but that did not last long. He did slap people whom he saw standing, conversing, horsing around, or being drunk. He would get mad.

Hilario Quispe:

The *hacendado* was a nice man. He gave generously, food, tips, everything he gave as he should. He lived well. His friends came from Cusco, because he was social and treated them well. He did not live in great luxury, only normal.

Paulino Sairitupac:

I could not go to school during the hacienda times. Do you think that "they" would let us? [*With indignation*] The hacienda owners said to my parents, "*Carajo*, if you educate your son, he is going to be a thief, he is going to kill you, he is going to hit you. Don't send him to school, he is going to be lazy, a vagabond, a thief." That is what they said.

Since the *hacendado* did not want education for us, we all were in the same ignorant state. But secretly I went to night school. Like a thief I sneaked out at night and went to school and I learned at least something. But when the cooperative came, they put up the school. In the times of the hacienda only the children of the *hacendado* got to go to school.

Federico García:

I want to make a gentlemanly confession, because age brings a certain peace. After what has happened to me with the slew of slanders, mocking, and persecution, I have learned that one should not be so open to what people say.

I have no doubt that in the Cusco region of those times, there was an enormous conflict between *gamonales* and peasants, and that the *gamonales* were cruel and insanely diabolical against their Indians. *Gamonalismo* was one of the principal causes for the underdevelopment of the region. In the case of Mr. Fernández, I only guided myself by what the peasants said of him. Today it would not surprise me if in their testimonies there were not a great dose of exaggeration, and that the peasants did to Fernández what they later accomplished with me. So, I have regretted that in the film I named the landlord Oscar Fernández, and that I named the hacienda Huarán. I could have changed both to fictional names. That way perhaps the story would have been a more coherent narration about the agrarian reform and the struggle for land without having raised false testimony against people who may have deserved it, but not at that level.

For example, I believe that there is no real proof that Mariano Quispe was murdered through a conspiracy between Fernández, his daughter, and the poisoned *chicha*. It could be true or not. Also no one really knows what happened to Zúñiga. I put these in the film as proven facts, and I now regret that.

I knew Fernández, but from the other side of the political fence. I was also born in the Calca region, and one of my grandfathers had an hacienda called Manzanares. I belonged to that social group, so as a youth I often went to the hacienda Huarán. Marta had a bad reputation; she was a tough character. That I do remember, but we completely lost contact. My mother was friends with Fernández's wife, so we went to fiestas from hacienda to hacienda. Evidently obscure family secrets were not shown on those occasions. When I became a university student, I changed sides and out of conviction began to favor the peasants. I broke with those who had been close to me.

I have no doubt that the film was a terrible blow for the Fernández family. It is like undressing the intimacies of a family and probably with a degree of exaggeration about which I now feel extremely sorry. Had I been more prudent, it would have been good to investigate the theme further. That is my self-criticism.

Hugo Neira, who wrote the fascinating reports of land occupations in the 1960s, "discovered" Saturnino Huilca, pleaded for Hugo Blanco, and worked for the controlled press during the Velasco regime. I met him in 1982 in Mexico, where he had a research post at the Center for the Study of the Third World. Later he moved to France and became a sociologist. He was a professor at the University of Papette in Tahiti. In 1998, he published a lengthy book about Peru in which he wrote positively about the Velasco agrarian reform. In 2006, he became the director of the National Library in Lima. There he told me that he did not believe that Saturnino Huilca was the mystic Andean religious leader that Federico García painted in the film, a depiction that García reiterated in my interview with him.

Hugo Blanco returned to Perú in 1975 during the second phase of the military government, but he was re-deported in 1976. Nonetheless, even from exile until the last-minute amnesty that permitted him to run for election to the constituent assembly in 1978, he garnered the third-largest vote, the most any leftist had ever achieved as a member of the constituent assembly. He was personally responsible for the article in the Constitution that condoned the agrarian debt (a contentious part of Velasco's reform), thus fulfilling his long-held view that the peasants were to receive their land without having to make payment because they had amply paid already by working for free for their landowners or because they had had their land forcefully taken from them. His immense popularity helped the rise of the democratic left in 1978.

Blanco's subsequent political career, however, was more troubled. He still called himself a Trotskyite, was popular on television for wearing symbols of poverty (a rope instead of a belt and rubber sandals). He is blamed for spoiling the chances that the Left could have won the elections in 1980. Unable to reach an accord between extremist and moderates, all attempts at a united left failed. In the end, Blanco ran for president with his own splinter group. In his campaign, the press reported that he said of himself that "because he was the most popular, most charismatic, most combative, most persecuted, most often imprisoned or deported, and most voted leader, he was the only natural candidate for the Left for the post of president of the republic" (Pease and Filomeno 1982, 3,790, my translation).

He came in a distant fourth in the election that returned Fernando Belaúnde Terry to his second term as president. Any chances of a strong leftist political opposition in that government fizzled, and for this, many say, Blanco is to blame. However, he retained a parliamentary seat and served several terms as a senator in Parliament in the 1990s. His political star faded completely and was insignificant during the years of terror provoked by Shining Path and its military repression. During those years he lived in Sweden.

Hugo Blanco and I had a friendly and polite conversation in February 2001, although it was somewhat inhibited on my part. Because Blanco was so controversial, since the 1980s intellectuals of the Left have downplayed his role. They highlighted his errors and shunned him socially. Nonetheless, he still is politically active (with a very, very small following) and has maintained his line consistently for four decades. He has returned to the Cusco area, where he participates in community development programs with a distinct indigenous movement and pro-community autonomy flavor that is not very original.

Because of his protagonist role in the agrarian reform, Hugo Blanco has the last word in this chapter. It is a self-reflexive piece taken from his book, and it is about the dangers of heroic redeemers.

> The bourgeoisie, like the exploiting classes of the past, fosters a belief in redeemers. . . . It is not necessary that these leaders be right-wingers; the opportunists of the left, who are not controlled by the bourgeoisie, are also accustomed to make the masses believe that such leaders — and not the actions of the masses themselves — are responsible for winning victories for the exploited masses.
>
> The bourgeoisie will even exalt the authentic revolutionaries, even though it may be through insults and slander. They are eager to extol the individual at the expense of the masses. As long as the masses believe in a redeemer, no matter how revolutionary he may be, the bourgeoisie feels relatively secure. This redeemer can be bought off, jailed, or killed; they cannot do that to the masses. (Blanco 1972a, 88)

This chapter has shown how, as individuals, the reputation of heroes, local or national, rises and falls. In the next chapter, on landowners, I reverse the procedure. I start with a collective image held by progressives of the "evil" landowner and how landlords tried to counter it. Then the chapter describes how individuals remember the unforgettable moment in their lives when they were expropriated, and the effect it had on them personally and on their families. There is a lot of outrage and hate explored through stories landlords tell. There is also an account of the measures that landlords took to defend themselves from expropriation, as well as an interview/portrait of the new kind of agricultural businessman that has emerged after the Velasco reforms.

three

Cast of Characters in Order of Appearance

LUIS GALLEGOS, an anthropologist and social columnist in Puno who was interviewed in Puno, September 1996.

ELIANA SEMINARIO, the widow of a cotton and rice landowner in Piura who was interviewed in Piura, July 1994.

CARLOS SCHAEFER, the son of a landowner in Colcabamba, Huancavelica who was interviewed in Lima, February 1996.

LUIS ALAYZA GRUNDY, a cotton farmer and the owner of the medium-sized Hacienda Arona in Cañete who was interviewed in Arona, February 1996.

EFIGENIA ALARCO, an expropriated owner of the *fundo* Pacos in Colcabamba, Huancavelica. Now a divorced physical education teacher in El Augustino, a poor district in Lima, she was interviewed in Lima, February 1996.

VÍCTOR SANTILLÁN, the son of a small landowner in Colcabamba, Huancavelica. An anthropologist, occasional consultant, and NGO employee, he was interviewed in Huancayo, June 1996.

BETTY GONZÁLEZ, a worker, and a union and cooperative leader in Huando, Chancay, and Lima, then a *parcelera* and housewife living in Huaral. She was interviewed by Danny Pinedo in Huaral, May 1996.

LUCHO ALCÁZAR, an expropriated owner of the *fundo* San José in Pariahuanca, Junín who farmed what the reform left to him for about ten years and then moved to Lima where he became a businessman. He was interviewed in Lima, June 1994.

NO NAME, the son of an expropriated landowner in Zurite, Cusco, he requested that his name not be used. A businessman and construction entrepreneur, he was interviewed in Cusco, July 1996.

RAFAEL SEMINARIO, an expropriated landowner of several haciendas in Piura. At the time of the interview in Piura, June 1994, he was a businessman and the president of Piura's chamber of commerce.

JOSÉ DE LA PUENTE HAYA, an expropriated small landowner in Trujillo who became a businessman establishing a television cable service in the city. The nephew of Víctor Haya de la Torre and a relative of Luis de la Puente Uceda, the fallen guerrilla leader of the MIR (Movimiento de Izquierda Revolucionaria), he was interviewed in Trujillo, November 1996.

ZÓZIMO TORRES, a worker and union leader of Huando in Chancay, Lima, in an orange grove that the owners had legally subdivided in order to avoid expropriation. He rallied protests to get the government to reverse the law that had allowed owners to subdivide their estates under their own initiative. He was interviewed in Huando, April 1996.

ALFREDO ELÍAS, an expropriated landowner from Santa Rosita, Ica. Now a businessman, farmer, exporter, and the ex-mayor of Ica, he was interviewed in Lima, March 1996.

No One Wants to Be Identified as a Class Enemy

Class relations were reversed when the state decided to demonize landowners in 1969. A moral discourse was developed to justify expropriation, and thus landlords who once were the center of power and prestige became quite quickly defined as deserving the punitive acts organized by the state on behalf of the nation. I will focus here on the constructs of hacienda, *propietario*, *patrón*, and *gamonal* that circulated with the reform process. They provide the context to how landlords as individuals—characterized as class enemies—responded in my interviews.

Expropriation converts a class definition into an accusation leveled at individuals who then have to deal with a very real sense of injustice and outrage committed against them in a very personal way. To be told that the lifestyle one has been leading is suddenly morally wrong is a deeply wounding and humiliating psychological shock. The reaction is anger, and it poured into my tape recorder. While I do think that the agrarian reform should have happened, I realize there is no agrarian reform without expropriating land. Here I want to give landlords a sympathetic venue for their outrage. No one likes being expropriated, let alone being labeled an enemy. My father's lifelong bitterness toward the Nazis, who took my Jewish grandfather's coffee import firm, his house in Hamburg, every other personal possession, and in the end my grandparents' lives, was a palpable festering wound throughout his life even in remote Huancayo, Peru.

I also need to state at the outset that it has been hard for me to write this chapter, since I did not derive glee or joy from the ex-landowners' suffering. Quite candidly, as I listened to these outpourings, I had to work very hard to reach some sort of empathy for them. At the same time, the landowners were very eager to provide me with their points of view as they felt that since the reform no one had given them a chance to express them. I trust that I accomplished the task they asked me to perform.

My father remembered Senator Alonso, the owner of the hacienda La Punta, riding into town down the main street of Huancayo in the 1940s. He would stop in front of Mr. Guerra's hardware store and shout until one of the store's employees came running out with a chair, helped the man get off his horse, and led it away. The *hacendado* would then sit astride the chair in the middle of the street, his arms folded over the back of the chair. Then he would shout out orders for someone to go to the bank and bring him cash, another to get him a newspaper, a third to bring him a drink, a fourth to summon the lawyer, and so on; he ran his business from the middle of the street, attended by scurrying attendants. Traffic, not that there was much in those days, was diverted around him. Memorable indeed.

Hacienda

The hacienda, an enclosed estate, as the exclusive dominion of the *hacendado*, evokes not only the land but also a world of refined privilege. It associates a family surname with a place; for example, the Pugas of La Pauca in Cajamarca in a long line of descent sometimes claimed to come from colonial nobility or military *caudillos*. In the case of the Pugas, their fame came from breeding fighting bulls. Losing the connection between hacienda and surname was indeed a wrenching experience.

In Puno, Luis Gallegos, the chronicler of the city's social page, recalled that in the bar of the Puno Club, Don Alberto Eduardo Amat cried, "'Aaaay, La Galaca! La Galaquiiiita!' he wailed. 'I have been stabbed right here in the heart! La Galaca, La Galaquiiita!' It was his best hacienda."

The memory is also fused with a building, the *casa hacienda*, constructed on an imposing place as the exclusive domain of the family and guests, filled with inherited furniture, collections of memorabilia such as pre-Hispanic ceramic vases, crucifixes, hunting guns, or portraits of ancestors and photos of prize breeding stock that provided visual elements for self-assurance and ostentation. The house was connected to gardens, orchards, stables, storerooms, and a chapel where religious services were conducted.

After expropriation, workers under the orders of agrarian reform officials guarded the house of Eliana Seminario on one of her husband's haciendas in Piura. Shielding herself through loyal employees, she would nonetheless go back to secretly remove a couple of forks and spoons, just so that the dinner set they left there would be incomplete. Using her own sense of propriety, she felt she was resisting and maintaining her dignity. Eliana Seminario was terribly pained when she later saw some of her deteriorated furniture being sold in a secondhand market in the streets of Piura.

The hacienda was a place where traditions were kept, continuity with the past was affirmed, privilege was underlined, and refinement was cultivated. It was an intensely private world with sharply defined boundaries and rigidly enforced patterns of exclusivity. The loss of these qualitative aspects in the process of expropriation loomed large in the memories of my interviewees. It was not so much the property but the intangibles that were bound up with them that provoked intense, melancholy responses.

Carlos Schaefer, of Colcabamba, Huancavelica, shared such a memory: "There were fruit trees, beautiful avocados, with which my father won prizes every year. Believe me, the most beautiful avocados! Our maid in Lima took a seed from one of the hacienda avocados and planted it in the garden and I still have our own avocados to eat. Delicious!"

A luxurious coffee-table book published by the Banco Latino in 1997, *La hacienda en el Perú: Historia y leyenda*, has essays by architects and historians interspersed with breathtaking photographs of beautiful examples of the restored rural architecture of hacienda houses, some of them now hostels. Arona, which I visited in the coastal Cañete Valley, is featured in this book (fig. 8). In 1996, I was shown around by Luis Alayza Grundy, a landlord who managed to retain seventy hectares as well as the house. It is a historical monument because it once belonged to Hipólito Unanue (Alayza is a descendant), a national hero whose statue is on display in the colonnaded interior corridor with vast expanses of polished wax floors and exquisite views of a beautifully maintained enclosed garden. There is also a large chapel where mass is still officiated once a day. The furniture, ac-

Figure 8 The interior of the hacienda house Arona. The caption in the original reads: "On the haciendas on the coast the ample and breezy corridors with columns served as a transition between the public exterior and the private familial world of the *hacendado*, in the back, the closed entrance door to the chapel of San Juan de Arona" (Banco Latino 1997, 92–3). © Raúl Rey.

cording to Don Luis, is not the original because the hacienda was sacked by the Chileans in the war of 1879. At the time of my visit he lived there quite alone during the week, because he also has a house and active family life in Lima, two hours away by car. During the summer vacations relatives came to stay there. For Luis Alayza, the *casa hacienda* is a white elephant because it is so expensive to maintain, but he will not allow it to be used for tourism because it would lose its tranquility, and he himself notes that he does not have the character to be a smiling innkeeper.

That coffee-table book is one example of unashamed selective memorializing of good times past. Leafing through it, one does not see a single picture of the dwellings of servants, workers, or peasant huts. Absent, on purpose, are photos of decayed and abandoned hacienda houses. Seeing those ruins was for me a far more impressive image of the passing of an era than anything else.

In my field notes of May 5, 1996, I noted the following:

Casablanca, Tarma, Junín (part of the ex-SAIS Ramón Castilla). The house still stands but is stripped, all the windows are broken, the floorboards are being torn out to use as firewood, no furniture. Electric connections gone. The Pelton turbine is scrap iron. The house sits on the lands left to the owner but he does not work them nor does he come back. The *mayordomo* still hangs around. He remembers that Sr. Otero used to live there all the time; he ran the hacienda with one accountant and a few *caporales* in contrast to the large number of employees of the SAIS. His wife was incredibly strict, passing a finger over the furniture to check for dust. Women who were sent to her house in Lima did not like being her servants.

In memory and in myth, the hacienda may have been much larger and more beautiful and peaceful than it really was.[1] The decay is what hurt the *hacendados* more than anything else. In my interviews and notes, there are many lists (of extreme emotional significance to those who recite them) of hectares of land, numbers of fruit trees, cattle, sheep, and alpacas taken away, of kilometers of fences and telephone wires they had invested in ripped out. Owners regret that they cannot go back to their haciendas because it is too heart wrenching. Efigenia Alarco remembered the eighty beehives they kept at her small property, the *fundo* Pacos. They had a beekeeper and he produced the honey, fumigated the hives, and maintained them. After the expropriation, she returned one day and found that no one had cared for the bees, they had swarmed, and honey dripped down the trunks of trees: [*Almost in tears*] "Poor bees!"

In the Paucartambo Valley, Cusco, in 1985, I came across a dilapidated hacienda compound in Challabamba. The thatched roof was sagging, the interior rooms empty, the patio overgrown and unkempt. In the middle of the patio stood a garish tomb. Surprised, because Peruvians are always buried in cemeteries, I found out from beneficiaries of the hacienda who continued to live in shacks behind the hacienda house that it was the ex-owner who was buried there. I was told that upon expropriation, the *hacendado* had moved to Cusco. There his life was miserable. He did not get along with his children, had no income, and began drinking. Gradually he had drifted back to Challabamba. He asked his ex-peons if he could live out his days there. They accepted and fed him, and when he died they buried him right there in the patio. But the ex-peons did not want to use the building. Roland Anrup's book *El taita y el toro*, a study of the cultural and affective aspects of Cusco haciendas, points out how frequently the ex-serfs do not want to go near the hacienda houses and prefer to let them become ruins: "We cannot live in the *casa hacienda* because the ghosts would not let us sleep. When one sleeps there one night one's dreams are haunted by these manifestations. So many people have lived in these old houses. We prefer to live in our own houses because for a long time we have lived in them and we are comfortable and we are the owners. The only people who have had the courage to enter the *casa hacienda* are outsiders" (Anrup 1990, 141–42, my translation).

Propietario

At the end of the nineteenth century, when the hacienda system was in its heyday, the word *propietario* connoted more than just the ownership of a collection of resources or things. It meant people who had wealth in contrast with those who had nothing. It signified the assurance with which one could command and dispose, rule and punish, take and bestow. Control over things implied trampling on people. In the highlands at one time, haciendas were valued not so much by the number of hectares as by the number of serfs who lived on them and provided labor. Haciendas on the coast monopolized water for irrigation, haciendas in the *punas* dispossessed herders of their animals whenever they wanted and evicted peasants if they were found to be inconvenient. Through rights of trespass on their lands, haciendas controlled market activities by monopolizing sales and purchases, or forbidding traders on their properties. Coastal haciendas used to issue their own specie in lieu of money for internal circulation, redeemable only at the company store. Boundary patrols kept the peasants' cattle from using hacienda pasturage, and if they were caught doing it anyway, the penal consequences for the owner of the cattle loomed larger than the offense. Haciendas could charge tolls, or they could close off transit through their lands. Debts were unregulated and allowed the impounding of personal property or arbitrary impositions as to how they would be repaid. Property in the larger sense created the conditions by which the owners could impose contracts on people within the hacienda and punish them for noncompliance, while leaving them little legal recourse. The defense of property entailed the creation within haciendas of their own policing systems, guards, *caporales*, jails, and the imposition of punitive measures subject to no limitations from outside regulation or control.

Historians such as Nils Jacobsen (1993) and David Nugent (1997) agree that the restraints that the colonial system had imposed on landowners collapsed with independence, while the new state was incapable of imposing

Figure 9 A confrontation between peasants and landlords in Cusco, January 20, 1964. The caption in the original reads: "In the offices of the peasant federation, the peasant Turqui and the *hacendado* Aedo [and his wife] attempt to negotiate an accord" (Neira 1964, 41). Courtesy of Hugo Neira.

its own. Hacienda power reached its peak in the 1930s. Coastal haciendas gradually modernized and some became owned by foreigners. In the highlands, however, modernization was slow. Gradually, as the twentieth century moved along, the state began drafting legislation to curb landowners, but it also had great difficulty in obtaining compliance. By the 1950s, when agitation for agrarian reform began, the process that eroded and limited landowner's immense powers of absolute control over their properties began to accelerate rapidly.

In the process of positioning themselves in the changing climate of impending reforms, landlords began under pressure to limit the extent of their arbitrary use of property rights. After highland peasant movements became active in the 1950s and 1960s, landlords often negotiated with their peasants, sometimes even in the offices of the Federation of Peasants in Cusco (fig. 9). This negotiation meant concessions toward the peasants. On the coast, workers began to unionize, and sharecroppers won certain rights. The Belaúnde agrarian reform, with its long and public parliamentary debate about what needed to be reformed, signaled to *hacendados* that *colonato* (the practice of granting a subsistence plot in exchange for work) was becoming illegal. Many haciendas "liberated" their *colonos*, gave or sold them the land on which they had settled, and paid them wages if they worked for the hacienda. Pasturage rights began to be clarified as well. Carmen Diana Deere's *Household and Class Relations: Peasants and Landlords in Northern Peru* draws attention to a "private" agrarian reform undertaken by *hacendados* in Cajamarca by converting their best lands into dairy operations and selling off the rest: "In the land sales of the 1960's landlords clearly were motivated to terminate the feudal obligations. As landlords scrambled to reduce the size of their estates, they also rid themselves of peasants who could claim *feudatario* status under the impending (Belaúnde) agrarian reform" (1990, 174). Wages and Social Security payments began to be required for permanent workers, and inspectors demanded proper bookkeeping to verify compliance.

During the Belaúnde regime, many *hacendados* changed their behavior and their outward personae. They worked hard to define themselves by the positive attributes of a modernizing elite, and they were unanimous in telling me that at that time they had been strictly "legal" and that everything was according to law—and, therefore, they felt secure that they were going to be able to accommodate to the agrarian reform. Their domination of Parliament assured them that they could control the process.

It was only the Velasco reform that led a frontal assault against rural property. To landowners this came as a shock. When the new agrarian law was declared and the military moved quickly to expropriate the sugar estates two days afterward, landlords woke up and realized to their horror that the state was going to expel landowners from their lands. Having too much land, owning the best plantations, and being wealthy was enough to expose oneself to expropriation. As happens in revolutions, the irony is that landlords, as they complained about the lack of due legal process in expropriation, were the ones whose parents and grandparents had so patently disregarded laws or arbitrarily manipulated them.

Patrón

Patrón has two main meanings: one is the boss of an enterprise who gives orders and must be obeyed, and the other is the protector of a person to whom one can appeal when needed in exchange for loyalty. The term easily migrated from traditional "feudal" haciendas in the highlands to the capitalist estates on the coast, even though they were worlds apart. Agrarian reform posters quoted Velasco's speech: "*Campesinos*, the *patrón* will no longer eat from your poverty." *Patrón* has different connotations when used by a serf, a worker, a union leader or leftist organizer, and last but not least, the landowner in a self-reflexive way.

Let me start with the view of an outsider. Thomas R. Ford, an American observer of conditions in the highlands in the 1950s, noted the following:

> The *patrón* of a Peruvian hacienda is likely to exhibit a great deal of personal kindness, to allow indulgences, so long as the work of his Indian laborers and tenants is carried out to his satisfaction. At the same time he will loudly voice his vexation at their slowness, laziness, stupidity, and general inefficiency. His display of injured righteousness in response to the exploitation charges of would-be reformers is not feigned, but quite genuine . . . Like the plantation owner of the Old South, he is puzzled, hurt and angered at the condemnation of his paternalism, which he regards as Christian charity in the fullest sense. (1962, 111)

There is a third, more subjacent element of *patrón* in the sense of a family unit, a kind of patriarchal hierarchy with the *patrón*, who is both loved and feared, at the apex of a pyramid (fig. 10). The familial aspect was underlined in that the serfs addressed the owner as *papay* (my father, in Quechua), while he responded invariably with *hijo* (son, in Spanish) or *hijito* (little son). Patterns of affection and discipline were modeled on family relations, but never in the sense of family solidarity. Affection and favors could be bestowed or withdrawn depending on the behavior of the worker. *Patrones* used these codes to divide and rule, to instill in the minds of the peasants that more could be gained in currying favor with the *patrón* than in collective action among themselves. Asymmetrical reciprocity with long-term mutual expectations of gift exchange were also characteristic of this relationship. Mutual evaluations of behavior between *patrón* and serf depended on the maintenance of these expectations. If the *patrón* responded properly he was a "good" *patrón*; if he did not live up to them, he was "bad." Vice versa, if the serf was obedient, meek, and obsequious he was a "good" serf; if he resisted or was contrary, he was labeled as "rebellious" and viciously persecuted.

Figure 10 The *hacendado* Blas Aguilar in his hacienda in Sicuani, Cusco, circa 1923. Photograph by Martín Chambi. Courtesy of Archivo Fotográfico Martín Chambi, Cusco, Perú.

Here I want to contrast Ford's description with that of another observer of roughly the same period, who stressed the weakness of the *patrón* and the inherent complexities of the *patrón* relationship. François Bourricaud's work on the department of Puno of the 1960s still stands out as an exemplary work of observation. In *Cambios en Puno*, there is a careful description of the hierarchy and power relationships of haciendas, including some startling comments:

> What is notable—even surprising—is that the two sides feel that they are being exploited. The Indian [serf] complains that the lands allotted to him yield poorly, that his neighbor has been given better, or that the *patrón* has abusively reserved the best lands for himself. In sum, the Indio feels that his work is "worth" more than the remuneration [in kind] that he receives. The *patrón* insists on the poor results of Indian labor, the negligence of his herders who let his sheep die, on the craftiness of the Indians who secretly substitute their own animals for those of the hacienda. Mistrust is the tone that colors the relationships between the owner and his serfs. . . .
>
> The patrón and the Indians have bad relationships, hostility prevails . . . he feels that the little control he can exercise over the management

of his patrimony is so vague and weak that he permanently fears ruin. (1967, 138–39, 148, my translation)

Paternalism as a component of the *patrón* relationship complicated landowners' self-image. On the one hand, they knew that it was being questioned on a national level and they were aware of its limitations within the confines of the hacienda, as well as glad to terminate the relationship if they could. On the other hand, in many places in the highlands such as in Colcabamba, Huancavelica, landowners were declining to quasi-peasant status in the 1960s and 1970s, turning the patron-client relationship upside down.

Víctor Santillán (in his youth a leftist anthropology student), the son of a small *hacendado* in Colcabamba, Huancavelica, laughs ruefully when he remembers his father's moans—Job-like—about the three disasters that befell him: 1) to have gotten mixed up with a second woman, a peasant; 2) to have had a communist son; and 3) to have had his land taken by the agrarian reform. "There was a *colono* on my father's hacienda who had more sheep than he," said Víctor. "Apo Robles lived on the *punas* of the hacienda and he was richer than my father. When my father had difficulty paying my school fees he would go to Apo Robles and borrow from him."

Víctor's father took the ten hectares that the agrarian reform left him and joined the *colonos* in a lifestyle not very different from theirs until his death. Actually, Víctor says, he was content.

In the 1960s, peasant federations struggled hard against the paternalism of the *patrón*, as the *patrón* himself did his best to discredit any real discontent as the product of outside agitators. In the 1970s, with the Velasco reform, landlords blamed agitation by SINAMOS for turning their serfs against them. They rarely acknowledged that peasants might have any genuine grievances of their own.

So when ex-landlords reminisced with me, they still used this code, and proof of having been a good *patrona* or *patrón* was the affection that some of their ex-workers still show for them. Efigenia Alarco, a landlady in Colcabamba, Huancavelica, said that her serfs defended her by telling the reform officials, "No, she is not like other *patrones* because she even eats from the same pot that we cook in. We all eat from the same pot; we do not choose the best piece of meat for her. No it was all equal."

In coastal haciendas, the personal familial element was not present.

Rather, from the 1940s until the agrarian reform, landlords faced increasing waves of worker unionization. From their point of view, resisting union leaders' growth and influence, isolating them, and controlling them were regular strategic behaviors. Although the state would frequently send police to break up strikes, it also promoted better labor relations through labor legislation. Because unionized workers voted, political parties also had an interest in allowing them to grow. The extent and limitations of *patrón*-worker relations were regulated through collective bargaining (the worker's term *la patronal* as "management" is significant). Permanent workers on the sugar estates were a well-paid, elite labor aristocracy until they were transformed into members of cooperatives, and they were reluctant to give up their unions.

From the landlord's point of view, then, the coastal *patrón* did not carry the connotation of paternalism, but rather of the quality of their good labor relations in a quasi-industrial setting. Betty González, a worker, remembers how strict the owner Don Fernando Graña was with her on the hacienda Huando in Chancay, Lima.

> Once he caught me in the field eating an orange. When I saw him coming from a distance, bam! I threw the orange away, but my mouth was still stained with the juices.
>
> "Did you put," he asked, "an egg yolk into your mouth?"
>
> "No, Don Fernando."
>
> "Why did you throw away the orange? Pick it up."
>
> I picked it up.
>
> "Now eat it," he said. "If you are going to eat it, eat it. Never throw it away. It costs me from the seedling, to germination, to pruning, until the tree bears fruit. And you are going to eat the orange and not throw it away."
>
> "Yes, Don Fernando."

Yet, Betty also remembers another facet of Don Fernando's eating admonitions. Her mother was a seamstress, and he would come into their house to have shirts and pants altered. Smelling the food simmering on the stove, he would lift the lid off the pot and, using the wooden cooking spoon, shovel beans into his mouth, saying, "Mmm, how good."

When they brought up the subject in conversation with me, coastal landowners invariably said that they got along well with their workers and their unions, that they were legal. As managers, they scoffed at agrarian reform propaganda that said that production on a commercial coastal plantation could function in a world without *patrones*. Dissatisfied cooperative members frequently complained that the government had become their new *patrón*.

Gamonal

Gamonal is a negative and critical word that became popular around the 1920s in Peru; it was used to portray the rural landowning class for its arbitrary exercise of power. "The term *gamonal* derives from the name of a virtually indestructible perennial plant of the Lilly family, the *gamón* (*asphodel*) . . . As a metaphor for the particular class of bilingual, bicultural and horrendously abusive landlords it describes, this name could not be more precise" (Poole 1988, 372). Popularized by the anarchist Manuel Gonzales Prada (1848–1918), it acquired political significance after a series of rebellions that arose against haciendas in the south of Peru from 1911 to the 1920s. Although repressed by the *hacendados* in the usual way with pillage, vandalism, arbitrary jail, and killings, this time the owners were denounced by intellectuals in Lima for perpetrating them. A commission created by the government of Leguía (1919–30) described them as abuses, terror, and illegal violence.

In the 1930s, with the strong collaboration of José Carlos Mariátegui, *indigenistas* and members of the Sociedad Pro Indígena developed the label *gamonal* to denounce the system. *Gamonalismo* was the elite control of local- and regional-level politics based on race, landed property ownership, and collusion to dominate and exploit the Indian population. Landowners considered themselves to be white (no matter what their skin color was), as superior members of the civilized race placed to rule over an inferior race of Indians. They enforced a strict code of behavior. The Indian had to lower and humble himself, always supplicant; the *gamonal* was strict, commanding, and authoritarian, but also distantly charitable. As the historian Flores Galindo puts it, "men on foot against men on horses; barefoot men against men with high boots" (1986, 527). Indians, *gamonales* asserted, were ignorant savages who were prone to atavistic violent outbreaks that only *hacendados* could control through strict disciplinary measures, by brutal punishment combined with the paternalistic protection of their childlike primitive inferior servants. Mariátegui's writings enshrined the word *gamo-*

nal in leftist discourse, but importantly he stressed *gamonales'* alliance with the rural coastal capitalist haciendas. Together, he said, they formed the oligarchy that ran the state. Velasco's agrarian reform explicitly targeted the political link between backward highland hacienda systems and the capitalist ones on the coast in the reform that expropriated both, in order to break "the spine of the rural oligarchy."

Gamonales as distinct historical individuals or legendary figures and stereotypes were proud of their reputation. They cultivated a wild bravado outlaw image associated with manliness, a penchant for individual violence and defiant criminality not unlike some mythical outlaws of the Wild West.[2] Colorful figures were converted into vibrant characters in literature, folklore, and popular legends. In many an influential *indigenista* novel, the *gamonal* plays the quintessential role of the bad guy.

Until well into the 1970s, peasants and leftists did not hesitate to use the word as a descriptive insult against landowners in agrarian conflicts. In speeches and denunciations the label was no longer restricted to the highland conditions for which it was originally devised. But when capitalist entrepreneurs on the coast were described by this pejorative and archaic term, it was akin to accusing a modern farmer in the southern United States of being an antebellum slaveholder. They, of course, were outraged. In my interviews I never asked ex-landlords if they considered themselves *gamonales*, for it was clear that they distanced themselves from the term. However, especially in the highlands, they readily acknowledged that *gamonalismo* did exist. They named other landowners in their region and their times whom they considered to live up to the stereotype, mostly by using violence as a means to run their haciendas. Implicitly this meant that abusive landlords (not the ones interviewed, but the others) did deserve to be expropriated. Thus even when denied, an undercurrent of solidarity and regret in terms of lost power and perverse prestige is present in the shuddering acknowledgment and celebration of the fabled *gamonal* of yesteryear. Thus the term also carries with it a certain kind of pleasurable memory of past pure bravado power. When I met Pio Yabar in the town of Paucartambo in 1985 (by all accounts the most clearly typical), he thoroughly enjoyed putting on the mantle of the *gamonal* for my benefit: "I drove (*arreaba*) the *indios* like cattle," he told me, smirking, but that phrase is in the public domain.

How then did landowners position themselves in their public personae to defend their lands? In what forms and ways did they distance themselves from the stereotypes? Downsizing, minimization, and denial were the means they used. Landowners struggled to appear before the agrarian reform officers as if their lands were small (haciendas were now deemed to be *fundos*); that they were just as poor as their *colonos*, treating them as their equals; or that their estates were efficient and their operations legal within the parameters established by the new laws. In other words, other landowners might be liable for expropriation, but not me![3]

Expropriation

Lucho Alcázar of Pariahuanca, in the department of Junín, describes the shock:

> The agrarian reform came on November 28, 1973. I just happened to be with my father when the notification of expropriation came. It hit us like a bucket of cold water. I will never forget it because it was most unpleasant. For three years we had lived with the anguish of knowing that one day it would be our turn. When it did, it came in a Ministry of Agriculture pickup truck carrying a couple of most unpleasant *ingenieros*, who handed us this paper, which . . . how can one put it? . . . It was like magic, no?
>
> With that paper I ceased to be an owner of what had been mine for so many years, something that had belonged to my grandparents. And that paper said that it was because of the social system that I would cease to be the owner of the hacienda that had cost us so much work to bring about. That paper made it clear that I had very few options, very little that I could do about it.
>
> We had hoped we would be left with about 40 hectares, corresponding to the legal minimum that landowners could keep. There were twelve properties in the valley and we were the last to be notified. Some were abandoned and the ministry took it all, but in another one near us, they let the owners keep one part. It raised the hope that in our case they might respect the minimum that could not be expropriated. But no, it was not to be like that according to that little paper; it said, "total expropriation."
>
> The agrarian reform agency had previously taken an inventory of the lands, the house, the cattle, and the distillery. At that time it would have

been possible to deceive them, I say it truthfully, but I did not because I had hopes that we could hold on to the house and its 20 or so hectares, plus an area higher up for the cattle. My father and I trusted that the process would be fair and legal, and we thought we were within our rights. I did not think of the possibilities of bribing because I felt that it was not necessary. We went back to the agrarian reform to negotiate, but they let us know through rumors that we would not get our minimum.

As our hopes were sinking, the government set up the agrarian tribunal and while an appeal was in process, the expropriation was halted. It was only then that my father and I decided to do it the way we should have right from the beginning. I got a lawyer—I will never forget him. Dr. Carrera in Lima was known to have good contacts in the tribunal. And it cost us a lot, let me tell you. He was expensive! But in truth, it was our last chance. We were allotted 16.7 hectares, the distillery (considered as part of the house), and half the cattle. To stand by helplessly while an *ingeniero* pointed to one cow and said "yes," pointed to another, "no," was terrible. Of course they took the best ones and there was no way to object. There was a lengthy bureaucratic process to be done in Huancayo to pick up a miserably small compensation check. Dealing with that disgusting bureaucracy was revolting.

Ingeniero No Name, son of a landlord in Cusco, who requested anonymity, tells of the reform's arbitrary reasons for expropriation:

My father had long ago settled with the *comuneros* as a consequence of a lawsuit in the 1960s. In that settlement, he gave his ex-serfs thirty-two hectares and abolished all the obligations, the payment for pasturage rights, all of that. In other words, we had completely severed our relationship to the peasant community. Up to the Velasco reform we paid proper wages, kept records of our workers, and were in compliance with all the Social Security contributions and taxes. We did not need that many people: a herder, a couple of employees, and women to milk the cows. Occasional labor was hired according to law. So the agrarian reform had no motive to give us trouble.

But those SINAMOS agents made a list of all the *comuneros*, with about two hundred families, of whom we perhaps might have known 5 percent. We demonstrated that people on that list were not from there but from distant places. An abuse! The SINAMOS agents toured the region with its pickup trucks and put up posters—LIBERATE THE COMMUNITY and things like that—trying to provoke confrontation between the communities and us. A girl who had been our domestic employee many years before came to Cusco and told us that SINAMOS agitators had asked her people to name the grievances they had against the owner. And the people had said, "We have no complaints, because the owner pays us salaries." The agents apparently admonished, "You have to lie, to slander, say anything, otherwise you won't get a thing. If you keep telling the truth you will not benefit. You have to lie, the more you lie, the more you will be given."

Efigenia Alarco's father had subdivided his properties in Huancavelica among his children in anticipation of the reform. She was given a small *fundo* that she worked by herself:

Velasco had said, "The land is for those who work it," so I gave up my teacher's job and went to work in my *fundo* Pacos. I bought improved seed and with eight peasants we worked the land on a sharecrop basis. I worked with them wearing boots in the cold fog, the peasants made me chew coca and drink alcohol to combat the cold. They said, "*Mamita*, drink, otherwise you will get sick."

During harvest time the reform official came and insulted me and asked what the hell was I doing working on that land since it was no longer mine. I said, "In the first place do not disrespect me. In the second place, your papers are wrong, I am not the one listed in the expropriation papers."

The altercation got violent.

And the people who were with me got mad because he pushed me and almost slapped me. So I was taken to the police station and spent a night in jail. In Huancayo, the agrarian reform official denounced me as a saboteur and counterrevolutionary. They took my things to the police station, and there they lost them: my rings, my vicuña hats, and saddles. After jail, I left the farm. Truth is I was living under threat.

Landowners unanimously claim that the reform cheated them on the valuation of movable assets to lower the cash compensation that the law stipulated. For machinery they based the value according to amortization procedures on the book value of capital goods by which tractors, for example, were valued at one *sol*. The landlords I talked to claimed that the government made up fictitious lists of workers and deflated the values for cattle or crops in order to minimize the cash compensations for expropriated assets. However, landlords were either silent about the widespread sale of cattle and machinery with which owners tried to salvage their assets, or proud that they actually did so. "We ate sheep every day until they were all gone before they came to seize them," said another landlord in Cusco. Many an hacienda was stripped and abandoned before the bureaucrats even got there to start the expropriation process. Workers went without pay during lengthy periods in which they were in limbo because landlords had abandoned their estates and the units were not yet transferred to the government's special committee.

Víctor Santillán remembers the disappointment his father suffered the day they went to pick up his compensation check: "'Here are your liquidation papers,' the official said. 'Debts: So and so much to Social Security and for severance pay that you owe the workers, it comes to 900 *soles*.[4] Assets: Tools, cattle, and buildings valued according to law, just a little over 900 *soles*. Difference in your favor: seven *soles*. Sign here and go to the cashier's office to collect.'"

In Piura Rafael Seminario recalls one disaster after another. Social Security wanted back payments for the workers for the three years after he had already been expropriated. He was sued for supposedly failing to pay severance payments:

> It was enough for a worker to appear with two witnesses who said that they had seen this man working on my lands for six months for the judge to say that this man had the right to severance payments. Here is the story: I saw a poor man who told me he needed money for medicines. In a moment of pure pity I told the man to go get the medicines at a pharmacy. He had never worked for me and I never saw him again. Years later during the reform, this man sued me. I told the judge that I had given him the medicine out of a charitable impulse. The judge responded that he did not believe that I could be charitable. If I had given him the medicine, it was because he did work for me, and therefore he ruled that I owed the severance payments for five or six years. I lost all

cases they brought against me because they, the "poor" workers, had all the good reasons, and I, the "exploiter" had no rights whatsoever.

Once notified that I would be expropriated, I no longer could take the products out of the farm. Agrarian reform made the workers enemies of the *patrón*, telling them, "The *patrón* cannot take anything." And these people (it is not really their fault), they took it to heart. They obeyed, telling me, "No, *señor*, this belongs to agrarian reform, do not touch anything!"

I had a small airplane. I used to fly between my haciendas and I enjoyed being a pilot. I never thought that they would try to take it (although as a precaution I had transferred the property to a friend of mine, Kiko Dibos). One morning I went to the airport and I found the workers of my ex-hacienda Chapaya with the land judge surrounding the plane: "This airplane belongs to the agrarian reform; it is part of the capital of the hacienda Chapaya."

"This airplane is not mine!"

"But you fly it every day."

"This plane belongs to my friend Kiko Dibos, and Mr. Dibos has breakfast, lunch, and dinner with General Velasco. If you want to take the plane, take it, but you will have to tell Mr. Dibos that you confiscated his plane."

And the judge was not that dumb. After I showed him the registration he told the workers, "This airplane belongs to Mr. Dibos."

And I asked them, "Why in the devil's name do you want the plane?"

[Imitating local rural bumpkin accent] "To be like the patrón" (*pa'tar como el patrón pue*).

Everywhere I went I was hounded and cornered. My nonagricultural properties were embargoed, my bank accounts were frozen, and I could neither write nor cash checks. I was pushed to last resorts. I had stolen three or four truckloads of cattle from my expropriated hacienda. I stole my own cattle and sold it. The buyer wanted to pay me with a check but it could not be in my name. So I told him to make it out to an employee and loyal friend of mine. At nine o'clock in the morning this employee swore that he would rather chew on his fingernails than take something from me. At eleven o'clock the same day he disappeared with my $25,000. This is not a story; it is the truth.

I asked, "Can I use this material in my book?"

"Use anything you want. I can give you much, much more."

Part of these outpourings stem from a feeling of frustration and impotence because the landlords' opposition to Velasco was felt to be weak to nonexistent. Each landowner defended his own estate. Each made efforts to influence individual cases. Versions like this one from a Cusco landlord are legend. He asked a military friend of his to fix things so that his estate would be exonerated. The officer phoned the director general of the agrarian reform: "Do me a favor and attend to Sr. Santander's case. By tomorrow at eleven this problem has to be resolved." Although the director general of the agrarian reform, Benjamín Samanez, was related to several landlords, he is famously known to have resisted such pressures. The phone call on Santander's behalf was not returned.

José de la Puente Haya (of Trujillo) recalls the strategy of the agrarian reform:

> Velasco's people had it all figured out. They used the technique of slicing up the cake in stages (*la rebanada*). When they started with the big ones, the sugar estates, people thought, "Wow." The government would then announce, "We will stop here." So smaller owners said to themselves, "I am safe, I am small, it is only against the big ones."
>
> After that they went after the medium-sized farms and the small ones still felt that they would not be touched. In this way any coordinated resistance was undermined.

Ingeniero No Name in Cusco shared his thoughts: "The *hacendados* were not united. They should have been, but they were not."

Eliana Seminario in Piura remembered the following: "There was a traitor in our midst. The Agrarian League from Piura sent this man to Lima to see what he could do for the landowners about limiting the expropriations. In Lima he became a turncoat. He informed the officials who was who and who had what. He came back to Piura to work for 'them.' Landowner families have since then shunned that family."

Another prominent landlord in Piura wondered why the sugar barons further south had not assassinated the general when they had their chance, although he did not say that the cotton dukes in Piura should have tried to do the same.

Resentment and Pride

Rafael Seminario was contemptuous:

> I do not call this an agrarian reform, I call it an agrarian revenge. Velasco was a traitor. He came to Piura after the revolution and one of those leftists asked him, "General Velasco, when will you declare Piura an agrarian reform zone?"
>
> Hiding his real feelings, he is said to have responded, "I cannot declare Piura a reform zone because all land in Piura is distributed. There are no *gamonales*; there is not enough land to declare the agrarian reform here. We will need a lot of money to declare Piura an agrarian reform zone."
>
> And having said that he got on a ship. Within twenty-four hours there is the newspaper headline: "Piura Declared Agrarian Reform Zone!"
>
> Everyone says it. Velasco was a *resentido social*. It was not our fault that he was born poor, no?

In the landlords' view, Velasco was a *resentido social* (best translated as "one with a chip on his shoulder"). Landlords in Piura in particular have a story they often repeat to themselves because it provides a humorous explanation for their own behavior, but it insults the Velasco family at the same time. Velasco was born in a poor neighborhood called Castilla on the wrong side of the tracks in the city of Piura. His mother, aunts, and sisters are said to have run a shady bar that sold *chicha* and entertained rich people. As a young boy, Velasco must have seen the disdain with which high society treated people of his kind. Velasco left home at an early age, arriving in Lima without a penny, and with great ambitions he enrolled in the army. There he had a successful career. At one point he came back to Piura as commander in chief of the northern region. But the local elite, knowing his background, snubbed him by not inviting him to become a member of the Piura Club. Full of regret, the story suggests that things would have been different if club members had not rebuffed Velasco.

Landlords blame communists and label the reform as a communist plot. They eagerly pointed out how communism failed in the rest of the world but unfortunately took hold of Peru during Velasco's times. Communism equals revenge, according to Luis Alayza Grundy. He remembers other landowners saying that the agrarian reform officials told them, "You already made a lot of money," as a good enough reason to be subject to expropriation.

This landlord describes the agrarian reform officials as a group of timid, spineless *cholos* who were incapable of imposing their authority, but because of that, they were doubly dangerous and unpredictable. For him, Velasco's minions were uneducated people of low social class who were badly trained and full of resentment, and did not want to listen to reason. They were full of psychological complexes (*acomplejados*), but also chickenhearted and incapable of asserting their authority. Allowing themselves to be bought out, they were therefore without moral authority. Because of their low moral character they dedicated themselves to destroying everything, and to steal out of envy. The act of expropriation is the very beginning because it is an assault on property rights, and if one begins with that, he said, then all else follows. The highest generals and top government officers were immoral, setting an example for everybody else to follow. They established precedents by applying the law with sneaky trickery and twisting it arbitrarily according to their convenience.

And Rafael Seminario put his finger on a base sentiment where the insult hits hardest: "Here in Piura there is a saying about the three worst evils: 'A poor white, a black with money, an *indio* with power.' That general, he gave power to the Indians and they avenged themselves." One does not have to be a psychologist to intuit that if landowners felt that the agrarian reform was a revenge, then the avengers may have had enough reasons to motivate them to practice it.

Pure destructive revenge was the evident motive that lends credence to the following story. Versions of its basic point are endlessly repeated and everyone who tells it vouches that it is a true story. Here I quote the most explicit told by Manuel Luna, the ex-*hacendado* of Ninabamaba, Quispicanchis, Cusco, in 1990:

> I had a bull, a fantastic breeder. As soon as he was on top of a cow she was served. It was outstanding, from the best stock, and at a perfect age. I was proud of him. The bull garnered prizes every time I exhibited it. Here is a photo with my great bull . . . Look at it, look at it carefully . . . When the agrarian reform was launched the Indians invaded my hacienda. I did not even have time to rescue the furniture of the hacienda

house. And they stole all my cattle. Because of agrarian reform they kept it all, including all my cattle. And the first thing that these brutish Indians did was to slaughter my breeding bull. They killed it. Do you know what they did with it? They ate it! Just like that. They ate it. When I found out, I felt such an impotent rage as I have never felt before. Not even when we had to abandon the hacienda house. I felt that if at that moment I had had a machine gun, I would have used it to kill them all. (cited in Anrup 1990, 207, my translation)

Roland Anrup, who at first did not lend credence to the story, did find evidence that similar events did occur in several instances, and one where agrarian reform officials had partaken of this meat.[5] More cattle were probably slaughtered than just prize breeding stock. Peasants have many stories of impounded cattle of their own that the *patrón* wantonly killed, and they also point out that hacienda cattle were stolen not by them but by reform officials or venal cooperative employees.

What interests me here is something else: the anger of the owners as they watched the ex-hacienda being torn apart by the mismanaged cooperative of the beneficiaries. It was not evident to them that a cooperative or community would not necessarily prioritize those aspects of hacienda production that the landlords valued the most but were also the most costly to maintain. I remember coming across a newly adjudicated small cooperative in the Cañete Valley in 1974 and watching how cooperative members were tearing up the *fundo*'s established vineyard with tractors. Amazed, I asked why. The *campesino* said that the reason the landlord had been expropriated was that he had run out of credit waiting for those grape stocks to become productive. He had not paid them wages for years, and they were starving. There was no other source of credit to preserve the vineyard and pay the workers at the same time. They had to produce a quick-maturing marketable crop so as to have income with which to eat.

Lucho Alcázar was disappointed in the use of expropriated land: "If the cooperative that was made up of my expropriated land would have been managed well or even better than the way I and my father ran the hacienda, then I could have resigned myself about the agrarian reform. But it was not like that at all. I often thought what kinds of brutes they were, because if they had produced a lot they would have had that much more to steal than by just grabbing what there was and running it into the ground."

No Name in Cusco felt similarly:

When we were expropriated it was a tremendous blow to our family, it was chaos from which we still have not fully recovered. Because of that I left for Argentina. When we saw how the cooperative failed, we knew that our sacrifice had been in vain. We felt greater frustration knowing that the plunder we were subjected to could have benefited many people and the country, but it did not. We felt more embittered.

We were thrown out on the street. We were left with nothing. None-theless, over the years we have lifted ourselves up through the discipline and hard work that my father had inculcated in us and the workers on the hacienda. I remember the day not long after the government took our property; I went to town to see to some paperwork. I met one of our ex-workers and he asked me, "And now, what are you going to do? You do not have anything anymore. Your car is going to get old and you will end up with nothing." I answered, "Look here, do you think I will stay down and out? You know us. We have worked hard together. We have struggled. Do you really think that I will end up being a pauper?" "No *papay*, you are right, you will never be a poor man." That is how he answered.

Eliana Seminario in Piura thought that the cooperatives failed because they lacked people who could exercise authority. Her husband liked to de-claim, "One has to know how to command." And some of the people of the ex-hacienda did recognize this. They greeted her husband with great affection. "We miss you a lot, Don Pedro," they would say, and ask him to come back with them to the hacienda in order to give them advice on how to run the cooperative. But he did not; he went into business instead, first canning fish, then import/export and banking. Eliana Seminario remarks that her husband was a man with a positive attitude: "There were no tears." He looked ahead instead of backward. Like her husband, most expropri-ated families changed quite rapidly and adjusted to the new situation. Out-wardly they showed nothing but quiet dignity.

Plots and Bonds

Although *hacendados* may remember that there was no resistance to expro-priation, it is not true that landowners did not defend themselves against the reform both individually and collectively. There was a loophole in the

Velasco law that landowners seized on to salvage part of their lands. Title IX of the agrarian reform law permitted landowners to subdivide their farms into smaller units that could not be expropriated. This part of the law had been a carryover from the Belaúnde law, which was created with the intent to speed up the reform. It allowed landlords to reform their estates "under their own initiative." It was meant to encourage the modernization of traditional haciendas, letting landlords emancipate their serfs by abolishing traditional free labor, providing serfs with individual titles to their subsistence plots within the confines of the estate. It also permitted sales of land. Coastal landowners, once they discovered the loophole, tried very quickly to downsize their operations by subdividing their properties among heirs, selling off parts to relatives, and, in order to "comply" with the law, selling a small portion of their estate to some of their workers. Although these parcellations were dubious, it gave some glimmer of hope to landlords for one year. The government rapidly rewrote Title IX in such a way that the incentive to do this vanished. Meanwhile, during 1969, approximately two hundred partitions had already taken place on the coast near Lima, Cañete, and Ica (Cleaves and Scurrah 1980, 112). Workers and leftist groups vigorously denounced them. Landlords also organized and lobbied hard to defend themselves.

The most famous test case of private initiative revolved around an orange grove called Huando (with 1,347 hectares), which belonged to the Graña family, in the Chancay Valley near Lima. Its luscious Washington Navel seedless oranges (that Betty González furtively enjoyed) were a marvel of modern agricultural technology. The owners subdivided the hacienda, assigning 700 hectares to various members of the Graña family and 160 hectares to employees; 200 hectares were sold to investors in Lima; and only 300 hectares were sold (on credit) to fifty of the most loyal workers of the hacienda. Five hundred workers were displaced and scattered to work on the smaller plots for new owners. The workers union, so the many new owners argued, lost its raison d'être since now there was no single *patrón* with whom to engage in collective bargaining.

The Huando case divided the nation. Unions, peasants, and left-wing politicians denounced this as a mean trick that undermined the reform and demanded the annulment of this parcellation. Zózimo Torres was the union leader of Huando, and he has co-written his memoirs with Charlotte

Burenius (the granddaughter of the owners) in a wonderful book called *Testimonio de un fracaso Huando* (Burenius 2001).[6] He remembers that move very well because getting the government to reverse this parcellation made him famous.

Zózimo tells how the lawyer representing the Graña interests told him: "We have done it with the law in our hands, and no one is going to remove us" (Burenius 2001, 138; my translation). The marvel was the speed with which all these transfers were accomplished, given Peru's notoriously slow legal bureaucracies. Huando workers went on a five-month strike and mobilized in Lima with the support of urban unions and workers' federations. The protesting agricultural workers were invited by the students to camp out on the grounds of the National Agrarian University. Many middle-class students from Lima remember getting radicalized by participating in protests against this parcellation. Zózimo Torres and a delegation of workers even succeeded in entering the presidential palace in their protest, earning television publicity and popularity out of it.

On the principle that laws could not be applied retroactively, landowners defended their position and lobbied very strongly. Pressure was mounting as landlords were able to rally the conservative segments of the army and navy in the government. Yielding, the agrarian reform set up a commission to investigate all private-initiative parcellations. This commission took several months and found both legal and illegal parcellations, but the legal ones were described as "unethical." It argued that even if legal, the private initiative was contrary to the spirit of the reform, and it recommended that all private initiative parcellations be annulled. The issue was so contentious that the report was kept secret until a high-level cabinet meeting took place (Cleaves and Scurrah 1980, 117). Landowners had also hoped to be able to topple the director of the agrarian reform through this process, but the cabinet decision vindicated him instead. During those crucial days, Zózimo Torres made another bold attempt to tilt the balance in the workers' favor. As he tells it, for a second time he sneaked into the presidential palace at a public swearing-in ceremony for a new minister.

> Dressed in nothing more than my humble blue jeans I tried to scurry as close to the balcony as possible. And the *Chino* appeared. How well do I remember! And right in front of me he performed the ceremony—"Do you swear before God etc., etc."—and then stepped closer to the public

gallery. I picked up my courage and shouted really loudly: "My general! My general! My general! Mr. President!"

And all of a sudden he turned around and looked at me. I met his strong stare and returned it firmly: "Excuse me, General," I said, "for us *campesinos* it is very hard to get to your office."

As the other ministers began to surround the general to guide him away, I shouted: "General Velasco! I am from Huando!"

He turned again, looked at me, and signaled that I should go upstairs. But when I got to the foot of the stairs a cordon of plainclothes policemen blocked my way. The Chino popped out between their bodies and said to me: "Hey *viejo*, you want to speak to me, no?"

Petrified and amazed, since I did not expect such a friendly tone, I only managed to mumble a few words: "My General, the Huando case . . ."

And the Chino smiled and told me, "Do not worry *viejo*, do not worry, everything is going to come out all right. We are studying it, I assure you it is going to come out all right." He repeated it while he shook my hand.

With that handshake we took leave of each other and I breathed my biggest sigh of relief. (Burenius 2001, 155–56; my translation)

In March 1971, according to Cleaves and Scurrah, Velasco's personal sympathies were clearly made evident by the kinds of supportive questions he asked of the commissioners at the cabinet meeting. "At Velasco's urging, the Council of Ministers cancelled all parcellations, whether legal or illegal. For landlords this was the clarion call that the reform was radicalizing and that they were losing the battle" (1980, 117). In a newspaper communication, the Association of Farmers of the Cañete Valley denounced the agrarian reform directorate: "To have reversed the parcellation is not allowable in a civilized nation and it only achieves sowing mistrust in the agricultural sector and other economic activities" (*La Prensa*, Lima, February 19, 1971; cited in Cleaves and Scurrah 1980, 115).

As the pressure against the reform was mounting, the Velasco government reacted in its characteristic military style. On May 12, 1972, it dissolved the Sociedad Nacional Agraria, the principal business lobby of the capitalist agricultural sector. Landowners and leftists coincided in the diagnosis. The intent of the reform was not only to benefit peasants or workers but as

Velasco is said to have said, to "break the backbone of the rural oligarchy." Political analysts by and large agree. Henry Pease summed it up nicely in his book *El ocaso del poder oligárquico* (1977):

> On October 3, 1968 the oligarchy lost its representatives in government. Soon after it lost its economic base: the agro-industrial complexes, the control of international trade, of banking, etc. In the following years the power of subordinate groups to this oligarchy was further reduced. Large and medium farmers on the coast, landowners and *gamonales* and merchants in the highlands confronted the inevitable expansion of state enterprises. Power, once oligarchic, ended up concentrated in the state, which also expanded its sphere of action as it sought to redefine its relationship with imperial capitalism. (1977, 51)

In the memories I collected in 1996, ex-landlords do remember the loophole of the private initiative very clearly. Some told me that they had considered using it when it was already too late, while others recognized that it was a ploy from which they were dissuaded by the quick and strong reaction of the government.

By July 1971, landowners were using the press to describe the expropriations as "confiscation," thus heralding the shaky future of property rights throughout the nation. They noted the contradiction in the reform's stated aims of supporting medium and small family farms while seeing that the government was more intent on creating cooperatives with the workers on these farms, which was tantamount to Soviet-style "collectivization." Several movements in defense of medium and small rural properties arose very quickly and protested vigorously, remaining active until 1976. They had good reasons to object. Cleaves and Scurrah list seventy downward modifications to the minimum size permitted (between 1969 and 1976). Each time the law was modified, the government declared that "this was it," that there wouldn't "be any more confusion." The initial law allowed 150 hectares minimum, but ended up with 50. Yet, the minimum could be overruled if labor laws had been infringed, if the owner was deemed absentee, or if land scarcity in surrounding areas warranted it.

The government's response to the increasing agitation that was dragging the smallest peasants into the fold of the middle farmers' opposition group was to issue certificates of nonaffectability guaranteeing the owner that his land would not be subject to expropriation. In an attempt to drive a wedge between owners of the smallest plots and those with medium-sized holdings, the certificates were mainly issued to the very small plot owners, those who had up to one hectare. This movement continued to press the government until 1976, when Velasco was overthrown. The Morales Bermúdez regime then declared that the expropriation phase was finished. By these means, a number of medium and small owners were given their minimum. But in the memories of the landowners I talked to, the amount, size, and location of these allotments were arbitrary. In their eyes, they were not only insufficient, but unfair and unjust. One landowner would succeed in retaining some land, while the one next to him didn't get any.

And then there was the issue of the agrarian bonds to pay for the expropriated land. The law had declared that beyond maximum cash payments of 10,000 *soles* (U.S.$300) for best-quality land, the owners were to be compensated for the rest of their land in bonds redeemable in twenty years (at 6 percent), twenty-five years (at 5 percent), and thirty years (at 4 percent). These were fixed interest rates, with yearly interest disbursements. The bonds could be redeemed earlier if the landowner decided to use them to invest in industry. A few large entrepreneurs did use them this way, notably the Romero family in Piura, but for medium and small farmers the small amount involved in the bonds was not worth the insurmountable effort of finding the co-funding and the paperwork to get them redeemed.

The value of the land was determined by the landowners' tax declarations (which they themselves had grossly undervalued), and this was regarded by owners as a crafty, mean, and dirty trick. The government agencies also took their time in issuing the bonds, so many landowners I interviewed said that they never bothered or refused to pick them up because they felt that by so doing they were showing conformity with the expropriation. Others hated dealing with a hostile bureaucracy. Eliana Seminario remembers how her husband used to give the green documents with detachable coupons for the yearly interest payments to their daughter to play with because the cardboard was so nicely perforated to cut out the yearly interest stub. She actually showed them to me neatly packed away, one folder for each of the properties they used to have, willed to her children as part of her husband's testament. Efigenia Alarco said that she did not pick up her interest payments because they were less than the bus fare downtown to get to the bank. With hyperinflation in Alan García's regime and two devaluations in the late 1980s (the *sol* was replaced by the *inti*, and the *inti* by the *nuevo sol*, each change removing three zeros), the bonds issued in original *soles* became worthless.

José María Caballero and Elena Alvarez, who analyzed the financial aspects of the agrarian reform in *Aspectos cuantitativos de la reforma agraria* (1980), confirm that landowners did not get properly compensated by the reform. By using "technical" experts in valuing installations, cattle, and plantations instead of using market price, a biased tendency toward low assessment was established. Equipment was appraised at the depreciated value in the hacienda's accounts (leading to the oft repeated "one *sol* for a tractor" diatribe), and the land, as mentioned above, by the owner's self-evaluation in tax matters. The total amount in compensation that the government assumed came to 15,000 million *soles* (U.S.$300 million), 73 percent of which were in bonds. Comparing the fair market value of land in 1967 with the value of the compensation resulted in a per-hectare amount of one-tenth of the market price. The authors also point out that most of the government's debt against expropriated owners was concentrated among the top-notch sugar and cotton plantations (some of them foreign owned), amounting to 42 percent of the compensations the government recognized. A colleague in Lima commented that because of this, the Peruvian agrarian reform also turned out to be the cheapest, in terms of government expenditure, in the Andean countries. The expropriated landowners I interviewed were correct in their complaints that they got peanuts or nothing. The only thing they got cash for was cattle, but it was more expedient to sell the animals before the officials arrived at the farm.

It was only with Fujimori's government in 1990 that there was a small, incipient move by bondholders to complain about the injustice committed against them and demand some kind of redress. Fujimori offered desert land to be developed by private initiative with future irrigation projects, but that proposal did not prosper. Bondholders pressured the administration to have the bonds revalued to current values, but no concrete measures were enacted. Toward the end of Fujimori's long reign, his advisor, Vladimiro Montesinos, a spy master and corruption specialist, was caught on television paying out politicians in hard cash. When the scandal broke and Fujimori was in real trouble, one of his final decrees was to revaluate agrarian bonds to current real values. But this decree was issued while he was on the airplane fleeing the country, hours before he faxed his resignation in 2000, and therefore did not go into effect.[7]

Businessmen

With the return to civilian rule under Belaúnde, García, and Fujimori, farmers with medium-sized holdings became a dynamic sector in coastal agriculture. They quickly recuperated their previous leadership position in terms of innovation, productivity, and market dominance. They also regained or never quite lost social ascendancy in the towns and regions where they operated, but they still were rancorous about Velasco. The social and economic distance between them and the ex-members of the dissolved cooperatives (called *parceleros*) remains an important and negative division even today. The *medianos* (those with mid-sized holdings) now see themselves as *empresarios* (entrepreneurs), while the *parceleros* still struggle with very small holdings, lack of training and credit, and the stigma of being *campesinos*.

Alfredo Elías is one of those *empresarios*, a dynamic promoter of asparagus production for export to the United States. He was, at the time of my interview in 1996, fighting for the return of his expropriated *fundo* Santa Rosita in Ica on the southern coast. Elías was appointed mayor of the city of Ica during the Velasco regime and earned a certain degree of respect from that administration. His story is interesting:

> I had 150 hectares in two *fundos*. I obeyed the law, even though the agrarian reform did not. They expropriated as they wanted, legally or not. They took the best *fundo*, Santa Rosita with 90-some hectares. But I did not accept it. I never responded to any notifications; I did not accept their payments; I rejected the bonds, or any other contact with them. Since I did not respond, their case against me remained pending during all these years. Then the government issued a law [a revised civil law code that said that any legal action not resolved in twenty-five years lapsed] in which one could thus argue that all actions undertaken by the agrarian reform that had not been concluded were to be annulled. Since the government was the initiator of the litigation, the act of expropriation was therefore nullified. Because the government dropped its case against me, the land was mine, and I demanded that the government return Santa Rosita to me.

But the land had been given to the workers of Santa Rosita a long time ago. After many years, the workers of Santa Rosita separated from the larger cooperative into which they were merged but nonetheless ended up broke. In recent years the beneficiaries of Santa Rosita had fallen into the hands of an unscrupulous businessman who had lent them money, fertilizers, and so on. They owed him. To clear the debt, this man then persuaded the *parceleros* to sell him land. Thus Elías was litigating against the government on the one hand, and against the new owner who had bought land from the *parceleros* on the other. In Elías's view, this man was not legally entitled to have done so. And he was having a conflict with the *parceleros*—his ex-workers, but also the adjudicated official owners. He thought he was going to win his case and was even more assured that he could get to some arrangement with the *parceleros*: "I can give them money, I can give them work, and recuperate my *fundo*."

It was an interesting case of the return of the *patrón*. The workers ended up with the prospect of reverting back to the position they were in 1969.

Elías blamed the agrarian reform for this situation.

> There was much talk about how the land has to perform a social func-
> tion, but social function, my friend, is not generating poverty, sowing
> misery. Land today is in this condition. So the key now is to get the land
> to produce at its highest possible level. Peruvians have to seek com-
> parative advantage and produce high-quality products and sell them
> at good prices. Peru's lands have to become agribusiness and generate
> work, generate wealth and well-being for the country. It is not a question
> of taking the little land there is to distribute them so that people have
> something to eat. No, we have to be like Chile. We in Ica have done what
> Chile did with fruit in counter season [selling fresh table grapes during
> the winter months of the United States]. We introduced asparagus, and
> it is saving agriculture in Ica. We process the vegetable, package it nicely,
> and airship it to the United States, where it is greatly appreciated. We can
> do this with grapes, with fruit, and many, many other products.

He presented his recipe for the broken-down cooperatives:

> Parceling up the cooperatives, making individual property owners, is
> only an intermediate step. It is a necessary step to finish off the coopera-
> tives. But then the laws of supply and demand will have to kick in. The
> *parcelero* who does not work or produce will have to sell his land to his
> neighbor. And that neighbor will go concentrating land until he be-

comes an enterprise. There is no other way. Peru cannot have the luxury of leaving its scarce lands in the hands of those who cannot produce.

His final judgment was the following:

We in Peru were stuck for thirty years. We have remained in the era of the agrarian reform. Distributing lands, fighting about land, taking land away from each other, litigating about land. We have invoked and curried favor with the state so it would take land away from someone and give it to whomever they chose to favor. The agrarian reform contributed to the introduction of politics in rural land and labor relations and implemented policies that are totally outmoded, useless, socializing, left wing, that have not succeeded anywhere in the world. Even the leftists themselves have realized that this was not the way.

Men like Alfredo Elías have shed the connotations of *hacendado*; they have reasserted their rights to property by defining them in productivist entrepreneurial ways. *Patrón* now means being a good business manager and innovator in globalized agro-industrial settings that hire a lot of female casual labor. Oligarchs or *gamonales* they are not, but yes lobbyists, power brokers, and active members of the business sector, playing by the new rules of the game set by the free market and international trade. Landowners who survived agrarian reform have become the "good" guys in the global neoliberal age.

There is no doubt that landowners were treated badly during the agrarian reform process, but there was no violence, no persecution of their relatives, nor, as in Russia or China for example, systematic generational disenfranchisement of landowners as a class. The hacienda system in the *sierra* had been in serious decline for a long time, and the agrarian reform there liquidated it. Most of the families that were expropriated were able to move into other sectors of modernizing society, and their children and grandchildren today may be grateful to the Velasco government to have given their grandparents the final push to abandon the hacienda. On the coast, the impact against landowners was stronger, and the sense of injustice committed against them therefore greater. Yet, as we shall see in the next chapter, there were more continuities between pre- and post-reform conditions than expected. I will focus on the intertwined stories of two people who in real life did not know of each other's existence. One is a member of the landowning and professional class who continued to work on the very same estate after its expropriation; the other is a worker and union leader who fought hard for expropriation and then ended up dismantling the very cooperative that he had worked so hard to establish. We also hear a meek voice of a woman, a landless laborer for whom the agrarian reform did very little. In that chapter, while I trace the rise and fall of cotton cooperatives on the coast, I also want to point out that in many fundamental ways changes brought about by the reform were neither deep nor permanent enough to alter power, class relations, or social mores in the coastal countryside.

four

MANAGERS AND UNION LEADERS

Cast of Characters in Order of Appearance

> MARIO GINOCCHIO, an agronomist, an administrator of an hacienda and then of the Cooperativa Mallares, Sullana, Piura. He was interviewed in Piura, July 1994.

> GERMÁN GUTIÉRREZ, a union and peasant leader in Cañete, and the employee of a service cooperative. He was interviewed in Cañete, March 1996.

> MARÍA VILLARRUBIA, the leader of temporary labor gangs to harvest cotton. She was interviewed in Quilmaná, Cañete, March 1966.

Cooperatives

There were many reasons why the agrarian reform preferred to adjudicate expropriated haciendas as cooperative enterprises rather than distribute land to individuals, but this turned out to be a hidden agenda as well as an expedient administrative measure. Neither the law nor Velasco's speeches had stressed collectivization; instead, they had projected a nation of prosperous small- and medium-sized family farms as their goal. The quick decision to expropriate the conservative opposition from their sugar estates gave the issue of what to do with them afterward some urgency. The speed with which the government proceeded and the radical nature of its confiscatory zeal contrasted with the preceding Belaúnde agrarian reform, which had been handicapped by the power that landowners had been able to exert on Parliament to tone down the laws. Landlords had had the ability to pressure the courts to slow down the expropriation process and to insure hefty compensation payments for surrendering land.

There were also powerful technical arguments against breaking up the best estates, such as losing advantages and economies of scale once an expropriated estate was in the government's hands. The reform effort was also pushed by its own dynamic. Because landowners started dividing up their own lands under "private initiative," facing massive organized protests from the workers, the agrarian reform began to favor the worker-managed cooperative of the whole estate as a solution. This decision left out temporary workers and the thousands of peasants who had been dispossessed by expansion of the haciendas.

Adjudicating land as cooperatives was a good political solution as well, because had the government started to divide up land there would not have been enough to distribute among the many deserving smallholders, nearly landless, and totally landless rural people whose expectations were raised by the regime's propaganda. Administratively the task of turning expropriated haciendas into cooperatives seemed easier. Expropriation could quickly be followed up by adjudication to the same workers on intact estates.

Clearly, the imposed reform model was not of peasant design or desire. It came from above and from outside the peasants' own milieu. It was invented in urban contexts. The economist José María Caballero, in his critical analysis of the agrarian reform, thinks that important aspects of the model of adjudication were not born out of the initial military reformist impulses, but rather, originated from the military's urban, left-leaning, petit-bourgeois civilian advisors. "Taking advantage of the ideological and programmatic vacuum of the military reform model, they were able to introduce, and sometimes even execute, their own conceptualizations, even when these often were neither understood nor completely assumed by their officer friends" (1980, 77, my translation). Models and diagrams on blackboards they remained, removed very far from reality. But, then, those were revolutionary years when all sorts of models were imposed on Peruvian society, the people of which then became subjects of experiments in social engineering. The ministry fell in love with variants of its cooperative models; it invented a whole series of institutional organizations and imagined how prosperity, equality, and development would be generated from their implementation. It joined several haciendas into huge "overdesigned" giant cooperatives. Far from distributing land, agrarian reform therefore consolidated land holdings, most often into unwieldy, large, territorially disperse units that incorporated within their boundaries a diverse mixture of forms of land tenure and production systems. The problems associated with pre-reform conditions were thus transferred, unsolved, from the old unjust system onto the newly adjudicated units. By the end of the adjudication phase 563 cooperatives were created, of which 360 were on the coast, including the 12 sugar estates. Those incorporated into cooperatives included 94,000 families (nearly a million people), representing 4.5 percent of the economically active agricultural population. Cooperatives received 271,000 hectares, representing 49 percent of irrigated land. On the coast, about half the land was expropriated and turned over to the workers.[1]

The memories of three people who lived on haciendas and had to adjust to the cooperative mode between 1970 and 1980 are presented here. I focus on cotton production in two coastal regions, the Piura Valley in the north and the Cañete Valley two hundred kilometers south of Lima.

Mario Ginocchio, agronomist (Piura)

I was born in Paita on February 29, 1924. I studied in the Italian school in Lima, and agronomy at the Agrarian University of La Molina. Then in 1947 I returned home to look for work. Dionisio Romero, the cotton king of Piura, offered me a post in the hacienda Mallares and my mother persuaded me to take it: "There is a future because you will work with the Romeros, who are your relatives."

I used to call Dionisio "Uncle." Beginning with a technical job, after fifteen years in the company, I became the administrator of Mallares and they gave me 5 percent profit sharing after taxes. That was a lot of money!

I am a methodical and quiet person, used to living on the haciendas. I do not like drinking, and am not a very social person; I prefer watching television and reading books. My only vice is cigarettes, up to three packs a day, but thanks to God I have quit that, too.

Germán Gutiérrez, labor and peasant leader (Cañete)

I was born in 1941 on the hacienda San Benito, which belonged to the Rizo Patrón family; it was one of the larger haciendas in the Cañete Valley. My mother's family was black, very humble, very Catholic, and always in the service of landowners. As a child I would go to the hacienda house with my aunts, the cooks, to play with the children of the landlords. We called them *gringuitos* or *blanquitos*. I attended the school on the hacienda and then finished primary [school] in the city of San Vicente de Cañete. The children of the landowners went to a very elegant seminary, San Patricio, and from there to Lima. When they vacationed on the hacienda, they rode their ponies and played soccer with us, but we were told not to be rough with them because they were more delicate than us coarse boys.

My father was from Arequipa. He had an independent spirit and a hot temper too. He thought that the workers, whose beliefs in the *llorona*, witches, and ghosts he ridiculed, were too submissive and superstitious. He was the head of the mechanical division of the hacienda in charge of all the machinery and enjoyed the trust of the owners, but ended up disgusted with them because of a dispute about a small plot of land the hacienda had given him on the uncultivated edges of its estate.

I was a restless and intelligent kid; I learned well and had good teachers who helped me develop my leadership skills, and soccer. We played a lot and each game ended in fights, and I was a good brawler and managed to get other kids to respect me. Because of soccer, I injured my knee, which ruled out professional sports or a career in the police force for me.

German lived in a rented two-room apartment in downtown Imperial, the bustling commercial center of the Cañete Valley. He had a piece of land, which he cultivated, but he also was drawing a modest salary as an employee. It kept him very busy.

María Villarrubia labor recruiter (Quilmaná, Cañete)

Quilmaná is a new settlement built on the edges of agricultural land in the desert. Smallholders, laborers, and immigrants inhabit it. Its streets are broad, but only the main one is paved and well lit. The houses are in various stages of construction, and I found Maria's house because a storekeeper in the neighborhood had told me to look for a large pile of bricks stacked in front of it. Her brightly painted house is a large and roomy square with ironwork windows but no glass. María wears a cotton dress and plastic flip-flops, her black- and reddish-dyed hair is in a ponytail, and she has an unusual receding hairline that gives her a broad forehead. Short and stocky, she exudes good humor, self-confidence, and after an initial nervousness, a straightforward, to-the-point answering style. The interview takes place in her bare living room. The family brings chairs and the tape recorder is placed on one of them. Adults and children watch. I am conscious that I am interrupting the dinner hour because the kids get impatient. The tape recorder picks up their whistles and giggles.

I was born in Lima in 1957 in the elegant district of San Isidro, where my mother worked as a domestic servant. We came back to Cañete because my father had an accident. Here we had no land. I did go to school both in Lima and here in the valley. I worked as a rural laborer hired by the day. My mother had experience in organizing work gangs, and I have followed her steps.

Cotton Was King

On the coast of Peru, cotton played a key role as an industrial and export crop. Dependent on irrigation and seasonal labor for intensive hand harvesting, its production was in the hands of a national rather than foreign landowning class. A plant native to the Andes, cotton was developed into a competitive industrial export crop through the work of the landowner Fermín Tianguis in Ica. It now flourishes in the Cañete Valley, and was further improved through the introduction in Piura of Pima varieties developed in the United States. Cotton supported a growing textile, soap, candle, cottonseed paste, and vegetable oil industry. It was a source of foreign exchange, with British and U.S. markets as the main buyers, throughout the nineteenth and twentieth centuries.

Labor relations evolved from slavery until 1854 through forms of sharecropping, fixed tenancy, and indentured Chinese and Japanese coolie labor. In the twentieth century, mechanization brought about an expansion of capitalist plantations with a relatively small, stable, unionized labor force, and a large segment of seasonal harvesters. The expansion of cotton production came first from privately sponsored irrigation schemes, and later was also funded by the Leguía and Odría governments. Cotton production competed with sugar, displacing its dominance in the Cañete Valley, and with rice in Piura. It was grown by smallholders, sharecroppers, and medium-sized farms; eventually, spurred by the boom in world prices brought about by the Korean War, it also became a highly mechanized agro-industrial crop. The exploitation and eviction of sharecroppers and the process of consolidation of large haciendas led to the formation of protest movements from the 1920s to the 1940s, notably in Piura. As in other regions of the coast, with capitalist production also came the creation of unionized labor for permanent workers, but not for temporary workers and seasonal harvesters.

Mario Ginocchio administered the hacienda Mallares in Sullana, Piura, 1947–69

I remember that before the agrarian reform Mallares was the largest estate in coastal Peru, and one of the six haciendas of the Romero group with more or less six thousand hectares. In those times a good harvest was twenty *cargas* of cotton per hectare and with that yield there was money to be made. In rainy years the river swelled and there were good harvests. The Romero family made a lot of money with cotton. Who provided the inputs? A store called Almacenes Romero. Who bought the cotton? Calixto Romero Exporter. How did they export? Through the Romero Paita Agency. They also had the second-largest cotton gin and a seed oil press. The only missing link was the textile part, but the Romeros installed a huge textile factory after the agrarian reform with money they cashed in from the compensation of their expropriated haciendas. The Romero group was to become the wealthiest and most dynamic corporation and financial group in Peru after the agrarian reform, branching into banking, construction, palm oil plantations, and more.

In 1930 the Romero group bought the hacienda Mallares from the Arrese family, who were seriously in debt. By the time Dionisio Romero hired me in 1947 they were investing heavily, opening newly leveled fields for irrigated cotton production. They were also expanding their orchards, bringing in grafts for avocados and oranges from Lima. Vast areas for cattle were fenced, and irrigation was extended.

The hacienda had rights to fifteen hundred liters of irrigation water from the Chira Canal. These were insufficient, and we installed pumps in the Chira River at Mallaritos. Originally this pump was an old steam pump fired by wood and gas. When I came, the pumps already were Sulzer diesels, and later we had five gasoline pumps, which were subsequently upgraded to diesel engines. We pumped as much as we could to compensate for the lack of water from the canal. Depending on how swollen the river was, we could move the pumps away from the danger of flooding. We almost doubled agricultural land from fifteen hundred hectares to twenty-five hundred by the time I left.

We worked hard. The administrator's task involved riding on horseback all day to oversee work and to control pests and diseases. We used to detect the development of the leaf-eating worm pest (*gorgojo de la chupadera*) by the characteristic smell we learned to diagnose, until I introduced the scientific counting method that I had developed in my thesis at the Agrarian University. An administrator had four horses: One for the morning, another for the afternoon. Next day we used horses three and four. The sweat of the horses permeated our own bodies because we rode them hard.

Each year we started irrigating the fields on December 4 or 5 because the integrated pest-management laws stipulated that the period of germination was to be between January 1 and 31, which meant that one could sow up until one week before the end of December. We had a very complex schedule starting with those fields that dried out faster and ending with those that took longer to dry out to be suitable for seeding. In 1968 we worked with nine or ten Caterpillar tractors with nine Farmall seeders, which could do four rows simultaneously. It was a race to get two thousand hectares planted. Some years we did not make it.

Anyone can say what they want about exploitation. But the Romeros were scrupulous about wages and the workers' Social Security obligations as stipulated by law. There were five hundred permanent workers. There were attempts to unionize. The workers had a lawyer, Dr. Luciano Castillo, a really correct man, who was the son of Melquiades Castillo, the founder of Peru's Socialist Party.[2] Management and the union organized the hacienda into delegates by departments. There were two delegates for cotton, two for rice, one for cattle, one for the orchard, one for pumps, one for tractors.

Every year there was a prolonged two- or three-week negotiation process, and the union came with its list of demands with thirty to forty points. They always left their stipulations for raises, the most important point, to the end. We focused on that. Discussions lasted one, two, or three hours. Once agreement was reached on that, the other thirty points on the union's list could be resolved in half an hour. There never was a strike.

I was often asked, "Why do you get on so well with your workers?" even though I was strict. If I caught someone stealing, I would fire him. But if the management was in error, then we recognized it and compensated the worker. I worked with two principles: first, to be just; second, I never got involved with their women.

Cotton was picked by hand and we hired up to five thousand temporary workers from Catacaos for about three months. We worked with about forty labor contractors (*mayorales*) for cotton picking. We signed contracts with them stipulating the places they were to harvest, the price to be paid for each quintal, and the transportation from the field to the cotton gin. We gave them drinking water and firewood for their camps. The labor contractor kept 10 percent of what his workers earned. In Mallares we paid better than other haciendas. And they knew that we did not cheat with the weighing. There were advantages to this practice: first, you have more people; second, you avoid trouble. Because if the quintal weighs a quintal, but you write down less, then we would have had complaints because the picker did not believe that we weighed it correctly. But if the quintal weighed a quintal and you paid him for a quintal, then he was happy. It also made record keeping easier.

By 1968, the year before the reform, we produced twenty quintals per hectare, up from ten when I started. On average we considered a good harvest to be twenty quintals, a normal one fifteen, and a poor one ten. Today a good harvest is considered to be ten quintals per hectare. We have gone back to the levels of productivity of 1947!! The department of Piura used to be able to produce five hundred thousand to six hundred thousand quintals, and in a bad year, three hundred thousand to four hundred thousand. Today they do not reach three hundred thousand. The area under cultivation in cotton has shrunk and productivity has fallen. Piura used to export vast quantities of cotton. Today exports are minimal.[3]

German Gutiérrez on labor relations on the haciendas of Cañete, 1940–65

There was a union on the hacienda where I was born. In those times the permanent workers only thought about better wages and working conditions. That was what the unions were about, and my father belonged to the union, but he saw that in the union there was much hot-air discussion without too many concrete results. He was not a militant, but he did not like it when he saw abuses. The hacienda owners were not really abusive, but some of the administrators were.

My father was seventy-five years old and pensioned when the trouble between him and the hacienda administration reached its peak. By that time the real owners were already living in Lima, and the owner's nephews were running the hacienda. One of them we called El Mechón (because that is what we called his ponytail, with which he came back from the United States). He was haughty, and from the time he took over my father had several problems with him. El Mechón questioned some plowing work my father's tractor drivers had done that had not come out right. My father responded to these criticisms: "You are not aware what is happening, you know less about agriculture here than your uncles, who were conscious of how things need to be done. You just want to cut corners to fill your pockets with quick money and it is not going to work."

From that time on, El Mechón began to mark my father and seek revenge. So when my father retired, he evicted him from the small plot of land the hacienda had given to him with the intention of giving it to others.

My father loved that piece of land. He worked on it on weekends and although he could have, he did not use the hacienda tractors, he used his own horse. We kids had to go and help after school and at dawn on Saturdays. We planted yucca, sweet potatoes, tomatoes, onions, and fodder for our animals.

After my dad destroyed the markers the hacienda topographers had placed on the fields, he marched into the office of El Mechón to confront him. He was really angry. My father almost beat the *patrón*, and El Mechón took out his revolver but shook so badly that he could not shoot, while my father stood stock still staring at the barrel. My father insulted the owner really badly using ugly swear words: "When you were still in diapers, I destroyed my lungs to enrich your family," he said. "If these accursed landowners want to evict me, they will have to remove me out of here as a dead man." He told me, "This plot of land is as old as you, *¡carajo!* Go to Lima and defend it in any way you can. There is a law that entitles any peasant who is using land within the hacienda property to keep it."

From that incident in 1967, the love of social justice came to me. My brother had found out where the agrarian reform office was, and I presented my complaint to an official. He commented, "Rizo Patrón? Wow! That is going to be a tough one."

After consulting with other bureaucrats in the ministry, it was clear that the ministry did not want to get involved with these oligarchs. Instead the man told me, "Go and find a private lawyer. Here is her address. She is a red."

"A red?" I had not understood what he meant.

"She is a communist and not afraid even of the devil."

And when I got to her office, the plaque on the door said Laura Caller Iberico [fig. 11]. So when she heard my story and found out that the case was against the Rizo Patrón family, she showed me a book by Carlos Malpica,[4] and in it the Rizo Patrón family was listed as one of the one hundred families that owned Peru. Doctora Caller told me, "I like this! I will take up the case against Rizo Patrón."

She traveled to Cañete and from a hill in the desert we could see the huge extensions of the private hacienda fields compared to the puny little plots that people like my father worked on the margins of their irrigation canals. Together with my father's case, Doctora Caller defended many other people who were in similar situations, sharecroppers, *yanaconas*, and others facing eviction for nonpayment of debts.

I did not know until later why she was called "the red doctor," but the owners did, and they were afraid of her. They tried to divide us by offering my father a bigger plot of land elsewhere. But Laura Caller told us to stay together and not to budge. And we won, because the first Belaúnde law was on our side, guaranteeing sharecroppers and hacienda servants their plots of land.

María Villarrubia describes cotton picking, 1996

You have to recruit people to form a gang of about forty to fifty people [fig. 12]. I make a contract with the owner for a whole field or a portion of a field. The payment is by the quintal. A person can pick two, some two and a half in a day. It depends on the person, and how good their hands are. If a child works alongside the person they can get three or three and a half quintals. It looks easy enough, but it takes skill and endurance.

We work really hard. We get together at my house at five thirty in the

Figure 11 Laura Caller, a lawyer who defended peasants and workers, in her studio in Lima, August 1986. Archive of the photographer Carlos Domínguez. © Carlos Domínguez.

Figure 12 A gang of cotton pickers in the Cañete Valley, 1982. Photograph by E. Mayer.

morning and I hire a truck to take the pickers to the place they have to work. I have to give them their large cloths, where they accumulate the harvested cotton. One has to keep a list so that by the end of the day the sacks and tarpaulins are returned to me. These belong to the crop owner, and I am responsible if something is lost. We start early with only a short break for lunch, which they bring with them. My job is to make sure the work is well done. There are some pickers who leave cotton on the plants, and I have to pick them clean. We work until three thirty in the afternoon. Then we have to sort the cotton and weigh it. At about five we can go home.

I keep the records. Payday is on Saturday. The *ingeniero* comes and pays everyone according to a list I keep. There are no deductions for Social Security or other obligations. There is neither a union nor even any attempt to organize. I get a commission, which is also paid on Saturdays. The gang stays with me more or less during the season. I have to find places to work for them. There is no difference in the way we picked cotton in the times of the haciendas and the times of the cooperative or today.

Mario Ginocchio tells of the rumblings before the agrarian reform, 1969–70

When the agrarian reform came there were talks here in my house in Piura in 1969: "What shall we do?"

Since there had been several laws that went back and forth, the threat of expropriation did not come as a surprise. I said, "I think we must do something preemptive."

And we thought about letting the workers have half the land. By dividing 2,500 hectares, there would be enough to give four hectares to each one of three hundred workers. Their severance pay could be used by the workers to pay for their land, and the remainder they could pay over time. We could reduce their number by retiring the older ones. The other two hundred workers would remain as workers on the land that the landowners would keep. I even kept a notebook in which I wrote down the names of those who were likely to stay and those who were likely to buy. At that time there were credible rumors that the landowners of Piura had heard Velasco say that landowners could proceed with reforming on their own initiative, as the first decree had stipulated, and keep up to 150 hectares per owner.

So we made an agreement, and our lawyer had found a flaw in the agrarian reform law: while it prohibited sales of land, it was silent about the sale of shares. So the Romeros' lawyers planned to transfer shares between themselves to reduce the number of owners, and then three of the remaining owners could claim the minimum 150 hectares each. My mother's share of the inheritance added to my own entitled me to 20 hectares of orchards, which she empowered me to administer.

In the end, these proposals never prospered. But the Romeros began to dismantle their operation and to reduce their staff and their salaries. Employees were promised continued employment in the nonagricultural enterprises of the family. Then they eliminated the profit-sharing clause that some employees like myself had had and because of that, on January 30, 1970, I resigned. I had a big argument with my relatives about that. In the meantime, the Romeros struck a deal with the agrarian reform. They turned over to the government all their land and machinery, which was appraised at a fair price in 1970.

I was forty years old. What to do now? I went to Lima. I thought of leaving Peru and went to the Australian embassy to inquire about emigrating. Another option was distasteful because I did not really want to become an insecticide salesman. So I remembered that the minister of agriculture at that time was General Valdéz Angulo, who at one time had been stationed near the hacienda at Sullana, and even though we were not friends, we used to greet each other. I had never worked for the government and I did not know how to find a job in the bureaucracy, but I decided to start at the top. I got as far the minister's personal secretary: "Señorita, I want to present myself to the minister."

"Do you have an appointment?"

"No."

"Then what?"

"Tell the minister that I am Ingeniero Ginocchio from Sullana and I want to talk to him about a job."

A few minutes later she came back. She had consulted with the minister and he told her to tell me that I should inquire at either the directorate for agrarian reform or the directorate for agricultural production back in Piura. With the minister's recommendation, the officials offered me a choice between two high-ranking jobs, either in expropriating haciendas or in managing the ones that had been taken over. I said, "Expropriation? No, the owners are all my friends, so I better not work in that. I'll take production." They asked me if I would like to return to Mallares.

"Do you think you have the authority and also the acceptance of the members of the cooperative?"

"If they vote on it, I will get 80 to 90 percent approval."

"You seem to be very confident."

"Yes, I am."

The members of the cooperative did approve my candidacy and I got the job. Mallares was the first officially adjudicated cooperative in Piura.

German Gutiérrez organized a protest movement against the landowner's attempts to delay in the expropriation of the haciendas in Cañete, 1970–72

I became well known in the Cañete Valley, and Doctora Caller oriented us. The people in the unions began to think according to the way she had planted ideas in our heads: "Forget about fighting for pay raises of a few cents. Fight for the land itself!"

In 1969–71 after the Velasco decree of agrarian reform, there were problems with the agrarian reform. The law gave the option to owners to divide up their lands "by their own initiative." There were also clauses in the law that allowed the landowners to keep a minimum of 150 hectares. We workers wanted these reduced or eliminated altogether. In addition, many owners had abandoned the land and stopped paying wages during the period of uncertainty between the time the decree became valid and the time an estate was actually expropriated, which lasted for about four years. The landowners fought politically to defend their property.

The workers feared that they were about to be left out of any benefits of the reform if they did not get the government to reverse its own laws. It took a lot of political organizing to get Velasco to change his mind and reverse himself on the issue of letting landowners divide out lands on their own initiative. Laura Caller told me to go and organize the workers on the haciendas. I took a job as a primary school teacher at the Hacienda Casablanca, where the Rizo Patrón family also had other properties, as a cover to organize the workers there. The workers there were having a hard time, no pay for months, no Social Security, and the place was half abandoned awaiting the outcome of all the legal representations the owners had initiated to avoid being expropriated.

We organized a march to Lima, with the women and their children in front following Doctora Caller's instructions. "Put the babies in the front and the men in the back. If the men are at the front, the police are going to beat them up."

The women were really combative and brave. Months before when we were getting tired of awaiting government resolutions, the men started to get discouraged. Some faltered in their resolve to hang on without wages. They said things like this: "I will become a fisherman, because I can't stand it anymore." And it was a woman, I remember her well, she was from Ayacucho, who stood firm: "¡*Compañeros!* If the men want to leave, let them go, but we women will stay on. However, when the day comes when we shall be victorious, if any of you who leave now ever come back, we will throw you out with sticks!"

So we marched to Lima to pressure the government to reverse its laws. And the children were so sick and hungry that the government commiserated and gave us relief food and medicines. The march to Lima was coordinated with representatives from all the valleys of the coast. There was an inspection in Cañete and a general came here with great sensitivity toward us. And he walked around and looked at the bathrooms, the houses of the workers, and the living conditions. He came to Casablanca where the owners, alerted, had organized a group of women who were faithful to them. They faked a child-care center. It was nice, with uniforms for the women and the children all neat. When the general came the people told him that it was a sham. They had put this up at the last minute for his visit. In the end the government eliminated the private initiative clause, it reduced the minimum that landowners could keep from 150 hectares to 50.

The hacienda Casa Blanca Oeste was the first one to be adjudicated in full to the workers after the government reversed itself on the issue of the private initiative. When the ministerial resolution came in 1972, each one of the workers was mentioned by name on a list of qualified beneficiaries in whose name the hacienda was expropriated.

We put up a Peruvian flag on a hill to celebrate. People were so happy they cried. They did not believe that they had become the owners of something they had never in their wildest dreams envisioned. To be owners of 500 hectares, when before they did not even have one furrow! That was a real experience of a personal triumph.

Laura Caller then instructed us that the next step was to capture the Peasant Federation of the entire Cañete Valley to make the people see that now the issue was to get all the haciendas expropriated quickly. Victories like the Casa Blanca case were eye-openers to the rest of the workers in the valley. With two other companions, we became the visible heads of the movement. Under cover we organized people in all the haciendas of the valley. The landlords called me a Communist agitator. Despite the fact that we had a revolutionary government, if the owners found their workers organizing, they would be fired, so we carefully moved around at night to protect them and ourselves. The police were in line with the authorities, and the local authorities . . . they identified with the landowners.

In 1971 we mobilized the whole valley and called for a strike. The hacienda of San Benito, where I grew up, became our headquarters, and there were pickets to convince the workers to stop working for their *patrones* and to jeer the scabs. Doctora Caller represented the workers in petitions to have all the estates expropriated outright.

To salvage some of their capital, the owners had also begun to sell land in small pieces to local people around here. Our fight was to get these sales declared null and void. We succeeded in that as well. In the end, the government expropriated just about every estate in the valley and on all the coast of Peru.[5] All those sales of land that had taken place, while the old law was in effect, got annulled. And this success we owe to Laura Caller and the worker mobilization we were able to mount in those years from 1969 to 1972.

Living on Credit

An adjudicated cooperative was a legal entity subject to the civil code, to be governed by the ideals and values of the cooperative movement. Property was adjudicated collectively to the legal unit, but never individualized among its members. There was no limited liability. Management was to operate on the principles of a democratic corporation. In theory it had complete autonomy, but in practice it had to conform to government designs and dictates. Decision making was split between an "executive" branch and a "legislative" one. Officers to directive posts were elected among the members.

The general assembly was the maximum authority of the unit, with ultimate decision-making powers. All members had one vote, and they elected the members of the councils and the special committees. The assembly approved the general plans of operation of the units, hired and fired employees, approved the accounts, and voted on investment plans and the way profits were to be distributed. At the same time, the government provided mandatory funds for reinvestment, severance pay, education, and social development.

The administrative and vigilance councils were made up of a president, treasurer, secretary, and members. They were the legal representatives of the unit who could sign checks and contracts. However, unlike corporations, authorities were selected from members of the general assembly for fixed periods of time. As elected officials they were responsible to the general assembly and could be deposed by it, though being deposed did not imply losing membership in the cooperative.

The technical and managerial staff personnel were not included as members of the cooperative, but their role was crucially important to the success or failure of the enterprise. They were considered employees of the cooperative and responsible to the administrative and vigilance councils. This technical staff was to provide the proper advice and expertise that the workers lacked in the technical operation of the cooperatives, as well as the best way of implementing policies decided upon by the councils and assemblies. The government reserved the right to choose the administrator (*gerente*) from a list submitted by the general assembly until the agrarian debt was paid to the government in twenty years. Full title was to be transferred after that.

Mario Ginocchio administered the new cooperative, 1970–74

I began to work as *gerente* in the Mallares Cooperative on November 1, 1970. First mistake of the reform. The government should have started with expropriating the worst haciendas, because then the mistreated and exploited peons would have been happy with the improvements the reform could bring. Instead they took Romero's estates, which were the region's "filet mignon." That meant that our well-treated workers were not necessarily happy with the expropriation. They were used to punctual wage payments under the Romero administration, and when the cooperative had difficulties paying wages on time, they began to resent it.

Second mistake. The so-called carrying capacity (*cabida*) of the cooperative was a calculation as to how many workers could be included within it.[6] There was a technician in the ministry who calculated this and he was under pressure to incorporate as many people as possible. He figured yields, total production, net income, and divided it by a given number of wage slots; and that gave him a number of approved worker beneficiaries who would then be qualified to become members of the cooperative. His mistake was to optimistically take the highest possible yields instead of an average. Under the Romeros we could keep five hundred permanent workers comfortably employed. The rest we made up of temporary hires. But the cooperative admitted nine hundred members who would have to be employed all year and receive full wages, Social Security, and benefits. There was no hacienda in Piura that could sustain nine hundred full-time workers!

Then we had to elect the delegates to form the provisional administrative and vigilance councils to be approved by the general assembly. I organized the electoral committee with nominations by employee and worker representatives, following the delegate system that had worked for labor negotiations. They also needed a worker representative. I nominated a person who no one believed I would.

I will tell why. A long time ago during my time as administrator, I found a woman stealing a sack of cotton. I requisitioned the bag and took it with me, and I asked the guards why they had not detained her. They answered that this woman was the wife of one of the socialist leaders among the workers. I notified the police and they searched her house and found three more bags. The case went to the office of the labor inspector and they ruled that he should be fired. He appealed, alleging that the woman was not his wife (only his mistress) and that he was not responsible for that woman's actions. We did not want to persecute the woman, so he won his appeal and we had to reinstate him. Anyway, time passed and I continued to treat him with utmost respect. Once a child of his died and he came to borrow money: "Very well, how much do you want?"

Fifteen years later, when I nominated him, he understood perfectly well what was required of him: "Just tell me what I have to do."

Problems quickly piled up. It was impossible to work with nine hundred men. Then they did not want to go and chop cotton. They were used to other kinds of work on the hacienda, but they never had had to pick the harvest themselves. There was no capital to work with. We depended on the seasonal credit that the agrarian bank gave us. In truth, we were not administrators, but just managers of the little money the bank gave us. The bank would say, "You have so and so much for this week."

And with that we had to work. There was no way to do anything, no projections, no leveling of fields, none of that. The bank only gave credit for cotton and rice production. The contrast with the time when I worked with the Romeros could not be clearer. The Romeros kept a reserve of 50 million [*soles*] in short-term working capital just to run Mallares. We used to review cash needs for Mallares on a weekly basis. If an unexpected event occurred, all I had to do was to pick up the phone: "*¿Aló?* Don Guillermo? I need so and so much for tomorrow." Don Guillermo, the cashier of the Romero Export enterprises, ever so solicitous, would respond, "Very well, it will be delivered by pickup truck at six in the morning."

Despite all these troubles, we ended the first year of the cooperative with a profit. It was a small profit, but a profit nonetheless. We had started planting late, we had not fertilized enough. We had an earthquake that destroyed our irrigation facilities. But this profit, where was it? *Whisssht*, the bank sucked it all up in interest payments owed. So there was no distribution to the workers as promised, no capitalization, no nothing. The people actually did not take their disappointment so badly. They had been paid punctually and a good wage at that. They trusted me. They knew I was not going to steal.

The second year was also profitable in agronomic terms. But we had debts; we needed to cover wages during the dead period after the harvest and the provision of the new bank loan. We needed to deposit funds for severance pay, and we started to spend on social services, supposedly to be financed out of profits. The payments for the tractors were due. Thus there was no distribution in the second year either.

The third year we began to feel the negative effects of SINAMOS. They used to say to the cooperative members, "You are the owners!" forcing me to respond, "No, *señores*: you are not the owners until you have finished paying the agrarian debt and the title is transferred to you."

Then SINAMOS incited them by saying, "The assembly can do what it wants. You are the maximum authority in the cooperative!"

I stood up and responded, "No, you cannot do what you want. You have to respect the statutes that govern the cooperative. You have to respect the agrarian reform."

They wanted to raise their wages. I objected, "There is not going to be enough money to pay. The bank will not give us that much."

The *socios* had their own system of calculation. They figured the cooperative's needs. So and so much for wages, this for materials, this much for seed and fertilizer. This is how much the bank should give us and that is that, insistently. But the bank would not budge. Instead, the bankers assigned costs per hectare based on their own calculations, decided the probably safe selling price, and then they gave us 80 percent of what they had calculated. There was a great discrepancy. The members of the cooperative wanted their raise nonetheless.

In a series of meetings of the general assembly in April 1974, there was a motion to expel a *socio*, the accountant, because he "had worked for Romero." He had worked with me in the hacienda times and was reliable. I reminded them that they could not fire anybody, let alone expel one of their own members. I said that there were laws against arbitrary dismissal. It was evident to everyone where this came from. They got advice from outside the cooperative and it showed because they were well trained. For me it came from people who were far left, more left than Velasco. I warned the assembly that I and everyone else also had worked for Romero, and if they were to remove him, I would resign too. Nonetheless he was expelled and I also resigned.

Suppose, for a moment, that this design would have worked. It meant that the cooperatives needed to generate enough profits to be able to pay wages, pay their taxes, Social Security, and agrarian debt obligations, and in addition, distribute profit shares to keep their members satisfied. Profits could only be generated by expanding and deepening the pre-reform conditions of profitability. This has been described as the "schizophrenia" between capital and labor imposed on the cooperative members. Success of the cooperative, defined by increased profits, implied that worker members impose on themselves, in the Marxist words of Rosa Luxemburg, "the discipline of capital" (1937, 35–36), which often worked against them. José María Caballero (1978) mentions, for example, that in many cooperatives there were too many workers. A capitalist solution would have been to fire

20 percent to 30 percent of their workers, but the *socios* of a cooperative could not contemplate such a measure.

Caballero's summary of how the state controlled the cooperatives is compelling. The state imposed its own priorities, such as cheap prices for staple crops to feed the cities and emphasizing exports to earn foreign exchange, taxes, and agrarian debt repayment. It imposed obligatory schedules for the disbursement of profits into reinvestment, education, and social expenditures (which was as high as 53 percent of gross earnings altogether). It dictated the crops to be grown and had a heavy influence on the price paid for the crops. Its bank mandated the forms and amounts of credit. The state controlled the process politically, as well. Beneficiaries of the reform were told to be content with the model imposed from above and were not allowed any maneuvering to invent other ways of acting than that which was officially laid down. Caballero observes that participation in the political process was granted, not gained, and was never self-defined. But the state also wanted the members of cooperatives to support the government through the vertical organizations it created and to dismantle their own unions and federations. Opposition was punished through administrative interventions. It is no wonder that critics on the right compared the cooperatives to the Soviet Union's collective farms, while those on the left called them examples of state capitalism.

This was not a grass-roots cooperative movement, nor really a self-managed enterprise, which its members could get to love, nurture, and grow. The beneficiaries remembered hacienda times and their bread-and-butter unions as not such bad times after all and continued to behave as if they were wage laborers rather than as owners of the enterprise. Any movement in the desired direction of expansion of profitability could only exacerbate the political problems of a cooperative. Many workers thus felt that nothing had changed, only that their new *patrones* were now different people imposed on them by the government (fig. 13).

German Gutiérrez, president of his cooperative, 1974–76

> The people did not reject the forced cooperative form that the government imposed because they had no choice. Workers were trained by government institutions to learn how to manage cooperative enterprises. I was the elected president of the Cooperative Túpac Amaru in the years 1974 to 1976. We were 173 members in that cooperative.

Figure 13 An agrarian cooperative in the Cañete Valley, 1982. Visible are the administrative quarters, housing, the chapel, and the cooperative's irrigated fields. Photograph by E. Mayer.

There was government support, bank credit, and the interest rates were not as high as they are today. The lands in Cañete are fertile and irrigation water is available the whole year, and we did well. We did not dismantle the productive structure of the hacienda. The tractor drivers stayed on in their jobs, other specialists continued doing what they had done under the hacienda, and even some employees stayed with us. We did not hire a manager, and I earned the confidence of the majority of the members. We elected those who used to be more in favor of the *patrón* to be members of the vigilance committee, because they were critical of us all the time, and thus kept us administrators in line. I was scrupulous with information, so everyone knew what was going on and why. We bought new tractors and I kept in touch with the agrarian bank, with which we made the yearly production plans and got our credit. We used our social fund well. We started remodeling the church to thank God because we are good Catholics. Then we built decent housing for our members. We built a good school and implemented the best technical training workshop because Doctora Caller said we should not neglect education. During my time as president, the cooperative always earned profits and it was well managed.

All in all the performance of the cooperative sector, having been given the best land, credit, and state support, cannot be said to have been in any way remarkable. It is not a great claim for this sector ten years afterward to have achieved levels of production similar to those of the haciendas from which they were created, a claim that is valid only for some cooperatives.

Once they were declared owners of the estate, workers did immediately raise their wages. I cite aspects of Douglas Horton's study: "On centrally managed estates wages have risen and profits have been distributed. Prior to the reform the sugar workers were the most prosperous rural workers in Peru. After the reform 82 percent were in the highest quartile of income distribution [up from 66 percent]. Their wages increased by about 80 percent. On other coastal estates [such as cotton] where the profit margin was less substantial, incomes have increased by less than 50 percent" (1976, 322).

But wage levels began to fall when post-Velasco governments introduced devaluation and wage-reduction measures. Inflation that came during the García administration further reduced them. Thus, the effect was temporary.

Against expectations, the reformed sector did not become a remarkable growth pole, nor an area of innovation and economic expansion. It is true that despite all the favored treatment it received from the state, there were also heavy constraints in terms of policy measures that siphoned surplus to other sectors of the economy, thus stifling growth in the cooperative sector. The price of cotton was kept low as an incentive for the textile industry. The government's cheap food policy for urban sectors militated against profitability for its producers. Bureaucratic mechanisms imposed by state monopolies maintained rigidities for the cooperative sector, so that cooperatives could not branch out into other crops or seek different markets. They were stuck with growing the crops with which they were created, even as market conditions became adverse. While the state cotton-buying monopoly delayed the checks for delivered cotton, the agrarian bank kept charging interest rates and penalties for late payments. It took many demonstrations and forms of political pressure to get the government to change the buying price of cotton. Defenders of the cooperatives claim, quite rightly, that under those conditions the mere fact that they survived and were able to take care of their members constituted sort of an achievement. This is also true.[7]

Blaming the very government that created them was a difficult thing to do. Politically, it can also be said that the reformed cooperative sector did not become a dynamic social and cultural pole to spread the Velasco revolution, nor a model to emulate elsewhere in Peruvian society. Despite the fact that together the cooperatives now monopolized the land on the coast, their unified political impact did not match that of pre-reform bourgeois landowners.

Unlike the Mexican Revolution, or the Movimento dos Trabalhadores Rurais Sem Terra (MST) in Brazil, which put a great deal of emphasis on the *mística* of its movement, there is no legacy in song, storytelling, popular culture, or even consciousness-raising "political" theater, music, or poetry that projected any kind of happy society that can be catalogued as the cultural product of the cooperatives of this period. The benefits the cooperatives were to generate for the excluded sectors in their areas did not materialize in the economy, society, or politics. Schools in cooperatives were not open to the children of temporary workers. Instead, tensions within the cooperative and among the cooperative, temporary workers, and landless peasants were exacerbated. Cooperative members were in bitter conflict with the organizations that represented the temporary workers and landless peasants who had been left out of the agrarian reform.

The isolation of the cooperatives was as pronounced as it was during the times of the haciendas. Their fences and guards were real as well as social. Cooperatives members faced fierce opposition, discrimination, and exclusionary practices by those *hacendados* who had managed to retain some land, the town merchants, and the elite of the provincial capitals of their regions. They were laughed at and treated as "*cholos*" in a racist, classist society, and because in hacienda times the owners had recruited *serranos* from the highlands to whom they paid lower wages, cooperative membership was associated by the rest of coastal society with the stink of the highland Indian. Worse, all the hostility associated with deep anti-*velasquismo* was unloaded on the cooperative members. They were not welcome anywhere. Instead, they lived in encapsulated infernos of conflict and strife.[8]

Maria Villarrubia worked for the cooperatives in the Cañete Valley, 1970–80

I worked as a temporary laborer in the Cooperative of Casa Pintada for about thirteen years. I had good pay and my Social Security card. Later I also worked in another cooperative, José Carlos Mariátegui, but because I did not bring my Social Security card, I was not insured in that cooperative. I was hired only on a temporary basis. They did not accept me as a permanent member of the cooperative because I did not bring my card. It is my fault, because I should have picked up my Social Security card from the Casa Pintada cooperative, but by the time I thought about it they had had problems and their offices were burned down and all the papers got lost.

Maria's modest statement about a bureaucratic impediment actually alludes darkly to the exclusionary practices practiced by the cooperatives. They refused to incorporate her to full membership, even as cooperative members relied increasingly on temporary workers to perform agricultural stoop labor they were unwilling to perform themselves.[9]

Troubled Times

The list of what went wrong with cooperatives is long. It is difficult to sort out among the many factors the ones that were responsible for creating discontent among the beneficiaries and those that caused the cooperatives to suffer diminishing profitability. Scholars divide them into external and internal factors. Fernando Eguren (1988), in a thorough review of those who studied the process of cooperative decline, counts the following among the external causes: falling prices of products and rising costs of inputs; cash flow problems and changes in lending policies by the agrarian bank; contributing factors of high-interest payments and agrarian debt obligations. Cooperatives could not compete with non-reformed farmers who engaged in a flexible, seasonal, casual hiring process, because the former had the obligation of assuming large fixed payrolls for their members as imposed by the agrarian reform model. Claire Auzemery and Michel Eresue (1986) point to inflexible production schedules and crop choices in cooperatives, while medium and small non-reformed farms branched out into more profitable lines. María Julia Méndez (1982, 1986), a defender of the cooperatives, showed that until the financial crunch of 1981–82, most cooperatives in the department of Lima were profitable and meeting their obligations. As for the internal causes of the decline of cooperatives, there were severe management problems (Martínez Arellano 1980; Horton 1976; Martínez et al. 1989). Among these, much touted in anti-reform propaganda was the slacking off by workers and the free-rider problem of members helping themselves to collective resources for individual benefit.

Another approach to the failure of the cooperative model is to analyze the internal contradictions with which these reformed agrarian enterprises were born. This method implies that a diversity of incompatible interests existed within cooperatives that pulled in opposite directions. Faced with conflict, members were forced to compromise and make concessions. These introduced instability, inefficiency, and a tendency for cooperatives to degenerate.

Such self-indulgent behavioral patterns, as described by Ginocchio, could only last until the coffers of the cooperative ran really dry and credit and bailouts ceased. Then the members had to face tougher choices. By the early 1980s, as the sociologist Giovanni Bonfiglio (1986) notes, ultimately the workers had two unpleasant options. One was to assume with greater discipline the rigors of a capitalist enterprise, forgoing wage increases and easier working conditions to keep the cooperative operating, at least to be assured of job security. The other was to delegate their role as managers and "abdicate" their power to a group of *técnicos* hired from outside. The *técnicos* would "usurp" the ideals of self-management, but would run the cooperative in autocratic ways, introducing greater work discipline and cost-cutting measures. Both courses of action meant a reorganization that produced better economic results for the cooperative, at the expense of wages, fringe benefits, democracy, and self-management.

Smaller coastal cooperatives such as Germán's resorted to increased self-management, dismissal of *técnicos*, and a tendency to slide toward peasant forms of production. Larger cooperatives like Mallares, in contrast, remained intact but fell more and more under the autocratic direction of *técnicos* and state control; some of them, especially the sugar cooperatives, became totally chaotic institutions. Critics of the Velasco reform have used these spectacular disasters as examples to show how the agrarian reform was a total failure. Satanization of the "Communist Velasco" government was widespread with the return of the Belaúnde government, and the cooperative movement had a hard time defending itself in the media.

Either way, cost cutting was undertaken on a massive scale. Wages dropped drastically, and investments were discontinued or postponed. On smaller cooperatives, there were also significant changes in the crops grown, with a tendency to replace export or industrial crops with marketable food crops with shorter growing seasons, fewer technical requirements, lower costs, and fewer price controls. Unable to pay good wages, they started distributing small pieces of land for workers to fend for themselves. In this way large and small cooperatives limped along, meeting payrolls with difficulty, becoming more credit dependent, and fostering a persistent feeling of unease among members.

Mario Ginocchio became administrator of Mallares for a second time, 1984–86

One morning in Piura, in 1984, I found a delegation of thirty men from the cooperative of Mallares in front of my house.

"*Ingeniero*, we are coming to look for you. Mallares is in trouble."

"But don't you have your own administrator?"

"Yes, but we are in trouble. We want you to return."

I accepted. When I got there I saw that everything was destroyed. They had had three continuous years of heavy losses. In 1983, the workers had eaten only coconuts. They said, "Yes, here all we ate was coconuts, because that is the only thing there was."

Horrible! The fruit trees had been destroyed. They said that it was the fault of the bank, because the bank gave loans for cotton production but not for the orchards. Since they ate with the loans, they destroyed the orchards in order to plant cotton to get the credit. The cattle were mostly gone, too. The hundreds of kilometers of fencing was gone, the wire sold, the posts used up for firewood. In sum, a brutal decapitalization.

We started working under adverse conditions. Instead of finishing by December 31, we started planting on January 6 and continued through February. That is a crime, a crime because of infestations. But the members' wages were dependent on our promise to the bank to plant 480 hectares of cotton and 200 hectares of rice, so if we did not plant it they would revoke the credit. But it was a year of heavy El Niño, and God was great with us. The Niño destroyed the cotton crops of all those who had planted on schedule, but spared us because we were so late due to the administrative chaos. We got a bumper crop. That year I again saved the cooperative. There was some money left over; they got paid on a regular basis. And the next year, too, we did well.

There was a surplus. I went to the bank and tried to negotiate. "Let me keep some to distribute among the *socios*; they worked hard and they need the incentive." The bankers said, "How can we pardon your debts? You owe for the years 1980, 1981, 1982, 1983. No way!"

So in reaction, in 1986 (in the midst of double-digit inflation), the members voted themselves a doubling of their wages. In my logic this could not work. "You are distributing to yourselves the profits you have not yet made." But they reasoned in a different way: "When we have profits, the bank takes them away, so we are going to make sure we use the profits before the bank gets them. There is no use in making profits for we do not see any of the benefits.

"But I warned them, "I am going to be very clear with you. If you raise the wages, in three months we will have depleted the loan, and then we cannot pay any more wages."

They responded, "The bank has to give!"

They had already had several clashes with the agrarian bank. These became a common occurrence, protesting about the delay when their credits were awarded and the way the money dribbled in in small amounts. Undoubtedly, the worse off the cooperative, the greater the tension between them and the bank. Sometimes the cooperatives took action, such as blocking the highways. Because Mallares was the largest and best organized, it took a lead in these protests. Once they even wanted to take over the bank building, but I advised them against it. Instead, they blocked off the street where the bank was and did not allow it to open its doors. These actions did have results, because ultimately and under pressure, the managers and the representatives of the cooperatives would reach certain short-term agreements.

The chaos continued that year of inflation. By May the cooperative had no more money; the bank was adamant. So they decided to pick their own cotton instead of hiring the temporary workers. But they were not very good at that.

But the *socios* had found other ways to survive. They started working unused land to feed themselves and keep goats and cattle. By that time, stealing from the cooperative became a frequent occurrence in contrast to the early years. Thefts began to increase because of low pay and the quantity of people without employment. At the end, the cooperative was practically abandoned, and those who stole knew that the cooperative was defenseless. And perhaps at night the *socios* stole too, but this we will never know.[10]

However, the numbers of unemployed people who lived in the shanties (*rancherías*) of the cooperative were evident to everyone. In hacienda times there were about 1,000 people in them. In 1986 there were 2,000 people living there. New shanties full of people sprang up all over the place. Some of the people in these settlements worked on the cooperative as temporary labor with some kind of preference on being hired when needed, others became *golondrinos* [swallows, landless temporary laborers] who had to find work wherever they could. During the hacienda times we could hire 150 to 200 temporary workers for fifteen days a turn. In 1986 fewer were hired from the shanties here, because there was less to harvest. The *socios* feared that these people would invade the cooperative.

Unable to pay for its accumulated debts, Mallares gradually disintegrated. First, the large cooperative was divided into fourteen smaller ones. But the financial and administrative problems continued. So in the end, the *socios* parceled out their land and possessions. Mario Ginocchio had resigned from the cooperative at the end of 1986, before this happened.

In 1980, Fernando Belaúnde was reelected president when the military decided to withdraw into its barracks. Although he claimed that he would not reverse the agrarian reform, he promulgated a law that simply stated that cooperatives could dissolve if a majority of their members so decided. He cut loose state control of the cooperatives. This law was accompanied by fiscal measures that withdrew the remaining privileges and supports the cooperatives had enjoyed (which had been eroding, anyway, since General Morales Bermúdez had replaced Velasco). Although most cooperatives in the Cañete Valley had posted profits from 1976 to 1979, by 1981 and 1982 they faced a fiscal crisis with lower productivity, falling prices for their products, rising costs (among them the oil crisis of 1979), and rising interest rates. The study by the French scholars Claire Auzemery and Michel Eresue (1986) showed that all seventeen cooperatives of the Cañete Valley were suddenly in the red and deeply in debt in 1981. The cooperatives could not expect a new government bailout from the Belaúnde regime, and the prospect of going broke would imply the loss of land and livelihood.

German Gutiérrez described the collapse of the cooperatives in Cañete, 1981–85

With the Morales Bermúdez government that no longer was revolutionary, the problems began to arise in regard to the support it was giving to the cooperatives. His administration was tantamount to a process of the dismantling of the agrarian reform, and the Belaúnde government did nothing to stop this trend.

There were criticisms about the way we ran the cooperatives as well.

And it is true that in some cases the criticisms leveled at us did happen. It is perhaps because my *compañeros* placed too much trust in professionals, especially our reliance on their financial advice. There was too much reliance on credit. They bought things, they spent too much and let the debt mount and mount, and because they were not acting in transparent fashion, they ran into trouble.

My cooperative was the first one to parcel out land among individual members in 1981. Why? Because by that time we saw that things were getting very difficult. It was the first time we had ever faced a loss and had a mounting debt. We saw how the Mariátegui Cooperative, because it was broke, was about to be put on the auction block, and we had to mobilize all the other cooperatives to prevent that. My companions were getting older and getting worried about retirement. My father also influenced me.

He used to come and visit us at the cooperative on his horse. Mockingly, he looked at the fields and said, "How beautiful your maize. Give me some."

"No *papá*, I can't. I have to ask permission from the other members of the cooperative."

"You dumb stupid ass!" my father said. "You are owners of everything and of nothing. You can't even give me some maize. You depend on each other, and it might be that the owner comes back and takes his land back. Before long you will be up to your necks in debts with the bank and when the repossession comes, where are you going to be, huh? Look at us small property owners. We are safe with our one hectare. It is going to be hard for the bank or the owners to take our small plots away from us, and we don't owe them a penny!"

Many retired workers were standing in line to get their pensions, and because the cooperatives had defaulted on their Social Security payments, the men could not pick up their checks. The banks even wanted to evict them from their houses. And they warned me, "You too will end up in the streets."

So I began to think that my father was right. But how to do it? There was a cooperative in Chincha. It was very different than ours because it had been created by the first Belaúnde government. Each member was the owner of his land. But there was also an area that was communal and they all participated in running it. They used the proceeds of this area for maintenance of the machinery, to cover collective administrative costs, for educational and health expenses, and so on. This gave us the idea on how to do it. We did not want our cooperative to sink and fall into the hands of the enemies of the *campesinos*. We went to the Ministry of Agriculture and requested its authorization to reorganize ourselves along the lines of the model of the service cooperative in Chincha, whose leaders together with personnel from the ministry then helped us redesign our own cooperative.

We parceled out the land among our members. By that time some members had retired, quit, or died so we created 109 lots, one per member. We kept a communal area of fifty hectares and formed a service cooperative that had the tractors and did the marketing, the administrative and financial work. It became a user cooperative. The miracle of boosts in productivity in each plot was amazing. Yields rose dramatically compared to the times when we worked the fields collectively. With one truckload of sweet potatoes, a *parcelero* (as the ex-*socios* are now called) paid off his individualized loan, and the other two loads were for him. No more wages, but payment by results.

However, the service cooperative and the communal area began to seriously falter after a couple of years. What we planted there was badly done because the members were not interested in working it and tended to hire others to do it. Those who worked there then wanted land allotments. So the communal area did not last long. Soon it, too, was subdivided. Each one of us now rents tractors from private operators, and we pay for the services of agronomists who give us advice on how to fertilize and fumigate, each one out of his own pocket.

We were strict and legal in the parceling out of the land. Even though there were some members whom we called scabs because they had made life difficult for the cooperative, they got their land. Each member got four hectares. If his wife was also a qualified member of the cooperative, the family got six hectares. Even though I was a leader I only got my base allotment, because I did not want the people to say, "How come he has six hectares? His wife is not a *socia*." One has to be honest. This is the way I have always lived my life.

With the example of Germán's cooperative, all the others in the Cañete Valley followed suit and quickly reorganized into private parcels and a service cooperative. The government had a hands-off attitude. The agrarian reform bureaucracy shrank, and discharged ministry officials offered their services to write the projects with which the cooperatives could request their disaffiliation. María Julia Méndez (1982, 1986) alludes darkly to macroeconomic policies intended to bring down the cooperatives. She charges the ministry with a lack of neutrality, including, among other things, the heavy fees charged by the ministry to provide a feasibility study for parcellation. It became a good business for ex-ministry employees to write the proposal, and some venal ex-employees wrote themselves into the project to get land.

Parcellation did not resolve all the juridical questions about property, until the Fujimori government implemented a titling program and passed a law allowing the free sale of land, which the Velasco laws had forbidden. Questions regarding the loss of economies of scale and the problems of dividing irrigation water also ensued. Landless workers also threatened cooperatives with land invasions. The division of the cooperatives was fast and chaotic. Many rights of members were trampled, and conflicts arose. Belatedly, in 1984, the government issued regulations that provided rules on how to liquidate cooperatives. Those cooperatives that had denied land to their "enemies" had to redivide the land to reincorporate them. As Germán described, the service cooperatives disintegrated rapidly. In order to clear their debts with the banks, *parceleros* shared out the obligations among themselves as a precondition for obtaining their parcels. The final incentive toward the complete privatization of agriculture was the Belaúnde government's decree revoking the obligatory sale of cotton to the state enterprise, allowing a free market to operate. Later, the Fujimori government closed down the government agrarian bank and cancelled all subsidies. All the trappings of state control that came with the agrarian reform were dismantled. A *parcelero* had his small property and became a free agent.

To the amazement of many observers, land productivity and production bounced back after the subdivision of cooperative lands into individual properties. Despite their fame as lazy *cooperativistas*, the new smallholders worked very hard. Their small pieces of land were then and are now cultivated very intensely, with a quick rotation of rapidly maturing marketable food crops. Many farmers started keeping milk cows and goats that eat the stubble on their fields. They cultivate subsistence crops and fodder between the rows of cotton. They rely less and less on bank credit and on sophisticated and costly technology, and they have gone back to using mules and horses as draft animals. Family labor is used intensively, and wage labor has diminished. Many crops are sold to middlemen in the field, so it is the middlemen who are in charge of the costs of harvesting. Various studies of *parcelero* efficiency show that costs of production fell dramatically, and productivity rose following subdivision into individual properties. As these small-family farms evolve and are able to save, they are diversifying into fruit plantations and contract farming for asparagus production for export. Without a government to dictate the terms of cooperation, many *parceleros* develop reciprocal collaborative relationships with their neighbors to overcome the diseconomies of their small scale. It is not uncommon to see four or five farmers joining their fields together to hire one tractor, and to cultivate the joint extension under technical supervision for which they pay. Thus, economies of scale are achieved for one season.[11]

María Villarrubia described current conditions, 1996

We now work for any kind of farmer who needs work: the medium-size farms run by the ex-owners of their haciendas; we also work with *parceleros* or with merchants who buy the standing crops. We work on any kind of job they give us, harvesting cotton, potatoes, or maize. We plant sweet potatoes, pick tomatoes, whatever job presents itself. I split up my gang among several smaller jobs depending on what is needed. Now that the price of cotton is so low, they also want to lower the piece rate they pay us, but that is really not enough. We can't live on that.

My gang is more or less a permanent one. They are people who have been working with me for a long time. They live around here, but they mostly come from the highlands, from Ayacucho, from Huancayo, Huancavelica. They are nice people, *gente humilde*, as we say around here. When people want to work with me, I have to know where they live and I ask around, I make sure they have their documents. They are mostly people who know each other and I know something about them.

Nowadays there are more women in the gangs than men; I have about sixty women and thirty men working with me. I do not think that the women come to ask for work with me because I am a woman, but because they have confidence in me and they know that.

It had become impossible to build a more collective and egalitarian dream on the basis of a capitalist system with extensive land use coupled with costly machinery, highly technical systems of production for a few industrial crops, extreme vulnerability to price fluctuations, and constricting state policies and interventions. Faced with the option of losing everything, the workers of the cooperatives finally took General Velasco at his word. He had said, and this is quoted all over, "La tierra para el quien la trabaja" (Land for those who work it), which is exactly what they did and so they took it. The 563 cooperatives of the agrarian reform are now a brief blip in the rural history of the country. One million *cooperativistas* are now *parceleros* with about three to six hectares per family. The smallholder household economy (E. Mayer 2002) is now numerically the largest sector of coastal Peru, and it has about half the irrigated fertile land.

Epilogue

In 1996 I attended a meeting at which the parceleros protested low cotton prices. The excerpt is from my fieldnotes.

> The ex-cooperative El Chilcal in Cañete was once one of the model cooperatives of the valley. Since the 1970s, the beautiful workers' houses, clean, elegant units built on the middle-class style of apartment complexes, had been showcased all over Peru. Each apartment has a small garden today already overgrown with flowering purple and yellow bougainvillea. But certain neglect is already visible: broken windows, the lack of fresh paint, unfinished second floors. I attend a valley-wide meeting sponsored by an NGO on the subject, called "What price for our cotton?" It is organized by Germán Gutiérrez.
>
> There is a big meeting room simply built with a large flat roof. For the event, organizers have rented sound equipment. Outside, a sign of hacienda times, a closed chapel. In the plaza where, symbolizing a new town, cement walkways and an ornamental fountain are not yet finished, people have set up food kiosks selling sandwiches and soft drinks to those attending the meeting. A police vehicle is present during the whole event.
>
> People begin to file into the meeting hall. They are all smallholders (*parceleros*), their average holding about five hectares. Once they had been proletarian workers, then they became members of a collectively

owned cooperative, and now they are independent smallholders. I realize that I am meeting the beneficiaries of the agrarian reform. The majority of the people are already past middle age with gray hair, wrinkled faces, skin burned dark by the scorching desert sun. The skin colors reflect all shadings of a Peru of *todas las sangres*: blacks, Asians, mulattoes, mestizos, Indians. One-third are women. They are more visible because those that still cling to their highland costumes (with wide skirts, synthetic silk blouses, long braids, and straw hats) tend to sit together. They do not say much, nor let their faces show what they think. Other women, dressed in more coastal styles with dresses and short hairstyles, conspicuously carrying handbags and showing expensive dental work, are more active participants. They easily comment, applaud, agree, laugh, or get indignant. The men all dress in the same way: long pants made of cheap materials, tennis shoes or plastic flip-flops, and T-shirts with the most variegated globalization logos—Chicago Bulls, New York Yankees, Aruba, Flacos—evidence of the process of worldwide recycling of used clothing. Terse faces, short-cut hair, and baseball caps prevail. That is why the members of the fundamentalist Peruvian sect, the Israelitas del Nuevo Pacto de Dios, stand out with their straggly beards and long hair hidden under turban-like cloths. Few farmers still don the traditional coastal broad-brimmed straw hats. Visibly absent are the well-to-do middle-level farmers, sons and heirs of the landowners who were left with their "minimum" un-expropriatable land, and absent too are members of the dynamic, business-oriented, commercial farmer class who have bought land since the collapse of the cooperatives. Even though most of these new farmers have given up on cotton, the protest meeting against low cotton prices would have been of interest to those who still cultivate the crop; yet, they do not participate, because they consider this meeting ineffective and they despise *parceleros* as usurpers of their land.[12]

The CECOCAN (Central de Cooperativas Cañete) is the cooperative of the now-defunct cooperatives. It still survives because it owns an industrial cotton gin that processes the harvest of the individualized smallholders. It is in economic difficulties, having to face competition with two commercial plants while price and demand are falling. It has a small office in downtown Cañete, a leftover of what once was a vast bureaucracy in support of the reform process, where Germán Gutiérrez works. It still has a fax, a secretary with access to a telephone, a meeting room, and a roster of freelance agronomists who provide, for a fee, technical advice on how to grow the crops. It also has a store that stocks agricultural inputs, fertilizers, and expensive deadly fungicides and pesticides to sell to the members of a credit program that the CECOCAN has managed to wrangle from a foreign donor.

The meeting begins. An emcee, who is also the local correspondent of Peru's radio news services, injects to the event all the pomposity he can muster. He knows the names, titles, and ranks of the dignitaries. The formalities of these meetings are also a legacy of the reform. They have been learned from years of participation in government-sponsored "base" organizations, and also from the opposition movements of trade unions and general assemblies in the cooperatives. On stage is a long table with a green baize tablecloth, above it a banner announcing sponsors and the title of the event. The hierarchy of elected leaders is seated in strictly ranked order, and, as a special honor, next to them, are the delegates from other valleys. In the first row of the auditorium below are important people who will speak later, and who will follow the proceedings closely. They are those who hold real but informal power. Behind, in the middle of the room, sit the more skeptical participants, observers and those who come to disturb. Working with prearranged cues, murmurs start at the back and become louder, eventually moving forward until a spokesperson gets up and obtains the microphone to give voice to the issue. Outside the room are those who are simply bored, those who have come to meet up with friends, those who know that the crucial moments of the meeting are still hours away and want to gossip or to find out who has come and who has not come. They buy soft drinks and sandwiches.

The formal objective is to run a pre-harvest training workshop to improve yields and quality of product. Agronomists take the stage and give instructions. But no one is fooled that this is a protest against the impending low cotton prices that the buyers' cartel (national textile mills) has announced, and which, the *parceleros* claim, do not cover production costs.

The *parceleros* don't speak up much. More vocal are the new professionals, agronomists, local employees of NGOs based in Lima. They have telling surnames—Mamani, Llactayoc, López, Lau—revealing their highland, coastal, or Chinese poor peasant origins, rather than the high-sounding surnames of Beltrán or Rizo Patrón of the once-aristocratic landowning class. Many of these professionals are sons of workers, and the way they earn their living is very different from that of agronomists who worked for the landlords or for the government reform service. So are their low and insecure earnings. They are surrounded by an aura of suspicion about involvement in shady dealings. The slight difference in their clothing from that of the *parceleros* is revealing. The immaculately clean shirts, pressed pants, the leather cases that hold their dark glasses secured to their belts. When they talk, there is clear evidence of keeping rank and hierarchy distinctions, mixed with terms that still carry over from the "class war" revolutionary days.

To navigate the implications of politically charged words like *compañero* (comrade), *campesino* (peasant), *ingeniero* (degree-holding agronomist) is difficult. These words alternate in their speeches with more neutral ones, such as *agricultores* (farmers, which encompasses them all), and *señores y señoras* (ladies and gentlemen), an insinuation of real citizenship and equality not yet really granted because of the paternalistic tone in which they are uttered. The speeches emphasize the many formal organizations, the cooperatives, the user cooperatives, the peasant leagues and federations as if they still were the powerful economic and political units that once were able to block roads, organize protest marches, and ultimately negotiate conditions with past ministers of agriculture. None of this is true anymore. Most of the people are attending the meeting as individuals, but the emcee refers to them as delegates of organizations that at best exist only on paper. At the end of the meeting, another organization is born, the Committee in Defense of a Just Price for Cotton.

Germán Gutiérrez gives the speech: "Today," he says, "we begin the fight for a just price for our products, a price that will reflect the real value of our work." He demands, "The state should intervene! . . . When government support services existed, these entities could intervene to balance the prices." ·

Germán denounces the collusion of the buyers and the "dumping" policies of the Fujimori government, which allows the importation of used clothing as a false application of neoliberalism. The speech is nostalgic and pleads with the increasingly indifferent state to support the cause of the farmers. In exchange, Germán offers the government the *parceleros'* political support. The policies they want implemented are memories of the past. Fujimori has other ways of gathering support and does not need them.

"The state should give us credit!"

"The state should protect us!"

"The state should give us a place!"

And if not, there is the threat that they will again block the roads and take up the combative stance that many so well remember. Even so, those attending are doubtful that any viable protest will result.

When the buying price is revealed to the audience, it is the lowest that anyone can ever remember or even imagine. The awful price quotation is confirmed at the height of Germán's speech, "65 *nuevo soles* a quintal!" The announcement causes an uproar: frustrated moans, disbelieving shaking heads, gestures of throat slitting, and grimaces of bitterness and frustration.

Consensus is quickly reached: they are going to present a petition to the government to take a stand, to guarantee better prices; if it won't, they threaten to mobilize. A second accord is to *warrantear* the harvest. This English word is used as an economic transaction that the CECOCAN wanted to encourage farmers to do—namely, that they should hand in their harvest to the gin but without accepting the current low prices. The CECOCAN could then bulk the harvest and use it as collateral to obtain a loan to pay the producers, while the cooperative holds on to the stock to wait for higher prices or to find customers abroad willing to pay higher. They would later reimburse the farmers for the difference.

In general, although the assembly approves the measure, most are pessimistic that this strategy will work. Leaders are skeptical about the farmers delivering the cotton rather than selling now to other intermediaries because they need the cash. Farmers are skeptical about the credit being secured. Economists doubt that the price will rise. Mistrustful participants fear embezzlement. Outside, I talk to one bored farmer at the sandwich kiosk who laughs at his companions for still growing cotton. He only planted one hectare of it, and the rest in sweet potatoes, which cost less to produce.

The meeting closes with a very emotional ceremony. Germán Gutiérrez leads everyone to stand up and keep one minute of silence in honor of the dead General Juan Velasco Alvarado, the general who single-mindedly pushed through the agrarian reform. It is done with all respect and much emotion. Not even the cynics abstain.

After the minute of silence, I walked away from that meeting on February 2, 1996, anguished and sad. I had an acute feeling that the agrarian reform processes of the past twenty-seven years had betrayed those who were present that day. Neoliberal and free-market policies implemented by Belaúnde, García, and Fujimori had certainly put the *pareceleros* in a disadvantageous position regarding prices, income, security, and benefits. Apart from the small plots of land that they had gained, the change in regimes and economic policies was not working in the *parceleros*' favor. I wondered how soon it would be before some of them would sell their parcels to the emerging entrepreneurial class of middle-class farmers, who in turn would plant asparagus on those plots and then hire the *parceleros*' daughters and sons to plant, weed, pick, clean, and package them to prepare them for export.

In the epilogue I have deliberately kept the ethnographic present from my fieldnotes because it seemed to me, then and now, that it was largely a memorializing event. Memorializing does refer to the past, but it is intensely felt in the present tense. The meeting's ritualistic aspects struck me as a rather hopeless collective effort to revive good times.

The next chapter describes the undoing of a supercooperative, this one in the highlands near the city of Cusco, where peasant communities organized confrontational invasions of cooperative lands. Storytelling about *tomas de tierras* (land occupations) and the glory days of the peasant confederations that challenged the military regime are the themes for memory-making in that chapter. It was a time when leftist intellectuals and peasants collaborated to undermine the reform, the peasants struggling to really get a hold of the land they had been told had been given to them, the leftists hoping to use the rural unrest to push toward a real revolution.

five

MACHU ASNU COOPERATIVA

Cast of Characters in Order of Appearance

> GENARO PANIAGUA, an anthropologist and the director of his own NGO who was interviewed in Cusco, October 1996.

> ISIDORO FRANCO, a peasant leader in Eqeqo Chacán who was interviewed in Eqeqo Chacán, October 1996.

> MARCELINA MENDOZA, the wife of a peasant leader in Circa Kajlla who was interviewed in Circa Kajlla, October 1996.

> ADRIEL VILLENA, a retired director of the agrarian reform office in Cusco who was interviewed in Cusco, October 1996.

> COMUNEROS OF TAMBO REAL, ZURITE who were interviewed in Tambo Real, October 1996.

> ESTEBAN PUMA, a peasant leader and the mayor of Anta who was interviewed in Anta, October 1996.

> CARLOS IVÁN DEGREGORI, an anthropologist who was interviewed in Lima, December 2006.

Machu Asnu Cooperativa

"Old donkey cooperative" is the euphemism for the white elephant that was created in the Cusco region on the high plateau of the Pampa de Anta, a prosperous agricultural plain near the imperial city. It was Velasco's first important attempt at making the reform visible in the southern sierra of Peru. He visited the headquarters in the ex-hacienda Sullupuquio in September 1971 on the day the cooperative was established. Techno-bureaucratic factors had influenced the choice to make it a collective "entrepreneurial" productivist model of enormous proportions and to honor Cusco's hero; it was called the Túpac Amaru II Cooperative. All expropriated haciendas of the region were transferred to this single cooperative, starting with 65 haciendas in 1971 and continuing with additional expropriations that were added until 1973. In all, the cooperative ended up including 105 separate units, with a total of 35,000 hectares dispersed over three districts of the Pampa de Anta. The number of beneficiaries counting serfs and vetted qualified members came to five thousand families, of which 79 percent were members of communities who did not work on the haciendas, 10 percent were *comuneros* but also part of the previous hacienda system (principally through access to pastures in exchange for money or work), 10 percent were resident serfs, and 2 percent other individuals. Whether one could become a member in the cooperative was decided by the agrarian reform offices, and also required an individual application, a monetary contribution, and a process of approval.

In 1973 I was co-directing a research seminar in the master's program in the Anthropology Department of the Catholic University in Lima. Jorge Villafuerte, one of our students from the University of Cusco whose research topic was on the agrarian reform in Cusco, took a critical position on why the cooperative was not achieving the objectives of the agrarian reform. Other participants defended the reform model, and the argument was lively. Villafuerte pointed out that the cooperative was becoming a very large, chaotic, encapsulated, and isolated enterprise that used expensive technology for mechanized agricultural production. It employed only a small, reluctant, undisciplined, and occasional labor force recruited from the ex-serfs of the hacienda and from the surrounding communities. Workers were paid in money, but due to cash flow problems, payment was often months late. Communities also contributed free labor in the early days in order to get the cooperative started. Operational difficulties in managing the monster cooperative also created bad image problems. For example, one year saw overproduction, with tons of potatoes and barley spoiling in storehouses right next to undernourished peasants who were forbidden to touch them. In another year, the air force provided transport planes to fly potatoes to markets. Another source of unpopularity was the inability to get production going, so that in some places, large tracts of land were left lying idle right next to overcrowded member communities that wondered what the slogan, "The land is for those who work it," really meant. Villafuerte cited pundits' worries about the viability of the "model" and pointed to its inbuilt weaknesses.[1]

To comply with the "participatory" objectives of the reform, the cooperative had created many peasant councils, committees, and oversight bodies that, as Villafuerte and others pointed out, never really functioned.[2] Instead of raising interest in participating in what the government called the revolutionary transformation of the countryside, most peasants developed an indifferent if not downright hostile attitude toward the cooperative. Those people who did occupy some of the high-, mid-, or low-ranking positions within it had greater loyalties toward their own interests and those of their families than to their peasant communities or to the different opposition political parties proselytizing in the region. Under these circumstances, the ability to make a go of the objectives for which each committee was supposedly responsible became impossible. Older conflicts between communities as well as village and regional affiliations were not resolved; nor were those whom they affected given a platform in which they could be discussed. Instead, all these people were lumped together into one single unit spread far and wide over three districts and told to "cooperate" (euphemism for compliance), to express solidarity with the agrarian reform principles that the military had developed for them in a top-down fashion. They were told to join the CNA, a pro-government national peasant confederation that demanded adherence to Velasco's ideology of what constituted approved revolutionary behavior. *Comuneros*, as the supposed beneficiaries, had very little commitment to the corporation.

Implementation of development projects and programs beyond the cooperative's lands was poor and nominal at best, although the purpose of the cooperative was to spearhead increased production, spread improved technology beyond its boundaries, and prepare the peasants for development and self-management. Enthusiastic promises that it would undertake the electrification of the whole area, distribute monetary benefits to its members, and build a regional hospital never materialized. The newly installed manager of the cooperative had promised General Velasco at Sullupuquio on the day of the inauguration that he would turn the Pampa de Anta into a flourishing garden, but many of those attending the event doubted even then that it could be done.

In an early evaluation of the process, based on fieldwork in 1972–73, David Guillet (1979) stressed that instead of distributing land, expanding participation, or generating growth poles for economic development, the Túpac Amaru II Cooperative had blatantly concentrated land, centralized power and decision making, and reinforced state control of the peasantry from its very inception instead of becoming an autonomous worker-managed institution.

Therefore, the *comuneros*' view of the cooperative as an old but also big, powerful, and male donkey, as embodied in the Quechua words *machu asnu*, was a gentle criticism compared with other more vicious descriptions from the Left that called it a clear example of state capitalism that cheated the peasants of the land for which they had fought—and which the reform had promised. The expropriated elite concurred with the Cold War assessment that the cooperative was indeed a perfect example of communism, or worse, that the cooperative became an institution set up to steal as much as possible. Their favorite nickname for Túpac Amaru II was a *pericotiva*, derived from *pericote*, the thieving mouse. I learned all this from Villafuerte's vigorous and well-argued positions in that seminar in 1973.

In 1996—twenty-three years later—I contacted Jorge Villafuerte, who by then was vice rector of the University of Cusco, and asked him to help me in my project to interview people about the experience of agrarian reform in Anta. He was happy to do this. He introduced me to the anthropologist Genaro Paniagua Gomez, who spent his whole professional life on the Pampa de Anta, grappling with an understanding of the process and collaborating actively in trying to transform it into something more viable. Like many *cusqueños* of those times, he had sympathized with the growing left-wing opposition that the military government and its agrarian reform had unsuccessfully tried to repress. He had worked with an institution funded by the Dutch government, CENCIRA-Holanda (Centro Nacional de Capacitación e Investigación para la Reforma Agraria; the Holanda part was that the Dutch government had, in financing this project in Cusco, insisted on more autonomy from the office in Lima).[3] Genaro introduced me to appropriate people to interview and provided me with his own thesis and copious studies, reams of statistics, collected pamphlets, and other publications upon our return to Cusco—much of which is incorporated into this text.

The cooperative of Pampa de Anta was brought down by the peasant communities through a series of land occupations beginning in 1976 and ending in 1979, by that time under Morales Bermúdez's "second phase." Students and teachers in Cusco were very active in opposition to the government, while the riot police were equally engaged in suppressing demonstrations, throwing tear gas, filling jails with dissenters, and deporting activists. Leftist parties sent support forces to what was then hopefully called "red Cusco" to further destabilize the regime. One participant told me that it was his impression that the regime was no longer interested in making a big effort to defend its supercooperative. It had other problems on hand. Rural and urban demonstrations and strikes were rampant in those days. Workers, teachers, and peasant unions were collaborating and challenging the government.[4] Morales Bermúdez's second phase of the revolution meant that the expropriation phase of the agrarian reform was finished. Efforts from then on were to consolidate the institutions that the reform had generated, but that did not occur. By the time Morales Bermúdez handed over the government to Fernando Belaúnde in 1980, the Machu Asnu cooperative had ceased to exist.

Eqeqo Chacán

By 1975 communities had already begun to challenge the cooperative's right to keep adjudicated land. The first one was the community of Eqeqo Chacán because even before the Velasco reform it had brought suit to have the lands of two haciendas, Huaypo Grande and Huaypo Chico, returned to it. Huaypo Grande was returned to Eqeqo Chacán under the earlier Belaúnde reform, but even though the courts had ruled that Huaypo Chico should also be given to this community, the lands were transferred to the cooperative. With colonial, republican, and recent court rulings in their favor, prior experience in organizing, the positive effects of a previous supervised improved potato production credit program, and the presence of Peace Corps volunteers in the 1960s, Eqeqo Chacán was in a good position to challenge Machu Asnu.[5]

Isidoro Franco, a combative peasant leader of legendary fame, turned out to be a jolly elderly gentleman full of humor when we met him. As a peasant leader with much experience, he had told the story of Eqeqo Chacán many times and my retelling here is based on the translation/transcription of an interview I conducted with him in Quechua, combined with Diego García Sayán's discussions with him in 1980, which were subsequently published in García Sayán's *Tomas de tierras en el Perú* (1982).

Isidoro told García Sayán that prior to the occupation he had made contact with the cooperative about Huaypo Chico's lands:

Before the takeover there was a dialogue with the members of the cooperative, especially with the president of the administrative council and with other *campesino* brothers of the council. We told them, "Return the land, it is in our titles, and nothing else will happen (*y nada va a pasar*)." "*Bueno pues*, we will give it to you," they said. We even wrote a letter to the administrator, the *ingeniero* of the cooperative. From January to December the *ingeniero* said that they would return the land. With those things they kept us waiting. But later, he said that they did not have time to attend to our business, that it was not possible since the government from Lima had not authorized him to return any land. They told us that in any case we would receive money in lieu of the land. "That money you can distribute among yourselves, but the land you will not be able to see," they said. They also said, "That cooperative is yours; work for the cooperative!" But they did not want to return the land. (García Sayán 1982, 135, my translation)

Isidoro told me that they thought about this and decided,

"We do not want the money; we want the land to work. We live off the land, and we do not want to have to go to other places to work. We do not want to live in the poverty of our fathers."

That is why we began to think about taking the land. I was invited to attend a meeting of the Confederación Campesina del Peru (CCP) in Querecotillo, Piura. Saturnino Acostupa and I went and we showed photos and how all of the cooperative was mismanaged. They began to be convinced that we would have to take the land. There the CCP, in the person of Andrés Luna Vargas, its president, began to help us plan the action against the cooperative. On the day of the occupation, several prominent leaders from Lima were present and helped us to plow and sow. I remember Javier Diez Canseco, but I have now forgotten who else was there.

It took the whole year. The preparations were concealed from the authorities. Franco and Acostupa built up a group of trustworthy *comuneros* in the separate sectors of the community, who in turn also recruited and organized. In each sector each enlisted clandestine squads made up of five or six trustworthy members. They invented pseudonyms for themselves. Franco chose Pumacahua; others protected themselves with the names of famous soccer players. The general command unit also organized peasant guards, a youth command, and a women's group. Some general decisions were made. When the day of the occupation came, every member of the community would have to participate and it was the job of each sector's squad commander to insure that. Each family had to contribute its own seeds and tools. The takeover would comprise the immediate plowing and sowing of barley on the recuperated land. They also decided that if there was repression and should people die, the community would take care of the orphans and widows. Everyone should start moving out of the village at four in the morning when a certain *huayno* tune was to be broadcast through the community loudspeakers. Isidoro remembers how over two thousand people, organized into orderly battalions with women and children in front and men in back, all carrying tools, seed, Peruvian flags, and banners, marched onto Huaypo Chico on December 5, 1976:

> We all entered the land with our cattle and tools to work our lands, while our wives, in the women's squad, stayed near the road to protect us. We tied up the cows and began to work, Saturday, Sunday. On Monday we rested. We continued working on Tuesday and Wednesday until we finished. On Wednesday men from the agrarian reform arrived. "Why are you doing this?" they asked. We told them that we were doing this because they did not give us the land that we had legitimately won in a lawsuit. "We have the right," we said to them. "We can't eat the money that you are offering us and this money is not enough to go around for all the people that there are within the community. It is by necessity that we are forced to do this," we said. (García Sayán 1982, 137, my translation)

García Sayán goes on to describe how on the second day, a small detachment of police arrived. Lookouts from the peasant guards alerted the community. Surrounded by the women's command repeating slogans and pleading, the leaders parlayed with the police. They politely explained to them how resolute they were in what they were doing, even willing to die. They showed their titles, the resolutions from the judges to emphasize the legalities of their case. The police opted to retreat from the scene. This success further invigorated them in their resolve to make the land takeover be respected.

Galvanized by their success on September 11, 1976, the peasant federations organized a meeting in the provincial capital announcing their intentions to take more land and to insist that those of their leaders who were in jail be freed. In a speech cited by Genaro Paniagua, their leaders proclaimed, "The state has stolen our land through a giant bureaucratized cooperative without our participation and has pushed the great masses of peasants on to the margins with reduced and insufficient lands" (1984, 54, my translation).

In 1977, aided by peasant leaders from Eqeqo Chacán and supported by peasant federations and their political advisors, nine other communities invaded cooperative lands, and took some six thousand hectares from the cooperative. Among them was the community of Circa Kajlla. There, with Genaro's contact, we recorded the experiences of Marcelina Mendoza.

Circa Kajlla

Marcelina is short and thin, with an affable smile. She is a great storyteller and not afraid. She remembers the date—December 31, 1977—when the peasants repossessed cooperative lands very well, since she was the right-hand person of her husband, Juan Ovalle, a community leader. There were many times when the police and the judiciary system sought her husband. Trying to elude them, he often had to hide, and it was Marcelina's task to feed him, protect him, and look for means to pay lawyers. Juan Ovalle spent much time organizing the community and petitioning government agencies for help. He was also involved in the underground movements that coordinated land occupations in other places. The day we interviewed Marcelina, he was irrigating his maize field and greeted us politely, but he left us alone.

The community of Circa Kajlla is expanding onto the flatlands, which before the reform had only haciendas. The peasant's old residences were stuck against a barren hill far away from any irrigated fertile land. There they had survived on minute plots for subsistence and raised animals pastured on the hacienda lands for a fee or in exchange for work. After the invasion, people began to move to the plain and build new houses there. There is a new village center, but the Ovalle-Mendozas built their house next to the lands they conquered for themselves, near the road and close to the ruins of the old hacienda house. The place where they live is called, appropriately, El Triunfo (Triumph), and forms part of a new peasant community that came to being during the struggles against the state/landlord. The great triumph is no more than 367 hectares of lands for a group of two hundred families.

Theirs is a large house with two stories, stucco walls, metallic windows, and an electric doorbell that works. Although there is evidence of well-being, one does not see opulence. They have about eight cows. Ex-leaders are often accused of grabbing the best and enriching themselves during the times of the land invasions. Their house, however, is modest, but not poor. Marcelina has one daughter and various adopted children from a sister who is not doing so well. She says about her daughter that even if she breaks her head, she is going to make sure that she finishes high school in Cusco. As for herself, she said that when she was a child her dream was to become a policewoman.

The ruins of the ex-hacienda are a few hundred yards from her house. Huge crumbling adobe walls still remain, the second-story wooden balcony is collapsing, the roof is sunken in, and tiles are spilled all over the patio. Even so, some people do live there, including Marcelina's sister. The chapel on the side is in total ruin, but across the road there is a modern school, which is going to act as a magnet for future families to build their homes near it.

Marcelina's Early Memories

Marcelina's father was the *mayordomo* on the hacienda and that is why, as a child, she could go to school in Zurite via six kilometers of daily walking back and forth. The only land they had was what the hacienda had given to them. The owner was a woman, an old woman, and she used to have herself carried on the back of a preferred servant to oversee her fields, check boundaries, and get around. Marcelina got to know her because her father went to pay his respects to the old lady once a year at Christmas, and she used to give out some candy. Marcelina and her siblings gathered wild mushrooms from the hills and brought them to her as a gift. The house, Marcelina remembers, was beautiful, with a well-kept garden: "Sure, why not, she had *pongos* (servants), she had fierce dogs too, and no one entered, only the *mayordomos* and the *pongos*."

It was Marcelina's father who started the paperwork to get the community recognized by the Belaúnde government. Because of that, in those days, Marcelina's father was sent to jail. Her mother had to sell cattle to pay lawyers to get him out. Since then, her father could no longer be a *mayordomo*: "The *hacendada* became my father's enemy."

Times of the Cooperative

Opening her arms wide to indicate dimensions, Marcelina gestures about the division of land between what was part of the cooperative and what she indicates by bringing her arms back together to form a small cup with her hands as the parcels that were left for the members. The administrators dictated, "From here to here, the cooperative, from there to there, the portion for the community."

> And as before, the community lands remained the same small size. My father became a member and continued to work for the cooperative for wages. He had to walk far to La Joya and Santa Rita when there was work. There were tractors, threshers, everything, but it was all for the cooperative. But our community stayed small. And when the cooperative was already in crisis, and seeing that the communities were engaged in a fight against the cooperative, my father then left the cooperative.

Her husband, Juan Ovalle, only completed primary school, yet he was hired as an agrarian social and education promoter by the Dutch organization set up in support of the reform process. This organization gradually became critical of the cooperative model and used its funds and foreign position to extend projects beyond the core of the powerful cooperative enterprise and even to undermine it. According to Marcelina,

> My husband found that in every community he visited there was inequality among the people. There were some who were all right, others remained the same, and there were also some who wanted to grab more. There were some who were more educated who saw that there was not enough land for the communities and they used to complain to my husband:
>
> "The cooperative has turned into an abusive institution and does not allow us to pasture our animals on its lands."
>
> "We work, but the wages we earn are not enough, and for our animals, there is no room to pasture them. All the land, all the barley is for the

cooperative. Tons of barley, oats and we do not even get the straw for pasture."

[*Gesturing toward the ruins of the hacienda*] There, in the storage rooms, inside there we found rooms full of barley and oats. The doors were open, and rainwater came in and damaged the grains. And those that worked there, their pigs were fattened with it. Enormous big fat pigs that ate it all. All of it for them only. And, anyway, with only barley and oats, what were people supposed to eat? The big combine harvester cuts the stalks very close to the ground; it leaves no grass for our animals. And because of that, people rose up in rebellion against the cooperative.

Marcelina quotes the people's complaints, which she heard from her husband:

"The cooperative screws us up worse than the hacienda."

"Worse than the hacienda because with them we used to have a plot of land in exchange for our work. Now we have nothing and there is nowhere where we can expand. We have no land, anywhere to work. People are unemployed; we do not have one single furrow to work. Nothing!"

So my husband said that we should petition for land. "We should ask for communal land. We need a school, we do not have anything."

When the manager of the cooperative heard about this, he was furious with my husband. He accused him in an aggressive tone: "You, you are the one who is agitating the people! Why should the people want land? Why? They are being paid a wage for their work, what more do they want? What do you want?"

So when we saw that the manager was not going to give us land, my husband said to us, "Then we will take it by force."

Secretly my husband had a parcel of land irrigated at night. And on an appointed day, the invaders came with their teams of oxen and plowed it. The whole community was there. The next day, the management of the cooperative responded with a threat to replow the occupied land with a tractor, and so we decided, "If they fight, we fight."

"Let us take more land!"

"If they do not want to do it in a peaceful manner, then let us invade more land."

At the head of the invaders, I shouted, "We want land to work, we want the cooperative to vacate the buildings of the ex-hacienda! This is our house; we also want to work there!"

The managers got tough. They sent workers from the cooperative to dislodge us. They came in two Volvo trucks full of men armed with stones, sticks, and slingshots.

The *comuneros* told Marcelina to try to talk to the managers because she was bilingual while the engineers could only speak Spanish. They told her to "tell the *ingeniero* that we need a place to create our community, that he should hand over the land and the ex-hacienda house, that it should be empty, that the cooperative should take its things away."

And then the fight began. The *ingeniero* got out of the cabin of the truck and slapped my face real hard. Yes, yes, he slapped me!!

And I, I had a small stick I used to herd animals, and waving it in the air, I said, "*¡Ingeniero!* Why, ah?! I am being reasonable and talking to you in a civilized manner, why are you hitting me? Am I your wife to be hit by you?"

And then one other person got out of the truck and screamed at me, "*¡Carajo!* What the fuck do you want here? What the shit do you want? Go back to your community. You have nothing to do here!"

And with a metal-tipped hose he had taken out of the engine of a tractor, he hit me on the head, twice. And I fell. And then many women surrounded me and screamed, "She is being hit! Help! Help! *Compañeros*, come here!"

The people came and massed around the truck and began to force it to go in reverse. And I was recuperating. I wanted to get up, but I could not. It was as if I was drunk. So on all fours, I pushed myself up, and I saw that the people were forcing the truck to go back. I wanted to catch up, and stood up and tried to join my *compañeros*. I was trembling all over, but I went on to help push the truck back.

There were many wounded that day. A cousin was almost moribund; he looked like a dying chicken. Another man was bloodied all over from a broken head. There were seven severely wounded people that day, three women and four men. They took us to Cusco to get treated. The truck returned to the cooperative's headquarters. But the *campesinos*, they invaded more land that day. They took all the grains stored in the old hacienda house.

In the fight, the people had smashed the windscreen of the Volvo. The cooperative lodged a complaint with the court, and Marcelina and her husband had arrest warrants. Police came looking for him, shouting aggressively at Marcelina:

"Where is he hiding? You have to tell me!"

"Look for yourself. Here is my house, look then. Why should he hide? He has not killed anyone; he has already testified that he was not there that day. Why are there arrest warrants at every turn?"

"He has to go before a judge. The judge has ordered another appearance.

Marcelina and ten others were taken by the police to confront the manager of the cooperative, and later to a judge. Imitating the manager's choleric voice, she recounts his words:

"You have busted the windscreen, you have to pay, and it costs so much."

And we responded, "Us, abusive? We were a small group of people; would we commit abuses? You are the abusive one, you brought truckloads of thugs in your truck to beat us up!"

So the *gerente* demanded, "Sign that you will be responsible to pay the damage done to the truck!"

"Then you, too, sign a document acknowledging that you broke our bones. Have you paid for what it cost us to get healed in Cusco? We want compensation for the medicines. We won't pay for damages to the truck or anything!"

[Imitating the manager] "Then you can rot in jail! On such a day you have to respond to criminal charges of destruction of property."

So we went to court and the judge said, "You are under arrest."

Then the whole community, all the *compañeros* who had come with me, said, "No, she is not going to stay alone. If you arrest her you arrest all of us. We will stay here, take us all to jail!"

"We will not let her go."

"We will not let her go."

So we all stayed in the courthouse the whole afternoon, till five o'clock.

"We will not move until she is set free."

"All right then, if you want, one of us men will stay instead of her."

The judge did not accept that either, so we suggested that the whole community be arrested. "Since you have your jail, Mr. Judge, let your jail burst with our people in it. Arrest us all."

[Marcelina laughs as she remembers how the judge threatened her in vain.] "You are very '*macho*,' no? You are not afraid to die."

"*¿Qué cosa, señor?* What am I going to die of? Why am I going to die?"

"You are not afraid? I will arrest you!"

"If you want to, take us all."

No one left the judge's office, we stood there until five in the afternoon. And the judge, he sat at his desk because we did not get out of his office. And so we forced him to let us go.

Liquidation

In March 1978 the Túpac Amaru II Cooperative resolved that it needed to restructure in order to contain the wave of invasions and to reduce confrontations. Here I summarize Paniagua's description (1984). The cooperative decided to restrict itself to dairy operations and close down its agricultural division. A great deal of land was rapidly distributed to communities and to peasant groups, principally to the most combative communities. Circa Kajlla among them received additional land, adding to what they had taken the year before. Túpac Amaru II reduced itself from thirty-eight thousand hectares to seven thousand hectares, keeping only irrigated lands in concentrated areas for its dairy operations. Of the twenty-six original communities, seventeen were released from formal affiliation with the cooperative. Only nine communities remained within the cooperative system. The restructuring program also promised to provide technical assistance to those who received land and to the remaining nine partner communities, so that they would be able to run the operations themselves in the future. The CEN-CIRA-Holanda and PRODERM programs of the Dutch government helped the other seventeen communities to set up communal enterprises on parts of the newly returned lands.

In Cusco, I interviewed Adriel Villena, a retired agrarian reform official. According to him, the cooperative was willfully brought down by agitators who had infiltrated it from the outside, but it was also undermined by rival organizations within the government. He told me, "I was adamantly opposed to the restructuring of the cooperative. I believe that those who worked with the Dutch program CENCIRA-Holanda used their position as a smokescreen to ultimately bring down the cooperative. I do not know why, but I do know that the officials who worked for them did lend themselves to the campaign to critique the cooperative. Some of the Peruvian staff was even invited to travel to Holland."

A high-level commission had been sent from Lima from the Ministry of Agriculture to deal with the crisis in the Pampa de Anta. It began a discussion with a restructuring proposal. And *ingeniero* Villena remembers expressing his views against this in the most vigorous terms. He remembers saying, "There have to be good legal reasons to liquidate a cooperative or to restructure it. There are no legal reasons. You are inventing them. You are going to crucify the cooperative like Christ who is without sin."

He continued his conversation with me: "I find it hard to understand how come they were so eager to liquidate the cooperatives that just started and had not yet had time to reach a certain level of success. It was like judging a newborn."

At that time, *ingeniero* Villena was the subdirector of the Agrarian Reform office of the Cusco region. His participation was important in that meeting. He remembers saying to the head of the delegation from Lima, "I am completely in disagreement. But I don't want to make your work more difficult. Since you have the rank of minister, please excuse me." And he walked out, followed by a couple of other supporters, creating a small uproar.

Villena thought that the problems could be fixed rather than ending in liquidation. If there had been thefts, it was the ministry's fault for closing down the supervisory body in Cusco. If the workers were out of control because they had been given too much freedom, that could be fixed, too. If there were agitators who organized meetings against the cooperative, so be it, but that was not the real sentiment of the people. It was not necessary to give in to agitation. I asked Villena what he thought of the land occupations like the one in Eqeqo Chacán: "Those invasions were practically theft. It was done to steal the crops. Those politicians took part in that pantomime to cover up the real motive, theft. And in part, too, CENCIRA-Holanda had a leadership in all that. They even provided transportation. Who benefited from liquidation? No one."

At the same time, on the left side of the political spectrum, the CCP spon-

Figure 14 The Fourth Peasant Congress of the Confederación Campesina del Perú (CCP) in Eqeqo Chacán, August 26–29, 1978 (Del Mastro 1979, 25). © CEPES.

sored a national congress in the community of Eqeqo Chacán on August 26–29, 1978 (fig. 14). My anthropologist colleague Carlos Iván Degregori attended it as a delegate of a leftist militant political party. He remembers it most vividly:

> Chacaaaan, of course I remember! One of my best memories. It was huge, more than one thousand delegates from all over the country converged on this tiny village. We urbanites of those times felt really authentic, because of Mao's dictum that popular wars start in the countryside and end in the city. While we were not yet in the stage of the popular war, we felt that the closer a congress was to the real countryside, the more authentic it was. It was like Arguedas's novel *Todas las sangres*, and there for the first time I saw this made real. There we were, the urban intellectuals with pro-peasant sympathies interacting with delegates from all over Cusco in ponchos and earflap caps, there were the shepherds from Puno and the cotton growers from the northern coast. It was great to observe the amazement with which the Piura coastal men met the highlanders. Each delegation presented its report, and the Spanish-speaking *piuranos* were astounded at how well the *sierra* peasants expressed themselves in Quechua (which was translated). There were jungle Ashaninka representatives, too, and they could not speak

well in either language. The delegate tried haltingly in a mixture of deficient Spanish and worse Quechua. The audience asked him to speak in his own language and the delegate demurred, saying that then no one would understand. Nonetheless, the crowd shouted, "Let him speak. Let him speak" [in his own language]. And he spoke so fluently and eloquently and no one understood one word, but they all applauded. It was symbolically very inclusive. And then the photographs. The Piura delegates had brought their Instamatics. "*Compañero, compañero*, a photograph." And they all posed, exchanging headgear, the *piurano* putting on the Ashaninka's feathered crown and the Ashaninka, the *piurano*'s broad-brimmed straw hat. It was all very moving and emotional, the CCP's high point.

Apart from publicity, solidarity, and the symbolics of hosting such an important event in a tiny *campesino* community, two significant things happened. The Cusco branch of the military regime's Confederación Nacional Agraria peasant federation, the FARTAC — rivals of the CCP — participated and agreed to act on a common platform. First, the two rival federations planned to form a united antigovernment front, sponsoring road blocks throughout the country and participating in the general strikes against the Morales Bermúdez regime. Second, this platform called for a national program to organize land occupations (*tomas de tierras*). Extracts of their resolution are summed up below, taken from the Appendix 21 published in García Sayán's book, *Tomas de tierras en el Perú* (fig. 15):

Why do we need to take land?

Because these lands are ours. Because our well-being comes principally from the land. Because the agrarian reform has usurped our lands. The landlords, already weakened by our preceding peasant movements, have been expropriated by the military government, and these lands have become concentrated and under the control of the state. Because land occupation is the peasant movement's main struggle, which strengthens it. With land occupations, along with other struggles, the great majority of our *campesino* brothers understand the path to confront oppression and exploitation.

Which lands do we take?

The lands belonging to the Production Cooperatives (CAPs), and the Societies of Agrarian Interest (SAISes), but taking into consideration

PROGRAMA Y PLATAFORMA DE LUCHA C.C.P.

CONFEDERACION CAMPESINA DEL PERU

pedro atusparia

la izquierda y la reforma agraria peruana

TRES CUESTIONES FUNDAMENTALES

Figure 15 Pamphlet covers published by the CCP about the agrarian reform (Confederación Campesina del Perú 1979; Atusparia 1977). Reproduced from originals housed in Yale's Sterling Memorial Library.

the following orientations. Take over idle or abandoned land inside the enterprises created by the government. Take over land from enterprises created by the government, from those enterprises that are incapable of guaranteeing the stability of their workers. Take over lands in the hands of landowners and *gamonales* who have not yet been expropriated. Take over lands belonging to exploiters, of those belonging to agents who carry out anti-*campesino* activities. (García Sayán 1982, 290–92, my translation)

Although there was a short period of peace in 1978, during which *campesinos* had enough time to organize themselves on the lands that they had just been given, the end of the cooperative was imminent. During 1979, another wave of occupations spread throughout the region (fig. 16). This time the takeovers involved not only land, but cattle, buildings, machinery, and installations as well. They hit the core of the cooperative. Managers desperately tried to dislodge the invaders. They denounced the agitators in press conferences and to the police. Chaotic days followed, particularly in Zurite: the cooperative's main Ancashuro cattle operations, which had

Figure 16 "Peasant women from Chincheros plow the land after a land takeover" (Del Mastro 1979, 29). © CEPES.

already been occupied on October 5, were suddenly surprised on October 24 by the stealthy arrival of management, which brought trucks in order to rescue cattle and equipment. Minor squabbles erupted that turned into disorderly slingshot battles, stone-throwing, and physical aggression on the invaders' side, answered by a police response involving bullets, tear gas, and beatings.

The problem was exacerbated because the whole town of Zurite and its neighboring communities were mobilized to go out to the fields to battle the cooperative workers and the police. Two policemen were captured and badly beaten. Legend has it that the women took off their uniforms, but my interviewees denied this. They say that only the intervention of political leaders persuaded the enraged women to release the hostages. A town meeting in Zurite lasted until past midnight to calm the populace. The whole region was mobilized and in disarray. Soon after that, eighteen communities decided in a semi-secret meeting that this time they were going to press for the total liquidation of the cooperative. On October 11, more than four thousand peasants from eighteen communities ratified this decision. They also agreed to peacefully resolve among themselves any boundary disputes that would result from the distribution of new lands and equipment.

In October 1979, the government responded with yet another plan to downsize further. It proposed creating four "stables" with the remaining cattle, which it would hand over to the communities. Money for various development projects was also promised. In November, the peasant federations, community leaders, and even the locals were unanimously against that plan: "No more projects, no more promises, only total liquidation." A commission was named that included delegates from the communities, the Ministry of Agriculture, and a judge. They were given three months to finish the task. The remaining cattle, because many had vanished who knows where, were distributed to the communities, and the machinery was centralized in one service center. In 1980, Machu Asnu Cooperativa ended.[6]

I recorded many stories from different *comuneros* about the last days of the cooperative. This time is still fondly remembered in great detail regarding personal involvement and excitement. Grown men have memories of how, as children, they had belonged to the "stone-carrying squadron" in order to supply the slingshots with munitions. They remember their parents' admonition to avoid answering questions from outsiders: "What do you say when the policeman asks you, 'What is the name of your father?' 'Papá.'"

Others describe intercommunity fights once the lands were handed over from the cooperative, wherein rival communities disagreed over the boundaries between them. Delegations from neutral communities intervened to mediate, sometimes marching in columns between opposed lines while carrying a white flag and urging the leaders to parlay and negotiate. People can still remember the slogans, the songs, and the dates of particularly heroic local acts. Women remember cooking many shared meals in an *olla común* and leafleting at mass protests in the towns of Anta and Izcuchaca. They recount with glee the image of innocence and "ignorance" they feigned when detained for questioning. The police found their insolence galling, and it provoked beatings, insults, and physical punishment. Also gratefully remembered is the solidarity of townspeople who brought food and medicine, the lawyers and leaders who worked for their release, and the relatives and community members who cared for their children while the mothers were in detention. In photographs of the period, the women clearly are in the foreground of events. The *toma de tierras* evokes the excitement that came from the acts of civil disobedience that achieved its objectives. For many leftists, this was the "real" revolution in the making.

Tambo Real

By 1976, everyone agreed that the Túpac Amaru II donkey cooperative suffered from *sobredimensionamiento* (overly large design). For Marxist ideologues, the question of what was to happen after the land was taken became contentious. In strict Marxist doctrine, a restructuring of land tenure required (as in China, for example) the collectivization of land and the development of the technical relations of production to increase productivity. However, they knew that to do this would be unpopular among the peasants who wanted to divide up the land among themselves into individual household units. While the Marxist groups knew they were gaining political ground in helping to organize land invasions, they also knew that they would lose that ground if collective forms of production were to be enforced yet again on the land that was taken. Some political parties were for the consolidation of recuperated land into smaller communal cooperatives, while others were for outright distribution. Technical experts were again worried about losing economies of scale and productivity, difficulties in transferring technology when it came to *minifundización*, and the potential for regression into poorly managed subsistence plots. For *campesinos* the issue was more practical, that of finding a proper mix between collective production and individual household production within the boundaries of their own communities. Genaro Paniagua and members of his political camp picked up on this tendency and suggested a more pragmatic solution. It was called *la vía campesina* (peasant way). Political support groups worked hard to persuade community members to reserve some land for collective or associative use by providing technical and financial support, again funded by the Dutch government. Paniagua gave us the successful example of the community of Tambo Real and instructed us to visit it. Danny and I conducted a collective "focus" meeting with about twelve *comuneros* a few days after we had talked to Marcelina.

Tambo Real was another cornered community stuck against the unproductive hillsides without access to the plains. It was unusual in that two landowners shared the people in it. One hacienda was in the process of modernization through the introduction of fenced pastures and high-quality cattle in a classic enclosure movement. The other hacienda remained more traditional, until expropriation, allowing access to its pastures in exchange for work or fees. In the memory of the *comuneros*, the modernizing landlord was the more "cruel" of the two because he was more of a taskmaster in requiring harder work, and because he denied access to his lands for *comuneros*' animals. *Comuneros* had litigated against him for six years in the 1960s. After the lawsuit, Tambo Real got some land and the hacienda got rid of its serfs. With the little land they had, the *comuneros* established a small common pasture, but it clearly was not enough as each family began expanding its herds after the reform. When the Túpac Amaru II Cooperative was created, the denial of access to pastures became the real problem, and this was the main reason for the push to invade land.

Tambo Real invaded lands twice and received more during the process of cooperative liquidation, ending up with 574 hectares for two hundred families (Paniagua Gomez 1984, 84). It also gained some extra hectares in a boundary dispute with a neighboring community after the cooperative collapsed. Members of the community told me that now they have on average 1.5 hectares in usufruct per family. Each family grows the usual highland crops and keeps animals. Portions of the harvests are marketed to cover the family's cash needs, and the animals function as self-reproducing savings accounts convertible to cash when needed. The community also has kept an area of 254 hectares in common, which is worked cooperatively, although for political reasons at the time of its creation it was decided that it would be called the "collective area" (*area asociativa*) rather than a cooperative or a communal enterprise.

The associative enterprise started with contributions of one cow per family, and when it calved the offspring became part of the enterprise while the mother cow was returned to the *comunero*. When they had eighty cattle, the members organized a dairy operation with regular salaries for its permanent workers. Stock was improved through a donation of ten purebreds. The community also grew crops on communal lands, initially by requiring free *faena* (corvée labor) contributions from all the family members. Later on, even though the work still was obligatory for all (by turns allowing the intercalation of individual and communal work schedules), members received monetary compensation for their work. Harvests were divided into those "for sale" and those "for distribution." Top-quality potatoes were shipped to market; excess seed and smaller ones were distributed among members according to how punctually they had performed their duties. Rations of grains were offered at cost to the *comuneros*. If a *comunero* wanted to buy more than the established limit, he would have to pay market price. The community also bought machinery (four tractors, a small combine harvester, a stationary thresher, a trailer cart, and a truck), which was used to work on collective areas. The machines were also available for *comuneros* to rent at half the market price—enough to cover fuel, operator wages, and maintenance costs—to plow or thrash individual plots. The year we were there, all the machinery was completely paid off. The collective enterprise also had a healthy cash reserve in a savings account.

The *comuneros* were emphatic that the objective of the associative area was not to pursue profits per se, but "to maintain" services and subsidies:

> For example, when one tractor becomes old, we think about selling it and buying a new one. For this we need to start saving to renew it. We do want to be able to offer reduced-rate services for our *comuneros*. We want to offer working opportunities to our *comuneros* by running collective enterprises and producing communal crops so we can pay wages. We also want to build up our community. For example, we have electrified the whole village without any loans or outside donations. We did the same thing with drinking water in each house. We want to improve the bridges and the streets. All this can be paid through the associative area. We also give gifts. At Christmas the *comuneros* get some sugar, a cake, and a little bit of cash. During carnival we sell meat at half price. When a *comunero* dies, the community contributes toward the burial costs.

In our group discussion, Danny and I asked about discipline, accounting, and sanctions, since these were crucial problems described in all studies of communal enterprises. Their answers were candid:

> Work is obligatory. The person who does not attend is subject to sanctions. Sanctions consist mostly of restricting access to machinery, and we also restrict them in the distribution of produce. When we call on twenty people to show up, we have a turnout fluctuating between fifteen and eighteen. But one has to use discretion. A leader cannot be so drastic, so authoritarian. It is hard to say to someone, "You do not get any because you did not show up for work." They often are older than us and we recognize this. They have struggled, they have put in a lot of effort to

build up Tambo Real and we cannot always exclude them. It hurts them when on payday they are not allowed to pick up produce, and they reflect on this and think to themselves, "I have to go in order to receive."

To my question about corruption, stealing, and efficient management, the *comuneros* replied that they had training from professionals affiliated with NGOs. They adapted organizational models that these professionals discussed with them. They had several committees—one to supervise the dairy, another to keep records for the agricultural division—and they were held to their responsibilities. They reported to the president every Sunday, rain or shine. There was also a general assembly to appraise the community as a whole. The *comuneros* also told us that a significant change had occurred during one year of crisis, in 1982, when a new generation with better education took over from the founders. A university-trained agronomist born in the community and then a member were also advising the enterprise at the time of our visit. They paid an outside accountant to keep the books in order, and a desktop computer in the room where the meeting took place was about to be made operational to improve logistics and data management. The *comuneros* also commented on the fact that they were a small community, with few divisions between them. They got along with each other, using persuasion and moral pressure rather than drastic sanctions. When elections to community officers took place every two years, it was done by lists (written on different-colored posters). People voted their preferences through colors. And party politics in running the internal affairs of the community were "practically forbidden": "We are all more or less in tune with one tendency. Everything here is in common. We all have to work, we have to share burdens, and all of us have to participate equally as well."

Winding Down

Danny and I were euphoric after this interview. Here, finally, in half a year of fieldwork, we heard a beautiful story of the Peruvian agrarian reform. The *campesinos*' self-confidence and air of assurance about the autonomy of Tambo Real's not-for-profit development model impressed us.

Our enthusiasm was dampened somewhat when, on our way back, we stopped at the provincial capital of Anta to interview the mayor of the town, Esteban Puma. He was a famous ex-peasant leader, a member of the

CCP, the Vanguardia Revolucionaria, and later of the unified left party Partido Unificado Marxista (PUM). Puma had won elections to be provincial mayor three times, the last one on the independent ticket Unidad Campesino Popular, garnering the votes from all the *campesinos* of Anta. Born in Eqeqo Chacán, he at one time was a member of the government's provisional administration of the expropriated haciendas, and later on of the administrative council of the Túpac Amaru II Cooperative. He told us that in his role as a co-opted peasant leader on the government's provisional committee, he had opposed the model and instead had advocated the creation of three cooperatives, one for each district in the Pampa de Anta, which would be tied together under a single service cooperative. However, military planners in Lima overruled this proposal; it was to be one super-cooperative. In those days many feared Puma. He had participated in the destruction of an *hacendado*'s house and was sent to jail.

The son of a Quechua-speaking family of *campesino* origins, he had graduated from high school and had some university training. He was picked to be on the committee because he was a skilled agricultural extensionist. Short in stature and heavy, with small eyes set in an enormous head, a white beard, and contrasting black hair, he looked like a *campesino* version of a filmic Moses. When said I wanted to talk to him about Machu Asnu, he responded,

> It was not so much a *machu asnu*. The agrarian reform has had a positive impact with me and with the peasantry. They gained liberty and freedom. There is no more *patrón*. The cooperative taught us certain things. Things like administration, training for leadership. The cooperative also taught us to see how *ingenieros* steal, so it taught us how to beware of *ingenieros*. It opened our eyes to the iniquity of those who came to administer us. We learned to understand the craftiness inherent in people. It transferred that craftiness, the cheating, and the thievery to everyone. It removed our innocence. We became like them.
>
> I interrupted, "But it also brought citizenship, no? The *campesinos* now have an electoral card, they have land, they have possibilities to buy and sell in the market. They are no longer a group of people set apart. They vote for you."
>
> He responded, "May the lord have pity on them!" (*Pobrecitos.*)
>
> "Do you really think this?" I asked.

"Yes, in part."

He said, amused at seeing my shocked face, "It is not over; it will never finish."

Wondering whether Esteban Puma had put on a cynical performance for our benefit, Danny and I nonetheless concluded that we could count the fact that a peasant leader had managed to rise to important levels of local leadership and administration as yet one more piece of evidence of positive effects of the agrarian reform.[7] We caught the train to Cusco, eager to get together with Genaro Paniagua to hear his comments on our experiences during two weeks of intensive interviewing.

We told him of how impressed we were with the achievement of Tambo Real. Genaro said that he and the CENCIRA-Holanda program had helped to set up twelve such associative enterprises, and more than twenty smaller ones. Of these, only Tambo Real was still in operation. All the other associative enterprises had disintegrated since then. The *empresas* had reproduced on a smaller scale the problems of the larger cooperative. The administrative and vigilance councils did not function well. There was bad administration, no accounting, and much suspicion, along with bad experiences with marketing, difficulties with participation in credit schemes, overextended credit, and too much enthusiasm in buying tractors. These problems caused endless internal conflicts within communities. Again, two tendencies emerged. One was to keep maintaining the associative enterprises; the other was to divide up the reserved land into parcels and to dispense with any development projects. The poorer and landless peasants were for division, while the leadership and the wealthier peasants were for keeping communal enterprises. Genaro also stressed that during the six years of the second Belaúnde government, outside NGOs did support the formation and maintenance of community enterprises, and provided credit for them. It was a decade later when CENCIRA-Holanda and PRODERM closed their offices that outside support all but vanished.

The political parties also abandoned the *campesinos*. After inciting them to take lands, and seeing that running the associative areas was generating problems that they could not solve, the politicos left the *campesinos* to their own fate. The peasant federations fizzled when they could no longer mobilize *campesinos* for any other cause beyond land invasions. Feeling betrayed, political organizers looking back on those times think that the peasants lost interest in transforming the country into a better society: "The peasants, once they got what they wanted, they went home to cultivate their plots."

As each community yielded to internal pressures for more land distribution, support for collective enterprises all but vanished in the Pampa de Anta. In a way, dissolving the supercooperative also reduced internal conflicts. Genaro pointed to his thesis, saying that he had predicted this result. In the thesis, where the words *Vía campesina* were in the subtitle in order to point to the specific choices peasants had made while struggling with issues of land tenure and production systems. He had said,

> Throughout their experiences in the past and those lived through their struggles, the *vía campesina* always opposed the process of concentration of land. First against the haciendas, then against the cooperative, and finally against the communal enterprise. Their long-term aim has been directed toward the individualization of land, especially cultivable land. They did this in the past and will continue to do so in the future. (Paniagua 1984, 99, my translation)

Thus, the ultimate mini-agrarian reform took place inside the communities with the distribution of the last few hectares of communal agricultural land into tiny parcels, while no one was looking, and no one objected. This story was nearing its end.

As Genaro handed me the bound photocopy of his *memoria*, I looked at the thesis and asked how he had come to write it. He said,

> In those days I was at the University of Cusco and I was interested in agrarian reform. There were students there who said that we should not only be in the university but also project ourselves to the political countryside. Agreeing, I ended up being befriended by the *comuneros* of Tambo Real, whom I have helped numerous times. But after a while I became interested in the process of the whole Pampa [de Anta], the relationship between the cooperative and the communities. I participated in the federation meetings and realized that there were many things that one needed to know.
>
> I resolved to do some research. I teamed up with two first-rate economists, Bruno Kervyn and Efraín Gonzales de Olarte,[8] who were also interested in *campesino* problems. They designed a questionnaire and

I participated in taking the survey. I used to sit in the CENCIRA office at night and write my notes of what I experienced during the days. I gathered a lot of data that people are always interested in. I published several papers on the Pampa de Anta. But I finally decided to get the thesis done and defend it out of pragmatic reasons. I needed a higher degree to seek better employment. I graduated on July 28, 1981.

Taking the Land

This is the appropriate place to evaluate the tremendous influence that peasant initiative had in dismantling Velasco's overdesigned model cooperatives. While the agrarian reform in Peru will go down in history as Velasco's agrarian reform, one must also give a great deal of credit to the *campesinos* who decollectivized the land. What Velasco expropriated, the peasants took from him. Diego García Sayán's book on land occupations, *Tomas de tierras en el Perú* (1982), is a thorough investigation of how, from the very beginning of the Velasco reform, the peasants' struggle against the reform included the tactic of invading adjudicated lands. Based on extensive fieldwork, local testimonies, and archives, it provides a superb opportunity to understand the use of this "weapon of the weak" (Scott 1985) in its struggle to make the reform more responsive to farmers' needs. Invasion of hacienda lands had been the principal tactic by peasants before the reform, but to turn the same weapon against the government itself was more complicated because it created confrontations between those whom the agrarian reform had benefited and those whom had been left out. In pre-reform occupations, the government played a mediating role between the invading peasants and the invaded landlords, sometimes favoring the peasants and sometimes not. In the post-reform cases, the government's role was more difficult since an invasion was a direct attack on the government. If it conceded to the peasants by admitting mistakes in adjudication, those invasions encouraged others, and with that the growth of clandestine opposition political parties. Admitting mistakes severely undermined the model of development the government had worked hard to legitimize.

Tomas de tierras were dramatic performances with uncertain outcomes. Unity and resolve by the invading groups were countered by attempts to divide them and by the threat of repression (there were laws against sabotaging the agrarian reform). Peasant federations grew as land occupations expanded, and left-wing political parties sought to direct and benefit from them. Factionalism and infighting among the different groups was endemic, and a competitive race to attack agrarian reform cooperatives certainly did not contribute to orderly transitions, increased productivity, or the consolidation of the agrarian reform to develop rural areas of the country productively. But in a positive view, by politicizing the countryside, citizenship was rapidly expanded to a class of previously excluded persons. Land invasions mobilized thousands of peasants, the left-wing political parties taught them democratic ways through their system of delegates and congresses, and when President Morales Bermúdez called for an election for a constitutent assembly, the Left garnered over 30 percent of the vote. In that constituent assembly, the right to vote was given to those who could not read or write, and that meant the Quechua- and Aymara-speaking Indians, the members of the rural communities, the serfs on the ex-haciendas, and the members of the dismantled cooperatives. Belaúnde reinstated municipal elections, so that many peasant leaders who had gained experience in taking the land were later to become elected mayors in their towns and districts. Most importantly, dismantling the agrarian reform did not result in any deaths, despite conflicts and confrontations. Civil disobedience by the invading peasants was countered by restraint and willingness to negotiate and to concede by the state.

In García Sayán's book, there is a chronological sequence and a rationale given for each period of land invasions. Early occupations in the period 1972–75 were aimed at making a sluggish government speed up expropriations and/or change adjudications, thus forcing it to live up to the expectations it had created. The most impressive and controversial land occupations were the invasions of haciendas in June–August 1974 in Andahuaylas, in the backwater department of Apurimac where local connections and an indifferent agrarian reform office had not yet expropriated any estates. The political party Vanguardia Revolucionaria (VR) had worked hard to prepare a simultaneous occupation of more than twenty haciendas in two days. Caught unprepared, the government negotiated with peasant leaders of Andahuaylas and their advisors first, but then carried out severe repression campaigns later (despite promises that it would not) when further occupations exploded in the same department after the signing of these agreements (García Sayán 1982, chapter 2; Sánchez 1981). Lino Quintanilla (1981), a member of Vanguardia Revolucionaria, became a peasant in order to organize the *campesinos* of Andahuaylas. His excellent memoirs are an invaluable first-person account of the complexities of this particular struggle. Another middle-class student, Julio César Mezzich, also married a peasant woman from Andahuaylas. He became more radical after this experience, later joined Shining Path, and is presumed to be dead (Berg 1994, 114).

García Sayán describes that in their second phase, land occupations were, of course, also carried out against already adjudicated units such as cooperatives, pre-cooperatives, or provisionally administrated units. These moves expressed discontent with the way the reform had adjudicated land, the rejection of imposed models, and the frustration of people whom the reform had not benefited. These occupations began in coastal Piura as early as 1972, but continued as late as the 1990s, long after the publication of his book in 1982. They occurred in many places and were organized by peasants who had been excluded from the reform or by groups that were not in agreement over the way in which adjudication had been carried out. In many parts of the highlands, these invasions were so local and so clandestine that they were not even noticed by the Ministry of Agriculture or any federation. Often they were the expression of ancient conflicts between communities over land. However, the spectacular success in the Pampa de Anta strengthened the Confederación Campesina del Perú (CCP) (fig. 17). *Tomas de tierras* continued to dismantle the agrarian reform adjudications throughout the Belaúnde and García administrations whenever cooperatives or SAISES showed weaknesses and local movements got organized. The final wave of land occupations occurred in Puno in 1987 (Caballero Martín 1990a, 1990b; del Pozo-Vergnes 2004; Rénique 2004; Martínez Arellano 1990) where the agrarian reform had created many large reform enterprises. *Tomas de tierras* distributed more land more widely, and to poorer peasants, than any of Velasco's agents.

García Sayán ends his book with a crucial question for the then-growing left-wing parties. "What to do after land invasions?" First, while recognizing that land occupations strengthened regional and national movements, as well as the political parties vying to direct and control them, García Sayán regrets that this impulse was not properly articulated into a more permanent political force. Second, he notes that after the euphoria of a successful occupation, the peasants distributed the land among themselves instead of maintaining higher-level collective organizations. Third, he points out that land invasions were followed by the demobilization of

Figure 17 Land occupation in Ayaviri, Puno, 1989. The community photographer Melchor Lima describes the event: "Sacrificial march on the boundary with the enterprise to recuperate communal lands." © Archivo Fotográfico TAFOS/PUCP.

peasant federations, to the consternation of leftists. Peasants went home with their conquered land and forgot politics. And with that, "The expectations aroused in certain sectors of the Left who saw in land occupations the beginning of a powerful hurricane that could drag in its wake the foundations of the bourgeois state were proved to be profoundly idealist and in error" (1982, 205, my translation). García Sayán finds fault with political parties for not having been able to build up stronger local groups organized around other issues that affected land reform, and for their faulty attempts to build up alternative, permanent, political power bases at the local and regional levels. Nonetheless, he concludes that "*tomas de tierras* had the enormous virtue of mobilizing thousands of peasants around a concrete and perceptible objective that they achieved" (1982, 211, my translation).

In the next chapter I focus on people's memories around the efforts to close down the SAIS Cahuide in the central highlands of the department of Junín, ten years after Machu Asnu's collapse. Unlike the Pampa de Anta case, protest and confrontation there turned violent due to the intervention of radicalized members of the Sendero Luminoso. The chapter begins with an exploration of the growth of modern capitalist sheep ranching in the region, the subsequent expansion of these ranches into community lands, and the setting up of agrarian reform supercooperatives (SAISes). Administrators and employees of the SAISes reminisce about what it was like to work on the reformed haciendas. The chapter ends with the painful memories of the appalling collapse of the SAIS Cahuide, as remembered from the point of view of its employees and two residents of the community of Chongos Alto during the dark days of *desactivación total* (total deactivation).

six

VETERINARIANS AND *COMUNEROS*

Cast of Characters in Order of Appearance

VÍCTOR CABALLERO MARTÍN, a sociologist and a former advisor to the CCP peasant confederation who was interviewed in Lima, June 1994.

MÁXIMO GAMARRA ROJAS, a veterinarian and the former chief executive officer of the SAIS Túpac Amaru I who was interviewed in Lima, June 1996.

PLINIO DIONISIO, a veterinarian, a professor at the University of Huancayo, and the former director of production of the SAIS Cahuide who was interviewed in Huasicancha, April 1996.

ROLANDO QUISPE, a zootechnician, a professor at the University of Huancayo, the former director of the department of development and the last executive officer of the SAIS Cahuide who was interviewed in Huasicancha, April 1996.

MANUEL ORTIZ, an anthropologist, a professor at the University of Huancayo, and a former employee of the department of development for the SAIS Túpac Amaru I who was interviewed in Huancayo, April 1996.

JUVENAL CHANCO, a community leader of Chongos Alto who was interviewed in Chongos Alto, April 1996.

SIMÓN MEZA, a accountant for Bebidas Venus and the ex-cashier of the SAIS Cahuide who was interviewed in Huancayo, April 1996.

LUZ GOYZUETA, a law student and the daughter of a resident of Chongos Alto who was interviewed in Chongos Alto, April 1996.

Inventing the SAIS

Víctor Caballero Martín is a true organic intellectual. A sociologist born in Trujillo, his passion has been in understanding and helping to transform rural societies in the highlands. A well-trained Marxist and activist in the Vanguardia Revolucionaria Party, he was associated with the Instituto de Apoyo Agrario, an NGO that supported peasant issues and was also a base for left-wing political activism and intellectual debate. His main role, nonetheless, was as advisor of the Confederación Campesina del Perú (CCP), where he helped pilot the organization through its many confrontations with successive governments. A small and intense person with vivacious eyes twinkling through black-rimmed glasses, he delivered his comments with a sardonic sense of humor, and immense experience coupled with doctrinaire righteousness. At the time of the interview, in June 1994, the CCP was floundering badly, the Instituto de Apoyo Agrario (the NGO that provided income and cover to the CCP) had dissolved, and he was out of a job. In his office, about to be closed down, we reviewed events relating to the fate of this peculiar agrarian reform institution, the SAIS, and he handed me several folders of unfinished research. "I hope you can use them," he said.

They contained a manuscript describing the response of peasants to a classic enclosure movement on the part of the sheep-ranching division of the North American Cerro de Pasco Copper Corporation mining conglomerate in the central highlands of Pasco and Junín.[1] The well-documented text is full of Marxist moral indignation eager to expose the true nature of capitalism and imperialism. These extensive land holdings in the high *punas* were everybody's favorite for expropriation, and in the case of the Cerro de Pasco Corporation, the clearest example of "imperialism" to expose. In the manuscript, the questionable way in which the company had acquired the lands around 1911, the enormous size of its holdings, and the conflicts it had generated with surrounding neighboring communities were amply documented.[2] Reporting on the ruthless way in which the modernization and capitalist reorganization of sheep ranching was carried out at the expense of peasant communities, Víctor argued for expropriation of the *yanki* company in the atmosphere of growing nationalism of the 1960s.

As documented in that manuscript, *Imperialismo y campesinado en la sierra central* (Caballero Martín 1981, 141–49), and in his other publications, W. K. Snyder, a graduate in animal husbandry from the University of Wyoming who was hired in 1954, transformed the conditions of operations on the haciendas that were so cheaply acquired. The Cerro de Pasco Corporation became the leading scientific ranching operation in the central *sierra*.

Through careful selection and crossbreeding with imported stock, a new prize-bearing type of sheep called the Junín breed was developed. These robust animals were adapted to the high altitude, climate, and pasture conditions of the Andes, and yielded meat and wool at a level of productivity that was exceptionally high for the region. The propagation of the Junín breed on the Cerro de Pasco's own lands required a drastic reduction of preexisting animal-to-land ratios (one animal per hectare), careful rotation schemes for areas in which they were to graze, controlled breeding conditions, and isolation from the local *chusco* breeds. In a seven-year period (1957 to 1964), the total number of sheep was reduced from 233,000 to 204,000, average costs of production per sheep fell from 0.23 *soles* to 0.06 *soles*, yields of wool per animal rose from six pounds to nine, and average meat output increased from 18 kilos to 25. Isolation of hacienda stock from other animals grazing on the lands was achieved by eliminating renters (*huacchilleros*), and buying out sheep belonging to herders who, until this program was implemented, had been allowed to pasture their sheep alongside the hacienda's own. Sixteen thousand mangy and relatively puny stock sheep were eliminated in the same seven-year period. With this new breed came a fencing program to keep other people's animals out of hacienda lands and to consolidate property.[3] In true capitalist fashion, rationalization of the work force vastly reduced the number of workers, and those who remained were subordinated to a cadre of technically oriented and, originally, largely foreign management. At the same time, those who stayed were provided with better wages, health benefits, and pension schemes.

To Peruvian middle-class eyes, Pachacayo, the administrative headquarters of these sheep operations, was a North American gated community from which they were definitely and clearly excluded. Any Cerro de Pasco mining or ranching camp had its Midwestern-style bungalows, curved streets, yellow school buses, and English-speaking Protestant churches. Company dining facilities were open to lower-level Peruvian employees such as accountants, but these in turn were exclusive employee areas from which manual workers were barred. The real backbone of the system, the Indian herders and their wives and children who spent months in the tundra in straw huts, were considered so rustic that they were only allowed on the premises on official business and were directed to the designated side of the counters in offices and storehouses. They were never fed, but they were given rights to different amounts of mutton.

Opposition to the Cerro de Pasco haciendas and those of other sheep ranches in the province of Junín and the department of Cerro de Pasco had generated, during the 1950s and 1960s, a series of well-coordinated independent peasant movements organized by the indigenous communities that were being pushed to the margins in the process of hacienda expansion. Víctor breaks this process into three phases of resistance actions. The first, dating from the 1940s to the 1950s, consisted of spontaneous reactions to the company's fencing policy. Fence cutting, challenges to hacienda actions to prohibit transit along customary rights of way, and localized actions of peasant resistance were common. The management responded with company-enforced, quasi-legal, and criminal procedures enacted within the hacienda's vigilance organization (headed by *caporales*), or in extreme cases, by the company's requests for police action and sentences to town jails for protestors. Local police and provincial justices were compliant with the company's requests since good relations between the company and the government came from the highest levels in Lima.

The second phase dates from 1958 to 1963 and involved five years of organized protests against haciendas. Action always started with legal suits questioning the very property rights of the haciendas, and the cases dragged on in courts. These were followed by land occupations, which provoked stern repression and, in turn, provided a platform for political mobilization. One of the haciendas, San Juan de Paria (very close to the mining city of Cerro de Pasco) was subjected to systematic assault by at least six surrounding communities over an eight-year period.

In 1963, Fernando Belaúnde won the elections. He had campaigned vigorously in every village and town promising an agrarian reform. Upon assuming power, he was greeted by a renewed spate of invasions. According to Víctor, this third phase was the preparatory phase for the agrarian reform, in which all sectors sought to position themselves in relation to the threatened/promised reform. Belaúnde was caught in a bind: having taken sides with the invaders during his election campaign, he could not easily order the police to push them back now that he was president, nor could he condone occupations prior to the promulgation of his reform laws. Meanwhile, keeping up the pressure, the *comuneros* of the Departments of Junín and Pasco carried out about eighty land occupations during that one year alone (1963). Howard Handelman's book *Struggle in the Andes* gives cogent descriptions of how spectacular these invasions were. "By dramatically retaking property that they felt was theirs, these peasants challenged a pattern of domination that had existed for hundreds of years. Their behavior indicated to the national government that the needs and demands of the *campesinos* could no longer be easily ignored" (1975, 6). The effect was to pressure the government to enact the agrarian reform laws of 1964.

During the first Belaúnde regime, attempts at expropriating lands belonging to the Cerro de Pasco Corporation had begun, but the company had enormous legal and political resources that enabled it to stall the process. The issue was still unresolved when Belaúnde was ousted by General Velasco. Within two months of the military takeover, the Cerro de Pasco Corporation's lands were expropriated on December 11, 1968, six full months before the new radical agrarian reform law was promulgated. The military government was under extreme pressure to come up with a viable adjudication scheme fast, lest it provoke another wave of invasions.

At the same time, officials in the Ministry of Agriculture were having serious second thoughts about handing over land and improved sheep stock to *indios* in the *comunidades*. They were under strong pressure that a potent lobby had brought to bear against dividing up the expropriated lands. Its spokesmen were able to paint harrowing scenarios as to what happened after communities invaded other haciendas, and how the projects undertaken by the Belaúnde regime, which had let *comuneros* keep invaded lands, had failed. Fences, they said, were dismantled, grasses impoverished and contaminated with parasites, pedigree breeding stock killed for meat, and new generations of lambs degenerated through miscegenation with the peasants' inferior flocks.

How was one to adjudicate the most efficient ranching operation of the country to such backward and ignorant *comuneros*? Máximo Gamarra, who at that time was still an employee of the División Ganadera (Ranching Division) of the Cerro de Pasco Corporation, clearly remembers the debate, as well as the outcome—for, had the lobby been unsuccessful, he would not be sitting in the elegant chief executive office of the SAIS Túpac Amaru I in Lima in 1996 as we talked (fig. 18). He told me that the most important decision that had needed to be made was whether to divide up the lands or not. Against dividing the land were those who considered it important to preserve this modern ranching system, a place where top-notch technology was being created and was successfully competing with such places as Australia. Among those who were against distributing the

Figure 18 Máximo Gamarra Rojas, on the left, receives a silver platter in recognition for his work in breeding the prize-winning sheep held by the worker H. Zárate on the right. In the center is H. W. Allen, the executive officer of the Cerro de Pasco Corporation. Pachacayo, 1968. Courtesy of Máximo Gamarra. © Máximo Gamarra Rojas.

land, there were strong arguments to maintain or even expand the economies of scale that had already been achieved by corporations such as Cerro de Pasco's consolidated multi-hacienda system. The commission that was created to decide what to do was headed by a local expert, Renato Rosi. A *ganadero* from Tarma familiar with the area, he suggested the participation of professors from the National Agrarian University, members of the prestigious Instituto Veterinario de Investigaciones Tropicales y de Altura (IVITA) research institute, and some ex-ranchers.

The committee discussed four models of adjudication (Martínez Arellano 1990, 76–89). The first was to break up the units into smaller yet efficient units to be administered by the communities who would receive them in adjudication because they had historical and legal claims to the land. One of these units would be kept by the state to be run as a leading high-technology ranch to provide support for the others. The second was to return much land to the communities, but to retain a core of advanced ranching units from which technical support and profits could be shared with the adjudicated communities. These first two models implied the loss of technological advantages, since communities were deemed incapable of sustaining the modern ranch system. The third model was to create a centralized cooperative that would include much of the hacienda lands, which would eventually be handed over to the individual community members as they educated themselves in the technology of ranching and the principles of cooperativism. The objections to this model were the cumbersome legislation pertaining to the organization of cooperatives and the long time it would take to organize and train the indigenous *comuneros* to assume their functions. The fourth model was to create an equivalent of a company or corporation and adjudicate it to the communities, who would become something like the shareholders or co-owners of that company. In other words, it would not distribute land, but ownership instead. Whole communities would be the beneficiaries, thus saving the agrarian reform the headache of actually distributing hotly contested land among communities and within them to individual herders. The company was to be run according to agreed upon technical criteria of efficiency, invest heavily in other profitable ventures in the area, and distribute the profits to its shareholders. Note that this last model redistributed no land, but made a symbolic transfer of ownership and left the infrastructure and operation of the ranches intact for them to be operated by Peruvian professionals. This model kept the existing system unchanged, and because of that it was the one that the government adopted.

Max Gamarra went on to say that, once they had decided against breaking up the Cerro de Pasco lands and infrastructure, it was only a matter of finding the right formula to make it palatable to the *comunidades*. The name for this arrangement, Sociedad Agrícola de Interés Social (Society of Agrarian Interest) was taken from the text of the old Belaúnde reform law, which in the preamble said that any agrarian reform's raison d'être was to promote the social interest of the larger and poorer segments of society, and which had copied those same words from the Declaration of Punta del Este, which established the Alliance for Progress, urging Latin American governments to undertake agrarian reforms.

This is how the peculiar institution of the SAIS was born. Max Gamarra liked to pronounce the acronym in its most peasant brogue, as "*seis*," sounding like the Spanish six, and that is how it became known around the region (as "*la seis*"). The SAIS Túpac Amaru I was created in October 1969. A pamphlet produced by the propaganda department of the Agrarian Reform Office is full of the rhetorical tricks that touted the SAIS model as "a self-managed (*autogestionaria*) peasant economic enterprise that compensates for the socioeconomic inequalities of a region, whereby the benefits of the collective enterprise are distributed to the development needs of each of the member peasant groups who are its co-owners" (Caycho 1977, 9, my translation).

Observing that the communities seemed to accept this solution passively, six more SAISes were speedily created in the department of Junín soon afterward, and then a total of sixty throughout the country. Of these six SAISes in Junín, only two remained thirty-five years later in 2005: the SAIS Túpac Amaru I and the SAIS Pachacutec. Of those that disappeared, a small one, Mariscal Cáceres, was absorbed by its member communities in 1986; the second largest one, the SAIS Cahuide, was violently destroyed in 1988; the third, Ramón Castilla, dissolved after smaller acts of violence were committed against buildings and bridges in 1989; and the fourth, the mini-SAIS Heroínas Toledo, was parceled by its two neighboring communities soon after a person posing as a cattle buyer wishing to have a private word with the manager asked him to step aside and shot him point-blank in the middle of a weekly cattle fair in 1988.

Consolidation

The second largest SAIS, the SAIS Cahuide in central Peru, was made up of the lands of the Peruvian-owned Sociedad Ganadera del Centro, the lands of which were in the highland grassland areas surrounding Huancayo. As a child, I always found the drive to the *puna* to be a spectacular adventure. Within an hour, taking the road that passed our house, we would leave the warmer valley and wind uphill to reach Acopalca, one of the administrative units that concentrated the sheep shearing and cheese-making facilities on the right-hand side of the Mantaro Valley's enormous extensions of the corporation. February was sheep-shearing season, and I remember clearly how the intense activity of an organized assembly line of twenty or so simultaneous, mechanically driven clippers was handled with the precision of a military operation. Every two minutes a sheep was brought to one clipper, immobilized on its back with its feet tied together with a rubber thong, shorn of its wool, dabbled with a bit of iodine if the shearing produced a cut, and released to another corral. The din of the bleating of thousands of sheep, the clacking of the clippers, and the shouted orders of the workers was overpowering. I remember too, in another shed, the sorting tables where freshly shorn wool was classified into first-, second-, and third-class and put into large bins, supervised by a very thin, lab-coated, and carrot-haired Scottish expert wool sorter who came to Huancayo every year to make sure that his export company, Duncan Fox and Co., received the AAA–quality wool for which it had bargained. My father showed me off, as a six-year-old boy, to Don Alberto Chaparro, the general manager of the corporation and a former conservative senator of the Odría Party. Bald, blue-eyed, with red hair and mustache, he was like the archetype of the rural capitalist ranching class. Peasants remember Alberto Chaparro as a cold person mounted on a horse.

The Ganadera del Centro was a shareholding conglomerate, formed in 1910, of several landowners who had contributed their lands and capital to rationalize management and operations. The company's 106 shareholders included Lima's most aristocratic families, which were closely tied to other landed estates, mining, the textile industry, finance, commerce, and professional and diplomatic circles.

Located high in the treeless *puna* grasslands, the span of the corporation's lands was immense, extending over the jurisdiction of two departments and two provinces, most of it higher than four thousand meters above sea level. The eastern boundaries of one of the units, Runatullo, in the district of Comas, were unknown as they disappeared in the vicinity of snow-peaked caps in unexplored regions that dipped into the little-traveled eastern lowlands. Punto, another hacienda, was on the headwaters of a remote river behind Huancayo's big snow mountain, and Huari's southern borders lost themselves on the eastern fringes of the department of Huancavelica. On the other side of the Mantaro Valley, the more lucrative haciendas of Laive and Ingahuasi reached far into the western cordillera. The expropriation documentation declares 247,257 hectares in total (2,472 square kilometers, almost the size of the state of Massachusetts). In 1971, there were 113,000 sheep, 6,500 cattle, and 700 horses. The corporation employed 448 people and their families. The expropriation's monetary value of land, installations, and animals was calculated at 145 million *soles* (U.S.$3.7 million). With the addition of three smaller neighboring estates, Antapongo, Río de la Virgen, and Tucle, the SAIS Cahuide was created in 1971.

Twenty-nine peasant communities (as legal entities) and one cooperative, to include the workers in the production units, became the legal "owners" of the enterprise. Title was to be handed over in twenty years when the final installment of yearly payments of an assessed agrarian debt of 234 million *soles* (U.S.$6 million) was complete.

The contrast between the twenty-nine communities and the undivided production units that were now linked together could not be greater. In 1970, there were 3,500 families in the communities, which had unequal access to 11,618 hectares of land on which they grazed 70,000 sheep (about half as many as the corporation) and 7,000 cattle (about the same as the Ganadera). The SAIS controlled twenty-one times more land than the communities, while the communities had three times the number of families to sustain and a land-to-animal ratio of 0.16 hectares per sheep, in contrast to 2.1 hectares per sheep on the SAIS. Not one hectare of land was transferred from haciendas to communities in creating the SAIS.

Intellectuals from all political camps were intrigued as they visited the SAISes and published studies and critiques. Rodrigo Montoya, an anthropology professor at San Marcos University, produced the first monograph in 1974. In it, he noted right away that if the SAIS were to pay the agrarian debt, taxes, and distribute profits to the twenty-nine communities in the form of development funds, little development could possibly result (Montoya 1974, 81–84). Other leftist critics said that this truly was "state capitalism" and that the communities had been duped. A pseudonymous critic, Ramón Saldívar (1974, 58), qualified this critique even more by pointing to the victory of the middle and petit bourgeois technocrats who acquired complete control of the process against workers and peasants.

The SAISes became state-supervised shareholding corporations that were to run the production units inherited from the expropriated capitalist enterprises, in the same "advanced" technical way and with the very same managerial staff, the same workers and herders, and the same transferred stocks of animals. But management was now to be responsible to its new "owners," that is, the member communities (not individuals, but the communities as institutions) made up of "supposedly" uneducated Indian peasant farmers, pastoralists, and temporary migrants. Communities, too, remained the same in terms of their boundaries, social composition, and land shortages, which caused the poverty and social problems they had inherited from the colonial and republican past. On an elective basis, two delegates were given the privilege of representing each community on the SAIS board, and if that board then elected any of them to be president or treasurer, these men could live in Huancayo and sign checks as long as their mandate lasted. Once a year, the community delegates received a check that represented their share in the profits of the corporation, which they had to spend in approved ways that signified, in symbolic ways, development.

However, bear in mind that the collective unit — still an enterprise with a mandate to pursue profits — was a weakened capitalist institution. It was restricted by the supervision of a peasant board of directors, mandated to follow democratic procedures in reaching decisions with strong worker and peasant participation, and operated in a hostile business environment. Later, under the second Belaúnde regime and the García regime, it also had to contend with lukewarm to ice-cold levels of support by the government.

Víctor Caballero continued his vigilance over the SAIS Cahuide's performance during the years after the reform. He and others published reports in which they showed that overall, during the whole time of their existence, SAISes in central Peru did manage to keep and slightly improve their sheep stock, maintain the integrity of their enterprises, pay their taxes and agrarian debt, and return a steady stream of small but respectable profits, although profits declined in later years. Max Gamarra, in his interview with me, was even more forceful about the SAIS Túpac Amaru I's rate of profits. He emphatically denied my somewhat hostile question about how, reputedly, the SAIS Túpac Amaru I had experienced declining rates of profitability: "We never fell below 10 percent. With the exception of one year, though, we never were able to top 17 percent of net profits. Compare this to a company that lists its shares in the stock exchange, and we are clearly up there with them. A 10 to 20 percent of distributable profits to its shareholders over a 25-year period is respectable, even in the United States." On a minimalist scale of measurement, one can indeed conclude that if survival was a criterion, the new managers had indeed done no more than that.

In April 1996, I interviewed three professors from the University of Huancayo. Plinio Dionisio and Rolando Quispe were teaching in the department of zootechnology, while Manuel Ortiz specialized in political anthropology. All had made their previous careers in the SAISes as "technocrats." Plinio Dionisio had held a high managerial production position in Cahuide. Rolando Quispe and Manuel Ortiz had worked in the development divisions of Cahuide and Túpac Amaru I, respectively. They reminisced about their roles as administrators in SAIS organizations.

Plinio Dionisio explained that early on the SAIS managers had come to the conclusion that expanding the sheep operations had reached its physical and technical limits. But the price of wool was falling. The SAIS embarked on a risky and expensive venture of land intensification through the establishment of a high-tech dairy operation at high altitudes. He considers this to be an astounding achievement and remembers these days with pride. He described it: "We called it the Laive Project, which aimed to install more than a thousand hectares of irrigated and cultivated pasture lands on which we would adapt a special breed of highly productive Brown Swiss cattle. It was necessary to import new stock from the United States, because our own was not very productive. It was a daring project; it was the first time that such a venture was attempted at such high altitudes."

The Laive Project began in 1971–72, soon after the creation of the SAIS. A consortium of several organizations was put together. The Ministry of Agriculture, the agrarian bank, and a German development project worked on improving highland grasses and establishing a milk processing plant in the valley, which would absorb production. They obtained a loan from the Inter-American Development Bank. They began involving the communities through labor draft contributions to construct the irrigation canals. But the pace was too slow. With abundant money to spend, Plinio Dionisio said that the SAIS accelerated the construction of the canal, paying wages, and even subcontracted sections of the canal to member communities. The SAIS also built a dam with a storage capacity of eight million cubic meters. It hired a huge group of experts, engineers, topographers, and veterinarians to design and implement the Laive Project.

With shining eyes, he went on talking as he remembered his own moment of glory:

And it was a success! The trickiest part was the adaptation of the imported heifers to the high elevations of Laive. We had bought a small farm in Huancayo, La Esperanza (at three thousand meters), and there we had built a stable to serve as a pre-adaptation stage for the animals' acclimatization. Then we had to bring them to the four thousand meter altitude of Laive, where we had prepared everything: the first hectares of cultivated forage, the stables, the milking sheds, and so on. In 1976 we were ready to bring them up. Ten years later, the SAIS was shipping five thousand liters of milk a day. Before the reform, Laive cows gave an average of 1.5 liters, and after the project they produced 5.6 liters, and some prizewinning ones gave 9 liters. We had nine thousand milk cattle from the five thousand that we started with. And we repaid our loans as well! That was our achievement.

I next asked the ex-employees to remember what they considered to be the achievements of the development divisions of their respective SAISes. Rolando Quispe explained that each SAIS was mandated to create such a unit to provide communities with development assistance.

I started work in 1974. My first job was to visit all the partner communities to teach them about the objectives of an SAIS. So for a year, even though it was not my task, I supported the political work of disseminating knowledge about the SAIS system and getting their support. Some communities, especially those on the Acopalca and Runatullo side, did not want to have anything to do with the SAIS, and thought that it was just another hacienda. They thought that all those speeches we made about participating were only a ruse to continue to exploit them, or even to invade their community lands.

After that, we began to develop projects that would result in something of significance to the partner communities. We began with building roads to those communities that were not yet connected. And they said, "Well, now that we have a road, we want a car." And most communities bought their trucks. And here, sadly, I have to say that we made a mistake, because the people did not know how to administer the finances of a vehicle. There were errors and they lost their trucks; many were sold at a loss. Others continued operating, but not as frequently and they had expenses and no income; so, often, the truck was not usable because spare parts were too expensive. Some trucks fell down the mountainside, and that was that.

Then we worked on establishing smaller community-run cattle operations. Very few, perhaps four or five communities already had their own community operations. In those we helped with technical aspects, and in those that did not have them, we promoted their establishment. We taught them about animal sanitation and we tried to get the government agencies involved in promoting projects for our communities.

Manuel Ortiz, the anthropologist, had a cynically upbeat view of how the SAIS Túpac Amaru I operated its development division. He described how Max Gamarra strategically consolidated power relationships to become the undisputed king of the SAIS. Gamarra personally (together with a small group of loyal retainers) ran the whole SAIS. He was very popular, frequently visiting the partner communities, participating in their fiestas, and getting drunk with *comuneros*. He spoke Quechua with them and he personally resolved their private problems. He used the development division to enhance his political power.

The distribution of profits to the partner communities was well organized in the SAIS Túpac Amaru I. Half of each community's share was given to each one directly and they used it to defray the current expenses of the community's administration, such as salaries. The other half was pooled and given to the development division for expenditure, to be implemented in large projects by turns, one project for one community at a time, and then on to the next. There was a roster of priorities that Max Gamarra had convinced the delegates to accept. For example, first roads were built to the isolated partner communities. Then came electrification for all the villages by turn, and Max Gamarra was there to inaugurate it personally.

He was a master entrepreneur, and it never occurred to anyone during this whole time to suggest that he step down. He had the whole system galvanized, each year he invented something new to get everyone excited about: a new trout hatchery here, yet another anniversary to commemorate there, the completion of an electrification project to celebrate in a third place. He ran everything, he knew everyone by first name, and he had his loyal informers everywhere.

Manuel Ortiz warmed up as he described how the administration ensured easy compliance on the part of the elected community delegates (fig. 19). Given the intense contact with the communities, the personnel of the development division could provide Max Gamarra with lists from which he could pick likely candidates and campaign for their largely uncontested elections. They would arrive in Pachacayo headquarters for a two-year stint. There they had housing, a salary, and expense accounts. Little by little, Max would involve them in the administration of the SAIS. The system picked the smarter *comuneros*, and after two years the peasants had learned accounting, administration, and other skills that would permit them to get salaried jobs in towns and cities. They were eager apprentices, rather than

Figure 19 Máximo Gamarra Rojas (third from right), the *gerente* of the SAIS Túpac Amaru 1 with *campesino* leaders. From left to right: Daniel Jiménez Soto (community of Tanta), Pedro Huaringa (community of Huacapo), Timotéo Inga (community of Usibamba), Máximo Gamarra, Agapito Collachagua (community of Pachachaca), and a man whose name is not remembered (community of Canchayllo). Pachacayo, 1975. Courtesy of Máximo Gamarra. © Máximo Gamarra Rojas.

scrupulous auditors. Ortiz described how Gamarra would say, "Come, let's go to Lima to sell the wool." There they ate in fine restaurants, used the impressive futurist building that the SAIS had built, and were served coffee by the executive secretary (Gamarra's relative). Then they watched Gamarra bargain with the foreign brokers. Often he would switch to English, and thus Max Gamarra—thanks to his early experiences with the Cerro de Pasco—became the only one capable of defending the interests of the SAIS. The delegates were impressed. Little by little, they become indebted to Gamarra. He sometimes hired their sons for office jobs.

Max Gamarra would not necessarily find Manuel Ortíz's portrait of him unflattering. He said to me that over the twenty-five years of being the CEO of the SAIS, the corporate spirit (*espíritu empresarial*) had to be maintained; the *comuneros* were told about it from the very beginning, and most accepted it. "We began," he said, "with the background of the Cerro de Pasco, and since I had worked with them for sixteen years I knew how to run it, and since I was the *gerente*, it is logical that it was I who would recommend what had to be done."

One common memory of the higher-echelon employees is their low salaries, begrudged by peasant delegates whose incomes were one-tenth of what a *técnico* commanded. Management chafed under the tight control that delegates exercised over any possible perks, and they knew the workers resented them. A very common accusation was that the management was corrupt and lived off kickbacks. Plinio Dionisio reviews his experience this way:

> When they hired me, and up to 1973–74, I was one of the best-paid professionals. I earned three times what a ministry official got. But the inflation that came later and SAIS politics drove my salary down. [*Raising his voice*] Eventually, there were times when a common shepherd with his salary and benefits was making more than the administrator. Sure, on principle, we said that we would sacrifice ourselves because we had so much at stake with the Laive Project, but later on, we began to feel the pinch. When I left in 1985 to become a teacher in a technical school, I was earning 300 *soles* more than the general manager. It got that bad in the recession.

Scholarly evaluations of the performance of the SAISes by the 1980s partially support his memories. Although all point to low morale, according to the agricultural economists Corinne Valdivia and Juan Pichihua (1986, 159–60), there was capitalization and technological improvement in the beginning and up to 1977, and then decline when the national economy began to spin out of control. The SAIS Túpac Amaru I fared better in creating new employment opportunities than Cahuide. However, due to inflation, the real value of wages and salaries fell by 71 percent over a seven-year period (1973–79), and more with hyperinflation later (Valdivia and Pichihua 1986, 160–62). Víctor Caballero Martín's analysis was more negative (1990a). He shows how in constant *soles* Cahuide's gross income began to decline steadily from 1980 onward. Echoing critical *comunero* views, Víctor observes that the questionable nonagricultural investments of the SAIS Cahuide scarcely benefited the *comuneros* or created more employment. As gross income fell, from the 1980s onward 70 percent of income was spent on wages and salaries of no real benefit to the *comuneros*. While not yet broke, Cahuide was in serious economic difficulties in the late 1980s.

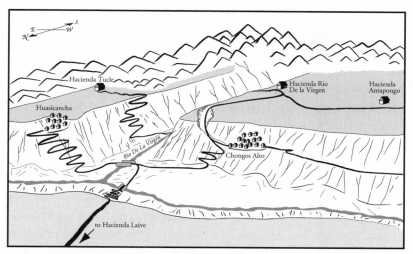

Map 2 Spatial relationships between Chongos, Huasicancha, and the lands of Tucle, Antapongo, and Laive of the SAIS Cahuide (based on Smith 1989, 2). Courtesy of University of California Press.

Though no pundit augured any bright future for the SAIS Cahuide, few predicted that it would implode the way it did.[4]

Chongos Alto

The community of Chongos Alto is at the headwaters of the Canipaco, a narrow little river that descends rapidly toward the Mantaro Valley (map 2). Cramped against a steep incline toward a spectacular landscape of enormous plateaus of *puna* flatlands, the agricultural plots of the *comuneros* form a very tiny fraction of usable land between 3,400 and 4,000 meters above sea level. During hacienda and SAIS times, the plateaus and mountain ranges were inaccessible to Chongos's herds. Instead, many children of the *comuneros* of Chongos and Huasicancha (its twin and rival, studied by Gavin A. Smith [1989]) emigrated to Huancayo, the mines in the central highlands, and Lima without ever losing their sense of community and their desire to recuperate the lands that the haciendas of Tucle, Rio de la Virgen, and Antapongo had usurped. Huasicancha had occupied lands from the hacienda Tucle in 1947 and in 1972 had refused to participate in the SAIS. In the 1980s, many young men from both communities made a living as shepherds on western U.S. ranches, recruited on five-year contracts. Migrants from both communities were successful in trade and professions. They settled in Huancayo, Lima, and the mines, providing a solid educational and financial base for community affairs back home, as well as a wide range of political contacts. Chongos is a district with its own secondary school, and an array of services such as a health post and a church. During the 1970s, a resident French Jesuit named Father Laguishe provided many social services and opened Chongos Alto to activities by NGOS.

When I went there in April 1996, the effects of the military's antiinsurgency campaign were still visible. The drive to Chongos took Danny and me past the military base of Vista Alegre along its barbed wire fence, down to a gully, and then back up to the boundary marker of Chongos, where there was a checkpoint. There, a woman dressed in local *pollera* costume emerged from a guardhouse with a shotgun in hand, asking what our business was. She was doing her duty as part of the peasant guard (*ronda campesina*) that protected the community. Because she was illiterate, she requested we write on a piece of paper our names, identity numbers, and the make, model, and license plates of our vehicle before she let us through.

Juvenal Chanco, the community leader of Chongos, had a rhetorical device I very much enjoyed. He tended to end his sentences with a "no?" question for emphasis, as if asking whether I sympathized with what he was trying to convey. From his *comunero* perspective, the employees and affairs of the SAIS were disdainfully referred to as the *empresa* (I translate it as company, enterprise, or administration). His pro-*comunero* position — independent of all political parties — may very well have been a new political position that he had recently developed, but it was very clear and well thought out, with a dose of neo-Indian ethnic politics thrown in for good measure. Juvenal Chanco reconstructed for me a coherent linear story about the need to liberate Chongos from the SAIS, and how it was clear from the beginning that only *chonguinos* should be running their own affairs on their own lands, as they were now doing. In his view, it was a long fight with unnecessary and very costly deviations.

He was forty-five years old, born in the village but educated in Huancayo, and had studied forest management at the university, although he did not complete his degree. His brothers and sisters live in Huancayo, Lima, and Italy and have become "thoroughly bourgeois." His love of the land and the community brought him back to Chongos.

I asked if he remembered the times of the hacienda. "Only by reference," he answered. His parents had refused to be herders for the *hacendado*. But his grandparents did work there. He remembers his grandmother's tales of exploitation. It was terrible, he said; the mistreatment of people was excessive. But it was not the *hacendado* who was the abusive person, it was the *caporal*, "no?," a local person like them.

I then asked how the community received the news of the agrarian reform. "With much approval and happiness," he said. But then, at that time, SINAMOS came as part of the government's scheme to promote these enterprises. "The military," he smiled, "they sweetened it, no?" He continued, "Sure, there were some *comuneros* who did say that they should occupy hacienda land. Other *comuneros* did say that was not an authentic agrarian reform, but a treacherous deception." Nevertheless, during the 1970s, the community did accept participation in the SAIS, but as the years passed, people came to realize that this was yet one more fraud. "Yes, it is true," he said, "that some profits were distributed, but they were insufficient for our needs. . . . Sure, the distributions came, well, for public buildings—cement, plaster, things like that, no? . . . But economic or technical improvement for the *comunero*, for the peasant, there was none." They realized that the way the SAIS was organized was getting them nowhere, that the *comuneros* had stagnated. They could not increase their animals, and the promised technological benefits never materialized.

As Juvenal warmed up, he lapsed into reported speech. "They would say to us, 'You are the owners, the ones who give the orders to the *empresa*.' Well, we the *comuneros* called them the 'technocrats,' no?; 'the sacred cows of the Parque 15 de Junio,' the address of the Huancayo offices of the SAIS Cahuide."

There were many other communities who accepted the *empresa*. The people of Chongos, instead, began to develop a critical stance against the *empresa*, sometimes supported by Chongos's three satellite communities of Llamapsillón, Palaco, and Palmayoc, and encouraged by the NGOs that started to work in the area. They eventually realized that the SAIS had to change and looked for support from other delegates to pressure for reforms.

Juvenal Chanco said that there were several attempts to change, in 1983, 1984, and 1985. The *empresa* formed a committee to reorganize, but all that came out of it stayed on paper. From the beginning, he insisted, Chongos proposed the breakup of the huge SAIS into smaller units under the direct administration of the production units closest to their communities—in Chongos's case, the ex-hacienda Antapongo with the four communities that surround it, and which are part of Chongos's ancestral land titles. The proposal also called for one central organization in Huancayo to market their products and to manage city affairs.

He continued his narration. Within this region, and even within the whole SAIS, Chongos had greater leadership skills. People born in Chongos but who were university-trained professionals had participated in strategizing sessions. They became aware of the dissatisfaction, and they began to look for ways in which the *empresa* could be transformed. So the Chongos elite began to propose that these professionals become delegates to the SAIS assemblies to work from within the system. They demanded that there be changes, or at the very least, that some advances toward fulfilling the real objectives of the SAIS be made. But in Juvenal's view, all their proposals fell on deaf ears, and when it came to election time, the SAIS *técnicos* manipulated the votes so that candidates from Chongos were never elected to executive positions. He was elected a delegate, Juvenal Chanco said, but never achieved a powerful position.

The SAIS experts shunted him aside because they perceived him as a thorn in their sides: too insistent. The *técnicos* were savvy at striking deals with more docile delegates. "It was horrible!" he said. "A form of prostitution." There was so much corruption within the SAIS. Once, he said to me, they offered to buy Juvenal out. They came to him with an organizational chart showing all those boxes and arrows, positions, and salary levels. To Juvenal's outrage, they sank so low as to use a fellow villager as an emissary to tempt him.

"Which of these positions would you like?" the emissary said. "These you can't have, they are reserved for professionals, but here, and here, those are available for you. Why don't you choose what you want?"

And I answered him, "No, until there are new winds blowing within the *empresa*, I will continue to refuse."

Juvenal was a university student at that time, and his fellow *chonguino* responded, "That is what others have also said. But when they finish their studies they come and beg us for a job."

Remembering this, Juvenal said to me, "It was like a slap in the face.

More than a slap in the face! It offended me. It enraged me. But it also filled me with pride. I swore to myself, 'I will never go to that *empresa* to beg for a job.'"

So, he went on, Chongos was always complaining and protesting and nothing ever came of it. Falling profit rates in the midst of an economic crisis induced fears that the *empresa* might go broke. The leadership saw that the political climate was changing and the *empresa* was weakening. It was the end of the second Belaúnde administration and the beginning of the Alan García regime, and the two regimes were not necessarily going defend the SAISes anymore. But the SAIS management kept saying that the SAIS was solid.[5] Around 1987, they were so disgusted that in one of Chongos's community assemblies they reached a consensus: "Even if they offer us leadership positions, we will no longer accept them."

In 1987, because Chongos and the other three communities were fearful that their archrival and neighboring community of Huasicancha would be tempted to invade lands belonging to the SAIS that Chongos also claimed ancestrally, the people of Chongos had quietly and defiantly begun to occupy lands inside the boundaries of the ex-hacienda Antapongo, a strategy designed to form a protective ring of Chongos herders and observers in case of trouble. The people of Chongos were, I realized, surreptitiously encroaching on Antapongo's lands, strategically positioning themselves to take advantage of the day when the SAIS would unravel. However, the SAIS delegates condemned Chongos for invading SAIS lands, and the police were called to expel them. From that time on, Chongos was to become a bitter enemy of the SAIS administration and a source of division among the delegates of the SAIS assembly.

By 1987, the communities that had been excluded from the original SAIS adjudication in 1971 began to press the peasant confederation, CCP, to help put pressure on a restructuring scheme so that they could gain access to SAIS lands. Víctor Caballero's organization helped frame a proposal and put it to the communities. But the presidents from the twenty-six original SAIS partner communities roundly rejected any designs of this kind, reasoning clearly that if the SAIS was to collapse, they did not want to share patrimony with anyone else. Also, in 1987, Huasicancha did sue the SAIS over some lands that Chongos also claimed as its own, and Chongos fortified the boundaries by defiantly posting herders inside Antapongo's lands again.

Juvenal Chanco told me he consulted a journalist in Huancayo who had studied the case, and who assured him that the SAIS was going to lose the suit that Huasicancha had brought to recuperate the contested lands, ergo Chongos would lose too. He also told Juvenal to watch out because everybody was against the SAIS, and worse, this journalist said, "Everyone is against Chongos, too." By that time, Shining Path's subversion was already heating up in Ayacucho, Huancayo, and Huancavelica, and was red-hot in and around the two main SAISes, Cahuide and Túpac Amaru I. This journalist had told Juvenal that neither the subversives nor the forces of repression had any use or liking for Chongos's recalcitrant attitudes. He explained to Juvenal that for the subversives' aims, the community of Chongos was an obstacle because it had an independent position that did not suit them, even though it was agitating for changes in the SAIS. The reactionaries did not much like Chongos's independent position either because they also wanted docile communities, which Chongos decidedly was not. Juvenal pointed out the logic to me: "It suits neither of them, no?"

On May 13, 1987, under the leadership of Chongos, there was a mass demonstration in Huancayo, in which participants of twelve secessionist communities from the Laive side of the SAIS clamored for restructuring (*reestructuración*). It had an effect, and discussions and negotiations began in earnest as to how the administration would proceed. But it was a losing battle because by then a growing group (among them many employees) was clamoring for a faster and easier solution, namely, the outright liquidation of the whole enterprise (*desactivación*) with the distribution of its assets to its shareholder communities, ex-workers, and employees. Shining Path,[6] too, had its own agenda, outright destruction, which it was actively pursuing through its assaults and threats. The political race was on as to which of the three "solutions" was going to be implemented. During that year, Shining Path stepped up its attacks. It blew up the police post in Chongos, destroyed community projects in the nearby village of Jarpa, and sent threats to community leaders, forcing them to resign and desist in discussions of restructuring. It issued ultimatums backed by assassination attempts against managers of the SAISes, and it used dynamite and arson as weapons. It also burned down parts of the installations of the SAIS in Runatullo, Punto, and Acopalca, and assassinated two men: Víctor Lozano, a peasant leader and NGO worker, and the anthropologist Manuel Soto.

On June 19, 1988, while the SAIS was really agonizing, the Chongos community formally entered Antapongo lands and took them over unopposed and without the fanfare usually associated with a land takeover. It was a preemptive move to insure that Chongos's interests would be kept alive in the chaos that was threatening the whole area. During the latter days, in January 1989, Shining Path forced a distribution of Laive cattle among community members and encouraged the looting of fences, roofing materials, and anything that could be carried away. On January 13, 1989, Shining Path blew up and burned all the buildings of the Laive hacienda house and milk processing facilities. A couple of days later, the same thing happened in Antapongo.[7]

Juvenal Chanco clearly wanted to convey to me that Chongos, despite its differences with the other member communities, was for restructuring and was firmly opposed to Shining Path, which combined its acts of destruction with military takeovers of the communities. However, it is clear that he was losing control over his *comuneros*, and Juvenal could only watch the looting authorized by Shining Path in dismay. In any case, Juvenal stated that by that time, Shining Path had already heavily infiltrated the SAIS workers and perpetrated many acts of vandalism. He accused the workers in the SAIS of bringing Shining Path into Chongos. And when they got there, the cadres deceived all three contending parties as to what Shining Path was going to do with Antapongo's lands. The Shining Path assured the Chongos people, "Antapongo is yours." To the workers in Antapongo, they said, "Antapongo is only for the workers, and not for the communities." To Huasicancha, they said, "You will recuperate Antapongo. The workers from Antapongo will not enter there."

"In other words," Juvenal Chanco said to me, "falsehoods, falsehoods." He went on to say that the looting of Laive was chaotic, with everyone grabbing what they could; while in Antapongo, the *comuneros* and the leadership of Chongos were able to persuade Shining Path cadres to enact a more orderly distribution of cattle and sheep. He said that the four communities gathered all the animals: one part was reserved for projected community enterprises, another part was given as compensation to the ex-workers, each one getting a number of sheep according to the years of service in the *empresa*, and the remainder was distributed among the *comuneros*. Even in that distribution, certain credentials of community commitment, activity, and residence were respected. Active *comuneros* got more sheep than those residents of Huancayo who maintained houses in Chongos or who were mere bystanders.

Figure 20 A destroyed installation in Laive with Shining Path graffiti. Courtesy of Brigitte Maass, 1996.

Juvenal turned emphatic. He said that the leadership strongly opposed any destruction of the installations of Antapongo. But the *comuneros* did not want to listen. They went there to destroy, to tear down the corrugated iron roofing sheets, to take the wood, to roll up as much of the wire from the fences as possible, to grab anything that was useful (fig. 20).

Living with Fear and Dying by Terror

At this stage it is useful to backtrack, to hear what the SAIS *técnicos* thought of troublemakers, terrorists, and *comuneros*. Plinio Dionisio picks up the story where we left him, gloating about his technological successes in establishing a huge dairy operation at Laive. Plinio admitted that there always were social problems, and that Laive was the principal target. There were, he said, people belonging to organizations in the communities who would sneak up to Laive to ask, how much is a shepherd earning? How many perks does an administrator have? Why is it that an administrator has to have a cook? Why does an administrator have to live in such luxurious housing? In his recollection, these people called themselves members of study groups, and Plinio Dionisio supposes they were encouraged by the NGOs that were operating in those communities, instigating a critical stance against the SAIS. Delegates constantly harped on notions of equality. They would say, for example, "Why doesn't a pregnant woman from Chongos get milk and meat? Why is it only the workers and employees of the SAIS who get meat and milk? Why is the milk being taken to Huancayo? Why is it not sold in Chongos Alto, in Huasicancha, and other villages?"

"Okay," the management responded. "We'll sell the milk at cost in the villages."

And milk was sold, and at the beginning people bought it, but later the trucks would return with large amounts unsold, so it was discontinued. Plinio Dionisio perceived that there was always some discontent. As the situation unfolded over time, subversives would pick management as a target.

Rolando Quispe, whose job was to monitor communities, supposes—like all administrators—that the origins of that discontent are to be traced back to SINAMOS promoters, who planted the seed among the *comuneros* by telling them, "It is yours. You have to administer, you are the rightful owners." The peasants would reply, "When are we going to feel like the owners. Why can't we decide now?"

The *técnicos* had to explain that they had to work according to established plans duly approved by peasant delegates. The *comuneros* contested this with mistrust and by suspecting corruption. If the *técnicos* sold some stock, they would question it.

"How come they are allowed to sell, and we aren't?"

"The administrator, he has an allowance of four or five kilos of meat a week, and I who am the owner, why can't I have it?"

Quispe supposed that relationships between the SAIS and neighboring communities were tense because everything they did was so visible. The SAIS's trucks drove out of the Laive gates loaded with cheese and milk, and *comuneros* saw all and got none. He went on to tell how in 1983–84, the SAIS Túpac Amaru I had requested police protection on its units against terrorist attacks. The SAIS Cahuide, equally threatened, did the same. So police contingents were placed on all production units. The police came in platoons of ten to twelve men, and the *empresa* supplied them with abundant meat and food, housing, transportation, and other facilities to keep them happy. Of course, the police did commit their usual share of abuses. They got drunk and had brawls, intimidated people by dangerously shooting their firearms, got involved with the women, requisitioned food from peasants, and extorted all the time. Thus *comunero* delegates pressed for a motion to expel them. The general manager admonished them: "Well, we have to make sure that the police don't abuse their position, but we need their protection; we can't let them go." "No!" said the delegates. "They are committing abuses." The delegates screamed, "Expel them! Expel them! This can't be!" Finally, the manager said, "Okay, let's vote." So, acting on democratic principles, the SAIS requested that the police leave, and the secret intelligence service left too, leaving them unprotected in wide open terrain.

As the actions of Shining Path become common nationwide, the group picked the SAISes as one of its favorite targets in central Peru. Between 1983 and 1990, by one count, Cahuide suffered thirteen attacks, and Túpac Amaru I, ten. Plinio Dionisio remembered one such attack on Laive in 1983, where people dynamited, burned, and destroyed the installations. But who were they? Plinio thinks that perhaps ten to fifteen members of Shining Path were there as leaders, but that there were sixty, eighty, or one hundred people involved. Who else could they be but people from this area? Perhaps even their own workers were involved. An informer had told Plinio that a worker from the SAIS unit Antapongo was seen pouring gasoline on a tractor to burn it. The next day, Plinio Dionisio gingerly explored possibilities in a conversation with that worker:

"You look all haggard," Plinio said. "Where were you last night?"

"I was here in my house, asleep," he answered.

"Not so, you are lying," Plinio said. "You were in Laive, right?"

"Yes, Doctor," the worker admitted.

"It was terrible," Plinio shuddered as he remembered. "We could not trust our delegates, we no longer knew which workers had what designs on us."

Both Plinio Dionisio and Rolando Quispe received anonymous threats during the years 1984 to 1988. Rolando told me his tale:

I remember clearly, I was in Huari at that time, and I got a paper telling me that I had to resign, and they gave me a deadline, and if not, they were going to liquidate me. So I thought to myself, "Is this for real?" I was not sure. It was a shabby piece of paper badly written with a red ballpoint pen. After keeping this to myself for a while, I decided, "I'll tell Lucho Salazar [the chief administrator of Cahuide]. After all, he is the boss, and should anything happen, he could reproach me." So I went and told him, and he replied, "Don't worry, Rolando, you have one letter, I have this many."

Rolando gestured wide, with both hands indicating a huge stack of papers. He laughed nervously. On April 4, 1988, Lucho Salazar was gunned down. Rolando Quispe was selected to replace him, and he was to be the last *gerente* of the SAIS. He continued,

> In those days we did not sleep in the same place. I had three different hiding places and would tell no one which one I would choose. I did not really sleep anyway. When we got back to town, we sighed in relief and blew it out with drinking bouts. But truly, I did not spend nights in my own house in Huancayo either. I moved around, my mother's, my mother-in-law's, friends' places. I developed psychological symptoms and applied my veterinary knowledge to cure myself, for we give cows massive doses of vitamins when they are under stress, so I gobbled vitamins. In the streets, if I saw someone running, I would duck!

Plinio Dionisio recalls that fear of being shot had a serious impact on how the *empresa* was being run. Most of the technical staff abandoned their workplaces in the production units. If Plinio had a scheduled visit to one of them, and he had any kind of hunch, he would postpone the trip and try to delegate responsibility. Those under him refused to go too, saying, "No, I won't go, it is too dangerous." No one was sure with whom they were talking anymore. Could the cashier, the accountant, or that guy be involved? One could not even have an opinion about anything. If one said something against them, well, one could get zapped, if one said something in their favor there was the possibility of military interrogations and torture. The workers became insolent, they had this menacing phrase that scared him: "Ya veremos" (We shall see).

But then around 1987 and 1988, just before the end of the SAIS, the symptoms became even more ominous. "The workers became very cooperative, the *comuneros* polite and complacent." He added, "But there was a silence, a kind of silence, that ¡carambas! made one very nervous. They did their work, they watched."

Plinio Dionisio, under pressure from his family, resigned before the SAIS collapsed. In contrast, Rolando Quispe, who was suddenly cast into an unwanted heroic role, timidly assumed it. When the *gerente* was assassinated, he became the general manager. He said that his wife was against this. She demanded of him, "What do you get from this *empresa*? Are you earning a fortune? Come on! Leave now!"

He ignored her. To me he said,

But, there it is, one can see how being a male, being a responsible man, how during the good times, I had risen in the ranks and how I had felt grateful. But the honor question was important too. I remembered how I had made spirited public statements that I would come to regret:

"The spirit of the *empresa*!"

"I volunteer for this or that!"

"I will defend it."

So, now, as we were losing it, was I going to run like a rat? As a man, how does one appear to others with whom one has worked? When they started attacking Lucho the *gerente*, I had stood by him, and now when they needed me, was I going to retreat? And say "no"?

Sheepishly looking at me, he said, "Well, there I was all alone, no choice!" Rolando Quispe described one of his last scary sorties to Runatullo. There had been thefts there, and the workers were very demoralized and needed him. "Well, okay," he said. "I will go." He requested two policemen to accompany him in the SAIS's easily recognizable Datsun double-cabin pickup. They left Huancayo early one morning. The police sat on each side of him in the backseat, with Rolando in the middle, their three faces covered with hoods during the whole six-hour trip. They drove through villages that were overrun by Shining Path, the situation was incendiary, and Rolando prayed.

On the way, they saw three young men walking along the road carrying things in the colorful handwoven cloths (*quipi*) wrapped on their backs. One of the policemen was so nervous he was foaming at the mouth. He jumped out of the car, pointing his machine gun at the youths, screamed and stammered in a voice of command that was mixed with spasms of fear, "Stop, *carajo*!! Show me those *quipis*!!!"

Rolando was sure those kids were about to die. But they opened up their bundles and showed the police that they were carrying soccer shoes. They were on their way back from a football match. He remembers how he felt great relief, because those boys so narrowly escaped being gunned down; but also for himself, as he imagined the consequences such an incident would have brought on him. Having arrived in Runatullo, he removed his hood. He acted out his leader's role, strutting around, spreading encouragement, dispelling fear, and trying to raise enthusiasm. But his heart was not in it. He was only thinking of the return trip.

He was acutely conscious that no matter how courageously he acted, soon he was going to be dead. He knew the SAIS was doomed, and yet he kept at it, playing his role cautiously and hoping to be able, at the very least, to carry out his responsibilities without too much dishonor until the moment of surrender: "That was it, to be, how can one say it? . . . heroic and defender of one's principles. But I accepted, no? That is how it was."

Parque 15 de Junio (the SAIS Cahuide, Huancayo)

Simón Meza is an accountant at Bebidas Venus, a bottled sweet drink company. Born in 1949 in Potaca, he was a member community of the SAIS Cahuide and one of the little communities under Chongos's sway. His grandfather had been a shepherd on Laive in hacienda times, and Simón was lucky to be sent to school and to graduate in the commercial section from the same high school in Huancayo I had also attended. He was hired by the SAIS in 1974, under an affirmative action policy of providing preferential employment opportunities for qualified sons of *comuneros* or workers. I found him accidentally in Huancayo in 1996.

I had gone to the ex-SAIS headquarters on the Parque 15 de Junio and saw that the building had been turned into a private commercial school (fig. 21). I inquired if anyone knew of any ex-SAIS employee I could talk to and was directed to Bebidas Venus, two blocks away from my father's office. When I was introduced to Simón Meza, who was sitting at his desk, I asked him if he knew where I could find the papers of the SAIS, since I was interested in the history of the agrarian reform. He looked at me and said, "We burned all the papers in the patio of the SAIS building." Aghast, I asked him to repeat what he had just said. "We burned those papers under orders of Shining Path," he repeated. Stunned, I asked him if he would care to tell me about it. Eventually, he did, after eluding me through several purposefully missed appointments. We met after his workday, and clearly in a state of controlled agitation, he suggested we go back to the Parque 15 de Junio SAIS building and borrow an empty classroom so we could talk undisturbed. We sat on school benches and he continued to be uneasy, terse with his answers, and scared throughout the interview. Nostalgic as I was,

Figure 21 The Parque 15 de Junio. The building in the background, once the headquarters of the SAIS Cahuide, is now the commercial school Eugenio Paccelly in Huancayo. Courtesy of Bricklin Dwyer, 2008.

stalking the streets for memories of my father in his old stomping grounds, I too was very emotional during this interview. (My father's office had been slightly damaged in a bomb attack, and once, walking along the main street, he had been showered with bits of plate glass as another bomb went off inside a store.) My own agitation helped Simón, though I prompted him by asking many questions.

Simón Meza had been a contented employee. He got rotated around several accounting tasks and rose in the ranks, and in 1987 when the troubles started, he was the chief cashier. At that time, there were eighty employees. The policy of hiring sons of *comuneros* had changed the social composition of the place. Sixty percent of the employees were sons of peasants, and those from the Laive side of the Mantaro Valley (Chongos included) tended to predominate. I asked if the place was rife with politics, and he answered that politics were always present. He described how the older employees from hacienda times would deride the sons of *comuneros*, and how the employees of the production side disparaged those from the development division as "tourists." He used to go with them to assemblies in the communities where the staff presented balance sheets, and he had to field hostile questions from the *comuneros*, since every worker and every employee was listed by name, rank, and salary level in the mimeographed reports they distributed. The *comuneros* loved nothing more than to pick a name from that list to disparage that person's skills, question the validity of his employment, and act outraged at the salary figures. However, when he visited his home community, he noted that many of his friends and relatives wanted opportunities to work for a fixed and secure salary and to get the meat and butter rations that the *empresa* distributed to its staff. There was always pressure to get them jobs.

In 1986, it was becoming evident that Shining Path had begun to infiltrate the workers in the SAIS, and it got worse and worse. Next he told me how in 1987 he had been a victim of an armed assault. Meza, several employees, and the driver were coming back from Laive after a stock sale, and they had lots of cash (380,000 old *soles*, equivalent to about U.S.$47,000) in the car. Already in darkness and winding down from the highlands on that narrow road, they came upon a stalled truck, which let them pass. Then they caught up with a second truck inching down the steep incline until it got to a hairpin curve and acted as though it could not complete the turn and had to back up to make it. The truck behind them rapidly caught up with them. They were trapped. Masked armed men jumped out of both trucks. "They were the *cumpas* [from *compañero*, a term used for *senderistas*], those who were fighting for the revolution, looking for the *ingeniero* Lucho Salazar," he said. They shot point-blank and the driver was hit. They knew about the money because they yanked the door open to grab the briefcase. Another car was also assaulted. The driver of that one had his hands tied, and the keys were taken from the SAIS Datsun. They were ordered to stay there for one and a half hours, and if they moved, a grenade would blow them up. The *cumpas* fled in the first truck. The wounded driver was bleeding. "Please, for my children! Save me! Save me! I am going to die!" he moaned.

Simón worked like mad to hotwire the car and took off, despite the menace. Nothing happened. They passed a police checkpoint in the valley to report the assault. But the scared policemen waved them on and hid inside their building rather than pursue the thieves. In Huancayo, Simón rushed the wounded man to the clinic where the workers were insured. There the staff refused to admit him because the law stipulated that a bullet wound required a police report before the patient could be treated. Meza tried another clinic and received the same rejection. Then he phoned *ingeniero* Lucho Salazar, who made some phone calls and then told Meza to hurry back to the first clinic. Then the car stalled! Anyway, the chauffeur lived, but the doctors could not get the bullet out of his brain. "He is okay now, but sometimes he loses his balance as if he were drunk," said Meza.

Responding to my question, Simón enumerated those who had died:

Ingeniero Capcha in Laive. Assassinated. They left him hanging from the lamppost in that little plaza.

A worker named Palomino. He was from Punto. They brought him and three others to the valley, and in a dark corner, in the village of Santa Rosa de Ocopa, near the Franciscan convent, they killed them.

Lucho Salazar and his bodyguard. He was caught leaving his house. A boy apparently trying to sell him a newspaper shot him point-blank and badly wounded him.

Two *comuneros* in the community of Rocchac.

Nine as a result of the attacks, but there are more. Those do not count; no?

I asked Simón if he had been threatened. "Yes. Twice," he said, "but they could not find me, so they went to my house and pointed a gun at my daughter."

He went on to recount the insistent demands in assemblies that the SAIS be deactivated, even as the management, belatedly, was proposing plans for restructuring. At a scheduled general assembly, the *comunidades* staged a building takeover instead. By then, Laive had been blown up and the other units too.

Simón responded to my question about what had happened at the office where we now were speaking: "Nothing, total deactivation, nobody showed their faces, the offices were deserted."

The employees quickly created an official union to protect their interests (pension funds, severance pay, and so on). Meza was elected representative. He ran to the police, seeking protection because there were important assets that needed to be secured—documents, bank accounts, the lands in La Esperanza, the machinery, the trucks—to no avail. He could not find the SAIS lawyer, who was hiding. The *gerente* resigned, everybody was unavailable, the community delegates had hastened back to their villages to get their share of the cattle distributions.

Who stayed at the office? "The porter," he giggled.

The members of the union hid too; they had to stay away from the building because they were also threatened. But in the end, Meza and other dedicated colleagues, working undercover and in fear of their lives, organized the distribution of what was left among the employees. They tracked down the people whose signatures were registered with the banks and made them sign so they could withdraw bank funds. Then they pooled the money. They distributed all the office furniture, the video machines from the development division, the typewriters and calculators among themselves. They started to work out a roster, intending to distribute funds according to seniority, but . . . the . . . how could he say it? . . . he hesitated, swallowing. Finally he could bring himself to say it. The terrorists had participated in the meeting and dictated the terms. The insistent clamor arose.

"It has to be equal shares!"

"Giving priority to those with more years of service is a double reward! They have had more time to steal!"

Simón attempted a laugh, but it did not come out right. Each employee got a share of land from La Esperanza, a potentially valuable piece of urban real estate since it was so close to the growing city. With my next question, Simón Meza got extremely uncomfortable. It was whether Shining Path had received any share of the booty. He looked desperately at me, and asked, "Is this interview confidential?" I assured him that it would be safe to tell me what he needed to say.[8] "They demanded it. They ordered me to sell the gas station, the trucks, the machinery. And they got their share too. Yes. They said, 'We need so and so much for our comrades who are walking in the highlands and they have to be fed.' They ordered me to sell a Volvo truck and a portion went to them. That's how it was."

And then the repression came to Huancayo, and Simón Meza began to fear for his life. He went into hiding, abandoned his family, and left Huancayo. Because two Shining Path operatives knew his name, his face, and where his house was, he could be implicated and it was dangerous. He roamed around southern Peru as an itinerant seller of used clothing. Two years later, he heard that the columns of Shining Path that had been the commandos of the deactivation of the SAIS had been caught by the army, and those two who knew him were in the high-security prison for terrorists near Huancayo. At that time, revenge killings between prisoners were very common inside the prison. Meza used his friends to make secret inquiries and found out that the two operatives who could identify him had died violent deaths inside that prison. Thus the situation changed for Simón and he decided to return to his family. He found a job with Bebidas Venus.

Even before Meza went underground, there was tension between ex-employees and delegates from the ex-member communities. The delegates marauded around Huancayo looking for SAIS property they could appropriate. They would ask the ex-employees, "What about the lands that the SAIS bought in the valley? What about the machine repair shop? Where are the funds from the bank accounts?"

The communities organized raiding parties to rescue those assets they rightfully considered theirs and not the employees'. A meeting was arranged between the representatives of the ex-employees and the representatives of the communities. The ex-employees made an offer. They would give them U.S.$10,000 and the two remaining trucks, and hand over the Huancayo building to legitimate representatives from all of the twenty-nine communities. The delegates refused; instead, they wanted to know exactly what had happened to all of the SAIS property: "Everything according to inventory! We want an exact accounting of everything you have done!"

The ex-employees responded that they would not acquiesce, but go to court instead. The lawyers made a killing out of this. A writ here, a petition there, the need to suborn the criminal investigation department over there. It went on and on. And while the court proceedings dragged, Meza hurriedly liquidated whatever was still around and distributed the money among the employees. They even had to defend the valuable urban parcels they had carved out of La Esperanza. The ex-SAIS community of Paccha was angry over the fact that the employees had grabbed La Esperanza. Paccha organized an invasion of La Esperanza, which had to be repelled by the ex-employees. Once again, the theater of land occupation was staged in full view of the Huancayo press, the judicial system, and the incredulous eyes of the city. The ex-employees had to defend it like poor invaders from other, poorer invaders. Day and night they took turns guarding their property; they suffered a lot while fending off the attempts of the *comuneros*.

In the end the only thing left was the building in the Parque 15 de Junio. The union had leased the building in the name of the ex-community members, and after a while, the people who were renting the building bought it from the communities. Meza was no longer around to participate in that transaction. That is how the SAIS ended, he said ruefully.

"And when did you burn the papers?" I asked.

The papers were burned in February 1989. It was done because Shining Path operatives ordered it. The command to congregate about ten ex-employees was transmitted to a couple of individuals who then let the rest know. They were to get together at three in the morning, and once there they received their orders.

"Look," a coworker said. "We have to burn all kinds of documents. If we don't, they say we will be implicated because of those documents. Nothing must remain."

At eight in the morning, the ten employees went to Parque 15 de Junio and carried all the folders, bound books, documents, accounts, and correspondence down to the patio, lit a huge bonfire, and burned it all. They were so docile that the event did not even require the actual presence of a cadre from Shining Path.

Meza described how he felt. "It was sad, but what could one do? [*laughs*] But when there is a threat, there are no alternatives. They were all watching each other, and if one person kept a piece of paper, the others said, "He is taking papers home." All the archives were burned, annual reports, minutes of assemblies, sales records, all those things that would have served later were burned."

It was quiet in the school of the Parque 15 de Junio when Simón Meza ended his story. I had smoked a whole pack of cigarettes, and he looked drained. I took him to a bar and asked for *pisco*. I was in a daze, but he relaxed. After a couple of drinks, he asked if I was going to pay for the information he had given me. I said, "No."

Chongos Alto Liberated

The six months of 1989 during which Shining Path brutally ruled Chongos and the immediate aftermath, the establishment of a military emergency zone, are the most painful memories for *chonguinos*, and I encountered much reluctance to talk about this period. At the time of my visit in 1994, it still was not safe to say too much beyond the official story that *chonguinos* and the government had jointly created. There were subjects about which the whole village had enforced a pall of silence among themselves and definitely to outsiders. "Normalization," as a Fujimori policy of not talking about or prosecuting anybody for human rights violations, was still in full swing in the area. Thus I was handicapped from a lack of what to local people was common knowledge, which they assumed I also knew, but which was too painful for them to explain to me. Absorbing the unease nervously, I often did not dare ask for clarification either.

Luz Goyzueta, a law student, did talk to Danny Pinedo and me in her mother's restaurant where we sought a meal after having concluded our interview with Juvenal Chanco. She stood behind the counter, dishcloth in hand, while Danny and I sat at one of the Formica-topped tables among our plates of half-finished food. We listened appalled and too intent to break the spell. Luz's mother is from Chongos and hankers for life in the *campo*, even though she runs a full-time middle-class home in Huancayo, where Luz is a university student. So whenever she can be, Luz's mother is in Chongos, organizing production in her fields and opening up her restaurant to sell meals to transient populations. On weekends, or when she is not involved with her studies, Luz comes to Chongos.

Luz Goyzueta told us that she had participated in the distribution of animals in Antapongo in December 1987. All members of the community were woken up at dawn and taken on foot up the hill and over the plains to Antapongo's headquarters (a walk of ten kilometers). First, Shining Path dynamited the hacienda house and the other buildings. Then they proceeded to distribute the animals following a list that the authorities of Chongos had provided. The distribution, according to her, favored those who had shown sympathies toward Shining Path, and for this reason, she thinks, she was given only one sheep. She couldn't manage the bucking animal, and exasperated, she gave it to a neighbor to do her the favor of bringing it to the village along with her share of sheep, but it got lost. She watched but did not participate in the looting of Antapongo and then returned to the village, tired and scared, at eight at night.

The *cumpas* gave strict orders as to what to do with the purebred cows they had distributed. The *chonguinos* had eight days to "disappear" them (sell, kill, take to remote areas in the *puna*, or find a place to conceal the animals elsewhere). During the following days Chongos was visited by merchants buying the animals for cash and carting them off. Most peasants were anxious to sell, scared about the incriminating evidence with which they were saddled. The merchants profited, buying animals for a song, and, to the consternation of newspaper editorialists in Huancayo and Lima, selling them to Huancayo's and Lima's slaughterhouses to be used for meat. One farmer refused to obey, and ten cows were blown up. Autocratic revolutionary rule was so strict that during the distribution days, neither alcohol nor coca was allowed.

Luz stated that Shining Path had worked in the schools in Chongos. In those days they acted openly, singing revolutionary songs, doing calisthenics, and conducting indoctrination sessions. Village people were forced to listen to lectures on revolution. Some older people emerged as Shining Path activists, she said, motivated more by envy than zeal, which exacerbated the feuding tendencies so rampant in the village. The Shining Path instituted its own system of quick justice. Luz was struck by the ideological extremes of women cadres. She gave an example of a case against a man who had a child with an unmarried woman. The cadres were ready to shoot the man, but the accusing woman pleaded for his life. The cadres asked what it was that she wanted. She said that she did not want to marry him, nor did she want to live with him anymore, as she said she was abused. She wanted child-support payments. So the cadres expropriated one hundred sheep from him and assigned them to her. In another trial, an old man complained that his jealous neighbor had been throwing stones across the fence onto his lands. The stone thrower was severely beaten.

During the time that the area was a "red zone," Shining Path blew up the beautiful colonial municipal building in the plaza, the branch of the Banco de la Nación, the health post, two buses, and a bridge to cut off a second access road to Chongos.

Luz Goyzueta also witnessed the executions of twelve community leaders of Chongos, Chicche, and Llamapsillón, conducted by Shining Path in the plaza on April 12, 1988. They were accused of treason, because one month earlier, Chongos and the three satellite villages had marched to the borders of their lands with Yauyos and expelled a group of people who had established themselves there under Shining Path's protection. There, the Chongos people had captured three men and turned them over to the police in Huancayo as "presumed subversives." In retaliation, Shining Path, with a list in hand, had rounded up twelve leaders at dawn and brought them to the plaza of Chongos.

Luz said that it was all directed by one woman terrorist who had her face covered in a ski mask, and in retrospect, she remembers that only two of the terrorists had real firearms, while the rest had wooden sticks carved and painted to resemble rifles. One of the accused, the vice president of the community council who was also a high school teacher, valiantly defended himself: "I know that you are going to kill me," he said.

The Shining Path leader shot him twice. He was hit in the leg and in the shoulder. Even so, the teacher continued haranguing the people congregated in the plaza. "Chongos is a combative village and Chongos will know how to defend itself. You can kill many, but you cannot kill the three hundred *comuneros*. We will prevail."

To shut him up, they slit his throat and left him dead, bleeding from the jugular. They ordered that nobody touch the bodies, and the cement walks of the plaza remained slimy with stinking pools of blood and spilled guts for ten days. The column fled the village in the same bus in which it had arrived.[9]

No one was allowed to leave the village. Luz was desperate to return to Huancayo, but Shining Path did not let her, suspecting her of being a possible informer. Finally on the tenth day, the fearful military dared to enter Chongos to pick up the bodies. They had come in their vehicles as far as the Vista Alegre junction, but from there they had used horses, since roads in the highlands can be cut off and travelers on them are easily ambushed.

The military presence was sporadic in the area until July 1989, when a base in Vista Alegre was established, and the military began its campaign to rout Shining Path. Luz Goyzueta described this phase, emphatically using the words "military counterterror." She says it was worse than Shining Path, and she had a harrowing personal experience to relate.

At two in the morning, soldiers broke open her door. She stood in the back of the house and screamed, "Stop or I'll shoot," hoping that they would go away, even though she had no weapons. They came in anyway and she saw a soldier. She admitted, "I don't have a gun. Search the house."

She was taken to the plaza and brutally interrogated until 3:30 a.m. She warned the soliders that she knew her constitutional rights, but the *comandante* responded that constitutional rights were suspended in emergency zones. Thus she consented to the interrogation. She was asked what she was doing there. She said that she was a descendant of Chongos people and that the house from which she had been taken was hers, and that there were relatives of hers in the village who could vouch for her and corroborate that she came to the village regularly. Desperately and with increasing insistence, she repeated this over and over; it was as if the interrogators didn't want to believe her. The *comandante* ordered her to kneel, to "give names," and then, he said, she would be able to go. She said that she did not know anyone. She protested loudly, over and over, until the priest hearing the commotion came out of his residence, rescued her, and took her to the sacristy. The *comandante* then accused the priest of covering for subversive students.

Luz described torture she saw and heard of. She mentioned that wires were used to gag people by the neck, and one can still recognize these victims by their scars. She saw how the military tied rows of suspects along a fence this way, leaving them visible for three days with little food or drink and no help. She was critical of the way the military ran the village in autocratic ways and how they interfered with everything, giving senseless orders.

"Today, all of you play soccer in the stadium!!"

"No, sir," the people responded, "it is threshing time, we have to go and tend the fields, we do not have time."

Nonetheless, soccer had to be played, and on Sundays, everyone had to come out to the plaza to sing the national anthem and march in a display of military-style patriotism that was supposed to magically ward off sympathies in favor of Shining Path. Just as with the occupation by Shining Path, lacking any of their own authorities, local people kept appealing to the military to resolve their interfamily disputes.

The priest who rescued Luz (he asked that his name not be used), conceded to me that there probably were people who identified with Shining Path in Chongos. The Shining Path's political propaganda was tolerated, but he did not detect widespread support for the group. The Shining Path's preaching included a mantra that the revolution had to break down three mountains, the first mountain being international capitalism, the second mountain, national capitalism, and the third mountain, regional capitalism—in this case, the SAIS Cahuide. It was obvious to him that people harbored expectations of being able to get something out of the SAIS, knowing that their leaders and Shining Path were in fierce competition to break it down. And once they saw that the leadership began to collaborate with Shining Path's initiative, the people tactically ended up going along with this, toward the material end of profiting from the breakup of the SAIS.

The priest said that the day that Shining Path killed those twelve leaders from Chongos, Chicche, and Llamapsillón was the real turning point, though friction had already emerged when Shining Path ordered the dynamiting of a bridge, which the village had counseled against. Villagers had had enough. After that, the villagers really began to get organized in secret to oust Shining Path from their midst. The village gradually reconstituted its own authority system, first reviving the old colonial *varayoc* system, the civil-religious hierarchy that used to be the peasants' own system of government and which had long ago been discontinued in favor of the government-sponsored system of elected officials.[10] Not even the parish priest found out about it until, one day, a group of people came and asked him to bless the ancient *varas*, or staffs.

No one mentioned arrests to us while we were there, and it was clear in our visit that people who had relatives in jail were not going to be pointed out to us in any explicit way. All denied that there were any *"arrepentidos"* (repentants) from Chongos. (Named after Fujimori's program to encourage desertion from Shining Path, this implied a public repentance of past involvement, no prosecution, and reincorporation into normal civilian life. Presumably, a more secret confession that gave names to the intelligence service was also a condition.) Somehow, in ways that were unfathomable for me to ferret out, a working reconciliation among *comuneros chonguinos* who had supported Shining Path and those who had opposed it had been worked out within the village. The official story we received from everywhere was that Shining Path was a nasty external incursion, that the subversion had beaten them in their attempts to deactivate the SAIS and had proceeded to break it up in ways that were against most *comunero* wishes, and that *chonguinos* thereby had become victims to outsider domination that had cost them dearly, and which they quickly rejected. Those who had supported the revolution, the official story has it, have seen the error of their ways and all now repudiate Shining Path.

At the beginning of my interview with Víctor Caballero in Lima, he had asked me if I knew what a black distribution was. Baffled, I said that I didn't. "It was a concept used by revolutionaries in Russia and China," he answered. In the Chinese revolution, Mao encouraged black harvests, letting peasants take the crops from the landlords' fields. The Shining Path did the same as it pursued its policy to eliminate local power holders: it encouraged looting and distributed harvests and animals, specifically targeting research stations in Alpachaca (Ayacucho), IVITA in La Raya (Cusco), Ayaviri (Puno), and SAIS installations in central Peru. Max Gamarra had described similar patterns. Outsider Shining Path platoons arrived in a village to round up people, guide them to an SAIS installation, attack and burn it, and let the participants loot it while the platoons then disappeared into the hills. What Shining Path did not realize, Víctor went on, was that the peasants were acutely aware that the political time was ripe for them to take the land, not just a harvest. Land distribution had not been, Víctor insisted, a policy of Shining Path, but was something that the peasants had pushed *Sendero* to go along with against its better judgment. He said that Abimael Guzmán, the chairman of Shining Path, had stated that land occupations tended to weaken peasant support for the long "popular war" that would put him in power, and therefore he was opposed to them. Thus, it was the peasants who took the initiative, it was they who used Shining Path for their immediate ends.

Víctor's analysis of why Shining Path attacked the SAISes in the first place was more tactical than political. Their columns needed safe havens and access to the Mantaro Valley, and therefore they had to cut a swath for themselves through SAIS territory that linked Lima, Huancavelica, and Ayacucho. With their assassinations, they could empty the area of SAIS administrators, and through the black harvests, they could secure peasant cooperation. When the tide of communities taking over the lands was unstoppable, Shining Path too began to occupy territory for itself and its supporters on the border with Yauyos, and that was intolerable for the *comuneros*, who had decided early on that ex-SAIS land was going to be exclusively for the twenty-nine original partner communities and no one else. Thus the Chongos, Chicche, and Llamapsillón *comuneros* had marched to the *Sendero*-sponsored occupation of their rightful lands, threw them out, beat them, and captured three of the men to turn them over to the police. It was in retaliation that Shining Path had killed the leaders in the plaza of Chongos, and the brief alliance between them was over.

After a time, the villagers got organized both to resist Shining Path and to establish a working relationship with the military, which also gave them more leeway. Eventually, *rondas campesinas* officially sponsored by the military were established, and the military operated from their barracks in Vista Alegre.

Juvenal Chanco, more intent on asserting his thesis of *campesino* self-reliance, had a more critical view of *rondero* glory. He said that the *comuneros* had participated in organizing peasant patrols as a concession to the army. His assessment of the menace of Shining Path was that its members were a few adventurers who took advantage of the social unrest created by the *comuneros* who wanted to recuperate SAIS lands. That is why, when asked to evaluate the degree of military repression in the Chongos area in comparison to other areas, he was of the opinion that the military repression was light, swift, and effective. "Shining Path operatives were caught quickly in those places because 'we' knew where they were hiding, no?" He said that only twenty people had been killed or disappeared, and that was mercifully light compared to other regions. He added that he was disappointed at how quickly the potential that *rondas* could have had in galvanizing the community and restoring some discipline had crumbled and dissipated.

Luz Goyzueta and Juvenal Chanco, I had by then realized, belonged to different factions in the village, and therefore both had an interest in giving me different versions. Chanco had campaigned for a candidate in the elections for mayor on a "genuine" *comunero* ticket and had been opposed by power-holding *chonguinos* who lived in cities and had professional credentials, who had become "*mistis.*" Now that Chongos was in possession of five thousand extra hectares, the internal struggle was to try to exclude emigrant villagers who had other sources of income and less need for land. The *comunero* faction was therefore doing its best to reject any influence from the powerful and more middle-class faction that had traditionally occupied positions of power in the municipality and community affairs. Luz Goyzueta belonged to this faction and tried to maintain her interests in community affairs. Her grandfather participated in the *varayoc* revival. Their respective assessments of the role of Shining Path therefore differed as they tried to represent their positions to me. For Juvenal it was a minor incursion; for Luz, a deeper involvement; for both of them and the whole village, a terrible disaster.

Finally, the Land

The next day, Juvenal Chanco and the mayor of Chongos offered to take us on a tour of the recuperated lands. Juvenal was keen to show Danny and me some ancient rock art in a secluded cave by a lovely spot along the river, which possibly could be developed by the community as an ecotourism destination to bring income to the village. After all, I was the anthropologist who could authenticate the ancient rock art and, besides, I had a car.

For him, the ride was like a ceremonial taking of possession of the newly acquired lands. As we drove he pointed out landmarks, rock formations, place names, and "historical sites." We drove several kilometers and then parked the Toyota Land Cruiser and started walking overland. We came across several *estancias* near water holes where cattle and sheep congregated at night and spread out during the daytime, guarded by herders and fierce dogs.

Important changes in the structure of herding practices had taken place since Chongos had occupied the land. The wire fences had all been taken out, and the herds were no longer the uniform sex- and age-segregated high-quality breed of SAIS and hacienda times, but decidedly mixed. Sheep were less in evidence and cows tended to predominate, but they did not look too healthy. Juvenal pointed out that sheep have too low a price. Even so, with government encouragement a portion of land had been reserved for a communal enterprise in which they hoped to restore some of the SAIS technology. I thought, though, that no matter how much faith was put into *empresas comunales* or with how much discipline they could be run, an *empresa comunal* would not be able to provide an adequate resource base for the many *comunero* families.

More important was the fact that the *estancias* had no "owners." Rather, each tended to center around an ex-SAIS shepherd who knew that particular territory well. The animals, it turned out, belonged to several people, often relatives but not always. Each *estancia* had become the locus of a sort of informal cooperative arrangement, with varying and changing animal ownership. Sometimes a friend in need of pasture would approach the group and suggest that they take in his or her animals. Owners of stock would come to an agreement to share the area of the *estancia* and herd all animals together under the guidance and leadership of experienced herders. Family members agreed to share herding time according to a strict schedule worked out in advance, in which the number of days of herding duty varied in direct proportion to the number of animals kept on that *estancia*. That is why, driving up, we had seen so many people on foot or pushing loaded donkeys coming and going, even schoolchildren, one of them reading his notebook as he rode the donkey.

As we reached the top of a ridge from which we had a panoramic view, Juvenal pointed out the historical boundaries of the ex-haciendas and explained the current boundary imbroglios. Antapongo's newly acquired lands had not yet been divided among the four communities, and they were still under joint and somewhat chaotic co-ownership. The tentative divisions and preliminary boundaries that had been made during the *desactivación* discussions were unacceptable to Chongos, and the people refused to abide by them. The reason was that the proposal gave proportionately smaller lands to Chongos, much of which were also very high, unproductive, and waterless. Chongos had instead proposed a joint administration with equal access for all four communities, something one of the smaller communities had agreed with so far, but which was opposed by the other two. The land dispute with Huasicancha was also a factor delaying the setting of the final boundaries among all of the communities, and it had already led to one bloody encounter between two of the villages and several court proceedings with no resolution yet in sight. As we walked, we had to make a detour through one area because Juvenal Chanco did not want to show his face lest it provoke a group of ex-SAIS employees who had set up a farm there and were opposed to being absorbed into the Chongos community. The situation certainly was chaotic, and Juvenal Chanco was unhappy.

Chanco was also unhappy about the social and psychological consequences of the whole recuperation process. "Individualism has become rampant," he complained. In response to a comment that I had heard over and over, that terrorism had induced a lack of discipline among the *comuneros*, Juvenal both agreed and disagreed. The rebellious spirit was what had saved them, he said, but it also had become a serious problem. It was the spirit of liberty that had led them to resist Shining Path. Nevertheless, he pointed out, "I have concluded that people here do not only want to be free, they want to be libertines. There is no more obedience, everyone wants to lead, nobody wants to obey. . . . There is an aftermath to Shining Path phenomenon here," he observed. "No one dares to confront anyone anymore, or to become strict with another person. There is this fear that there will be complaints against the leadership for abuse of power."

Chanco had a theory that all these bad experiences would eventually teach the people to develop a more cooperative spirit. The secret revival of the *varayoc* system during the time Shining Path ruled the village may have had something to do with reestablishing locally based discipline. *Varayoc* leaders who rose through the ranks of the civil and religious authority were in the past strict disciplinarians and commanded a great deal of respect.

The revival was part of the search for "roots" and authenticity to find ways of legitimating eroded authority. In matters of organization and discipline there was much to learn from the grandfathers, he had said. Sure, he conceded, he understood that every individual wanted to increase his or her stock of animals, but what they didn't see was the relationship between the quantity and quality of animals. Pointing to an *estancia*, he told us, "It all is going toward degradation of pastures." He said that the community had decided to create three areas to rotate the pastures, in order to combat this phenomenon. When the majority said that it was time to move to the higher grounds, many did go, while others stayed behind because it was too far. So, while in assemblies, everyone agreed on imposing sanctions, fines, and all that, those who refused to comply became unruly (*lisos*) and no one was capable of implementing the sanctions. The issue went back to the assembly. Again, the endlessly debated decision was that they had to move, but this time the resisters were even more numerous than before, so in the end the leaders decided that implementing unpopular decisions was worse because it eroded their legitimacy. And so they decided that it was better to "let everyone figure this out for themselves."

Juvenal described how the very process of letting them work it out by themselves was panning out. Gradually, as the lower areas were getting too crowded, those with more animals began moving out to the distant pastures in the higher zones, and in this way the animals were more evenly spread out. However, as of yet, no areas had been left fallow to allow natural grasses to recuperate. So Juvenal was vaguely hopeful that experience and experimentation would eventually teach the *comuneros* how to manage their newly acquired land in the long run. Still, he thought, it would take time and they would have to reach rock bottom first before they could see their way out of the tragedy of holding common pastures with private ownership of stock.

When we got to the lovely rock formation near the murmuring river, with stands of native bushes and *queñua* trees that sometimes harbored wild deer, much to Juvenal Chanco's chagrin, we found that the libertine spirit he had denounced had once more done its ugly thing. Next to and around the ancient rock art, modern *comuneros* had added their own graffiti. A heart pierced with arrows with the names of the lovers had been added to the ensemble.

On the way back, we made a detour to the former *casa hacienda* of Antapongo. Now it was my time to tell a story: I remembered how my father told us children that, a long time ago, he had passed by Antapongo late at night and requested shelter for the night. He was graciously received by the administrator of the hacienda, an Italian named Mario Valfré. The interiors were luxuriously appointed and my father spent a glorious, comfortable night. At suppertime he had been served by a waiter dressed impeccably in white and wearing gloves. This in the wild high *punas*! Juvenal then mentioned that Marcial Soto, Luz's grandfather (who had been a butter churner), also had memories of Mr. Valfré, the Italian *gringo*. Valfré never answered when a person spoke to him. He would continue walking bent forward (as with a military officer's gait), and only after he had walked quite a distance away from the person would he answer, looking straight ahead. Toscana was his warehouseman. If Valfré wanted to please someone, he would yell, "Toscaaanaaa, ah! Give him two pounds of coca."

I asked if he was a nasty person. "No, he was always a correct, cold, distant person." He had been in the Italian army and that was his style in dealing with people.

We reached Antapongo at sunset. Set along a lake turned pink by the rays of the setting sun, there was a huge ruin. Whitewash could still be seen on the enormously thick adobe walls, and the outline of the ceremonial patio in flagstones now covered with thick grass was still visible. Juvenal took pictures, and later he called me to his side as he was rummaging around a dilapidated side building next to the now useless stables. Juvenal said that the day they all came up to Antapongo for the distribution of the cattle, he had watched the looting from a distance. He saw an old woman rooting around where we were now standing. He became curious and walked up to her. "Here," she said. "This is the place where they kept my father prisoner, for several nights!"

We were looking at the remains of the *coso*, the hacienda jail. Juvenal said to me that lots of people must have accumulated a great deal of rancor against the hacienda house. The destruction of the place could be, he reflected, a natural reaction, a liberating moment, and a compensation for all the humiliation and abuse they had suffered in the past. "That is why," he said to me, "it was a pleasure for them to loot, to dismantle, and to destroy, no?"

Latin American agrarian reforms in the 1960s through the 1980s, in general, did not do much to transform skewed economies with extreme income inequalities and glaring rural-urban disparities. They did not resolve the problems of endemic poverty, nor cope with the tremendous population explosion in Latin America by providing more work opportunities in the countryside. Reform efforts were short lived because opportunities for action by the few enlightened leaders who were willing and able to overcome resistance to land expropriation came only in rare moments of political ferment. Reforms often were followed by counterreforms. In Peru, a rural insurrection by Maoists developed after its agrarian reform. In Chile, Nicaragua, and El Salvador, agrarian reforms were associated with revolutionary and counterrevolutionary conflict, as well as the direct or indirect involvement of the United States. Many people died in El Salvador and Nicaragua. As a whole agrarian reform that started off as a revolutionary idea became a conservative policy enacted as a palliative to stem potential unrest, or to provide demobilized soldiers with something to do after the conflicts.

In all of them, land distribution was problematic at best. Too little land was distributed, and land that was doled out went to the better off of the poorer classes. The reformed sectors were not provided sufficient or appropriate support by bureaucracies that were bungling and indifferent, a problem that was worsened by strapped government spending. Collective group farming on cooperatives has tended to collapse throughout the Latin American countries where it was implemented, even in Cuba's sugar cooperatives.

The Berkeley economist Alain de Janvri, whose overview of agrarian reforms and counterreforms in Latin America in *The Agrarian Question and Reformism in Latin America* described several theoretical paths that these movements could take, says that the combination of the Belaúnde and Velasco reforms in Peru constituted an effort to shift from precapitalist estates to capitalist "Junker" or elite estates in the highlands, and from estates to family farms on the coast (1981, 203–10). However, by the end of the 1980s, all forms of Junker and precapitalist estates were dismantled by the peasants themselves into smallholdings. Peru's case fits de Janvri's theoretical formulation of "functional dualism" that, he says, explains the persistence of a family farm capitalist sector combined with a peasant-based semi-proletarian sector, capable of lowering labor costs and producing cheap food for urban markets. The agrarian reform in Peru has strengthened the peasantry, a social class that Marxists and development specialists of the West had seen as a class doomed to disappear. De Janvri concludes that "new land reforms are unlikely to occur in the near future in Latin America" (1981, 223).

There are, as the twenty-first century begins, hints that a return to agrarian reforms may be possible. In Brazil, the Landless Rural Workers' Movement (MST) is forcing the expropriation of estates for distribution to landless people who then create small family farms or cooperatives. Venezuela is expropriating land and building cooperatives on them and Evo Morales, Bolivia's populist indigenous president, spoke in August 2006 about a need to implement agrarian reform in the eastern lowland areas of the country. Does this presage a new wave of reforms? It does not appear to be the case as of this writing, because these examples are small and tentative. However, land concentration is taking place on the coast of Peru, building up pressure if alternative forms of employment for the rural poor do not develop. Other issues will rise to the foreground to heat up political debates and protests in rural areas: Open free markets underwritten by the North American Free Trade Association (NAFTA), the Central American Free Trade Association (CAFTA), and MERCOSUR imply the flow of agricultural commodities across national boundaries with lowered tariffs inducing a more globalized competition that will affect small scale family farming throughout the continent. Pricing policies for farm goods, protection against competition from abroad, and legal rights of workers are issues that are placed on the agenda for this new century. In Mexico and Peru neoliberal reforms seek to dissolve the *ejidos* and the *comunidades campesinas* in Peru. As decentralization advances, communities have lost their direct link to the central government, which, for a century, provided them with some measure of protection. Potential mobilization to reconfigure this situation is sure to be on the agenda.

Yet one aspect of agrarian reforms in Latin America, most clearly illustrated by the Peruvian case and highlighted in this book, is not stressed enough in contemporary studies: namely, the fact that land ended up predominantly in the hands of smallholders was not by design of the reformers, but by the autonomous actions of its beneficiaries. In the final stages of agrarian reform in Peru, Nicaragua, Honduras, and El Salvador, much land was taken from the state by peasants in peaceful acts of civil disobedience that ran counter to the theoretical models or designs of their respective governments' intentions to concentrate land, and to maintain or expand land extensive, machine-based technology with monocrop agroindustrial tendencies. Agrarian reform is no longer on the agenda of the neoliberal order that has become hegemonic in the hemisphere since structural adjustments, privatization, and reduction of the state's functions have become the dominant economic models accompanying democratic political regimes. Reformed land is now predominantly farmed in private-smallholding individual family farms that struggle greatly against adverse market conditions, local and foreign competition, and lack of capital. Rural wage labor has lost its protections, its unions, and the capacity to bargain collectively or to stem the trend of falling wages. It has become casualized and feminized. Social security for rural workers and peasants is a largely unfulfilled wish. Rural capitalism no longer needs to expand in the form of exclusive estates that concentrate land, but can rely on contract farming to outsource costs and liabilities, dumping them on the rural household for it to absorb externalities amid adverse market conditions.

Many peasants in Latin America are now growing "fair trade" coffee, mangoes, asparagus, and broccoli for air freighting to urban markets in the United States, and I eat these products in solidarity. The peasants combine subsistence with market production, seek temporary employment, migrate to cities in their own countries and—illegally—abroad. The neoliberal ideology that replaced nationalist state and social programming now protects private property as sacred dogma. It encourages foreign investment, believes in the virtues of the self-regulating market in an uneven playing field, and tracks the creation of wealth without worrying about how unfairly it is distributed. Peru's case is no exception to these depressing conclusions.

Rural poverty in Peru hits the highlands hardest, and within that area, those who are indigenous, even after the drastic agrarian reform

Could it have turned out differently? Rosemary Thorpe and Geoffrey Bertram, the foremost economic historians on Peru, take a longer historical view in their book *Peru 1890–1977: Growth and Policy in an Open Economy*. In it they tell how in some ways the military government in the 1970s did have the unique opportunity to change the export-dependent economy into a more autonomous path of development in the face of powerful external constraints, but nonetheless failed to do so: "Perhaps the most important lesson of the Peruvian experiment is that it is not sufficient for a government to have its heart in the right place (if we can so describe the Velasco Government with respect to autonomous development). Oversimplified models of social reality run the risk of merely shifting the focus of social conflict, on the one hand, while leaving essential economic weaknesses untouched, on the other" (1978, 319).

Other chroniclers of that period cite indecision, "cold feet," improvisation, and the isolation and ouster of Juan Velasco by his military colleagues, who became scared enough of Communism to remove him. Because Velasco was a loner, his revolution was unfinished when he got sick and lost control.

Yet, because of Velasco, the hacienda system is history, both in the highlands and the coastal valleys. Although the "feudal" hacienda in the highlands was already in decline, Velasco's reform liquidated it for good. Leveling an ancien régime does require political action, even if it is crumbling. On irrigated and fertile lands on the coast, a more healthy mixture of medium-sized farms compete with a group of struggling agrarian reform beneficiaries who have very small plots in producing food crops for the city (Lima) and for export. In the highlands, the hacienda *runa* (indigenous workers; literally, people, in Quechua) became free *comuneros* and voting citizens when in 1979 the Constitution removed the literacy requirement from the right to vote. Indigenous people in Peru are not yet full citizens, but they are citizens nonetheless. During the military regime the Peruvian rural population participated in many class-based *campesino* federations; while in Ecuador during that time, the very same demographic group began to build up an indigenous political movement that outlasted Peruvian rural organizations. Peruvian peasants did wrest the land from cooperatives and SAISes, but unfortunately their movements did not develop perspectives beyond the immediate goal of getting the land. Nor did the Cinderella *comunidades campesinas*—undoubtedly the reform's clearest beneficiaries in the highlands—capitalize on their gains to build a stronger *comunero* political base. They got the land, but not much else. That peasant federations were incapable of building lasting institutions and becoming an important political force or a political party is another symptom of an incomplete revolution in Peru. Nonetheless, anywhere one goes in today's Peru, one has to start with what effects the agrarian reform has had on the local scene. It often brings surprises. In Cajamarca in 1996, as I was touring with an NGO focused on water problems, we stopped at a place where the farmer was constructing an amazing system of micro-irrigation to grow vegetables. In his house he was installing a tank and pipes for a running water system to catch rain water from the roof. This man was once a worker on an hacienda, and he got the karst-like land he was improving with much toil through the agrarian reform.

Hugo Neira, the newspaper reporter who authored *Cuzco: Tierra y muerte, reportaje al sur* in 1964, later took the opportunity to ponder the trends of his country from afar while he was a sociology professor in Tahiti. He wrote in *Hacia la tercera mitad: Perú XVI–XX* that "Velasquismo separates the before and the after in Peruvian life. It is not a rupture, it is *the* rupture . . ." (1996, 421, emphasis added).

He goes on to say that it was the moment when state, nation, and popular classes coincided. If that rupture required the top-down, technocratic, heavy-handed authoritarian method of pushing for change by marching into action with fife and drum, Neira asks, what kind of political society did Peru have before that needed the kind of Meji restoration that the military implemented? "If it was Peru's Meji restoration, it lacked the samurais, in other words an iron elite, continuity of purpose and honesty" (1996, 427). Like Pancho Guerra, the enthusiastic *velasquista* mentioned in chapter 1, Hugo Neira also claims that "without [Velasco's] land distribution, the Andes today would be *senderista*" (1996, 428). It is a rhetorical statement that cannot be answered, as is Mario Vargas Llosa's purported argument, according to Neira, that Velasco's leftism opened the way for Shining Path. It is a war of words but not really an analytical statement. Nonetheless, the question posed from the Left and the Right about the relationship between the agrarian reform and the rise and subsequent defeat of Shining Path needs some sort of debate that will undoubtedly be refined as more research on the impact of Shining Path brings new insights.

It is true that one of the consequences of the Velasco regime was the growth of a political left in Peru (Hinojosa 1998, 68). Thirty percent of Peruvians voted for the Left in the election of 1979. Many leftist political groups emerged and they tried to form united platforms while simultaneously engaging in bitter disputes among themselves, so badly that in the end they fizzled altogether in the late 1990s. In the 1980s and 1990s, the majority of left-wing groups embraced democracy and electoral platforms, even though some retained their radical tone. Others shifted to a middle-of-the-road model of Euro-Communism or electoral socialism, even seeking alliances with centrist parties. Only tiny fractions of the most extreme Maoist groups opted for armed struggle.

Maoist political groups grew in Latin America and in Peru after the Sino-Soviet split in the 1960s. Maoism appealed to Peruvians because of the Maoists claim that it was possible to leap to socialism directly from feudalism, as they had done in China, without having to pass through a capitalist phase of development. Peasants could, according to the Maoist argument, become the revolutionary vanguard, and the many peasant movements that accompanied the agrarian reforms were interpreted as indices of their revolutionary potential. Once Velasco had established diplomatic relations with Communist China, Peruvian intellectuals, among them Abimael Guzmán, the founder of the Maoist party splinter group in the University of Ayacucho, did visit that country during the Cultural Revolution. The cruel violence and intransigence of the young Revolutionary Guards impressed the visiting Peruvians. However, for many radicals in Peru, Chairman Mao's discourse was a rhetorical device they themselves did not really practice; Abimael Guzmán was the one loner who decided to follow Mao's example to start an Ayacucho version of a "long march" that would recruit a peasant revolutionary army in a war to topple the putrid government in Lima. The Shining Path phenomenon that came about as a result seemed, as argued by the Mexican scholar and politician Jorge Castañeda in *Utopia Unarmed* (1993), a totally new and dangerous phenomenon compared to previous trends and tendencies of the left in the rest of Latin America. Nor was Shining Path an ethnic Indian revolt, although European and U.S. scholars who were observing initially thought so when reports of violence in Ayacucho began to circulate. The vision of enraged Indians killing their landlords in justified outrage had terrorized the imagination of Peru's elites for decades, and it had been used by progressives to justify the need for agrarian reform. A carry-over of that image initially influenced foreign observers about Shining Path.

If one looks at Latin America during that period, one can see that military dictatorships did provoke armed struggles against them. For instance, the height of armed insurgency in Argentina occurred in 1977. While Morales Bermúdez was winding down Velasco's revolution, the Argentine *montoneros* were fighting against Videla's right-wing military regime. In Central America three armed struggles against extreme right-wing dictatorships took place: the Sandinistas' armed revolution in Nicaragua (1979–90) against Somoza; the near defeat of the extreme right by the FMLN (Frente Farabundo Martí para la Liberación Nacional) in El Salvador (1979–91); and in Guatemala the guerrilla movements of the Ejército de los Pobres and the Fuerzas Armadas Revolucionarias, which involved peasants and indigenous groups in rebellion and which suffered enormous human losses in 1980–81 when General Efraín Ríos Montt, who was then the president, pursued a vicious scorched earth campaign against them. Those movements struggled against extremely corrupt and reactionary military dictatorships that marked the "second wave" of armed insurgencies in Latin America (Castañeda 1994, 90). Also noteworthy is that in these three countries no significant agrarian reforms were implemented in the 1960s and 1970s (the Guatemalan agrarian reform was toppled in 1954 because it affected the interests of landlords and United Fruit, a U.S. company). If the argument is that military dictatorships spawn guerrilla uprisings, then there are more examples of right-wing dictatorships provoking them than of mildly left-wing military regimes, such as that of Velasco in Peru or Omar Torrijos (1968–81) in Panama; in the latter case, no guerrillas arose.

The Peruvian experience can also be compared to the case of Colombia. In Colombia no significant agrarian reform took place and several guerrilla movements arose and they continue to be active, although those guerrillas did not confront a military regime. Without Belaúnde's timid reforms in the 1960s and Velasco's more drastic expropriations in the 1970s, Peru could hypothetically have taken the path of Colombia, where landlords formed their own paramilitary armies to defend their properties from peasants and guerrillas. In Colombia, the illegal drug trade became a third element in the equation, and in Peru both Shining Path and the MRTA (Movimiento Revolucionario Túpac Amaru) took advantage of narcotics corruption to fill their purses. Would a paramilitary army of Peruvian landlords have stopped spontaneous peasant land occupations or have exacerbated armed conflicts? The issue, mercifully, never arose. Peasant uprisings in Peru throughout the forty-year period were peaceful social movements that used civil disobedience as their tactic. Peruvian landlords did not arm themselves against the peasants nor "disappear" their leaders with the connivance of the government. The Velasco government did not shoot at anybody during its agrarian reform.

What is implicit in the argument that Shining Path without Velasco would be surrounding Lima is that the group was so violent and seemingly unbeatable for observers in the 1990s. The horror of Mario Vargas Llosa, a conservative author and politician, would not only have Presidente Gonzalo's (Abimael Guzmán's) peasant armies surrounding Lima, but also have the whole nation caught up in a situation of generalized violence. Pessimism so pervaded Mario Vargas Llosa's novel *La historia de Mayta* (1984), which describes the deterioration of Peru of those times, that the novel ends with a terrible fantasy set in the future: a combined Bolivian-Chilean army incursion from the south is joined by an Ecuadorian military invasion from the north, both supported by the United States, to stop the insurgencies. That vision did not become reality because Shining Path was defeated fairly fast and effectively. Blaming Marxists or their military godfathers for the trouble is something one can say for political effect after the fear has dissipated.

Pancho Guerra and Hugo Neira limit their case to saying that peasants were unwilling to join guerrilla insurgencies en masse because they had already been liberated from hacienda oppression and been given the land. The same argument has also been made, quite correctly, about the failure of Ché Guevara's attempt to start a guerrilla-based revolution in Bolivia: there, while the CIA and the Bolivian army were hunting Ché and the Cubans in 1967, peasants were not interested in supporting or joining a guerrilla insurgency after the MNR (Movimiento Nacionalista Revolucionario) agrarian reform of 1952.

The case of the SAIS Cahuide described in chapter 6 reveals another angle. The insurgents took advantage of the chaotic situation in the SAIS, hoping to further their cause through tactical moves, but Shining Path gained nothing by provoking its collapse. José Luis Rénique's study of Puno (2004) similarly shows that an alliance of peasant federations, government agents, leftist parties, Maryknoll priests, and civilians in the cites of Puno and Ayaviri managed to bring down the supercooperatives while at the same time preventing the forces of Shining Path from gaining much ground in that area.

The uncomfortable truth, however, is that an unspeakable cycle of violence did follow quite quickly after the military rules of Velasco and Morales Bermúdez. The incubation period of Shining Path took place during the eleven-year rule of the military and the insurgent group's first public act was to burn the ballot boxes in the village of Chuschi in the department of Ayacucho in 1980 upon the return to democracy. The Shining Path did start in Ayacucho, and it had a chance to recruit members when anti-Velasco sentiment boiled over in protests in the town of Huanta in 1969, only eight months after he took the government. The protests were against Velasco's decree that abolished free education. Students and teachers organized them, and Velasco's police repressed the movement with violence in both Huanta and the city of Ayacucho. Many teachers become bitter enemies of the military regime and some may have joined the *senderistas*. Later on, in the 1980s, the Vanguardia Revolucionaria (VR) party split into factions, provoking the defection of some members of the party who had helped sponsor the land takeover of haciendas in Andahuaylas in 1973–74. The dissenters were angry because their leaders, so they say, had capitulated and negotiated with the military, thus dampening the revolutionary potential the radicals thought they were nurturing among the peasants. The best-known convert to *senderismo* is Julio César Mezzich, who disappeared from sight and is presumed to be dead (Mallon 1998).

Tactical entanglements and local enmities did provoke a decade of violence in much of south-central Peru, notably the Ayacucho region (Kirk 1997; Theidon 2004; Comisión de la Verdad y Reconciliación 2004), and an unprecedented number of killings in the vicious, violent reactions by local Shining Path cadres against the very peasants who were supposed to be recruits for their glorious cause. The violence we witnessed initially appeared to many of us to be a Chinese import on the part of the Maoists, and a "dirty war" Chilean-Argentine import on the part of the military. Peasants and civilians were caught in the middle and suffered immensely—both simultaneously and subsequently; this suffering in itself also unleashed further unprecedented waves of locally generated violence among civilians. Why this happened is beyond the scope of this book, and neither Vargas Llosa's fictions nor Hugo Neira's and Pancho Guerra's comebacks help answer this question.

But there is a concrete example that every Peruvian needs to remember. The Quechua-speaking *comuneros* of Huaychao and Uchuraccay in Ayacucho, liberated from the hacienda of the same name by an act of the agrarian reform, acted in accordance with their *papá gobierno* (father government) in January 1983, violently killing Shining Path cadres when the latter came to the community to boss them around, take sheep from them, and give them orders not to attend the market or sell their goods because the Maoist revolution needed to starve the cities. They responded to violence perpetrated against them with courageous violence of their own instead of cowering in terror. Expecting retaliation, the next day the members of Uchuraccay then killed eight journalists (seeking to report on this act) by mistake, thinking that they were also guerrillas. That mistake cost the *comuneros* dearly because Peruvian society was aghast and scandalized. The Shining Path, the army, and civil society took revenge on Uchuraccay. It took the government and its armed forces six more years to recognize that its impoverished, illiterate, and inarticulate peasants were not Communists, but rather valuable allies capable of fighting the Maoists.

Nightmares and Dreams

Uchuraccay was a nightmare, and that nightmare hit Peruvian anthropologists the hardest because we were called to explain it. The debate that enmeshed anthropologists pro and con as to what had happened or how to understand it was nightmarish indeed. Carlos Iván Degregori, an anthropologist of my generation, spent many years in the University of Ayacucho combining teaching with political militancy. He moved to Lima to teach at San Marcos University and became the leading scholar on political violence in Peru and reviewing anthropological studies in Peru. In a history of our discipline, *No hay país más diverso: Compendio de antropología peruana*, he says that Marxist anthropology and essentialized "Andean" structuralist cultural anthropology went into total bankruptcy when faced with the political violence of the 1980s: "That bankruptcy had an emblematic name: Uchuraccay" (Degregori 2000, 47). Uchuraccay became my own nightmare as I, too, became aware that a cycle of violence had started in Peru. I spent an anguished year writing an article analyzing what had gone wrong in Peru that could provoke a situation like Uchuraccay in which I stated that "Peru is in deep trouble" (1992).

In the 1970s, economic and Marxist class analysis informed most of the studies of agrarian reform in Peru and its contemporary effects during those years. At that time it was a reasonable and interesting approach, as the notes that use and cite these works in the preceding chapters amply testify. However, there is something missing in those analyses: people as human beings who are sentient, rational and irrational at the same time, culture bound and seeking other horizons simultaneously; actors engaged in a process that involved their energies, their emotions, their passions, and basest instincts. Those aspects were absent in the copious statistical tables and indexes, photocopies, government reports, and Web downloads on the Peruvian agrarian reform that cluttered my study. And they did make arid reading matter. So when I came to conceive this book, after many a false start, I decided to focus on people. My method was to be testimony; my expedient resource, memories; the end result a collection of stories linked together with an overall theme of the agrarian reform. I hope that what was barren is now alive and populated.

I have already indicated in the preface that at certain moments the acts of remembering become like bad dreams, partly due to the intense reliving of emotional states, but also because dreams when remembered do have a narrative structure in which the "I" sees the "I" in the dream at once both dissociated from and tightly bound up in him- or herself. As in dreams, but yet differently, in the act of remembering an emotional bridge links the present with past events. But memory making, gathering remembrances through testimony, memorializing, memoir writing, poetry, theater, fiction writing, and historicizing touch on dreams only by association or reference. Without an emotive content, the memories lose their evocative power. Revolutions, because they are moments in which emotions run high, can be evoked years afterward.

Not all dreams are bad dreams, and dream as metaphor is also apposite in the study of agrarian reform because, as Martin Luther King realized so well, people have forward-looking dreams of better lives and the possibility of overcoming the oppressive conditions against which they struggle. No agrarian reform can exist without a dream of what it will be like in the future; no politician or technocrat can engage in a policy or program without an image of the future. Unfortunately, Velasco's technocratic utopia was bland, ill defined, and kitschy. In action, it fed more on revenge and hate than in the construction of a tomorrow of solidarity. Hugo Neira (1996, 432) remembers the "Velasco state as a cold monster, a philanthropic ogre" (the latter a paraphrase of Julio Cotler). Agrarian utopias and dreams of the future had been hatched long before by the messianic thinkers of the 1930s. Velasco's lieutenants only executed cold plans without emotional content or an imaginative vision of future things to come. Equally, Shining Path's leader, Abimael Guzmán, never did sketch out what the "state of a new democracy" would look like. Both were revolutions without humor, both fed on hate, and both defined class enemies.

Nostalgia

Paying attention to people's emotional states as they remember personal events has its dangers. Empathy may cloud the mind's eye with tears of sympathy. The intensity of the relived and shared emotion certainly lacks objectivity. The sheer volume of moving stories can lead to pathos or even worse to bathos. Melodrama is a well-liked genre in Latin America's *telenovelas*, but these endlessly repeat themselves because of the need to watch the actors cry. For me, the collector of memories, the emotional wallowing in each story became an impediment in dealing with them, sorting them, ordering them, or forgetting them. Emoting is addictive and I have spent ten years doing this as I tried to convert them to text.

Now that these stories go to the printer, a few words of caution are necessary. I follow Peruvian events while residing in the United States. I did live through the Velasco years and I do want to mention that this writing project has been tinged by my nostalgia and imagining what my life would have been like if I had not decided to pursue my academic career in the United States, but had stayed in Peru and lived through the tumultuous but dark decades that followed the general's regime. Am I nostalgic about the days of Velasco? No, I am nostalgic about "home" and for *ceviche*, just like any other emigrant.

The other point is that I have not written this book with the intent of setting off a fashionable retro revival to recycle Velasco's revolution as we approach its fortieth anniversary of the agrarian reform. Retro is a feature of consumerist culture. It periodically recycles past fashions, music, dance styles, or car designs. It is happening now with East Germany's nostalgic invocations of its Communist culture in the humor of films such as *Goodbye Lenin* (Becker 2003). In today's Venezuela of Hugo Chávez there are also many allusions in rhetoric, action, and culture to Latin American revolutions led by strong military *caudillos* — not only Bolívar, but I also can see where Chávez imitates Velasco. Because Velasco's revolution has been deliberately placed in the category of things best forgotten, I have in this book endeavored to bring it back to the consciousness of today's readers. But the caveat I want to stress is that in evoking the period, the good, the bad, and the ugly be equally represented. Velasco's regime has not yet been historicized and opinion continues to be sharply divided, and in Peru politicians tend to recycle as well. Beware!

The Last Story

Carlos Iván Degregori, as a member of the Peruvian Truth and Reconciliation Committee, heard many, too many, terrible testimonies. In Lima in December 2006, he told me this story:

> The war came to Umaru and Bellavista in the Río Pampas of Ayacucho in the 1980s. Sendero came, the army came, and both caused havoc. The Shining Path controlled the upper zones of the area, the army the lower zones, and the people of Umaru and Bellavista were caught in the middle. They did not know where to go, because if they did not go up to the liberated territories, Sendero would have pursued them, calling them "collaborators," *yana uma* (black heads). If they didn't go down toward the lowlands, the army would have treated them as *terrucos* (terrorists). The war there was terrible and the village was abandoned for many years.
>
> So, this is a story about a small family that, much like the sacred family of the Bible (but a couple with a little girl), flees from this horror, because no one was left in the village. When I did get back, what I saw was horrible, and I will not tell you about it, because it is too terrible. But the family fled, saying, "Let's go to Huamanga" (another name for Ayacucho).
>
> And when they got to Huamanga they did not know anyone, except the daughter of their ex-landowner. She was a progressive university professor and my friend. It was her mother who had been the *patrona*. She had long ceased to charge them rent or personal services. But this

was the only place the fleeing family knew in the city and they were received by the landowner's daughter. And there, although they were given protection, the fugitive family was treated with this strange mixture of humane treatment combined with social distance that separates mestizos from Indians.

And when I went to visit my friend the professor, I found the girl watching television (the family called their television set and refrigerator "agrarian reform" because they had bought them with the little money the government had given them upon expropriation). And it was the classic situation, the girl thought that there were little dolls and animals inside the television box and she kept going behind the set to try to discover how they were caged. But the moving aspect of the story is that the fleeing family had sought out their *patrona*, the *mamita*, of the old hacienda and they were given shelter without question.

AP	Acción Popular (Popular Action), a political party
APRA	Alianza Popular Revolucionaria Americana (American Popular Revolutionary Alliance), a political party
CAFTA	Central American Free Trade Association
CCP	Confederación Campesina del Perú (Peruvian Peasant Confederation), an antigovernment peasant league
CECOCAN	Central de Cooperativas Cañete (Centralized Cooperative of All Cooperatives in Cañete)
CEDEP	Centro de Estudios para el Desarrollo y la Participación (Center for the Study of Development and Participation), an NGO
CENCIRA– Holanda	Centro Nacional de Capacitación e Investigación para la Reforma Agraria (Research and Training Center for the Agrarian Reform–Holland), an international development project in support of agrarian reform
CEPES	Centro Peruano de Estudios Sociales (Peruvian Center for Social Studies), an NGO in Lima
CGTP	Confederación General de Trabajadores del Perú (General Workers Confederation), an anti-Velasco organization
CIDA	Comité Interamericano de Desarrollo Agrícola (Interamerican Committee for Agricultural Development), an intergovernmental organization
CNA	Confederación Nacional Agraria (National Agrarian Confederation), a pro-government peasant league
COAP	Comité de Asesoramiento de la Presidencia de la República (Presidential Advisory Committee)
COMACRA	Comité de Apoyo a la Reforma Agraria (Support Committee to Agrarian Reform), unit that took over expropriated land until adjudication
DESCO	Centro de Estudios y Promoción del Desarrollo (Center for the Study and Promotion of Development), Peruvian NGO and think tank
ESAN	Escuela de Administración de Negocios, Lima's business school
FARTAC	Federación Agraria Revolucionaria Túpac Amaru Cusco (Túpac Amaru Revolutionary Agrarian Federation, Cusco)

IAA	Instituto de Apoyo Agrario (Agrarian Support Institute), an NGO
IEP	Instituto de Estudios Peruanos (Institute of Peruvian Studies), a research institute
IU	Izquierda Unida (United Left), political coalition
IVITA	Instituto Veterinario de Investigaciones Tropicales y de Altura (Tropical and High Altitude Veterinary Research Institute)
MERCOSUR	Mercado Común del Sur (Southern Common Market); Brazil, Argentina, Uruguay, and Paraguay
MNR	Movimiento Nacionalista Revolucionario (Nationalist Revolutionary Movement), a political party in Bolivia
MRTA	Movimiento Revolucionario Túpac Amaru (Túpac Amaru Revolutionary Movement), a political party and armed guerrilla movement
MST	Movimento dos Trabalhadores Rurais Sem Terra (Rural Landless Worker Movement), a Brazilian organization
NAFTA	North American Free Trade Association
PCP(SL)	Partido Comunista del Perú Sendero Luminoso (Shining Path Communist Party of Peru), a political party and guerrilla organization
PCR	Partido Comunista Revolucionario (Revolutionary Communist Party), Maoist
PRODERM	Proyecto de Desarrollo Rural en Micro-Regiones (Micro-Regional Rural Development Project), in Cusco
PSR	Partido Socialista Revolucionario (Velasquista Party)
PUM	Partido Unificado Marxista (United Marxist Party)
SAIS	Sociedades Agrararias de Interés Social (Agrarian Societies of Social Interest); enterprises instituted by the agrarian reform
SEPIA	Seminario Permanente de Investigación Agraria (Permanent Seminar for Research on Agrarian Issues), an academic association in Peru
SINAMOS	Sistema Nacional de Movilización Social (National System for Social Mobilization), Velasco's top-down system of organizing political support
SNA	Sociedad Nacional Agraria (National Agrarian Society), a landowners' institution and lobby
TAFOS	Talleres de Fotografía Social (Social Photography Workshops), a project from 1986 to 1998 that provided local groups with cameras to capture images of their preferences, now housed at the Pontificia Universidad Católica del Perú
UCP	Unidad Campesino Popular (Popular Peasant Unity), Esteban Puma's local political party
UNRISD	United Nations Research Institute for Social Development
VR	Vanguardia Revolucionaria (Revolutionary Vanguard), a political party

Introduction

1. Note on interview translations and the use of names: I was not able to incorporate all of the material from the interviews into this book. Once transcribed, I went over the text, adding notes and clarifications or deleting irrelevant digressions. These were then sent to the interviewees for comment. Translating and incorporating oral text into a written narrative has its own difficulties. My aim was to convey the story, the emotional tone of the narration, and its dramatic potential. Translation is therefore free and selective, without altering the intent of the interviewee's communication with me. I have resorted in some instances to re-narrating what I was told, in others to selecting a particularly cogent part and using block quotes to highlight important points or to re-create remembered dialogues with others that my interviewees produced on tape. In writing, I paid a lot of attention to trying to present different voices without necessarily having to resort to verbatim texts. In each chapter I opted to vary the form in which I presented people's memories.

   Names in Peru follow the rule of having Christian or given names first, followed by the father's surname and then the mother's paternal surname, with the emphasis on the father's surname. In daily speech and in narration many speakers dispense with the full-names rule, focusing on the paternal surname as a common form (as with Velasco), using given names to indicate more intimacy (Juan), and relying on the complete double surname to sometimes express contempt (as in Juan Francisco Velasco Alvarado). The full name can also be used to pull rank by mentioning genealogical links to important ancestors, or in official and legal contexts (*nombre completo*). There are also nicknames as compressions of given names (Pancho for Francisco) or as funny and expressive monikers (as in el Chino Velasco). Having so many people named in this book made it difficult to avoid tedium in keeping the form consistent. Therefore, the main characters at the beginning of each chapter are introduced with full names, if known; later in the text, first names alternate with paternal surnames. The mother's surname appears alongside the paternal surname in cases where the latter is common, since the person interviewed presumably would have wished to keep her or his persona distinct. There are also a few double-barreled paternal surnames, notably that of president Francisco Morales Bermúdez Cerruti.

   Transcriptions in Spanish of the interviews are available at CEPES in Lima and at Yale University Library.

Agrarian Reforms

1. Velasco was an intense person. Friend and foe recognized his genius and no one doubted his sincerity. He exercised a personal authority and expected others to follow. His personal life was modest and private: he lived at home, commuted to the presidential palace, and spent the weekends with his family. He was mistrustful. Born in Piura in 1910 from a family of humble origins, he was at ease with people on a personal level, particularly with peasants, workers, and teachers who came to the palace to pay their respects, but stiff in formal situations and a poor public speaker. The best portrait of Velasco as a leader is in chapter 4 of Dirk Kruijt's *La revolución por decreto* (1989, 1994), an excellent study of a charismatic military dictatorship. Alfonso Baella Tuesta, a journalist and newspaper director who was a bitter opponent of Velasco, compiled *El poder invisible* (1976). This book, with press photos, newspaper clippings, personal accounts, and skilled writing, composed an extremely negative depiction of the regime and its leader, and became a favorite read for the anti-Velasco segments of Peruvian society (it earned the author his deportation). For the political atmosphere of Lima during Velasco's times there is no better work than Guillermo Thorndike's *No, mi general* (1976). Written like a novel, it is an account of Thorndike's year as director of *La Crónica*, one of the expropriated newspapers. The journalist María Pilar Tello, in *¿Golpe o revolución?* (1983), published her lengthy interviews with fourteen retired military officers associated with the regime. For social science perspectives on those times there is Alfred Stepan's, *The State and Society: Peru in Comparative Perspective* (1978), and the edited volumes *The Peruvian Experiment* (Lowenthal 1975) and *The Peruvian Experiment Reconsidered* (McClintock and Lowenthal 1983), to cite but a few.

2. Mariátegui was of utmost importance during the 1960s and 1970s. In the second of the seven essays in *7 ensayos de intrepretación de la realidad peruana* (1928), "El problema de la tierra" ("The Land Problem"), his points about agrarian structure are clear: The republican liberal regime did not, as it should have upon independence from Spain, liquidate feudalism (*latifundium* and indigenous servitude). Dividing land into small private property units, which should have been accomplished by the independent liberal state, was already passé during his time (1930s). The specificities of the Incan past gave the agrarian system a special character: "the survival of the community and elements of a practical socialism in agriculture and in the lives of the Indians" (1979, 32, my translation). Mariátegui extensively quoted from Castro Pozo's (1924, 1936) studies to bolster the hypothesis that the indigenous *ayllu* (the pre-Hispanic kinship and territorial units that continued into the twentieth century) was capable of transforming itself into a socialist cooperative. Mariátegui also pointed out that the coastal sugar and cotton *latifundium*, though capitalist, depended on imperialist desires for its products and did not resolve the problem of an adequate labor force or the food needs of the nation. This is the basic template that fueled ideological debate during the 1930s, when Mariátegui vigorously disputed with the APRA thinkers Haya de la Torre and Luis Alberto Sánchez about how to understand

the agrarian problem and the role that Indian communities could have in agrarian restructuring. During Velasco's times, debate about Mariátegui's role in characterizing Peruvian society was one of the most important ideological revivals fueled by the regime's own claim to be revolutionary (without a solid theoretical backing) and was vigorously disputed by those who claimed to be the authentic ones. It is also the period of flowering of a second generation of Peruvian Marxists who needed to refer to their founder. On this, the most serious and important scholarly work is that of the historian Alberto Flores Galindo, *La agonía de Mariátegui* (1991). Every leftist group, regardless of internal ideological disagreement, started with Mariátegui, even the Sendero Luminoso, whose call to arms was to follow the "Shining Path" that Mariátegui had indicated.

3. Since my student days I have valued these early accounts of conditions in highland haciendas. Moisés Sáenz was a Mexican intellectual sent to Peru to report on the conditions of the Indians in 1933. See the English translation, Sáenz (1944), 76:

> Feudalism still exists. Anco is a small town situated on the road between Mejorada and Ayacucho, inhabited by the workers of two haciendas adjacent to this town and merely separated by a street. I have never been so reminded of medieval times than in this place. It is quite archaic and monastic; all the people seem to belong to a brotherhood of serfs. We met one strapping young fellow who, in appearance, might have taken the part of Manelich in Tierra baja [a play written in 1897 by the Catalán author Angel Guimera] to perfection. We enquired about his occupation; he could barely speak to us, but a woman told us in Quechua that he was a trusted worker of his master. "How much does he earn?" we asked her. "He does not earn anything," she answered. "His parents were also in the service of the master . . ." On the road we met an Indian who was walking with his daughter, a girl of some twenty years. Her hat was covered with yellow flowers which she had cut along the road; she looked like a shepherdess of the Middle Ages. We asked them from what town they came and they answered, "We belong to Guillermo Pacheco." This gentleman, the owner of people, is the owner of the Llaccria estate; his servants according to this, know to whom they belong, but not where they live. (1944, 76)

> Moisés Poblete Troncoso was commissioned by the International Labor Organization to report on working conditions of Peruvian Indians. His report, *Condiciones de vida y de trabajo de la población indígena del Perú* (1938) is a cold indictment in that he described the conditions under which Indians worked next to a long list of which laws in the civil code were being violated. The contradiction between the widespread practice of exploitation in the face of benevolent or protective legislation that no one enforces has always fascinated me. His recommendation was more legislation!

4. Solon Barraclough (1922–2002), an American economist, was the intellectual activist behind the movement for agrarian reforms in Latin America. Barraclough was an ardent New Dealer educated at Harvard who soon ran afoul for his equal-opportunity efforts in the forestry department of the state of Tennessee. In 1961 he was in Chile

working for the United Nation's Food and Agriculture Organization (FAO). Behind the scenes he masterminded the high priority that the Alliance for Progress program gave to agrarian reforms at the Punta del Este Conference, to which all Latin American governments gave their reluctant support. According to Richard Gott, writing his obituary, under Barraclough's direction the detailed CIDA studies of the land tenure situation in half a dozen Latin American countries "are now recognized as perhaps the most significant and valuable piece of socio-economic investigation in Latin America in the 20th Century. Without Barraclough's visionary insistence on research as a key to subsequent action, in the teeth of opposition on the ground and within the FAO bureaucracy, these studies would have never got off the ground" (Gott 2002, 2). He had also collaborated closely with Eduardo Frei's government in Chile, which started an agrarian reform that continued with Salvador Allende's administration. With the coup by Pinochet, the reform was reversed, land returned to its owners, and the institute closed. Barraclough then settled in Geneva, where he became director of UNRISD (United Nations Research Institute for Social Development). The article he wrote with Arthur Domike, "Agrarian Structure in Seven Latin American Countries" (1964), is key because it set out the argument for the desirability and feasibility of agrarian reforms.

5. With the benefit of hindsight, the comparison between the laws and implementations of Belaúnde's government and those of Velasco bring out certain ironies. On the one hand, many of my interviewees looked back remorsefully, thinking that perhaps the "milder" laws of Belaúnde would have been better than the "drastic" ones of Velasco. On the other hand, the Belaúnde regime was slow and superficial in implementing its program, while the Velasco regime was bent on action, on widespread expropriation, speedy adjudication, and prompt attention to production. Velasco's actions lacked a clear legal framework, and the regime modified and changed the laws as circumstances dictated. Perhaps it could have been a better agrarian reform if the Belaúnde law had been applied with the zeal of Velasco's army. Excellent comparisons of the two agrarian reforms are in Susana Lastarria-Cornhiel's essay "Agrarian Reforms of the 1960s and 1970s in Peru" (1989) and José María Caballero's aptly titled *From Belaúnde to Belaúnde* (1981b).

6. The radicalization of the agrarian reform law was the first action that the inner circle of Velasco's radical military and civilian advisors imposed on the more reluctant and traditional military men. A blow-by-blow account of how this was accomplished is in chapter 2 of Peter Cleaves and Martin Scurrah's *Agriculture, Bureaucracy and Military Government in Peru* (1980). The junta had at first appointed as minister of agriculture General José Benavides, the son of a military president and a relative of landowners. He convened a commission to rewrite the agrarian law. However, a group of civilian advisors, among them Benjamín Samanez and Guillermo Figallo—later to become key figures in the whole process—voiced their concerns about the watering down of the new laws to some military men close to Velasco. These generals, with the president's knowledge, then hatched a plot to undermine Benavides. His drafted law was rejected in a tense meeting of the council of ministers, and an

agreement that a new one be drafted under the supervision of the COAP (Comité de Asesoramiento de la Presidencia de la República) was accepted. The COAP was the most important policy-setting instrument of the regime and was made up of radical officers of the military close to Velasco, together with civilian advisors who were recruited on an ad hoc basis. While the new law was taking shape behind closed doors, Benavides was forced to resign. The new law was so secret that those who wrote it did not leave the presidential palace until it was approved in a tense meeting of the council of ministers that lasted through the night of June 23, 1969, the same day that Velasco unveiled it. The reason for the secrecy was the possible opposition from the Sociedad Nacional Agraria (SNA), at that time a powerful agricultural lobby capable of exerting pressure in policymaking, especially through relatives of military men. The government shut it down in 1972.

7. Post-reform evaluations of the agrarian reform come with numbers, each one with a number of years since the agrarian reform.

Seven years: Mariano Valderrama's *7 años de reforma agraria* (1976) stems from a seminar led by the sociologist at the Catholic University, with students collecting materials. In it, the early years and the conflicts that the process generated are analyzed and subdivided into phases and periods. Most useful is a year-by-year chronology. It describes the difficulties in setting up collective forms of production, landowners' initial resistance against expropriation, the mistrust of cooperative members, peasant protests, and the efforts by the state to consolidate the process.

Ten years: Edited by an institution, the CIC or Centro de Investigación y Capacitación, *Realidad del campo peruano después de la reforma agraria* (1980) contains the proceedings of a conference with ten participants. Extremely thoughtful and contextual, it nonetheless is very negative in its evaluation of the preceding military government's policies. The focus is on how misconceptions about preexisting conditions in the countryside twisted the agrarian reform process in the wrong directions, and how the reform was a failure incapable of achieving the goals set for it.

Twenty years: Edited by Angel Fernández and Alberto Gonzales, *La reforma agraria peruana, 20 años después* (1990) is also a symposium. Despite the figures and facts presented about the dissolution of all forms of collective production that by then had taken place, the editors tried to imprint a positive review of what had been accomplished and what could not have been done.

Thirty-seven years: Edited by Fernando Eguren (2006b), *Reforma agraria y desarrollo rural en la región andina* brought together specialists from the six Andean countries for a comparison. Eguren's (2006a) essay on Peru lists negative and positive consequences of the Peruvian case, and the lessons learned—among them, that one cannot impose cooperative forms from above.

There are, of course, innumerable other individual scholarly works and symposia that deal with the agrarian reform as it unfolded and disintegrated. To give some sense of their disciplinary area, content, regional character, and chronological and intellectual ordering is beyond the scope of this work. Below is a brief listing of general works I have regularly used in addition to the ones cited in the text. *As-*

pectos cuantitativos de la reforma agraria (1969–1979) by José María Caballero and Elena Alvarez (1980) is a pocket book with essential statistics. *La reforma agraria en el Perú* by José Matos Mar and Manuel Mejía (1980) rambles and oscillates from case studies to generalizations. Héctor Martínez Arellano's *Reforma agraria peruana: Las empresas asociativas altoandinas* (1990) is informed by his access to data in the Agrarian Reform Inspectorate where he worked, and it approaches the reform from the government's failure to make the institutions it implemented function properly. In English, apart from the works by Susana Lastarria-Cornhiel and José María Caballero already cited, Douglas Horton's *Haciendas and Cooperatives: A Study of Estate Organization, Land Reform and New Reform Enterprises* (1976) is an early survey of cooperatives and a frequently cited masterpiece. Peru's reform in context of other Latin American agrarian reforms is in Alain de Janvri's *The Agrarian Question and Reformism in Latin America* (1981). The University of Wisconsin's Land Tenure Center has been, for the past three decades, the main monitor of land reforms in Latin America. Studies sponsored by the center include Peter Dorner's *Latin American Land Reforms in Theory and Practice* (1992) and William Thiesenhusen's *Searching for Agrarian Reform in Latin America* (1989). The two-volume *Agrarian Reform in Latin America: An Annotated Bibliography* (1974) is a guide to a treasure trove of collected documents, journalistic accounts, monographs, pamphlets, and legislation. In Europe, there is the exiled Chilean scholar Cristóbal Kay's *The Complex Legacy of Latin America's Agrarian Reform* (1997), and for a comparison in world terms, David Lehmann's *Agrarian Reform and Agrarian Reformism: Studies of Peru, Chile, China and India* (1974) provides a different perspective. In the chapters that follow, other works are cited as appropriate.

8. State capitalism and state-sponsored cooperatives were different. The military regime expropriated oil, mining, fishing industries, transportation, banks, and the press; it created many state enterprises and marketing boards that were under direct control of the central government. The agrarian cooperatives and SAISes, though supervised and controlled, were nonetheless deemed to be autonomous civilian enterprises. It is true that nationalization and cooperativization did provide employment and power to the "new" middle class to which Ricardo Letts refers (1981). See Saulniers 1988, Fitzgerald 1976, and Thorp and Bertram 1978 for the overall economic policies.

9. The capture of Abimael Guzmán and the rescue of the hostages in the Japanese embassy were dramatic events that inspired two novels in English: Nicolas Shakespeare's *The Dancer Upstairs* (1995), also a film directed by John Malkovich (2003), and Ann Patchett's exploration of the notion of the Stockholm syndrome in *Bel Canto* (2001), inspired by the shock the hostages felt after special troops killed all the young guerrillas. Peruvian authors are now tinkering with thrillers that refer to the period of violence; see, for example, Santiago Roncagiolo's *Abril rojo* (2006), and Mario Vargas Llosa's *Lituma en los Andes* (1993) in the same vein.

10. In contrast to all other cooperatives, the members of the sugar cooperatives have refused to dissolve them and have been forced to privatize. Because of the unresolvable difficulties in which they find themselves, they are an embarrassment for those

who have pro-agrarian reform positions, and a boon to those who want to paint the reform in negative terms. Scholarly work on the crisis of the sugar cooperatives is scarce. Manuel Mejía became an advocate for their privatization in *Cooperativas azucareras: Crisis y alternativas* (1992); see also a defensive posture by Jorge Oroza in "Los problemas de gestión de las cooperativas azucareras y sus planteamientos de solución" (1990). Orlando Velásquez Benítez's *Reto final del agro azucarero peruano* (1998) is more of a historical ethnography of eight agro-industrial complexes. Symptomatically, while *limeño* and foreign scholars have looked away, the latter two works are by local professionals. It looks like no one wants to pick up the shattered pieces, but when they were being set up, national and international interest in the sugar cooperatives was intense. I confess that I too found it impossible to shape my interviews in the ex-cooperatives into a chapter for this book.

11. Intellectuals of SINAMOS reviewed the regime in a three-volume retrospective, edited by Carlos Franco. In *El Perú de Velasco* (1983) Francisco Guerra among fiteeen other collaborators spell out their case on how Velasco's regime should be seen as a transition from an oligarchic state to a process that laid the foundations of a national state. CEDEP also edits an extraordinary journal, *Socialismo y participación*, an invaluable source of debates and high-quality scholarly work.

Heroes and Antiheroes

1. There is a recurring theme of good Indian peasants fighting abusive gamonales in literature. In a recent novel, *Babilonia la grande* (1999), the social scientist Oscar Ugarteche used the reform as background. One of the characters, dissatisfied with social life in Lima, traveled to Ayacucho, where she was told one story after another of abuses by gamonales, which stirred her social sentiments so that she later became a militant with Shining Path. Classic indigenista novels from Peru include Clorinda Matto de Turner's *Aves sin nido* (1973), Ciro Alegría's *El mundo es ancho y ajeno* (1941), and José María Arguedas's *Yawar fiesta* (1941), *Todas las sangres* (1964), and a fantastic fable called *Temblar: El sueño del pongo* (1976).

Artistic treatment of the Velasco reform is very scarce. *Alpa Rayku*, a theatrical production by the prize-winning Grupo Cultural Yuyachkani (1983) about hacienda occupations, staged how peasant committees ran their own affairs after they took over fifty haciendas in Andahuyalas and it was not appreciated by officialdom. Based on the theatrical techniques of consciousness raising by the Brazilian Augusto Boal, the play included other ways of memory making in the form of songs, dances, and skits that celebrated the peasants' victory over the landlords and over the Velasco government, which repressed the movement. The performance was used to strengthen the spirit of antigovernment resistance in land occupations. A recurring image in people's memory that I was often told, that humane peasant women persuaded the hacendados to leave because their lives were in danger, is part of the performance. Although friendly, the admonition was carried out in a humiliating way by mounting the owner on a burro to speed his departure. There are a few songs composed during those days that mixed traditional tunes and verse with political content. Here is one that Rodrigo Montoya and his brothers Luis and Edwin (1987, 665–67) collected (Quechua and Spanish versions, the English one is mine) in Andahuaylas of those times:

Kay Peru Naciumpi (Carnaval de Tancayllo)	En Esta Nación Peruana	In This Peruvian Nation
1	1	1
Kay Peru naciunpi hambre y miseria *manana tukuq*	En esta nación peruana el hambre y la miseria no se terminaban	In this Peruvian nation hunger and misery had no end
2	2	2
Ay, *qaykakamaraq* *wakchalla kasun* pubri*lla kasun* *kay Peru naciumpi*	¡Ay! hasta cuándo seremos pobres y huérfanos en esta nación peruana	Oh! Until when shall we be poor and orphans In this Peruvian nation
3	3	3
Campesinu *runa* *hatarillasunña* vamos a la lucha	Hombres campesinos levántemonos vamos a la lucha	*Campesino* men let us rise let us struggle
4	4	4
Ay *qaykakamaraq* *wakchalla kasun* *gamonalista* sirvi*spa*	¡Ay! hasta cuándo seremos pobres sirviendo a los gamonales	Oh! until when shall we poor be serving the *gamonales*
5	5	5
Lima capital*pis* cojo Velasco llapan llaqtapi, sinamos	En Lima, la capital, el cojo Velasco; en todos los pueblos, Sinamos	In Lima, the capital, limping Velasco in all the towns, *sinamos*
6	6	6
Dulces palabras negra conciencia *Wakcha runata* engañan	Dulces palabras negra conciencia ¡Cómo engañan a los pobres!	Sweet words black conscience deceive poor people
7	7	7
Campesino, obrero alianza*kusunchic* Vamos a la lucha	Campesinos y obreros hagamos una alianza, vamos a la lucha	*Campesinos* and workers let us forge an alliance let us go to the struggle
8	8	8
Vamos a la lucha Definitiva hasta alcanzar nuestra liberación	Vamos a la lucha definitiva hasta alcanzar nuestra liberación	Let us go to definitive struggle until we achieve our liberation

A recent fictional account of the reform by the anthropologist Rodrigo Montoya, *El tiempo del descanso* (1997), used a strange case in which a landlord father and son of the Alencastre family were both murdered in separate Indian uprisings on the very same hacienda, El Descanso in Cusco. The roman à clef interweaves the period of 1921 to 1932 with the early 1980s, narrating the struggles of the Indians to open up markets and schools, and to resist the landowners in the earlier rebellion against Andrés Alencastre, with post-agrarian reform attempts by the second landlord (Gustavo Alencastre) to return to his hacienda. Written as an internal stream of consciousness, it allows the cast of characters to express (and the author to compress) their feelings of rage and hate of their landlords in the case of the Indians, and overbearing haughtiness in the case of the landlords. Thus, it is another variant of a good guys-versus-bad guys indigenista narrative. In the novel, hacendado father and son, apart from their self-interest in the total control over land and the hacienda people, are obsessed with raping young Indian virgins (a manifestation of the sometimes alleged right of Peruvian hacendados to the derecho de pernada [jus primae noctis], for which they got their just desserts in the end). Why, in real life, Gustavo Alencastre (also a Quechua poet and professor with leftist leanings at the university in Cusco) was brutally murdered by his compadre from the ex-hacienda has not been clearly established

2. *Kuntur Wachana* won three prizes: a prize from the FIPRESCI (Fédération Internationale de la Presse Cinématographique), awarded at the Moscow film festival in 1977; a prize from the World Council of Peace, also awarded in Moscow in 1977; and another prize at the Benalmádena Festival in 1977. Federico García Hurtado has an amusing anecdote about how he got the Moscow prizes. Anti-communist elements in the Peruvian government had attempted to block his submission of the film to the Moscow festival. When he tried to board the Aeroflot airplane in Lima en route to Moscow, he was detained and told that he had no permission to leave the country. His absence was noticed only in Havana, where the plane stopped for refueling, because a journalist who had witnessed García's detention had sent a cable. The Peruvian general who was heading the delegation phoned Lima and found out that a group of navy officers were intent on preventing the film's submission to the festival. But García had previously sent a copy of the film from Buenos Aires. There was no point in preventing his attendance. Nonetheless, insistent back-and-forth phone negotiations between generals and navy admirals were necessary to allow García to travel to Moscow on the next plane, where he was received with a bottle of vodka and advance publicity that may have positively influenced the awards.

3. García remembers with pleasure how he and his companion, Pilar, persuaded the famous musician to arrange the music for the film:

> We had finished the film but had no music and we had no money. We heard that the famous Peruvian composer Celso Garrido Lecca had just returned from a sojourn in Allende's Chile, and Pilar and I went to talk to him. He responded that he did music for films, but that he was an expensive composer. We told him that we had not one penny, but begged him to at least see the film and afterward we would talk. We took him to the lab, and I narrated the events as the soundless images were rolling on the screen. By the time the first part of the film had ended, Garrido was in tears. He said, 'Look here García. I am going to provide the music and the performers, and I will charge you nothing. Wrong, I will charge you one *sol!*"

4. An early organizer of peasant unions was Emiliano Huamantinca. Born to a mestizo family in Cusco, he appeared to Hugo Neira with his small mustache as if he could have been a traveling salesman, a mayor of a small town, or an anonymous school-

teacher. He was a textile worker and a union leader, a "member of the indigenous and mestizo politicized plebeian masses from which he himself had emerged" (Neira 1964, 14, my translation). Huamantinca built up the strategy to support mobilization on haciendas and provided them with legal aid. He died in 1963 in a bus accident as he traveled to attend a union conference.

5. The prophetic role that García gave to Huilca was intentional. I questioned García Hurtado about why he had chosen to portray Huilca in this fashion. He responded by assuring me that, in his opinion, Huilca was a high-ranking *misayoq* (a shaman) in the clandestine priesthood of Andean Indians of the Cusco region. Not only was he a practical organizer as is portrayed in the Neira version, but he was also a native prophetic sage. "I was a friend of Huilca's for many years, and, during the filming, he taught me a lot. The dialogue between Quispe and Huilca that appears in the film came from the very beautiful things he said. I remembered them and put them in the film." To reproduce Huilca's words was not easy, because the sound had to be dubbed onto the edited film. Neither Huilca nor the person who acted as Quispe knew Spanish, nor could either one read, and to remember exact dialogue lines was something totally outside their experience. The director remembers how he did it. "I took Huilca to my home in Cusco and placed the tape recorder where we had previously recorded improvised speech from him in front of him and told him to memorize exactly what he had said into the recorder. I said to Huilca, 'You will have to say exactly the same thing when we will go to the laboratory.'"

6. There is debate as to whether haciendas were feudal or capitalist institutions. An important distinction that was introduced by Eric Wolf and Sydney Mintz (1955) between the "plantation" economy of a modern capitalist rural enterprise found in Peru largely on the coast that produced export crops with a proletarian labor force and the "traditional" feudal hacienda of the highlands, such as those in the Cusco region, sets the stage for this debate. Henri Favre provided a succinct definition of the feudal hacienda: "A system of agricultural production and social relationships in which a stable population (of peons) is bound to the *patrón* or his representative by a series of personal obligations—actual or symbolic—which keeps him in a state of virtual servitude, or at least in a primitive state of dependency" (1967, 105, my translation).

Feudal aspects were shown in the social organization inside the hacienda based on the personal relationship between the *patrón* and the worker. Dutiful paternalism on the part of the owner was countered by respectful obedience on the part of the serf. When the unwritten rules were breached, an offense was committed by the worker, and he was punished by the *patrón*. Nevertheless, the relationship between the two of them continued. Therefore, the way to enforce discipline varied from case to case, and so did the punishment; conversely, there was no standardized procedure to deal with particularly recurring offenses. Punishment was short lived and tended to try to restore the status quo by enacting repentance and forgiveness performances at the end of each incident. Therefore, punishment was often corporal and violent, arbitrary, and terrorizing, to serve as an example to others. Under this system, landlords had little interest in using the laws of the nation and its judicial institutions, and ignored them with impunity. Hence the closed, arbitrary, authoritarian system that also enforced servile behavior on the part of the Indians had a distinct "feudal" odor, which was roundly denounced. Reform movements sought to de-feudalize the hacienda by insisting that universally applicable national laws also be valid inside it. On the other hand, *hacendados* defended themselves with rational, "capitalist" legal arguments. The hacienda was considered private property, and any threat was an unconstitutional attack against this. The landlords cast the unpaid labor obligations as perfectly legal rental agreements in which the right to the subsistence plot was to be paid in kind rather than in cash. In the Convención Valley, these often took the form of legally enforceable contractual agreements. Eric Hobsbawm, who traveled in the area during the reform period, called the system "neo-feudalism" (1969: 48), comparable to the European Middle Ages. "Landlords were essentially parasitic on their serfs . . . they had no incentive to improve productivity, they relied on powers of non-economic coercion. . . . and they were wasteful of manpower" (1969: 46–47) despite the fact that the region as a pioneer area had abundant land, scarce population, and a very poor transportation system.

By the 1960s, the system was in serious decline, questioned on ideological grounds, and disputed from below by peasants and their allies. The particular conditions in the Convención Valley accelerated its demise through the rapid growth of commercial agriculture in which the settler peasants soon could outproduce the landlord, and their interests did not only concern wages but producing and selling their own crop. By the time the movement became important, sociologist Eduardo Fioravanti points out, a real rural proletariat (both permanent and temporary) had inundated the region working for landlords, settlers, and subsettlers alike for miserable wages. Thus, even before the formation of unions, Fioravanti insists *contra* Hobsbawm, the "dominant mode of production was capitalist due to the character of the productive forces, to its linkage to national and international commodity markets, and for the existence of capitalist production relationships (paid wage workers). Those precapitalist relationships that still survived did not determine the agrarian social structure, but only created certain obstacles to the development of 'agrarian capitalism' that the unionization movement was able to break" (1974, 219, my translation).

7. Alfredo Romainville was known by the nickname "the monster of the Convención Valley." "Victims of his cruelty were the settlers Melquiades Bocangel, Cirilo Guzmán, Hernando Villena (who was maimed) and numerous women raped by him and his brothers. Andres González, Oscar Quiñones, and Constantino Gordillo, among others, spent many years in jail for organizing unions, because the owner together with this lawyer friends prepared the judicial proceedings in the courts of Cusco to keep them there" (Villanueva 1967, 30, my translation).

Hugo Blanco's portrayal of landlords as the bad guys against whom he crusaded is closely paralleled in the film as well:

Another example was the hacienda bordering Paltaybamba, Santa Rosa de Chaupimayo, the seat of my union. There the *gamonal* Alfredo Romainville strung up a naked peasant to a mango tree and, among other things, flogged him all day in the presence of his own daughters and other peasants. Another peasant could not find the horse his master had told him to find. Romainville forced him down on all fours, ordered him to put on the horse's harness, and compelled him to haul six *arrobas* (150 pounds) of coffee; he made him travel in this fashion, on hands and knees, around the patio where the coffee was dried, lashing him with his whip. (Blanco 1972a, 94)

8. Hugo Neira's book *Cuzco: Tierra y muerte* (1964) was based on actual reporting in the Cusco area in 1964. Written in a very lively style, with short chapters culled from a selection of his daily press reports and illustrated with excellent photographs, it depicted all sides of the conflict. It is an outstanding vivid document of those times, worthy of resuscitation. Neira became an enthusiastic supporter of the peasant movements as a result of his investigative reporting, and he contributed greatly to an understanding of the social and political causes of the land invasions taking place at that time. A second edition of his book, *Los Andes: Tierra o muerte* (1968), was expanded to include background and comparative information to make it accessible to a broader Latin American readership. A fourth edition of the original from 1968 appears with a new introduction in Neira 2008.

9. Regarding the symbolic power of *fútbol*, I asked Federico García Hurtado if he had intentionally used the soccer match because of its powerful symbolism. He responded that it served him to structure a dramatic sequence to the story because the game paired the contestants. To my comment that it was a stacked match with intentional foul play, he agreed that that too could be interpreted as a portentous message. But, he said, its primary force was because it was a real story known and commented upon all over the region. It had become a myth, and García just gave it dramatic potency.

10. Regarding the first notification of expropriation, Adriel Villena, the director of expropriation in the Agrarian Reform Office in Cusco, recalled, "I sent one of my functionaries to Huarán, and Marta Fernández threw him out."

11. Real life is more prosaic than cinematography. Mario Herrera, the leader in Huarán and later the author of an anthropological dissertation about Huarán (1994), writes that the takeover was as follows:

> During the night, a spy climbed a cypress tree that grew in the patio of the hacienda house to observe the landlord's movements (having previously silenced his dogs), because of a rumor that he had acquired arms from a cousin who was in the army. The spy was instructed to give an appropriate signal when everything was safe. In the morning, the landlord emerged from his rooms, walked past the room with the guns, and entered his pantry to get maize for his chickens. The daughter also came out and went directly to the kitchen to give orders to the cooks and then joined her father in the chicken coop. It was then that the signal was given, and the people entered the hacienda compound and surrounded them both. Initially, the landlord tried to get to his room where the arms were, but the

group that had been entrusted to secure it prevented anyone from entering it. Father and daughter were surrounded by peasants shouting, "Long live Zúñiga Letona!" The landlord became aggressive, and some peasants were motivated to take justice into their own hands, but the actions of others in the group prevented any excesses from being committed. Persons loyal to the landlord made it to the police station in Urubamba to get help. Meanwhile, SINAMOS officials in Cusco had also been notified by representatives of the peasants. Upon hearing the news, they could barely suppress their pleasure. They speedily sent a commission headed by a general to Huarán. The police arrived around noon and ordered the people to release Mr. Fernández and to leave the place within ten minutes. The leadership persuaded the police officers to wait until higher authorities would arrive. When they came, the police were told to desist. The outranked police officer interpreted the orders of the army general as an offense against his institution, but he nonetheless obeyed. (1994, 96, my translation)

12. Among those who made *cine campesino*, the Bolivian film director Jorge Sanginés is best known for his *Yawar Mallku* (Blood of the Condor) (1969), which is often shown in the United States. With Cuban support, Federico García Hurtado went on to make two more *campesino*-based films in which local people reenacted past events playing themselves. Some actors from Huarán also participated in these. *Laulico* (García Hurtado 1980), following Hobsbawm's (1963) concept of "primitive rebels," was about cattle thievery and the violent expulsion of the landlord of Fuerabamba in the department of Apurimac. It was criticized for the clumsy use of Andean mythology as a device to construct a retrograde vision of a simplistic, redeemed, primordial Andean past. Bedoya critiques the "primitive collectivism" that García's film evokes as "[a] collectivism that harks more to Eden and to origins than to the historical" (1992, 216). The other film, *El Caso Huayanay* (García Hurtado 1981), was also about communal vigilante action in the department of Huancavelica. In this case, the members of a community killed a violent social outcast whose connections with *gamonales* and the judicial system had twice freed him from jail. An epic version of *Túpac Amaru* (García Hurtado 1984) was, for the critic Bedoya, García's least successful film. A "secular hagiography" (Bedoya 1992, 225, my translation) of Peru's revolutionary saint," the scenes concentrated on solemn moments full of pathos in which the overacted hero had to enounce decisive phrases for viewers to memorize as if they were schoolchildren" (Bedoya 1997, 254). García himself, however, considers *Túpac Amaru* his most successful film and the one that made the most money, though he loves *Kuntur Wachana* more because it was his first feature film. The genre shared an ideological interest in unmasking the myth of idyllic life in rural areas, and using local people to film their own stories.

13. Huilca's conciliatory words dubbed onto footage from the documentary are translated: "New cooperatives are born and there is prosperity in the communities. I give faith as an old revolutionary that I have been given the privilege to see the new era, and in my heart there is no more place for hatred."

14. Other film treatments of agrarian issues include the feature film *La muralla verde*

(1970) by the talented director Armando Robles Godoy, which began in an optimistic tone about the virtues of pioneer agricultural colonizing in the jungles by an idealistic urban bureaucrat whose adventure later ended in personal grief, in part due to bureaucratic bungling. A second film, *Espejismo* (1973), was a more lyrical film that exploited the love theme between the *hacendado*'s daughter and one of the workers on the hacienda, an impossible crossing of social boundaries that was replicated in the friendship between the landlord's lonely son and the talented soccer-playing son of a worker.

15. Zúñiga was active in the Convención Valley after 1970. Eduardo Fioravanti both acknowledges Zúñiga's help in his research and dedicates the book to his memory.

16. The collectivist mystique of Huarán's early leadership was insightfully discussed by Herrera in his dissertation:

> These young men began their work with a socialist mysticism and an effort to implement a collective utopia in Huarán to make it a model of Peruvian socialism. It was easy, because most of them were single. They moved into the hacienda house, where they had the privilege of participating in communal life organized there. They had access to more resources than they could ever have hoped for in their own homes: free food and lodging, handsome salaries, and pleasant female companionship. The utopia lasted for about two years. Then the cadres began to marry and to think about forming their own homes. (1994, 132, my translation)

17. Marta Fernández was interviewed by Roland Anrup in 1978 and 1979 for his book *El taita y el toro* (1990, 103–11). She describes how her father and she had attempted to modernize the hacienda by becoming more strict, in accordance with capitalist rationale, and thereby generated more resentment for breaking with older social agreements. For example, they introduced an eight-hour work day, cash payment for use of pasturage, the use of written contracts, and so on. Anrup published the letters that Marta was sent by a "revolutionary committee" in 1960 threatening their lives and accusing them of expelling their serfs, an injustice also dramatized in *Kuntur Wachana*.

Landowners

1. Fictional accounts of life on a hacienda in memoir form include Miguel Gutierrez's *La violencia del tiempo* (1991), set in Piura and Lima, which reconstructs the doings of the Villar outlaws in three volumes. Haciendas figure prominently and the novel drips with resentment. Edgardo Rivera Martínez, in *País de Jauja* (1993), is far more gentle and evocative of the life of a young, poor son of a seamstress who sees the sad life of hacienda owners from a (social) distance. Laura Riesco's *Ximena de dos caminos* (1994) is an evocation of childhood spent in the mining camp off La Oroya as a middle-class daughter of an employee, and it includes episodes on haciendas of relatives in Tarma. In the Chilean novelist Isabel Allende's *La casa de los espíritus* (1983), agrarian conflict and forbidden love across social classes is one of the threads in the family saga. The farcical antics of an eccentric grandfather (an angry expropriated *hacendado*) form part of a caricature of Lima's middle classes in Jaime Bayly's

Los últimos días de La Prensa (1996). These writers are very different from the earlier *indigenista* genre.

2. *Gamonales* are alive and well in the Provincias Altas of Cusco. According to Deborah Poole (1988, 1994), the swaggering symbolic power styles of the Chumbivilcas *gamonales* are still admired in contemporary southern Peru. One characteristic was their refusal to bow to constituted state authority. When bands of *gamonales* openly defied state representatives, they gained local popularity. Smart craftiness was imputed to legendary cattle rustlers whose intrepid raids were gleefully retold with local pride. Intellectuals in Cusco wrote about these tales and thus created a positive image for the characterization of *chumbivilcanos* as fiercely autonomous, a regional identity that supposedly melds Indian fierceness with male *gamonal* bravado. Bolstering the myth of the *chumbivilcano* "cowboy" are the well-attended bullfights and rodeos celebrated in the region. Here *machismo* is demonstrated by facing not one but many bulls in the ring, with the accolades for valor going to those who actually get gored. These bloody festivals have gained legitimacy through contemporary state-sponsored educational and cultural institutions, under the rubric of folklore, celebrating cultural authenticity. Poole contends that even without their lands, *gamonales'* domination continues in many parts of remote *puna* land in southern Peru.

3. Landlords often pretended to be peasants in their arguments before expropriators in attempts to retain their lands. Linda Seligmann in *Between Reform and Revolution* states that "one of the most common stances they took was to present themselves as marginalized peasants to invoke the principle of reciprocity in their negotiations with peasants. In presenting themselves as peasants, they drew upon multiple images of peasants—prominently including the figure of the peasant [and themselves as well] as a downtrodden, uncivilized being who, once given the appropriate economic resources and education, could become a respectable Peruvian citizen, which coincided with the image promoted by the Velasco regime" (1995, 93).

4. Landlords in the highlands knew that personal service and unpaid labor had long ago been declared illegal, but compliance with expensive labor legislation would have caused them to go broke long before the reform. Therefore, retroactive collection of Social Security debts was regarded as a particularly punitive measure to reduce cash compensations. In many cases bribes were paid to "fix" this particular problem. I doubt that the highland workers ever received the severance pay or pensions the government collected.

5. *El taita y el toro* (1990) by Roland Anrup is an excellent study of the deep cultural and psychological structures of the patriarchal configuration of the old hacienda system. It combines historical and literary sources, particularly José María Arguedas, fieldwork, and interviews with serfs and many ex-landlords. Theoretically, Anrup imbues this particular topic with Freudian totemic parricide, Bakhtinian carnival, and a Lacanian deconstructionist psychological approach. "According to my interpretation when peasants kill and eat a breeding bull they are demonstrating their affective ambivalence towards the *hacendado*, their hate and respect for him, their desire to kill him, to eliminate him, to liberate themselves from his tyrannical power.

Once eliminated, it is possible to be like him, to replace him, to acquire his force and his potency" (1990, 229; my translation). The impotent fury of the ex-*hacendado* in retelling this story implies that the deposed patriarch shares this interpretation. The Shining Path's destructions of experimental breeding cattle at the University of Ayacucho in Alpachaca and the government camelid breeding station in La Raya in Cusco-Puno, and the subsequent distribution of the stock for meat to the peasants, may have partaken of this interpretation (see also chapter 6).

6. Zózimo Torres circulated in academic circles in Lima in the late 1990s, talking in an anguished way about how the Huando cooperative had collapsed and blaming himself quite a bit. This memoir is in a chronicler's style, with each short chapter presented as a visit to Charlotte Burenius in order to provide continuity to the story. Charlotte has a description of Huando from the landlord's family's point of view. Her transcription and literary conversion of taped conversations with the editorial help of the poet César Calvo makes this an extremely well-written book. I had also interviewed Zózimo Torres and Betty González for my own project.

7. Lobbying for the revaluation of the agrarian bonds cropped up occasionally in Lima's press. A collection of newspaper editorials by José Hernández de Agüero titled *La promesa* (2001) keeps hammering on this issue. He is the son of the ex-owner of El Carmelo in the Virú Valley, where he spent his youth.

Managers and Union Leaders

1. Sources of these statistics include Gonzales 1990, 43; and Eguren 1990, 28, which report the latest counts. Caballero and Alvarez 1980; and Matos Mar and Mejía 1980, 179 have earlier compilations.

2. Sharecroppers led a protest against the miserable conditions in the 1930s and 1940s. The movement to organize *yanacona* sharecroppers was led by early anarcho-syndicalists and the founder in Piura of Peru's Socialist Party, Melquiades Castillo. The early APRA also focused on how to protect them from eviction as the process of capital-intensive hacienda production gained speed. Hildebrando Castro Pozo (1947), also an early socialist, produced a study of sharecropping in Piura of the 1930s and 1940s, on the basis of which *La Ley del Yanaconaje* (the Sharecropper's Law) was promulgated under APRA auspices in 1947. See Matos Mar 1976 and Peloso 1999.

3. Cotton production experienced a boom in the 1950s but began to decline before the Velasco reform. According to Korovkin (1990, 28–29), the crop's share for exports fell sharply as the crop became an industrial input for Peru's nascent textile industry, with up to 40 percent of cotton produced being used for the national textile industry in the 1970s. Government policies regarding price, exchange controls, taxation, and incentives were responsible in subordinating the agricultural sector to the needs of industry. The Velasco government established a buying monopoly to insure a steady cheap supply of raw materials to the industry. See Revesz 1982 for a more detailed study of Piura cotton growing. Revesz emphasizes that cotton was not only produced by cooperatives but also largely by peasant smallholders. He contradicts the commonly held view that ignorant peasants on their farms or in disorganized coopera-

tives were responsible for declines in productivity, since the erratic yearly statistics of productivity show similar variations before and after the reform (1982, 65).

4. Carlos Malpica's book *Los dueños del Perú* (1968) was the leftists' bible on the concentration of wealth. Mainly, it is a carefully compiled list of companies with their family connections by economic sector (the Rizo Patrón family's landholdings are listed on pages 124–25). Yet, his conclusions went hand in hand with Velasco's expropriatory zeal: "The authentic owners of Peru are not the *latifundistas* on the coast called the 'barons of cotton and sugar' by a political party in its formative years; nor the Peruvian shareholders in banks and insurance companies, called by another political party the 'money *latifundistas*'; nor are they the 'Jews' who control the many retail stores and one or two banks; not least the big merchants. The true owners of Peru are a small group of foreign enterprises, especially those from the United States that control the principal economic sectors of the country" (1968, 67 my translation). An early Marxist of *aprista* parents, he was the senator who introduced the first agrarian reform laws to Parliament, was frequently jailed, and Velasco deported him. In the 1980s and 1990s, he was an honored and senior leftist parliamentarian in various coalitions.

5. In Cañete, seventeen cooperatives were established with ten thousand hectares and two thousand members (Auzemery and Eresue 1986, 182). Korovkin's study of the Cañete cooperatives is an outstanding and detailed work focusing on the combination of politics and economic factors. She points out,

> The first hacienda unions in the valley were organized by the moderate APRA party. . . . Shortly before the reform, however, many unions radicalized their demands and changed their affiliation to the Confederación General de Trabajadores del Perú (CGTP) controlled by the Communist Party. Rural mobilization peaked after the promulgation of the 1969 land reform. Many hacienda unions played an important role in curbing the resistance of local landlords and accelerating the expropriation and adjudication of haciendas. (1990, 59)

6. Many nonpermanent and landless laborers were left out of the cooperatives, creating a major political problem for the reform. Cooperatives refused to incorporate "*eventuales*" and land-hungry peasants around haciendas, providing ample opportunities for discontent, which was capitalized upon by antigovernment organizations. Most notably, the CCP peasant federation was very effective in Piura (Arce Espinoza 1983).

7. Ambivalence by members toward the cooperatives in Piura is reported by Emma Rubín de Celis (1977, 1978). In Cañete, Korovkin reports in one case study that "financial scandals became routine. During the ten years the cooperative conducted three audits at the request of its members, all three discovered serious financial irregularities involving the manager, the senior employees and the members of the administrative council" (1990, 73). My own interviews in other coastal ex-cooperatives also brought out stories of chaos, infighting, mistrust, and collusion. In Ica, political infighting between factions of elected leaders of the largest cooperative produced bullet injuries, mafia-like behavior, and the judicial persecution of whistle-blowers.

However, not all cooperatives were like this; particularly smaller ones did live up to the government's and their member's expectations. However, contentment does not produce interesting ugly stories.

8. With highland migration to the Cañete Valley, ethnic/racial tensions increased. People from the highlands (*serrano*) have for many years been subject to discriminatory treatment on the coast. In the Cañete Valley, the three towns reflect this well. San Vicente is a colonial town with the air of landowner distinction; San Luis is a tradition-keeping town of predominantly African-Peruvian descendents of slaves; Imperial is a bustling, disorganized *cholo* and *serrano* town of immigrants. The politics and patterns of social exclusion are reflected in Opus Dei's dominance in San Vicente, that of populists in Imperial, and the decline of San Luis as a viable municipality.

9. Despite lame attempts to improve the lot of temporary cotton pickers in the cooperatives of Cañete, their situation did not improve. Korovkin describes that during the "good" years, temporary laborers worked with written contracts guaranteeing income and social benefits. As cost-cutting measures became more imperative, cooperatives reverted to the pre-reform practice of *enganche* that María describes, but hiring recent migrants from the highlands. "As could be expected," writes Korovkin, "this measure soured relations between cooperatives and temporary workers, so much so that some of their leaders started talking about invading cooperative lands" (1990, 117).

10. Stealing from cooperatives had its consequences. When I gave a lecture at the University of Ayacucho on this and was asked why the cooperatives failed, I said, "Please raise your hand if you have not stolen from a cooperative." The audience laughed. The theory of the free-rider problem alludes to the costs of supervision to control the rider, while the general theory of Garrett Hardin (1968) of the tragedy of the commons gives a rational choice answer. If I believe everyone else is helping themselves to common resources, then I better grab my part before the bonanza is over. But in any social system, even helping yourself to freebies is rule bound and limited, as the studies on collective agriculture in the Eastern Bloc in Europe show. In Peru there were several levels and modalities in the cooperatives: the workers sloughing effort, the warehouse employee diverting fertilizer, the manager embezzling funds, and the elected officials expecting kickbacks and commissions are escalating levels of "corruption." Damage to the cooperative enterprise goes up as one moves up these levels. In anti-agrarian reform discourse, the accusation of stealing figures prominently. The ex-*socios* get blamed most, the administrators least. Even today *parceleros* face that stigma just because they—through no choice of their own—were members of a cooperative. In neoliberal theory, collective and socialist enterprises are more vulnerable to such illegal temptations than capitalist enterprises, but that too is decidedly a myth. Corruption as discourse is also ideologically motivated political talk.

11. Productivity and profitability increased after the cooperatives divided the land into individual plots. Michael Carter wrote a highly theoretical article that compared cooperatives with *parceleros*: "It may be concluded that the CAPS [production co-

operatives] produce less output than would the smaller private farms given the same observed inputs—perhaps as much as 15 percent–30 percent less" (1984, 843; see translation into Spanish 1985). Carter and Alvarez (1989) go over the same issues but take into account the political and economic context. Labor on cooperatives was more expensive than small-scale semi-proletarianized labor. When *cooperativistas* became *parceleros*, they drastically lowered their own self-employment wages by working harder, using family labor, and foregoing Social Security and other benefits. Gols (1988) is happy to report increased everything—production, productivity, income—for the Cañete *parceleros*. Fernández (1985) has a good title: "La reforma agraria no fracasa, tampoco los campesinos, lo único que fracasa es la cooperativa" (the agrarian reform is not a failure, nor the *campesinos*, the only failure is the cooperative). It contains excellent testimonies by all parties and points of view, much in the spirit of this book.

12. A deep rift remains in the Cañete. Landlords who kept their minimum and businesses that bought land have morphed into *agricultores medianos* and behave as the new agrarian bourgeoisie. They do not collaborate or make common cause with the *parceleros*. Figallo and Vega (1988) as well as Monge (1988) give details of the rise in the 1990s of new associations created by entrepreneurs to pressure the government to abolish legislative restrictions on land transfers that still remained on the books from the Velasco and Morales Bermúdez periods. Auzemery and Eresue (1986) describe how these middle farmers were capable of turning regional and national public opinion against the reform. The suppressed anti-Velasco feelings surfaced quickly and publicly with the return to democracy.

Machu Asnu Cooperativa

1. The design of the supercooperative was contentious from the beginning. Disjunctions between planners in Cusco and the agrarian reform planning office based in Lima forced the implementation of plans that local experts thought were unworkable. Officials in Cusco, who understood the socioeconomic characteristics of the Pampa de Anta, backed by experts from the Food and Agriculture Organization (FAO) and the United Nations, favored three smaller cooperatives with a central service for the communities surrounding them. But, as David Guillet reports, "These plans were scrapped by a political decision at the national level for a post-reform enterprise that would have more impact in the total picture of agrarian reform in Peru" (1979, 103–4). Raymond F. Watters adds, "It is important to note that not all of this land represented expropriated hacienda land: *Comunidades Campesinas* were persuaded to enter communal lands from each village, so that [for a while] the *comunidades* thus ceased to be formal entities. Indeed it is a moot point whether 'persuade' is an adequate description" (1994, 220). Héctor Martínez Arellano (1980, 111) posited that the choice of a single supercooperative by the Ministry of Agriculture planner represented a love the government had for "gigantism" and the protection of the sacrosanct principles of economies of scale. In Puno, one such unit was appropriately named the Cooperativa Agraria de Producción Gigante, and had two hundred

thousand hectares. In the seminar in which Jorge Villafuerte was the critical voice, those who were enamored with the design of the Túpac Amaru II Cooperative cited plans to expand agricultural land by draining stagnant lakes on the Pampa de Anta, the potential of the cooperative to restructure the whole productive and distributive system of agricultural goods, and the elimination of the inefficient *campesino* economy. One seminar member had attended a briefing in the ministry in which Captain Dante Castro expounded on the virtues of the supercooperative's design. He reported to the members of the seminar that he had been convinced. "The model is beautiful," he said. Villafuerte responded that the problem was that it ignored the people who lived there.

2. Sources on the Pampa de Anta and the cooperative include these theses: Paniagua Gomez (1984), as my main source, is the basis of this chapter; Canal Ccarhuarupay (1976) has a local student's fresh perspective in describing the enormous distance between the *comuneros*, the cooperative's executives, and its elected delegates; Roca Puchana (1990) talks about the role of women in the mobilization process against the cooperative; Vargas Chambi (1990) deals with Tambo Real. Since the "*machu asnu*" was an exceptional white elephant of the reform, it is worth reading Martínez Arellano's (1990) general indictment of the other associative enterprises the reform created in the highlands for comparison.

3. CENCIRA-Holanda (Centro Nacional de Capacitación e Investigación para la Reforma Agraria) and PRODERM (Proyecto de Desarrollo Rural en Micro-Regiones) were funded by the Dutch government, which invested heavily in Peruvian rural development. While the Ministry of Agriculture concentrated on shoring up the Túpac Amaru II Cooperative, extension agents of CENCIRA-Holanda worked in the communities and had opportunities to capitalize on *comuneros'* complaints against the cooperative, the intellectual means to propagate them, and the institutional means to undermine the cooperative. *Ingeniero* René Ramirez, the last *gerente* of the cooperative, was mightily resentful of the CENCIRA. In an interview in Cusco in 1996 he told me, "During the time of difficulties, CENCIRA was there to destroy the cooperative and to organize the communities by giving them money. They said to the communities, 'If you disaffiliate from the cooperative, we will give you this credit.'" CENCIRA-Holanda's *Plan de desarrollo de Antapampa diagnóstico* (1979) is a thorough statistical survey of the whole region that provided the program with its work plan: "To redistribute land to the poorer communities, above all redistribute those from the cooperative" (307); to establish an investment and credit program coupled with agricultural extension, and to work toward strengthening the capacity of the community in its relation to the peasants' household economy (308–18, my translations). Its companion volume (CENCIRA-Holanda 1980), coordinated by Genaro Paniagua, studied twenty associative areas like the one in Tambo Real that were established in communities after the disintegration of the cooperative. Its conclusions and recommendations nonetheless were skeptical of the possible success and functions that the associative areas in each community could perform. PRODERM (1979–91) was one of the early Integrated Rural Development programs established after the collapse of

the cooperative. A final self-report on its positive effects is available in Boada 1991. The hacienda-less Pampa de Anta today is a prosperous agricultural region of small-holders and communities.

4. For more on "red Cusco" under Morales Bermúdez, see Rénique 1991, chapters 9 and 10 for an excellent regional history that deals (in part 2) with the regimes of Velasco and Morales Bermúdez, and the second regime of Belaúnde. Velasco's expropriations and the contentious implementation of cooperatives played center stage in the years 1969–75. The influence of SINAMOS in town and countryside grew rapidly, spurring the growth of counterorganizations from the Left. In any case, the parties of the Left were engaged in an internal debate on what posture to take. Peasant federations had been severely repressed during the military regime of 1962 and were in a weak position. In the city in 1973, Velasco's confrontational encounters with students and teachers had already provoked the burning down of the SINAMOS office, signaling the beginning of its growing unpopularity. When Morales Bermúdez (under internal pressure) closed down SINAMOS in 1976, the field was left wide open for antigovernment organizations to regain lost territory. From the military's point of view, writes Rénique, "popular organizations began to mobilize showing a worrisome affinity toward an expanding revolutionary left" (1991, 282). Teachers, students, workers, government employees, and peasants became combative and aggressive. However, it was not easy to reconcile the peasants' concrete demands with the ideological struggles of the tiny factions of leftist political parties—whose leaders and intellectual backers talked in such difficult Marxistese—and their capacity to a provide a means to channel peasant mobilizations. The FARTAC (Federation Agraria Revolucionaria Túpac Amaru Cusco), which had been set up as part of the CNA's vertical support group for the Velasco reforms and which had dominated (with SINAMOS's help), became more radical and eventually cut its ties with the CNA to join the growing opposition peasant federation of the CCP in 1977. Two groups became influential in the Cusco countryside, Vanguardia Revolucionaria (VR, Revolutionary Vanguard) and the Maoist PCR (Partido Comunista Revolucionario, Revolutionary Communist Party), which though rivals aided and coordinated the growth of the ranks of the CCP in Cusco and participated in strategies for propitious land invasions in various places throughout the nation. They rejoiced in the unity achieved at the Eqeqo Chacan conference. The cooperative of Pampa de Anta was one opportune area for opposition forces to coalesce. See also del Mastro 1979 for a user-friendly tour of groups, a chronology of the rise and fall of diverse federations with complicated acronyms, and revealing photographs.

5. Sources on Eqeqo Chacán include José Carlos Gutiérrez Samanéz's (1969) economic ethnography of household economies and Alberto Vera Ardiles's (1972) evaluation of Eqeqo Chacán's prior experience, carried out under the University of North Carolina's supervised credit program and community development program. Among the changes he listed was the community's purchase of a public address system, which proved to be very useful. According to locals, its purchase and installation was encouraged by a group of Peace Corps volunteers (Vera Ardiles 1972, 52).

6. The director of Cusco's agrarian reform shared his regrets with me. *Ingeniero* Adriel Villena responded to my question as to which was the worst moment in his career. He said it was when the cooperative in Anta was liquidated. He took it personally: "I saw how the cattle were disappearing, how the sophisticated stables they had built were destroyed." I asked, "Do you think that we Peruvians are inherently dishonest and when we are given the opportunity, we will steal?" He responded, "In part, yes, because I did experience this. . . . There is a saying, 'Opportunity makes the thief,' and another one, 'With open coffers even the just person sins.' But it is embarrassing to admit to this."

7. Esteban Puma was no saint. A report on local-level politics, governmentality, and clientelism by the Peruvian political scientist Martin Tanaka (2001, 48) used Esteban Puma's political career as a case study. Tanaka describes how Puma constructed his own populist, socialist-leaning local political party (Unidad Campesino Popular). However, he was impeached for bad administration and misuse of public funds in 1998. Because of that, he moved to the city of Cusco and began studying at the university.

8. Statistical information from the Pampa de Anta gathered by CENCIRA-Holanda led to first-rate scholarly studies by economists Bruno Kervyn (1988, 1989) and Efraín Gonzales de Olarte (1984, 1987). The extreme difficulty the cooperative had in transforming peasant householders into "farmers" led both authors, in close collaboration, to search for an understanding of the specificities of household, family-based economies associated with communities. Gonzales posited a positive "community effect" that explained the persistence of communal organization despite the marked tendencies toward family individualism that both of them observed in their research in the Pampa de Anta. In his second book, Gonzales measured the impact of inflation on family economies that were supposedly weakly integrated into the market. Kervyn used institutional economics to describe choices between more collective and private systems of production within the same community. Peasant resistance to imposed development models in the Pampa de Anta finally alerted scholars to pay attention to their needs and specific cultural and social arrangements of local people.

Veterinarians and Comuneros

1. Several works have been published on the formation of ranching haciendas in the central *sierra*. Víctor Caballero Martín, I later realized, had published most of the material contained in the manuscript he gave me the day of the interview in two publications (1979, 1981). Nelson Manrique (1987, 1988) and Florencia Mallon (1983) show that the Peruvian-Chilean War of 1879 brought ruin to the regional landed oligarchy, and their estates were bought up at the turn of the century by merchants, miners, and capitalists established in Lima. Thus began the process of modernizing ranching haciendas through consolidation. Encroachment on community lands began in the 1920s with the growth of the international wool market. The construction of the smelter in La Oroya, with its huge smoke stacks billowing pollutants over a large area used for agriculture and pasturage became a cause célèbre in the 1920s. The Leguía

government forced the Cerro de Pasco Corporation to compensate owners, which it did by buying the contaminated land from haciendas and communities. When the company installed scrubbers in the refinery and the damage abated, it ended up with enormous extensions of pasture land bought, as Mallon puts it (1983, 227), at rock-bottom prices. Dora Mayer (no relation of mine), a prominent collaborator of José Carlos Mariátegui, published a denunciation of the company's labor practices in English (1913) and in Spanish. The Spanish pamphlet, issued in 1914, became a rare item until a second edition was published (D. Mayer 1984).

2. Protest and outrage among the peasants against the rationalization of ranching with fences was combined with repeated attempts by peasants and communities to recuperate lands lost to hacienda expansion. Peasant leaders sought alliances among neighboring communities and urban intellectual backing to dramatize their plight. They formed peasant federations. Local press reports in the mining unions' newspapers and radio stations, as well as protest marches in the cities, supported the actions of the *comuneros* and denounced government repression. The land issue and its anticapitalist stance was a left-wing "progressive" cause and provided opportunity for debate among Peru's intellectuals. Authoritative studies of these movements include Kapsoli 1975 and 1977; Caballero Martín 1979 and 1981; and in English, Handelman 1975. Manuel Scorza, a novelist writing in the late 1970s and a participant in the Latin American literary *boom*, used a mixture of *indigenismo* and magical realism to portray the conflicted relationships between virtuous *comuneros* in central Peru and their invisible and institutionalized corporate landlord. His widely read and translated novels include *Redoble por Rancas* (1970), *Historia de Garabombo el invisible* (1972), *El cantar de Agapito Robles* (1977a), and *El jinete insomne* (1977b).

3. Improved sheep breeds introduced to the *puna* zones of Peru had precedents among Peruvian *hacendados* in the highlands before the Cerro de Pasco's program (Mallon 1983, 175–76). Pierre de Zutter (1975, 63–72), a Belgian journalist who wrote propaganda in favor of the agrarian reform, is very dismissive of the Americans involved in Cerro de Pasco's contributions to improving stock breeds. However, after the agrarian reform, the marvel of the "Junín" breed was touted as one of its great achievements.

There is a kind of "sheep racism" involved in this discussion, whereby stock locally adapted since colonial times (*chusco*) is considered inferior to improved breeds. This may well be true with regard to the wool and meat quality needed for industrial processes. However, improved stock requires segregation from the local breeds, more land, better-quality pastures, fencing, and so on. The local *chusco* breed is hardy and adapted to the very poor land conditions of the crowded communities.

Herding activities on haciendas required a fully operational peasant household. Peasants successfully resisted becoming pure wage earners on the hacienda. Through the "right" of *huacchilla*, the hacienda acquired labor, while the herders gained the right to pasture their own sheep alongside those belonging to the hacienda. In daily acts of resistance, such as covertly but defiantly increasing the agreed-upon number of sheep permitted to graze on hacienda land, or systematically disregarding prohibitions against trespassing on hacienda pastures, or in withholding labor, villagers constantly confronted the hacienda. When such petty confrontations escalated, the hacienda responded by tightening the rules and their enforcement. It became more strict in capturing and punishing trespassers, curtailed the number of sheep allowed in *huacchilla* arrangements, and raised the fines against infractions. When improved sheep were introduced, the hacienda tried unsuccessfully to force the herders to get rid of their inferior and diseased animals. The more ruthless methods adopted by the División Ganadera (Ranching Division) of the American company made their estates the only ones that were free of *huacchos* by the time they were expropriated. The anthropologist Gavin A. Smith's (1989) studies of peasant resistance in the community of Huasicancha and the economist Joan Martínez Alier's (Spanish 1973, English 1977a) insightful analysis on the economics (rent versus wages) of *huacchilleros* on the haciendas of the Ganadera del Centro are the classic sources on this subject, in which they argue that haciendas were subject to external and internal siege (*asedio*). To veterinarians dreaming of cleared pastures, peasant resistance was irrational, and this attitude had an important influence in how the expropriated sheep ranches were to be adjudicated and managed. Zootechnicians wanted to make newly expropriated land available to *comunidades* on the condition that the latter get rid of their poor stock, and it was a source of friction throughout the agrarian reform. Rigoberto Calle (1989) decried the loss of high-quality stock that resulted from changes brought about by the agrarian reform. As the reform petered out, *chusco* breeds (although somewhat improved) have won out on the pasture lands of the Andes and are again the dominant species.

4. Studies that monitored the SAISes' performance during a twenty-year period included those by anthropologists, economists, sociologists, and social science students from local universities such as the one in Huancayo. Early analyses and reports on SAIS affairs are to be found in the work of Professor Rodrigo Montoya (1974), of the University of San Marcos, whose long list of oppositional forces (workers against management; management against communities; wages and salaries versus development for communities; investment in production versus investment in community development) and the impossibility of reconciling them set the tone for many a later interpretation. Hernán Caycho (1977), from the Escuela de Administración de Negocios para Graduados (ESAN) business school in Lima, analyzed the early economic performance of various SAISes. César Fonseca Martel (1975) reported on the SAIS Pachacútec from the perspective of the communities that were incorporated into the system. Bryan Roberts and Carlos Samaniego (1978) reported an early evaluation of the impact of the SAIS Cahuide on a member community. Cynthia McClintock (1981, 320) conducted attitudinal surveys in cooperatives and SAISes, and found that while workers adapted fairly well to the new cooperatives' more egalitarian management style, a kind of "group egoism" existed that excluded nonbeneficiaries of the reform. Agricultural economists kept the pulse of SAIS performance over time. Valdivia, in her master's theses at the University of Missouri (1983), and Valdivia and Pichihua (1986) compared cooperatives and SAISes and tracked the performance of SAISes in

the central *sierra*. Víctor Caballero Martín's periodic monitoring (1986 and 1990a) shows differences with Valdivia and Pichihua, which are highlighted in the main text here. Joel Jurado's, Corinne Valdivia's, and Juan Pichihua's (1986) policy options for the then incoming government of Alan García in 1985 predicted a deepening economic crisis for associative enterprises, and recommended downsizing, lowering objectives, and turning these units into multicommunity projects. Manuel Ortiz's dissertation from the University of Huancayo (Ortiz Espinar and Cruz Montero 1991) details the political management of Túpac Amaru I (Universidad Nacional del Centro), while Jonatán Valerio Laureano's (1985) thesis gives a dramatic account of how the community of Ondores recuperated the lands of Atojsaico from the SAIS Túpac Amaru I, with the consequent expulsion of Ondores from the SAIS.

Héctor Martínez Arellano noted that the stature of Túpac Amaru I, Cahuide, and Pachacutec as *la crème* of high technology and capitalization enabled their continuation (Martínez Arellano 1980, 1990; the latter was published after his death). He observed that SAISes elsewhere in Peru performed much more poorly, jeopardizing their chances for survival. He pointed to a lack of government support, poor administration, and an alarming decline of centralized production of quality stock against the growth of peasants' own *huaccho* herds. Management paid less than lip service to the democratic self-management principles that had been touted, and the reality included more clientelistic control of the enterprise by a small elite of administrators and workers, as well as widespread free-rider problems. Many SAISes and cooperatives in the high Andes became chaotic shells where workers and others had established, in one form or another, household herding systems not too different from those in traditional communities, or else functioned as independent smallholders. The land and resources of the corporate demesne were progressively encroached upon by SAIS members, *huaccho* herds outnumbered those of the central administration, and administrators too acquired vast *huaccho* herds. As far as the loftier objectives of the reform, such as reducing inequality, combating poverty, or producing development for partner communities, Martínez Arellano maintained that these were not achieved.

5. It was during Alan García's administration that the SAISes in the department of Puno also collapsed. Junín and Puno were the two departments in which highland sheep and cattle ranching were predominant, and where most of the SAISes were installed by the Velasco administration. There were chronological coincidences and tactical similarities, as well as differences, in the way in which the SAISes were dismantled in the two departments. In both cases, the SAISes were facing financial difficulties, among them the fall in prices for wool and lamb meat (Caballero Martín 1990b). In both departments, neighboring communities demanded the land, though more insistently in Puno, where the Velasco agrarian reform had marginalized them more so than in Junín. In Puno, the García administration played a more active role in forcing the SAISes to restructure than in Junín, and in both departments, the violent dynamiting actions of Shining Path played an important role in speeding up the process of collapse. The Shining Path was unable to repeat in Puno the spectacular case

of Cahuide's looting, but there were many incidents, such as blowing up sheds and burning down the Maryknoll priest's NGO, an institution supported by the peasants. Far more devastating in Puno was Shining Path's order issued to provincial, district, and community authorities to resign from their posts or face assassination. While the threat posed by Shining Path sped up the process of dissolution in both departments, it still remains unclear what exactly were the purposes behind Shining Path's actions. In this footnote I give a brief summary of how the drama played out in Puno, which contrasts with the story of the SAIS Cahuide in the main text. The detailed history involved in the end of the agrarian reform and the defeat of Shining Path in Puno can be read in José Luis Rénique's fascinating book, *La batalla por Puno* (2004).

By 1986, reacting to internal pressures and the growth of their federations, peasants demanded that SAISes give them land and threatened to invade them if they did not accede. They were supported by the Partido Unificado Marxista (PUM), a unified lefist political party that was a fusion of the VR, the PCR, and other smaller groups, as well as by technical experts broadcasting examples of the disastrous mismanagement of the SAISes—for example, those contained in a volume edited by Martin Scurrah: *Empresas asociativas y comunidades campesinas: Puno después de la reforma agraria* (1987). Even the government realized that the SAISes in Puno needed to be restructured. President García listened to the insistent demands of community leaders in a well-publicized meeting he held with them on September 21, 1986. He answered, "I want to be honest with you (all), we want to keep our promise to restructure without propitiating a social war, which is what some people want, some people said that we should signal freedom for communities to invade the empresas and the SAIS, invasion. I want restructuring, I do not want invasion, invasion signifies dead people, invasion signifies our wounded flesh, invasion signifies disorder, invasion signifies gain for those who trade in hate. I prefer a fair and just restructuring, a progressive and cumulative restructuring, little by little like a whole life and we will do it until we have satisfied the historical demands of the *parcialdidades* and the communities. That is the way we are going to do it, and that is the way I guarantee to you" (Rimana-kuy 1987, 216; my translation).

The demand to dissolve the cooperatives was supported by massive regional and urban progressive movements, which also sought more regional autonomy and economic relief during the economic crisis that was compounded by a severe El Niño drought in Puno. Even while parts of the department were militarized to deal with the growing insurgency by Shining Path, urban strikes, mass demonstrations, and land invasions were held defiantly.

In January 1986, the government had promised to distribute one million SAIS hectares to the communities. However, it could not meet the deadlines because it met with resistance from the entrenched SAIS management and its beneficiaries. Instead, land invasions began in June 1986, with a massive coordinated uprising that took half a million hectares on its own. Invasions continued for two more years until all of the SAISes were ultimately taken. According to Ethel del Pozo-Vergnes (2004, 140–42), the dissolution of the supercooperatives was messy, contested, nasty, and fast. Under initial pressure, the supercooperatives were forced to cede large tracts of land to their neighboring communities. Later the remaining lands were broken up into smaller units, to be run together with the neighboring communities. Ultimately, because the workers and managers continued to have a stake in the land and patrimony and complicated the process by resisting the restructuring, the peasants called for complete dissolution of the enterprises, partitioning of the remaining land, and distribution of animals.

As the government speedily designed the giveaway of the land, cries of corruption and featherbedding for ex-administrators and APRA party members further spurred more waves of post-restructuring land invasions. Some of the restructured communites were "paper" communities often made up of ex-employees of the cooperatives plus their friends. Thus, while the peasant federations claimed that they had peacefully taken the land, Alan Garcia personally flew to Puno to distribute the very lands that the peasants had invaded the day before under PUM banners so that he could claim that it was the government that gave the lands and not the peasants who took them (or vice versa, depending on which way one would want to interpret it).

6. The Shining Path and the Movimiento Revolucionarion Túpac Amaru (MRTA) were prevalent in the Mantaro Valley in the late 1980s to the early 1990s. After the severe military repression of Shining Path insurgency in the Ayacucho region, Shining Path spread quickly to the neighboring departments of Junín and Pasco. In the central highlands, Shining Path was present in schools and universities, and in urban and rural areas. It was also present in the eastern lowlands. The MRTA had a presence in urban areas universities, and it controlled two rural areas in the highlands, with some additional bases in the eastern lowlands. The MRTA and the Sendero Luminoso were bitter enemies and devoted much energy to fighting each other. During those years the number of attacks on infrastructure increased dramatically as their strength grew; they took over communal organizations, village administrations, and urban neighborhoods. The University of Huancayo was a fierce battleground among police, the university administration, and rival Shining Path and MRTA revolutionaries. The city of Huancayo was under military command, but despite the enforced curfew at night, gun and dynamite battles between insurgents and the military were frequent. Twice, Shining Path enforced an "armed strike" (*paro armado*) on the whole city, in which all businesses were ordered to close or face retaliation. On the street where my parents lived, every wall and house had Shining Path grafitti, including a death threat to anyone who erased them. Initiates who wanted to become militants had to prove themselves by covering walls with their grafitti (Starn 1991).

The guerrillas of the MRTA were decimated en masse when they were caught by the army in Molinos, near Jauja, as they were planning an incursion against the city of Tarma in April 1989. The army's tardy response to Shining Path was to form peasant defense committees (*rondas campesinas*) that patrolled their community territories in close alliance with the military. The Fujimori regime was more directly involved in providing the *rondas campesinas* with transportation and rifles to defend themselves, and its military occupied the University of Huancayo. Fujimori's government installed faceless judges in Huancayo and built and filled a high-security prison with presumed terrorists. In contrast with the Ayacucho region, in the central *sierra* Shining Path did not have as long of an incubation period since the initiative came from cadres fleeing Ayacucho; however, its actions were more widespread and desperate, despite being short lived. Statistical information on the high levels of violence during those years was collected and published by an NGO in Huancayo named Servicios Educativos Promoción y Apoyo Rural (1992).

7. Two accounts of the destruction of Laive and Antapongo corroborate the memories of Juvenal Chanco and Luz Goyzueta, which I am recounting here. Rodrigo Sánchez (1989), who has a long trajectory of research and NGO activities in the Huancayo region, wrote an insightful overview after the destruction of the SAIS Cahuide. Rather than ask why it collapsed, as so many pundits had predicted in years past, he asked why SAISes had survived for so long despite their inherent weakness. Sánchez notes that the communities' insistence on urgent restructuring was peaceful, democratic, nonviolent, and desperate as they attempted to thwart Shining Path's agenda of total destruction (1989, 97).

Nelson Manrique, a historian and also a native *huancaíno*, published two authoritative accounts (1989, 2002 in Spanish; and 1990–91, 1998 in English) of the insurrection in the central *sierra* that took place in 1982–89. Both authors concur that Shining Path's incursion on the SAISes was opportunistic, counted by them as acts of destruction against the state that were to be treated in the same fashion as the blowing up of transmission lines or bridges. In the case of Cahuide, Manrique concluded (in agreement with Sánchez) that the impasse between the communities and the intransigent managerial staff about restructuring was an opportunity for Shining Path, which aimed to break it. The Shining Path did not have any reformist plans other than destruction and total territorial control. Manrique supposes that its objectives were to completely clear the countryside of any other influence, hence its assassination of authorities, blowing up of communications, and attacks on the NGO in Jarpa, a village that Shining Path ruled for a month in order to create liberated territories in preparation for the final confrontation between it and the army.

Sánchez's and Manrique's accounts do not mention the degree of infiltration by Shining Path in the SAIS as described by the storytellers in this chapter.

8. Simón Meza has given me permission to publish this part. In December 2006, I phoned him from Lima asking if he felt that it was now safe to say what he had told me then confidentially. He agreed.

9. Oral testimonies by citizens from Chongos Alto before the Peruvian Truth and Reconciliation Committee in 2002–3 corroborate the accounts by Luz Goyzueta (1996), Juvenal Chanco (1996), and Nelson Manrique (1989) (Comisión de la Verdad y Reconciliación 2004, 299–301). A summary text recapitulates the relationship between Chongos and the SAIS, its land disputes with Huasicancha, and Chongos's relationships with Shining Path. When Shining Path abolished the community authorities and replaced them with its own *comités populares*, the authorities continued to operate clandestinely. Some testimonials surmise that Huasicancha *comuneros* (at that

time in bitter conflict with Chongos) may have tipped off Shining Path about these secret meetings and their presumed attempts to contact counterinsurgency forces. In a photograph reproduced by a local Chongos organization and shown to me, one could see that the posters left on the bodies of assasinated leaders read: "This is the way that the government's dogs die" and "Anyone who picks up this cadaver shall be assassinated." The Truth Commission heard twenty-five individual testimonies (not accessible to me as of this writing).

10. Don Marcial Soto, Luz's seventy-year-old grandfather, showed me the *vara* (staff) that had belonged to his father. Marcial's father had risen through all the *cargos* (posts) to culminate as *alcalde*. Marcial himself passed several of the lower-level positions such as *alcalde campo*. The staff was made of dark chonta palm wood and was about a meter high, with about a two-inch diameter at the top tapering toward a tip at the bottom. It was decorated at the top with copper and tin rings covered with designs, stars, and crosses. The iron tip, with which the staff could be planted in the ground, was missing. A tradition dating from colonial times, the *vara* was the symbol of authority and obedience. Marcial remembered that when the *alcalde* or his subalterns patrolled the village and found someone being disobedient or being lazy, they would plant the staff on the ground next to the person, and that meant punishment in the form of lashes on the back with a whip that had three tips. Afterward, the person had to kiss the hand of the person who had done the whipping and make the sign of the cross. The younger subordinates of the *varayocs* had specific tasks entrusted to them, for example delivering candles for a saint's fiesta or whatever was needed for a whole year while the *cargo* lasted. There were different tasks associated with each position. For example, those who entered in January had to organize the quail hunt (*chaco de perdíz*). The *varayoc* asked permission from the haciendas to cross into their lands, and the whole community went out to hunt the quail. It was great fun, like a fiesta. And the quail were brought to Huancayo to be presented to the authorities of the city and the government as gifts. The *vara* system of autonomous authorities was replaced in the 1950s.

Terms are Spanish unless indicated otherwise.

agricultor mediano: Mid-size landowner

agricultores: Farmers

alcalde, alcalde campo: Two positions in the civil-religious system of rank and authority

allegado: Relationship between a *colono* and another person to cultivate land and share obligations owed to the hacienda

area asociativa: Land reserved for collective production

arrepentidos: Repentants; deserters from Shining Path reincorporated into community life

autogestionaria: Self-managed enterprise, as opposed to state enterprise

ayllu (Quechua): Indigenous pre-Hispanic kinship and territorial unit

barrio: Neighborhood, usually of the poor

cacique: Indigenous hereditary authority in colonial Peru

campesino: Peasant

caporal: Private guard on an hacienda

carajo: Vulgar expletive

caramba(s): Expression of wonder and amazement

cargos: Positions in the civil-religious system of rank and authority in a community

casa hacienda: Hacienda house

caudillo: Strong-armed political leader in Latin America

ceviche: Raw seafood in lemon and chili sauce

chicha (Quechua): Home-brewed maize beer

cholo/a: Depending on context and tone of voice, a derogatory or endearing term for lower-class people of Indian background

chusco: Rough, of poor but hardy quality; used to refer to breeds of animals

colonato: The practice of granting a subsistence plot in exchange for work on an hacienda

colono: Resident serf on an hacienda

comandante: Officer in charge

comités populares: Popular committees, Shining Path's imposed rule in communities and shantytowns

compañero/a: Comrade

comunero: Member of a peasant community

comunidad campesina: Officially recognized peasant community after 1969

comunidad de indígenas: Officially recognized indigenous community until 1969

cooperativista: Dedicated member of the cooperative movement

coso: Hacienda jail

cumpas: From *compañeros* (comrades), a term used for *senderistas*

desactivación total: Total deactivation

División Ganadera de la Cerro de Pasco Mining Corporation: Ranching Division of the Cerro de Pasco Mining Corporation

El Niño: Recurring meteorological phenomenon that produces rain in the northern deserts about every decade

empresa: Business enterprise

empresario: Entrepreneur, businessperson

empresas comunales: Communal enterprises

enganche: System of temporary labor recruitment through advances

espíritu empresarial: Corporate spirit

estancia: Pasture with a small hut away from the main house

faena: Communal (corvée) labor

feudatario: Serf on an hacienda with rights to a subsistence plot in exchange for hacienda work

foco guerrillero: Guerrilla base in a rural area

fundo: Small farm, used often when hacienda became a negative term

gamonal: Powerful landlord in rural areas

gamonalismo: Landowner system of political domination

ganadero: Producer of sheep, cattle, and llamas and alpacas

gente humilde: Humble people

gerente: Chief executive officer in a corporation or an enterprise

golondrino/a: Landless temporary rural worker

gringuito/a: Upper-class white person or foreigner

grupo campesino: Peasant group, an association of peasants formed by agrarian reform

hacendado: Owner of an estate

hacienda runa (Spanish and Quechua): People of the hacienda

huacchilla (Quechua): From *orphan* or *poor*; the right to use someone else's pasture

huacchillero/a: Sheepherders on haciendas who had the right to pasture some of their own stock along with those of the hacienda

huacchos (Quechua and Spanish): Animals of a *huacchillero*

huayno (Quechua): Musical tune of a certain genre

indigenismo: Artistic and political movement favoring indigenous peoples

indio: Indian, usually in a pejorative sense

ingeniero: Degree-holding engineer (often agronomist); also a class status term for a professional in command of an office or an institution; a title and term of address

inti (Quechua): Currency denomination between 1985 and 1991

Israelitas del nuevo pacto de Dios: Religious sect

izquierdistas: Left-wingers

la vía campesina: The peasant way (tendency to divide land into small units)

latifundistas: Owners of large estates; a social class

latifundium (Latin): Large land property

limeño: Resident of the capital (Lima); used to refer to the point of view of its upper-class residents

llorona: Miracle-granting crying virgin of legend

machu asnu (Quechua): Old donkey

mamita (Spanish and Quechua): Literally, little mother; term used to address the wife of the hacienda owner

mayorales: Temporary labor contractors on cotton haciendas

mayordomo: Administrator on an hacienda

minifundium (Latin): Very small land property

minifundización: Process of land divisions leading to very small, unviable units

mistis (Quechua): Mestizos and local power holders

olla común: Communal food during strikes and demonstrations

papá: Father

papá gobierno: "Our father the government" (evokes paternalism)

papay (Quechua): Term of respect often used by serfs to address the owner

parcelero/a: Owner of a parcel of land as a result of the division of cooperatives

patrón/a: Boss

pericote: Petty thief (derived from *mouse*)

pericotiva: Cooperative of thieves

polleras: Wide woolen skirts associated with indigenous status

pongo (Quechua and Spanish): Servant in the hacienda system

propietario: Owner

puna: Plateau grasslands higher than 3,600 meters above sea level

quipi (Quechua): Colorful hand-woven cloth used to carry things

rancherías: Rural workers' slum-like settlements

reestructuración: Restructuring

resentido social: Resentful person; a term used by conservatives to attribute motivation for revolutionary feelings

rimanakuy (Quechua): "Let us talk to each other" meetings between community leaders and President Alan García

rondas campesinas: Peasant self-defense organizations

rondero: Member of the *rondas campesinas*

senderistas: Members of the insurgent Shining Path

serrano/a: Person from the *sierra* highlands

sierra: Highlands

Sociedad Ganadera del Centro: Ranching Society of Central Peru; a shareholding conglomerate

socio/a: Member of a cooperative

sol, nuevo sol: Currency denominations (the *nuevo sol* has circulated since 1991)

técnico: Trained technician

telenovelas: Soap operas

terrucos: Terrorists

testimonio: Literary genre based on personal testimony

tomas de tierras: Land occupations

tumbos de la vida: The way fate shapes one's life

vara: Staff, symbol of authority carried by a *varayoc*

varayoc (Quechua): Head of community authority system based on the civil-religious hierarchy imposed during colonial times

velasquistas: Supporters of Velasco

viejo: Lit. *old man*, but also a male-to-male term of endearment

warrantear (Spanglish): To warranty

yana uma (Quechua): Black head; term used by Shining Path for collaborators with the armed forces

yanacona (Quechua): Resident indigenous serf on an hacienda

Alegría, Ciro. 1941. *El mundo es ancho y ajeno*. Santiago: Ediciones Ercilla.

Allende, Isabel. 1983. *La casa de los espíritus*. Barcelona: Plaza y Janés.

Anrup, Roland. 1990. *El taita y el toro: En torno a la configuración patriarcal del régimen hacendario cuzqueño*. Stockholm: Departamento de Historia, Universidad de Gotemburgo; Instituto de Estudios Latinoamericanos, Universidad de Estocolmo.

Arce Espinoza, Elmer. 1983. *La reforma agraria en Piura: 1969-1977*. Lima: Centro de Estudios para el Desarrollo y la Participación (CEDEP).

Arguedas, José Maria. 1941. *Yawar fiesta*. Lima: Centro de Investigacíon y Capacitación (CIP).

———. 1964. *Todas las sangres*. Buenos Aires: Editorial Losada.

———. 1976. *Temblar: El sueño del pongo*. La Habana: Casa de las Américas.

Atusparia, Pedro (pseudonym). 1977. *La izquierda y la reforma agraria peruana*. Lima: Círculo de Estudios Artemio Zavala.

Auzemery, Claire, and Michel Eresue. 1986. "El proceso de parcelación de las cooperativas agrarias del valle de Cañete." *Boletín del Instituto Francés de Estudios Andinos* 15(1–2): 179–205.

Baella Tuesta, Alfonso. 1976. *El poder invisible*. Lima: Editorial Andina.

Bayly, Jaime. 1996. *Los últimos días de La Prensa*. Lima: PEISA.

Banco Latino, ed., 1997. *La hacienda en el Perú: Historia y leyenda*. Lima: Ediciones PEISA.

Barraclough, Solon L., and Arthur Domike. 1964. "Agrarian Structure in Seven Latin American Countries." *Land Economics* 42(4): 391–424.

Becker, Wolfgang, dir. 2003. *Goodbye Lenin* (film). Germany: Sony Classics.

Bedoya, Ricardo. 1992. *100 años de cine en el Perú: Una historia crítica*. Lima: Universidad de Lima.

———. 1997. *Un cine reencontrado: Diccionario ilustrado de las películas peruanas*. Lima: Universidad de Lima.

Berg, Ronald H. 1994. "Peasant Responses to Shining Path in Andahuaylas." In *Shining Path of Peru*, ed. D. S. Palmer, 83–104. New York: St. Martin's Press.

Blanco, Hugo. 1972a. *Land or Death: The Peasant Struggle in Peru*. New York: Pathfinder Press.

———. 1972b. *Tierra o muerte: Las luchas campesinas en Perú*. México: Siglo XXI.

Boada, Hugo. 1991. *PRODERM Acciones de desarrollo y cambios en Anta*. Cusco: Convenio Perú-Holanda/Comunidad Económica Europea.

Bonfiglio, Giovanni. 1986. "Gestión empresarial y cooperativas de la costa." In *Perú: El problema agrario en debate*, ed. V. Gómez, B. Revesz, E. Grillo, and R. Montoya, 181–200. Lima: Seminario Permanente de Investigación Agraria (SEPIA) I.

Bourricaud, François. 1967. *Cambios en Puno: Estudios de sociología andina*. Mexico City: Instituto Indigenista Interamericano.

Burenius, Charlotte. 2001. *Testimonio de un fracaso Huando: Habla el sindicalista Zózimo Torres*. Lima: Instituto de Estudios Peruanos.

Caballero, José María. 1978. *Los eventuales en las cooperativas costeñas peruanas: Un modelo analítico*. Lima: Departamento de Economía, Pontificia Universidad Católica del Perú.

———. 1980. "El fracaso del modelo agrario militar." In *Realidad del campo peruano después de la reforma agraria: 10 ensayos críticos*, ed. CIC, 67–104. Lima: Centro de Investigación y Capacitación (CIC).

———. 1981a. *Economía agraria de la sierra peruana antes de la reforma agraria de 1969*. Lima: Instituto de Estudios Peruanos.

———. 1981b. *From Belaúnde to Belaúnde: Peru's Military Experiment in Third-Roadism*. Centre of Latin American Studies and Wolfson College. Cambridge: Cambridge University Press.

Caballero, José María, and Elena Alvarez. 1980. *Aspectos cuantitativos de la reforma agraria (1969–1979)*. Lima: Instituto de Estudios Peruanos.

Caballero Martín, Victor. 1979. "Historia de las haciendas de la División Ganadera de la Cerro de Pasco." In *Campesinado y capitalismo: Ponencias en el primer seminario sobre campesinado y proceso regional en la sierra central*, 101–18. Huancayo: Instituto de Estudios Andinos.

———. 1981. *Imperialismo y campesinado en la sierra central*. Huancayo: Instituto de Estudios Andinos.

———. 1986. "La crisis de las empresas asociativas en el agro puneño." In *Perú: El problema agrario en debate*, ed. V. Gómez, B. Revesz, E. Grillo, and R. Montoya, 123–52. Lima: Seminario Permanente de Investigación Agraria (SEPIA) I.

———. 1990a. "El modelo asociativo en Junín y en Puno: Balance y perspectivas del problema de la tierra." In *La reforma agriara peruana, 20 años después*, ed. A. Fernández and A. Gonzales, 97–130. Chiclayo: Centro de Estudios Sociales Solidaridad.

———. 1990b. "La realidad de la reestructuración de las empresas asociativas en Puno." In *Puno Tierra y alernativa comunal: Experiencias y propuestas de política agraria*, ed. D. Zuirta and V. Caballero Martín, 135–57. Lima: Tarea.

Calle E., Rigoberto. 1989. "Evolución de la ovinocultura en el Perú en su relación con la tenencia de la tierra." Seminario Permanente de Investigación Agraria (SEPIA) III, Cusco. Not published.

Canal Ccarhuarupay, José F. 1976. "Movilización social en la Pampa de Anta." Universidad Nacional San Antonio Abad del Cusco.

Carter, Michael R. 1984. "Resource Allocation and Use under Collective Rights and Labor Management in Peruvian Coastal Agriculture." *Economic Journal* 94: 826–46.

———. 1985. "Parcelación y productividad del sector reformado: Cuestiones teoricas y una eficiente alternativa institucional mixta." In *Las parcelaciones de las cooperativas agrarias del Perú*, ed. A. Gonzalez and G. Torre, 303–10. Chiclayo: Centro de Estudios Sociales Solidaridad.

Carter, Michael R., and Elena Alvarez. 1989. "Changing Paths: The Decollectivization of Agrarian Reform Agriculture in Coastal Peru." In *Searching for Agrarian Reform in Latin America*, ed. W. Thiesenhusen, 156–87. Boston: Allen and Unwin.

Castañeda, Jorge G. 1993. *Utopia Unarmed: The Latin American Left after the Cold War*. New York: Vintage Books.

Castro Pozo, Hildebrando. 1924. *Nuestra comunidad indígena*. Lima: Editorial El Lucero.

———. 1936. *Del Ayllu al cooperativismo socialista*. Lima: Biblioteca de la Revista de Economía y Finanzas.

———. 1947. *El yanaconaje en las haciendas piuranas*. Lima: Compañía de Impresiones y Publicidad S.A.

Caycho, Hernán. 1977. *Las SAIS de la sierra central*. Lima: ESAN (Escuela de Administración de Negocios) Departamento de Investigación.

CENCIRA-Holanda, PRODERM, CENCICAP ANTA. 1979. *Plan de desarrollo de Antapampa diagnóstico*. Cusco.

———. 1980. *Las areas asociativas en las comunidades campesinas de Anta*. Cusco.

CIC, ed. 1980. *Realidad del campo peruano después de la reforma agraria: 10 ensayos críticos*. Lima: CIC (Centro de Investigación y Capacitación).

Cleaves, Peter S., and Martin Scurrah. 1980. *Agriculture, Bureaucracy and Military Government in Peru*. Ithaca, N.Y.: Cornell University Press.

Comisión de la Verdad y Reconciliación. 2004. *Informe final: Perú, 1980–2000*. Lima: Comisión de la Verdad y Reconciliación, Universidad Nacional Mayor de San Marcos, Pontificia Universidad Católica del Perú.

Confederación Campesina del Perú. 1979. *Programa y plataforma de lucha CCP*. Lima: Confederación Campesina del Perú.

de Izcue, Nora, dir. 1973. *Runan Caycu* (documentary film). Perú.

de Janvri, Alain. 1981. *The Agrarian Question and Reformism in Latin America*. Baltimore: Johns Hopkins University Press.

de Zutter, Pierre. 1975. *Campesinado y revolución*. Lima: Instituto Nacional de la Cultura.

Deere, Carmen Diana. 1990. *Household and Class Relations: Peasants and Landlords in Northern Peru*. Berkeley: University of California Press.

Degregori, Carlos Iván. 1990. *Ayacucho 1969–1979: El surgimiento de Sendero Luminoso*. Lima: Instituto de Estudios Peruanos.

———, ed. 2000. *No hay país más diverso: Compendio de antropología peruana*. Lima: Pontificia Universidad Católica del Perú, Universidad del Pacífico, Instituto de Estudios Peruanos.

del Mastro, Marco. 1979. *Luchas campesinas Cuzco: 1945–1980*. Lima: Centro Peruano de Estudios Sociales (CEPES).

del Pozo-Vergnes, Ethel. 2004. *De la hacienda a la mundialización: Sociedad, pastores y cambios en el altiplano peruano*. Lima: Instituto de Estudios Peruanos, Instituto Francés de Estudios Andinos.

Dorner, Peter. 1992. *Latin American Land Reforms in Theory and Practice: A Retrospective*. Madison: University of Wisconsin Press.

Eguren, Fernando. 1988. "Revisión y balance de los estudios sobre restucturación de empresas agrarias asociativas." In *Perú: Problema agrario en debate*, ed. F. Eguren, R. Hopkins, B. Kervyn, and R. Montoya, 197–240. Ayacucho: Universidad Nacional San Cristobal de Huamanga.

—————. 1990. "La reforma agraria y el nuevo orden en el campo." In *La reforma agraria peruana, 20 años después*, ed. A. Fernández and A. Gonzales, 19–36. Chiclayo: Centro de Estudios Sociales Solidaridad.

—————, ed. 2006a. *Reforma agraria y desarrollo rural en la región andina*. Lima: Centro Peruano de Estudios Sociales (CEPES).

—————. 2006b. "Reforma agraria y desarrollo rural en el Perú." In *Reforma agraria y desarrollo rural en la región andina*, ed. F. Eguren, 11–32. Lima: Centro Peruano de Estudios Sociales (CEPES).

Favre, Henri. 1967. "Evolución y situación de la hacienda tradicional de la región de Huancavelica." In *La hacienda, la comunidad y el campesino en el Perú*, ed. J. M. Mar, 105–39. Lima: Instituto de Estudios Peruanos.

Fernández, Angel. 1985. "La reforma agraria no fracasa, tampoco los campesinos, lo unico que fracasa es la cooperativa." In *Las parcelaciones de las cooperativas agrarias del Perú*, ed. A. Gonzalez and G. Torre, 271–303. Chiclayo: Centro de Estudios Sociales Solidaridad.

Fernández, Angel, and Alberto Gonzales. 1990. *La reforma agraria peruana, 20 años después*. Chiclayo: Centro de Estudios Sociales Solidaridad.

Figallo, Flavio, and Juan F. Vega. 1988. "ANAPA: ¿Qué clase de gremio y gremio de qué clase?" *Debate Agrario* 2: 51–69.

Fioravanti, Eduardo. 1974. *Latifundio y sindicalismo agrario en el Perú: El caso de los valles de La Convención y Lares (1958–1964)*. Lima: Instituto de Estudios Peruanos.

Fitzgerald, E. V. K. 1976. *The State and Economic Development: Peru since 1968*. Cambridge: Cambridge University Press.

Flores Galindo, Alberto. 1986. "El horizonte utópico." In *Estados y naciones en los Andes: Hacia una historia comparativa; Bolivia-Colombia-Ecuador-Perú*, ed. J. P. Deler and Y. Saint-Geours, 519–70. Lima: Instituto de Estudios Peruanos, Instituto Francés de Estudios Andinos.

—————. 1991. *La agonia de Mariátegui*. Madrid: Editorial Revolución.

Fonseca Martel, César. 1975. "Comunidad, hacienda y el modelo SAIS." *América Indígena* 25(2): 349–66.

Ford, Thomas R. 1962. *Man and Land in Peru*. Gainesville: University of Florida.

Franco, Carlos, Rolando Ames et al., ed. 1983. *El Perú de Velasco*. Lima: Centro de Estudios para el Desarrollo y la Participación (CEDEP).

García Hurtado, Federico, dir. 1972. *Huando* (documentary film). Perú: SINAMOS.

———. 1971. *Tierra sin patrones* (documentary film). Perú: SINAMOS.

———. 1977. *Kuntur Wachana* (film). Perú. Producciones Huarán.

———. 1980. *Laulico* (film). Perú: Producciones Cinematográficas Kausachum Perú S.A. Pilar Roca.

———. 1981. *El Caso Huayanay: Testimonio de parte* (film). Perú: Producciones Cinematográficas Kausachum Perú S.A. Pilar Roca.

———. 1984. *Túpac Amaru* (film). Perú: Cinematográfica Kuntur S.A.

García Sayán, Diego. 1982. *Tomas de tierras en el Perú*. Lima: DESCO.

Gogol, Nicolai. 1996. *Dead Souls*. Trans. B. G. Guerney. New Haven, Conn.: Yale University Press.

Gols, José. 1988. "La parcelación de las empresas asosiativas de la costa peruana (el caso de valle de Cañete)." In *Perú: El problema agrario en debate*, ed. F. Eguren, R. Hopkins, B. Kervyn, and R. Montoya, 241–59. Lima: Seminario Permanente de Investigación Agraria (SEPIA) II.

Gonzales, Alberto. 1990. "El agro asociativo en el Perú, veinte años después." In *La reforma agraria peruana, 20 años después*, ed. A. Fernández and A. Gonzales, 37–57. Chiclayo: Centro de Estudios Sociales Solidaridad.

Gonzales de Olarte, Efraín. 1984. *Economía de la comunidad campesina: Aproximación regional*. Lima: Instituto de Estudios Peruanos.

———. 1987. *Inflación y campesinado: Comunidades y microrregiones frente a la crisis*. Lima: Instituto de Estudios Peruanos.

Gott, Richard. 2002. "Solon Barraclough: The Man behind the Land Reform Programmes in 1960's Latin America Whose Work Became Essential to the Anti-globalization Movement." In *The Guardian*, London, Dec. 31.

Grupo Cultural Yuyachkani. 1983. *Alpa Rayku* (theatrical script). Lima: Grupo Cultural Yuyachkani, CIED.

Guillet, David. 1979. *Agrarian Reform and Peasant Economy in Southern Peru*. Columbia: University of Missouri Press.

Gutierrez, Miguel. 1991. *La violencia del tiempo*. 3 vols. Lima: Milla Batres.

Gutiérrez Samanéz, José Carlos. 1969. "La actividad económica en la comunidad de Eqeqo-Chacán." Universidad Nacional de San Antonio Abad del Cusco.

Handelman, Howard. 1975. *Struggle in the Andes: Peasant Political Mobilization in Peru*. Austin: University of Texas Press.

Hardin, Garrett. 1968. "The Tragedy of the Commons." *Science* 162: 1243–48.

Hernández de Agüero, José. 2001. *La promesa*. Lima: Jaime Campodónico.

Herrera Hidalgo, Mario. 1994. "El proceso social de tenencia de tierras en el Valle Sagrado de los Incas Caso Waran." Universidad Nacional San Antonio Abad.

Hinojosa, Iván. 1998. "On Poor Relations and the Nouveau Riche: Shining Path and the Radical Peruvian Left." In *Shining and Other Paths*, ed. S. Stern, 84–127. Durham, N.C.: Duke University Press.

Hinton, William. 1966. *Fanshen: A Documentary of Revolution in a Chinese Village*. New York: Vintage Books.

Hobsbawm, Eric J. 1963. *Primitive Rebels: Studies in Archaic Forms of Social Movement in the 19th and 20th Centuries*. New York: Praeger.

———. 1969. "A Case of Neo-feudalism: La Convención, Perú." *Journal of Latin American Studies* 1(1): 31–50.

Horton, Douglas. 1976. "Haciendas and Cooperatives: A Study of Estate Organization, Land Reform and New Reform Enterprises." Latin American Studies Dissertation Series 67. Ithaca, N.Y.: Cornell University.

Interamerican Committee for Agricultural Development. 1966. *Tenencia de la tierra y desarrollo socio-económico del sector agrícola—Perú*. Washington, D.C.: Unión Panamericana.

Jacobsen, Nils. 1993. *Mirages of Transition: The Peruvian Altiplano, 1780–1930*. Berkeley: University of California Press.

Jurado, Joel, Corinne Valdivia, and Juan Pichihua. 1986. "SAIS de la sierra: Aciertos, fracasos y alternativas." In *Priorización y desarrollo del sector agrario en el Perú*, ed. A. Figueroa, 305–24. Lima: Pontificia Universidad Católica del Perú, Fundación Fredrich Ebert.

Kapsoli, Wilfredo. 1975. *Movimientos campesinos en Cerro de Pasco: 1880–1913*. Huancayo: Instituto de Estudios Andinos.

———. 1977. *Los movimientos campesinos en el Perú: 1879–1965*. Lima: Delva Editores.

Kay, Cristóbal. 1997. *The Complex Legacy of Latin America's Agrarian Reform*. The Hague: Institute of Social Studies.

Kervyn, Bruno. 1988. "La economía campesina en el Perú: Teorías y políticas." In *Perú: El problema agrario en debate*, ed. F. Eguren, R. Hopkins, B. Kervyn, and R. Montoya, 29–92. Lima: Universidad Nacional San Cristóbal de Huamanga. SEPIA II.

———. 1989. "Campesinos y acción colectiva: La utilización del espacio en comunidades de la sierra sur del Perú." *Revista Andina* 7(1): 7–83.

Kirk, Robin. 1997. *The Monkey's Paw*. Amherst: University of Massachusetts Press.

Klaren, Peter F. 1973. *Modernization, Dislocation, and Aprismo: Origins of the Peruvian Aprista Party, 1870–1932*. Austin: University of Texas Press.

Korovkin, Tanya. 1990. *Politics of Agricultural Co-operativsm: Peru 1969–1983*. Vancouver: University of British Columbia Press.

Kruijt, Dirk. 1989. *La revolución por decreto*. Lima: Mosca Azul Editores.

———. 1994. *Revolution by Decree: Peru, 1968–1975*. Amsterdam: Thela.

Lastarria-Cornhiel, Susana. 1989. "Agrarian Reforms of the 1960s and 1970s in Peru." In *Searching for Agrarian Reform in Latin America*, ed. W. Thiesenhusen, 127–55. Boston: Allen and Unwin.

Lastarria-Cornhiel, Susana, and Grenville Barnes. 1999. *Formalizing Informality: The Praedial Registration System in Peru*. Madison: Land Tenure Center, University of Wisconsin.

Lehmann, David, ed. 1974. *Agrarian Reform and Agrarian Reformism: Studies of Peru, Chile, China and India*. London: Faber and Faber.

Letts, Ricardo. 1981. *La izquierda peruana: Organizaciones y tendencias*. Lima: Mosca Azul Editores.

Lowenthal, Abraham, ed. 1975. *The Peruvian Experiment: Continuity and Change under Military Rule.* Princeton, N.J.: Princeton University Press.

Luxemburg, Rosa. 1937. *Reform or Revolution.* Trans. Integer. New York: Three Arrows Press.

Malkovich, John, dir. 2002. *The Dancer Upstairs* (film). USA: Fox Searchlight Pictures.

Mallon, Florencia. 1983. *The Defense of Community in Peru's Central Highlands: Peasant Struggle and Capitalist Transition, 1840-1940.* Palo Alto, Calif.: Stanford University Press.

———. 1998. "Chronicle of a Path Foretold? Velasco's Revolution, Vanguardia Revolucionaria, and 'Shining Omens' in the Indigenous Communities of Andahuaylas." In *Shining and Other Paths*, ed. S. Stern, 84-117. Durham, N.C.: Duke University Press.

Malpica, Carlos. 1968. *Los dueños del Perú.* Lima: Edición Ensayos Sociales.

Manrique, Nelson. 1987. *Mercado interno y región: La Sierra Central 1820-1930.* Lima: DESCO.

———. 1988. *Yawar mayu: Sociedades terratenientes serranas, 1879-1910.* Lima: Instituto Francés de Estudios Andinos, DESCO.

———. 1989. "La década de la violencia." *Márgenes* 3(5/6): 137-83.

———. 1990-91. "Time of Fear." *NACLA Report on the Americas* 24(4).

———. 1998. "The War for the Central Sierra." In *Shining and Other Paths*, ed. S. Stern, 193-223. Durham, N.C.: Duke University Press.

———. 2002. *El tiempo del miedo: La violencia política en el Perú 1980-1996.* Lima: Fondo Editorial del Congreso del Perú.

Mariátegui, José Carlos. 1928. *7 ensayos de interpretación de la realidad peruana.* Lima: Biblioteca Amauta.

———. 1979. *7 ensayos de interpretación de la realidad peruana.* Prólogo por Anibal Quijano. Notas y cronología por Elizabeth Garrels. Caracas: Biblioteca Ayacucho.

Martínez, Daniel, et al. 1989. *El Agro Costeño: Empresas asociativas, realidad y desafíos.* Lima: Centro de Estudios Para el Desarrollo y la Participación (CEDEP).

Martínez Alier, Joan. 1973. *Los huacchilleros del Perú: Dos estudios de formaciones sociales agrarias.* Lima: Instituto de Estudios Peruanos, Ruedo Ibérico.

———. 1977a. "Relations of Production in Andean *haciendas*: Peru." In *Land and Labour in Latin America*, ed. K. Duncan and I. Rutledge, 141-64. Cambridge: Cambridge University Press.

———. 1977b. *Haciendas, Plantations and Communities.* London: Frank Cass.

Martínez Arellano, Héctor. 1980. "Las empresas asociativas agrícolas peruanas." In *Realidad del campo peruano después de la reforma agraria: 10 ensayos críticos*, ed. CIC, 105-50. Lima: Centro de Investigación y Capacitación (CIC).

———. 1990. *Reforma agraria peruana: Las empresas asociativas altoandinas.* Lima: Centro de Estudios para el Desarrollo y la Participación (CEDEP).

Matos Mar, José. 1976. *Yanaconaje y reforma agraria en el Perú.* Lima: Instituto the Estudios Peruanos.

Matos Mar, José, and José Manuel Mejía. 1980. *La reforma agraria en el Perú.* Lima: Instituto de Estudios Peruanos.

Matto de Turner, Clorinda. 1973. *Aves sin nido*. Lima: Promociones Editoriales Inca S.A. (PEISA).

Mayer, Dora. 1984. *La conducta de la compañia minera del Cerro de Pasco*. Lima: Fondo Editorial Labor. [Also see original pamphlet: Mayer de Zulen, Dora]

Mayer, Enrique. 1992. "Peru in Deep Trouble: Mario Vargas Llosa's 'Inquest in the Andes' Reexamined." In *Rereading Cultural Anthropology*, ed. G. E. Marcus, 181–219. Durham, N.C.: Duke University Press.

———. 2002. *The Articulated Peasant: Household Economies in the Andes*. Boulder, Colo.: Westview Press.

———. 2006. "Vicos as a Model: A Retrospective." Paper presented at the conference entitled "Sustainability and Development: Lessons from Vicos, Peru." Cornell University, Ithaca, N.Y., September 8–9.

Mayer de Zulen, Dora. 1913. *Coduct of the Cerro de Pasco Mining Company*. Lima: Imprenta El Progreso.

McClintock, Cynthia. 1981. *Peasant Cooperatives and Political Change in Peru*. Princeton, N.J.: Princeton University Press.

McClintock, Cynthia, and Abraham Lowenthal, eds. 1983. *The Peruvian Experiment Reconsidered*. Princeton, N.J.: Princeton University Press.

Mejía, José Manuel. 1992. *Cooperativas azucareras: Crisis y alternativas*. Lima: Cambio y Desarrollo.

Méndez, María Julia. 1982. "Las cooperativas agrarias de producción y las parcelaciones: Situación actual y perspectivas." In *Situación actual y perspectivas del problema agrario en el Perú*, ed. F. Eguren, 95–136. Lima: DESCO.

———. 1986. "Cooperativas agrarias y parcelación en la costa peruana." In *Priorización y desarrollo del sector agrario en el Perú*, ed. A. Figueroa and J. Portocarrero, 253–303. Lima: Pontificia Universidad Católica del Perú, Fundación Fredrich Ebert.

Monge, Carlos. 1988. "Características y representatividad de los gremios empresariales agrarios." *Debate Agrario* 2: 25–50.

Montoya, Rodrigo. 1974. *La SAIS Cahuide y sus contradicciones*. Lima: Universidad Nacional Mayor de San Marcos.

———. 1989. *La lucha por la tierra, reformas agrarias y capitalismo en el Perú del Siglo XX*. Lima: Mosca Azul Editores.

———. 1997. *El tiempo del descanso*. Lima: Sur Casa de Estudios del Socialismo.

Montoya, Rodrigo, Luis Montoya, and Edwin Montoya. 1987. *La sangre de los cerros: Antología de la poesía Quechua que se canta en el Perú*. Lima: Centro Peruano Estudios Sociales (CEPES), Mosca Azul Editores, Universidad Nacional Mayor de San Marcos.

Naipaul, V. S. 1990. *India: A Million Mutinies Now*. New York: Viking.

Neira, Hugo. 1964. *Cuzco: Tierra y muerte, reportaje al sur*. Lima: Problemas de Hoy.

———. 1968. *Los Andes: Tierra o muerte*. Madrid: Editorial ZYX S.A.

———. 1974. *Huillca: Habla un campesino peruano*. Lima: Promociones Editoriales Inca S.A. (PEISA).

————. 1996. *Hacia la tercera mitad: Perú XVI–XX*. Lima: Fondo Editorial SIDEA.

————. 2008. *Cusco: Tierra y muerte*. Lima: Editorial Herética.

Nugent, David. 1997. *Modernity at the Edge of Empire*. Palo Alto, Calif.: Stanford University Press.

Oroza, Jorge. 1990. "Los problemas de gestión de las cooperativas azucareras." In *La reforma agraria peruana, 20 años después*, ed. A. Fernández and A. Gonzales, 211–72. Chiclayo: Centro de Estudios Sociales Solidaridad.

Ortiz Espinar, Manuel, and Carlos Cruz Montero. 1991. "Estructura de poder en la SAIS Tupac Amaru I Ltda." MA thesis, Universidad Nacional del Centro, Huancayo.

Orwell, George. 1945. *Animal Farm: A Fairy Story*. London: Secker and Warburg.

Palmer, David Scott. 1973. "Revolution from Above: Military Government and Popular Participation in Peru." Latin American Studies Program Dissertation Series 47. Ithaca, N.Y.: Cornell University.

Paniagua Gomez, Genaro. 1984. "Anta: Toma de tierras y la via campesina de desarrollo." Universidad Nacional San Antonio Abad del Cusco.

Patchett, Ann. 2001. *Bel Canto*. New York: Harper and Collins.

Pease, Henry. 1977. *El ocaso del poder oligárquico: Lucha política en la escena oficial 1968–1975*. Lima: DESCO.

Pease, Henry, and Alfredo Filomeno. 1982. *Perú 1980: Cronología política*. Vol. 9. Lima: DESCO.

Peloso, Vincent C. 1999. *Peasants on Plantations: Subaltern Strategies of Labor and Resistance*. Durham, N.C.: Duke University Press.

Poblete Troncoso, Moisés. 1938. *Condiciones de vida y de trabajo de la población indígena del Perú*. Geneva: International Labor Organization.

Poole, Deborah. 1988. "Landscape of Power in a Cattle-Rustling Culture of Southern Andean Peru." *Dialectical Anthropology* 12: 367–98.

————. 1994. "Performance, Domination, and Identity in the *Tierras Bravas* of Chumbivilcas (Cusco)." In *Unruly Order: Violence, Power, and Cultural Identity in the High Provinces of Southern Peru*, ed. D. Poole, 97–132. Boulder, Colo.: Westview Press.

Quintanilla, Lino. 1981. *Andahuaylas, la lucha por la tierra (Testimonio de un militante)*. Lima: Mosca Azul Editores.

Rénique, José Luis. 1991. *Los sueños de la sierra: Cusco en el siglo XX*. Lima: Centro Peruano de Estudios Sociales (CEPES).

————. 2004. *La batalla por Puno*. Lima: Instituto de Estudios Peruanos, Casa de Estudios del Socialismo, Centro Peruano de Estudios Sociales (CEPES).

Revesz, Bruno. 1982. *Estado, algodón y productores agrarios*. Piura: CIPCA.

Riesco, Laura. 1994. *Ximena de dos caminos*. Lima: PEISA.

Rimanakuy. 1987. *Rimanakuy '86: Hablan los campesinos del Perú*. Cusco: Centro de Estudios Rurales Andinos "Bartolomé de las Casas."

Rivera Martínez, Edgardo. 1993. *País de Jauja*. Lima: La Voz.

Roberts, Bryan R., and Carlos Samaniego. 1978. "The Evolution of Pastoral Villages and the Significance of Agrarian Reform in the Highlands of Central Peru." In *Peasant Cooperation and Capitalist Expansion in Central Peru*, ed. N. Long and B. R. Roberts, 241–64. Austin: University of Texas Press.

Robles Godoy, Armando, dir. 1970. *La muralla verde* (film). Peru: Amaru Producciones Cinematográficas S.A.

————. 1973. *Espejismo* (film). Perú: Procine.

Roca Puchana, Andrea. 1990. "La mujer y las tomas de tierra—Anta." Universidad Nacional San Antonio Abad Cusco.

Roncagiolo, Santiago. 2006. *Abril rojo*. Madrid: Alfaguara.

Rubín de Celis, Emma. 1977. *Las CAP de Piura y sus contradicciones*. Piura: CIPCA.

————. 1978. *¿Qué piensa el campesino de la reforma agraria? Caso Piura*. Piura: CIPCA.

Sáenz, Moisés. 1944. "The Peruvian Indian (Sobre el indio peruano y su incorporación al medio nacional 1933)." In *Strategic Index of the Americas*. Washington, D.C.: Research Division Office for Emergency Management.

Saldívar, Ramón (César Benavides). 1974. "Agrarian Reform and Military Reformism in Perú." In *Agrarian Reform and Agrarian Reformism: Studies of Peru, Chile, China and India*, ed. D. Lehmann, 25–70. London: Faber and Faber.

Sánchez, Rodrigo. 1981. *Toma de tierras y conciencia política campesina: Las lecciones de Andahuaylas*. Lima: Instituto de Estudios Peruanos.

————. 1989. "Las SAIS de Junín y la alternativa comunal." *Debate Agrario* 7: 85–101.

Sanginés, Jorge, dir. 1969. *Yawar Mallku* (film). Bolivia: Ukumaru Lta.

Saulniers, Alfred H. 1988. *Public Enterprises in Peru: Public Sector Growth and Reform*. Boulder, Colo.: Westview Press.

Scorza, Manuel. 1970. *Redoble por Rancas*. Barcelona: Editorial Planeta.

————. 1972. *Historia de Garabombo el invisible*. Barcelona: Editorial Planeta.

————. 1977a. *El cantar de Agapito Torres*. Caracas: Monte Avila Editores.

————. 1977b. *El jinete insomne*. Caracas: Monte Avila Editores.

Scott, James C. 1985. *Weapons of the Weak: Everyday Forms of Peasant Resistance*. New Haven, Conn.: Yale University Press.

Scurrah, Martin, ed. 1987. *Empresas asociativas y comunidades campesinas: Puno después de la reforma agraria*. Lima: GREDES.

Seligmann, Linda J. 1995. *Between Reform and Revolution: Political Struggles in the Peruvian Andes*. Stanford, Calif.: Stanford University Press.

Servicios Educativos Promoción y Apoyo Rural (SERPAR). 1992. *Cifras y cronología de la violencia política en la región central del Perú (1980–1991)*. Huancayo: Servicios Educativos Promoción y Apoyo Rural.

Shakespeare, Nicholas. 1995. *The Dancer Upstairs*. London: Harvill Press.

Smith, Gavin A. 1989. *Livelihood and Resistance: Peasants and the Politics of Land in Peru*. Berkeley: University of California Press.

Starn, Orin. 1991. "Sendero, soldados y ronderos en el Mantaro." *Quehacer* 74: 60–68.

————. 1998. "Villagers at Arms: War and Counterrevolution in the Central-South Andes." In *Shining and Other Paths*, ed. S. Stern, 224–60. Durham, N.C.: Duke University Press.

————. 1999. *Nightwatch: The Politics of Protest in the Andes*. Durham, N.C.: Duke University Press.

Stepan, Alfred C. 1978. *The State and Society: Peru in Comparative Perspective*. Princeton, N.J.: Princeton University Press.

Tanaka, Martín. 2001. *Participación popular en políticas sociales. ¿Cómo y cuándo es democrática y eficiente, y por qué tambien puede ser lo contrario?* Lima: CIES (Consorcio de Investigación Economico Social), Instituto de Estudios Peruanos.

Tello, María del Pilar. 1983. *¿Golpe o revolución? Hablan los militares del 68*. Lima: Ediciones Sagsa.

Terkel, Studs. 1971. *Hard Times: An Oral History of the Great Depression*. New York: Avon.

Theidon, Kimberly. 2004. *Entre prójimos: El conflicto armado interno y la política de reconciliación en el Perú*. Lima: Instituto de Estudios Peruanos.

Thiesenhusen, William, ed. 1989. *Searching for Agrarian Reform in Latin America*. Boston: Allen and Unwin.

Thorndike, Guillermo. 1976. *No, mi general*. Lima: Mosca Azul Editores.

Thorpe, Rosemary, and Geoffrey Bertram. 1978. *Peru 1890-1977: Growth and Policy in an Open Economy*. New York: Columbia University Press.

Trivelli, Carolina. 1992. "Reconocimiento legal de comunidades campesinas: Una revisión estadística." *Debate Agrario* 14: 23–39.

Ugarteche, Oscar. 1999. *Babilonia la grande*. Lima: Alfaguara Eds.

University of Wisconsin, Madison, Land Tenure Center Library. 1974. *Agrarian Reform in Latin America: An Annotated Bibliography Complied by the Staff at the Land Tenure Center Library*. Land Economics Monographs 1 and 2(5).

Valderrama, Mariano. 1976. *7 años de reforma agraria peruana: 1969-1976*. Lima: Pontificia Universidad Católica del Perú.

Valderrama, Ricardo, and Carmen Escalante. 1986. "La hacienda vista por un pongo huancavelicano." *Quehacer* 41: 103–10.

Valdivia, Corinne. 1983. "A Comparative Analysis of Capital Accumulation in to Peruvian Sheep Associative Enterprises." MA thesis, University of Missouri, Columbia.

Valdivia, Corinne, and Juan Pichihua. 1986. "El proceso de acumulación de capital, desarrollo y contradicciones internas de las SAIS de la Sierra Central." In *Perú: El problema agrario en debate*, ed. V. Gómez, B. Revesz, E. Grillo, and R. Montoya, 153–80. Lima: Seminario Permanente de Investigación Agraria (SEPIA) I.

Valerio Laureano, Jonatán Homer. 1985. "Revindicación de tierras de la comunidad campesina de San Juan de Ondores 1979–1980." BA thesis, Universidad Nacional del Centro del Perú, Huancayo.

Vargas Chambi, Iván. 1990. "Las empresas comunales: ¿Fracaso o desarrollo? Empresa comunal de la comunidad de Tambo Real: Organizacion, desarrollo y eficacia." Zurite Anta, Universidad Nacional de San Antonio Abad.

Vargas Llosa, Mario. 1984. *La historia de Mayta*. Barcelona: Editorial Seix Barral.

————. 1993. *Lituma en los Andes*. Barcelona: Planeta.

Velásquez Benítez, Orlando. 1998. *Reto final del agro azucarero peruano*. Trujillo: Universidad Nacional de Trujillo, Facultad de Ciencias Sociales.

Vera Ardiles, Alberto. 1972. "Cambios dirigidos en la comunidad de Eqeqo-Chakan." BA thesis. Universidad Nacional de San Antonio Abad del Cusco.

Villanueva, Victor. 1967. *Hugo Blanco y la rebelión campesina*. Lima: Editorial Juan Mejía Baca.

Watters, Raymond F. 1994. *Poverty and Peasantry in Peru's Southern Andes*. London: McMillan Press.

Wolf, Eric, and Sydney Mintz. 1955. "Haciendas and Plantations in Middle America and the Antilles." *Social and Economic Studies* 6(33): 380–412.

Yambert, Karl. 1989. "The Peasant Community of Catacaos and the Peruvian Agrarian Reform." In *State, Capital and Rural Society: Anthropological Perspectives on Political Economy in Mexico and the Andes*, ed. B. S. Orlove, M. W. Foley, and T. F. Love, 181–209. Boulder, Colo.: Westview Press.

Page numbers in *italics* refer to illustrations.

Matos Mar, José, 4–5, 250 n. 7
mechanization, 115, 117, 173
memory, xvii, 78, 147, 148, 239
memory and dreams, xvii, 238–40; emotion and, xvii, 149, 202–3, 217, 239; narratives and, xix, 76, 86, 93, 97–98, 155, 200, 217; nostalgia and, 240–41
Méndez, María Julia, 135, 142
Mendoza, Marcelina, 151, 158–64
Mexican Revolution, xxiii, 134
Mexico, xxiii, 6, 8, 51, 72, 73, 230
Meza, Simón, 183, 211–17, 272 n. 8
military dictatorships, 30, 35, 53; in Argentina, 7, 235, 237; armed struggles against, 235; in Brazil, 7; in Chile, 7, 28, 107, 237; in Ecuador, 7; in El Salvador, 235; in Guatemala, 235; in Nicaragua, 235; in Panama, 235
Military Junta Peru (1962–63), 1, 17, 50
minifundium, 9, 16, 171
models, 4, 16, 36, 38, 112, 133–34, 152–53, 160, 174, 180, 231, 264 n. 1
modernization of agricultural enterprises, 16, 29, 82, 83, 153, 231
Montoya, Rodrigo, xiii, xxii, 192, 252 n. 1, 268 n. 4
Morales Bermúdez Cerutti, Francisco: presidency of, 1, 7–8, 27, 34, 104, 139, 154, 179
Movimento dos Trabalhadores Rurais Sem Terra (MST), 134
Movimiento Revolucionario Túpac Amaru (MRTA), 31, 236, 271 n. 6

Naipaul, V. S., xxi
narratives, xvii, xviii, 43, 55, 72, 95, 98, 155–57, 200, 256 n. 11; collective, 222; intentional, 224; versions of one story, 52–53
National Agrarian University (La Molina), 101, 113, 117, 188
nationalism, 2, 4
Neira, Hugo, 41, 46, 72, 233, 236, 238, 240, 256 n. 8

neoliberal reform, xix, 30, 31, 149, 230
NGO, 201, 206
Nicaragua, 229, 231
No Name, 76, 91–92, 99
nonexpropriatable minimum land, 90, 123, 145

Odría Amoretti, Manuel: presidency of, 1, 11, 17, 18
oligarchy, 11, 89, 97, 103, 120
Ortiz, Manuel, 183, 193, 196–98
Orwell, George, xxi, 68
Ovalle, Juan, 160–61

Pampa de Anta, 153, 154, 164–65, 174, 177, 178, 264 n. 2, 266 n. 8
Paniagua, Genaro, xiii, 151, 158, 164, 171, 176, 264 n. 2, 264 n. 3
paramilitary, 235–36, 241
parcelero, 106–7, 140, 143, 144–49, 262 n. 10
participatory, 56, 153, 158, 193
patrón, 76, 83, 83–88; affection or hate and, 84–86, 97–98, 241, 259 n. 5; family patriarch, 84; as good or bad, 84, 86, 172; hostile relations and, 85–86; righteous personalism, 84; as ruler, 88, 119, 131, 175, 186
Paucartambo, 29, 45, 80, 89
peasant federations (FARTAC), 45, 82, 158, 167, 170, 176, 178, 232
peasant leaders, 46–47, 74, 155–58, 175–76. *See also* Blanco, Hugo; Franco, Isidoro; Huilca, Saturnino; Mendoza, Marcelina; Puma, Esteban; Quispe, Hilario; Zúñiga Letona, José
peasant movements: xxiii, 17, 25, 27, 82, 101, 186–87; demobilized, 180–81; in La Convención y Lares, 47–51; peaceful, 236
peasants, 10, 33, 40, 171, 176, 178, 230, 237; political experience and, 179
peasant struggles, 3, 11, 71, 100, 149, 178–82, 267 n. 2

108, 167, 192, 263 n. 12; nostalgia for
and forgetting of, 240–41; the person,
4, 5, 7, 8, 39, 96, 101–2, 123, 139, 149,
153, 246 n. 1; regime of, xviii, 3–6, 23,
37, 108, 146, 232, 246 n. 1; revolution of,
2–4, 133, 233, 236, 248 n. 6
Velasco's agrarian reform, xxiii, 19–20,
73, 83, 111–13, 123, 201; as a failure, 136,
139, 149
Venezuela, 230, 241
vía campesina, 62, 171, 177
Villarrubia, María, 111, 114–15, 134–35
Villena, Adriel, 151, 164–65, 266 n. 6
violence, 181, 205, 208–11, 213–14, 236;
agrarian reform and, 234; on dead and
wounded people, 162, 214, 215, 219–20,
237, 238; psychological consequences

of, 226; as tactic, 237; on things, 217–19,
259 n. 5, 270 n. 5. *See also* black harvest
violent cycles, 237

wages, 22, 65, 91–92, 117, 123, 130, 133, 135–
37, 172; owed, 93; severance, 93, 122
White: as race category, 88, 97, 113–14
worker organizations (proagrarian reform), 123, 126, 131–32, 157, 170, 231,
264 n. 2
workers, 117, 118, 122, 128, 147, 231

yanacona. See servitude

Zuirte, 168
Zúñiga Letona, José, 41, 51, 57–60, 58, 69,
258 n. 15

Enrique Mayer is a professor of anthropology at Yale University.

Library of Congress Cataloging-in-Publication Data
Mayer, Enrique, 1944–
Ugly stories of the Peruvian agrarian reform / Enrique Mayer.
p. cm. — (Latin America otherwise)
Includes bibliographical references and index.
ISBN 978-0-8223-4453-7 (cloth : alk. paper)
ISBN 978-0-8223-4469-8 (pbk. : alk. paper)
1. Land reform—Peru—History—20th century. 2. Land tenure—Peru—History—
20th century. 3. Agriculture, Cooperative—Peru—History—20th century. I. Title.
II. Series: Latin America otherwise.
HD1333.P4M38 2009
333.3'185—dc22   2009029296